MANUFACTURE OF HOUSEHOLD SOAPS, TOILET SOAPS AND OTHER SOAPS WITH FORMULATIONS

(A Complete hand book of Soaps Manufacturing)

Written By

EIRI BOARD OF CONSULTANTS & ENGINEERS

ENGINEERS INDIA RESEARCH INSTITUTE

4449, Nai Sarak, Main Road, Delhi - 110 006 (India)

Ph:. 91-11-23918117, 23916431, 23840361, 31082370

Fax: 91-11-2391 6431, 2391 8117

*** E-Mail : eirisidi@bol.net.in**

***Website: www.startindustry.com**

Sole Distributor :

INDIAN INSTITUTE OF CONSULTANTS, 4/27 ROOP NAGAR, DELHI - 07

PRINTED & PUBLISHED BY

ENGINEERS INDIA RESEARCH INSTITUTE

4449, Nai Sarak, Main Road, Delhi - 110 006 (India)
Ph:. 91-11-23918117, 23916431, 23840361, 31082370
* Fax: 91-11-23916431, 23918117
* E-Mail : eirisidi@bol.net.in
* Website: www.startindustry.com

DISTRIBUTED BY

SMALL INDUSTRY RESEARCH INSTITUTE (SIRI)
INDIAN INSTITUTE OF CONSULTANTS

ISBN : 81- 86732-53-5
Printed in New Delhi (INDIA)

Rs. 750/-

Printed & Published by Sudhir Gupta for "Engineers India Research Institute" 4449 Nai Sarak, Main Road, New Delhi - 110 006

Preface

The book **Manufacture of Household Soaps, Toilet Soaps and Other Soaps with Formulations** *covers almost all the basic and advanced details to setup own Soap Industry/Unit. The new edition of the book is covering latest technology including Details of Soap base manufacture, Solid, household and toilet soaps manufacture, Raw materials for soap industry, Oils, fats and their pretreatment, Manufacture, purification of fatty acid and production of soap base, Recovery and refining of glycerine, Perfuming of soaps and detergents, Testing of soaps and detergents, Manufacturing process and formulations of various soaps, Miscellaneous formulae, Scourig bar, Detergent cake & powder, Toilet & herbal soap, Laundry soap, Liquid soap, Nerol laundry soap, Liquid shoe polish puff, Soap stone powder from raw soap stone, Complete plant Suppliers, Suppliers of fragrances, flavours, perfumes for soaps, Suppliers of soaps manufacturing chemicals, Present manufacturers etc.*

The book has been written for the benefit and to prove an asset and a handy reference guide in the hands of new entrepreneurs & well established industrialists.

Director

ENGINEERS INDIA RESEARCH INSTITUTE

Nai Sarak, New Delhi (INDIA)

E-Mail : eirisidi@bol.net.in

CONTENTS AND SUBJECT INDEX

CHAPTERS	PAGE NO.

CHAPTERS PAGE NO.

1
Soap Base Manufacture

Introduction

The chemical reaction in which an ester is heated with aqueous alkali such as sodium hydroxide, to form an alcohol (usually glycerol), and the sodium salt of the acid corresponding to the ester. The process is usually carried out on fats, (glyceryl esters of fatty acids). The sodium salt formed is called a soap. A typical saponification reaction is :

$$(C_{17}H_{35}COO)_3C_3H_5 + 3NaOH \rightarrow 3C_{17}H_{35}COONa + C_3H_5(OH)_3.$$

This chapter is concerned with the production of soap base from fats using the fully boiled process, and more modern processes derived from it.

SOME PRINCIPLES

Phase Diagram

Fig. 1.1 shows diagrammatically a simplified phase diagram for a typical soap (say 80% tallow and 20% coconut oil) at about 90-100ºC, indicating only phases which are relevant to the soapmaking process. The shapes of the various areas are influenced by the fat blend, particularly its content of lauric oils. The main electrolytes are salt (sodium chloride) and caustic soda (sodium hydroxide); but some sodium carbonate and sodium sulphate (derived from salt returned from the glycerine recovery process) may also be present. Figures quoted by various authorities for the relative salting out powers of these electrolytes vary, but roughly one part of salt is equivalent to 0.85 parts of caustic soda or 2.0 parts of sodium carbonate. The effects of the various electrolytes are additive, and are commonly expressed in terms of salt.

Area A on the diagram represents neat soap, or soap base, the product of the soapmaking operation, from which most products are made. It contains about 67-70% anhydrous soap, or 61-64% TFM.

Area J represents curd, or grained-out soap, sometimes called kettle wax. As discussed later, the high anhydrous soap (or TFM) content indicated on the diagram for this phase is somewhat misleading in that the curd soap produced by settling (or even centrifugal separation) contains a variable amount of enmeshed lye.

Area B represents 'middle soap'. This phase appears as 'water lumps' (possibly augmented by acid soap) if the electrolyte content is allowed to fall too low in any part of the vessel. The area is avoided by experienced soapmakers, as, once formed, water lumps are difficult to eliminate.

Area D is nigre, an impure solution of soap in water.

Area L, an extension of D, represents lye. As the electrolyte content increases, this phase changes from a thin, low soap, nigre, or nigre lye, to an aqueous solution which contains hardly any soap, known as lye.

Area M is a two-phase area which, theoretically at least, can separate into curd and lye. A mixture represented by point *x*, comprises cure x_1 and ly x_2. The proportions of the two phases are given by the relationship

$$\frac{\textit{quantity of curd}}{\textit{quantity of lye}} = \frac{xx_2}{xx_1}$$

that is the uantities of the phases are inversely proportional to the lengths of the tie lines from the mixture point *x* to the phase points x_1 and x_2.

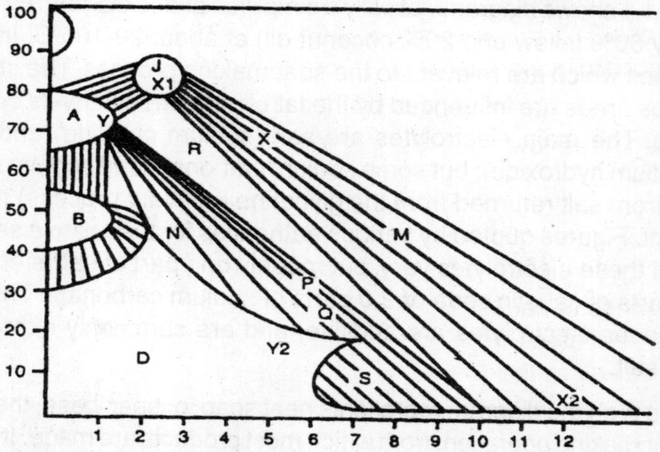

Fig. 1.1. Simplified diagram for phases significant in the production of soap base by the fully boiled process.

Similarly, area N is another two phase area representing mixtures of neat soap and nigre. Mixture of composition *y* can separate into neat soap y_1 and nigre y_2, in the ratio

$$\frac{\text{quantity of neat soap}}{\text{quantity of nigre}} = \frac{yy_2}{yy_1}$$

Area P represents the neat soap-lye zone. The so-called 'bay area', S, shows the equilibrium between nigre and lye.

The triangular area Q represents mixtures which separate into three phases of fixed compositions represented by the points of the triangle, neat soap, nigre and lye. Similarly, area R.

Saponification

Important practical points concerning saponification are :

(i) Fats and aqueous caustic soda are not miscible at temperatures which can be achieved without pressures well above atmospheric; and the reaction with neutral fats, particularly those other than the lauric oils, does not start readily. It is autocatalytic, that is catalysed by the product of the reaction, soap. Hence, the reaction rate accelerates greatly until most of the fat has reacted, when it slows down again. The soap formed/time curve is, therefore, somewhat S shaped as shown diagrammatically in Fig.1.2. The slow initial phase is a heterogeneous, surface, reaction helped by vigorous agitation and the formation of an emulsion stabilised by soap. The main part of the reaction is homogeneous, with the fat probably 'dissolved' in the soap micelles.

The final stage is slow because the concentration of residual fat becomes low. In factory practice, the slow initial stage rarely causes much difficulty because fatty acids present in most soapmaking fats react readily to provide some soap; and because saponification is commonly carried out in a way which adds the reactants to a mass of soap. As with other chemical reactions, an excess of caustic soda help to minimise the residual unreacted fat, but steps have to be taken to avoid an unnecessary excess of alkali in the lyes which are transferred from soapmaking to glycerine recovery. One way is to carry out the saponification in two stages; in the first an excess of fat is allowed so as to reduce the free alkali in the lye, and in the second the saponification is completed, using an excess of alkali, and the lye containing this excess is passed to the first stage. At one time, soapmakers used drastic treatments to minimise free fat in which the soap mass was boiled for long periods with a substantial excess of caustic soda, using either open,

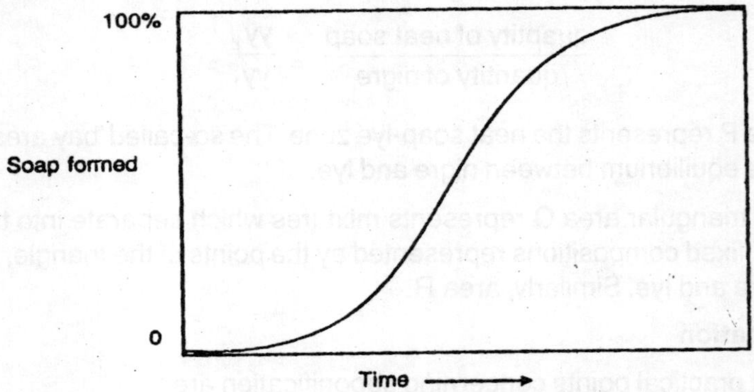

Fig. 1.2. Rate of saponification curve for neutral fat.

or closed, steam coils. This process certainly produced soaps with excellent keeping properties. Prolonged heating with caustic soda possibly breaks down some components in what is normally regarded as the unsaponifiable portion of the fat.

(ii) Like other reactions, saponification is accelerated by increases in temperature; and some processes use temperatures which can only be achieved in an aqueous system by the use of elevated pressures.

(iii) When some soap is present, too much electrolyte will salt, or grain, out the soap and greatly slow down the reaction. Too little will cause 'bunching', or thickening, so that it is important to ensure that the electrolyte content of the saponifying mass is within the correct range at all times. The actual requirement depends upon the composition of the fatty acids in the vessel, that is upon the fat blend. Caustic soda is a powerful electrolyte, but allowance must be made for the fact that it is continuously being removed by the reaction.

The '66%' Rule of Wigner; and Related Matters

This work is based upon examination of the results of large numbers of full scale boils of soap, as well as upon laboratory and pilot scale experiments, so-called '66% rule', which says 'a soap curd may be regarded as consisting of soap hydrate containing 66% of fatty acids, and of lye identical in composition with that from which it has separated'. This does not necessarily imply the physical existence of a soap hydrate not containing any salt; and the nearest approach achieved by Wigner in removing additional lye from a curd by settling and centrifuging in the laboratory contained about 64% TFM and 0.3% NaCl. Wigner deduced his rule as an empirical observation from a study of large numbers of boils, which showed that when a pan contents has been grained and settled.

$$\frac{\text{Percentage salt in soap curd}}{\text{Percentage salt in lye}} = 1 - K_s \frac{\text{Percentage TFM in curd}}{100}$$

K_s is nearly constant for almost all soaps, with a range of about 1.50 – 1.53, average 1.515. If electrolytes other than salt, particularly caustic soda, are present in significant quantities, equivalent salting out figures must be added to the salt concentrations. By substituting salt in soap curd = 0, it follows that for a salt-free curd, the percentage TFM in curd equals 100/*Ks* = 100/1.515 = 66%. Table 1.1 gives some analytical data for full scale boils of different types of soap presented by Wigner in support of his rule.

Wigner also found that the 66% rule could be applied to fitted pans using 'free solution' in place of lye. Free solution is defined as water which is not combined in the 66% TFM hydrate. For the neat soap which separates when a fitted pan is allowed to settle, Wigner says that 'neat soap is a soap hydrate of a composition which varies according to the concentration of salt in the free solution, always containing more water than the hypothetical 66% hydrate, and containing a small amount of salt which increases with the increase in the degree of hydration'. Figures in support are given in Table 1.1. It will be seen that as the concentration of electrolyte in free solution falls and the fit becomes 'finer', or 'closer'.

Table- 1.1 Data in support of the 66% rule for soap curds.

TFM% in soap	*NaCl% in lye*	*NaCl% in soap*		K_s†	*TFM% in soap hydrate*
		Found	*Calculated*		
53.7	9.5	1.76	1.76	1.518	66.0
52.3	9.1	1.87	1.89	1.520	65.9
54.6	9.0	1.44	1.56	1.538	65.0
57.8	8.8	1.10	1.10	1.514	66.0
56.0	8.7	1.33	1.71	1.513	66.1
53.5	9.1	1.69	1.71	1.522	65.7
57.1	8.2	1.17	1.10	1.501	66.6
57.8	9.4	1.17	1.17	1.516	66.0
58.0	9.1	1.12	1.10	1.512	66.2
56.7	9.2	1.34	1.30	1.506	66.3
54.7	9.6	1.68	1.65	1.508	66.3

† The column for K_s has been added by the present author

Table- 1.2. Data in support of the 66% rule in fitted soaps.

Sample	NaCl in free solution %	TFM%	Neat soap NaCl% on sample	NaCl% at 63% TFM	Nigre TFM%
1	11.0	63.2	0.47	0.47	<1
2	10.9	63.35	0.435	0.43	1.2
3	10.7	63.3	0.425	0.42	3.5
4	10.3	63.2	0.435	0.43	9.6
5	10.25	63.2	0.44	0.44	8.6
6	9.3	62.8	0.445	0.45	21.0
7	8.25	62.35	0.45	0.45	32.6
8	7.85	61.85	0.48	0.49	36.2
9	7.55	61.3	0.53	0.54	37.2
10	7.25	60.85	0.55	0.57	39.3

(i) The TFM content of the nigre increases very substantially.

(ii) The TFM content of the neat soap falls a little.

(iii) The salt content of the neat soap adjusted to the figures at 63% TFM, or any other fixed level such as 79% for a dried toilet soap, is nearly constant for samples 2-7, but tends to rise as the fit becomes finer. It is also a little higher for sample 1 separated from a nigre lye rather than a nigre.

It is also found that soap given a coarse, or open, fit settles much more rapidly than when the fit is close, or fine; this is due to the greater difference in density between the phases, as well as to changes in viscosity.

These results conflict slightly with what might be expected from the phase diagram as usually drawn, for example in Fig. 1.1, in that the electrolyte content of the neat soap, as well as its TFM content, should fall as the fit becomes finer. As shown in Table 1.3, this latter trend is found in results reported by Palmqvist for centrifugal separation of neat soap and nigre in a De Laval continuous soapmaking plant. Phase equilibrium is not necessarily reached with either gravity or centrifugal separation; and degree of separation can also affect the compositions obtained. Some practical implications are :

(i) Rapid separation and the low TFM content of the nigre/nigre lye, make open fits attractive whenever they can be used.

(ii) Household soaps made by the traditional frame process require fine fits with long settling times. On the other hand, household soaps made by the modern spray chill/vacuum plodding method usually benefit from an open fit and relatively incomplete separation, which leaves a high salt content in the soap. This type of soap is also generally acceptable for soap powder manufacture.

(iii) Traditionally, bases for toilet soaps and soap flakes were given rather more open fits than those for framed household soaps. This was understood to give lower electrolyte contents.

Table 1.3. Centrifugal separation of fitted soap in a continuous soapmaking plant.

Recorder	Fitting column (that is soap before separation)					From separator Neat soap		Nigre
Index	Distance from minimum	Composition by volume Neat soap%	Nigre %	Lye %	NaOH + NaCl %	NaOH + NaCl %	NaOH + NaCl %	TFM %
37	0	84	16	–	1.01	–	–	–
41	4	85	15	–	1.12	0.36	4.55	31.6
43	6	85	15	–	1.15	0.43	5.11	29.9
45	8	86	14	–	1.17	0.47	5.54	28.0
50	13	86	14	–	1.23	0.49	6.06	–
53	16	87	13	–	1.25	0.53	6.29	21.2
57	20	87.5	12	0.5	1.29	–	6.70	18.1
62	25	88.5	10	1.5	1.33	0.57	7.23	14.5

(iv) Modern continuous soapmaking plants using centrifuges for the final separation tend to use quite open fits, often with the separation of a very thin nigre, or nigre lye.

Some of these points are elaborated in subsequent sections. Wigner himself mentions that there are certain exceptions to the 66% rule; for example, when a groundnut oil soap is boiled for long periods with a lye having a high salt content in order to produce a curd soap which is as hard as is possible from GNO. The rule is, however, commonly accepted as applicable in all normal soapmaking operations; and some applications are mentioned later.

PRODUCTION OF SOAP BASE BY THE TRADITIONAL METHOD IN SINGLE VESSELS

Plant

Pans, sometimes called kettles (particularly if they are covered), for the manufacture of soap base can have a range of shapes and sizes. Cylindrical pans are common, but one major company standardised on 14 ft (4.27 m) cube vessels which fit conveniently together in groups of four, with alleyways between each group. Whatever the shape, they should have a slightly dished base so that lyes (or nigres) can be run-off completely from the bottom discharge valve, or cock. The heat loss should be as low as possible and the settling distance not too great; and the cube is probably a good compromise. Neat soap and nigre do not separate properly at temperatures below about 70-75°C, so that pans should not be too small and should be lagged for this reason, as well as to minimise steam consumption. Very small pans used for experimental boils should usually be steam jacketed, so that a little steam can be used to prevent unduly rapid cooling while neat soap and nigre are separating. Pan covers are also desirable to reduce heat loss from the soap surface, and to reduce risk of contamination with dirt from the atmosphere; but they are by no means always fitted. Pans are usually made of mild steel, but it has been found useful to lien the upper parts with stainless steel, or other corrosionresistant material, to reduce contamination of the soap with iron.

The usual fittings, in addition to a bottom discharge facility are :

(i) An open steam coil to provide both heat and agitation. Closed steam coils are no longer necessary, or usual.

(ii) A skimmer pipe, which can be raised or lowered, and through which the neat soap layer can be withdrawn when the settling is complete and the pan is 'cleansed'; that is the neat soap removed.

(iii) Pipes arranged to discharge into the pan above its contents for fat, caustic soda solution, water, and other materials. Salt can be shovelled over the side of the pan, but it is now commonly added in the form of saturated brine. Particularly in large panrooms making a variety of soap bases, a fairly comprehensive pipe system to permit transfer from pan to pan, and to other departments, is desirable.

Saponification

Traditionally, saponification is carried out by pumping the fat into the pan whilst the soapboiler adjusts the additions of caustic soda, salt, water and steam, so as to maintain the conditions necessary for steady reaction. This is a skilled operation; too much electrolyte can cause the soap mass to grain, and too little to bunch or thicken. If the pan contents are inadvertently grained with too much caustic soda, the reaction slows and great care is necessary when conditions are adjusted to re-establish it; otherwise the heat of reaction may cause the pan contents to boil over.

Nigre and other soap from the previous boil is often left in the pan to provide the soap needed to aid saponification; although it may be found desirable to remove some, or all, the nigre from time to time, for transfer to a lower quality base, or for it to be cleaned by graining, or fitting.

Rosin, which contains no glycerol, is preferably added to the rest of the soap after as much as possible of the glycerol has been removed. Solid rosin can be tipped into the pan, but, particularly when substantial proportions are to be included in the fat blend, it is better to partially saponify it separately. Rosin contains complex acids related to the terpenes, such as abietic and pimaric, which react readily with sodium carbonate solution. When rosin was widely used in soaps, it was common practice to saponify it partially with sodium carbonate in a separate vessel, grain, and discard the dirty lye (which rises to the top instead of sinking to the bottom as with ordinary soap lyes). The partially saponified rosin soap was added to the rest of the soap in the pan at a convenient stage, preferably after most of the glycerol had been removed; and some caustic soda was then needed to complete the saponification.

Saponification in a pan can be made easier by the use of a saponification jet, which can be made quite simply. One design which has been used widely is shown in fig. 1.3. The partially saponified emulsion of fat, soap and caustic soda solution is discharged through a flexible pipe, which can often be arranged to serve more than one pan; the metal hose being securely clamped to the pan in use. When the jet is used as an aid to saponification in a pan it is only necessary to regulate the flow of caustic soda solution roughly in proportion to the flow of fat. Steam is used in the jet as required, depending upon the temperature of the fat and the reaction rate. The mixture should flow into the pan as an emulsion in which saponification is taking place vigorously. The reaction is completed by boiling in the pan, with additions of caustic soda and salt as necessary.

Graining or Washing

After saponification has been completed, the pan content is grained with salt. When in the grained state, clear lye can be seen between the curds as the pan content boils gently, or in a sample lifted on a paddle. The pan is allowed to settle and the saponification lye is run off. The soap is 'closed' by addition of water and grained again with salt. During this operation sufficient water must be added to produce a wash lye of the desired size, say 0.3 tonnes of lye per tonne of soap curd; care being taken to avoid the formation of water lumps. The process is repeated as many times as is worthwhile, it being appreciated that the glycerol content of each wash is lower than that of the previous wash, so that, using this process, it is uneconomical to wash to reduce the glycerol in soap to a very low level. The capacity of the glycerine recovery plant may also be a limiting factor.

Dirt is removed from the soap mass in the washes, but the primary objective is to separate the glycerol. As indicated in the previous paragraph, there is an economic balance betwen the yield (percentage of the glycerol in the fats which is recovered) and the average concentration of glycerol in the lye produced, because the cost of lye treatment and evaporation is related to the lye concentration; that is to the quantity of lye which must be purified and the quantity of water which must be evaporated to produce a tonne of crude glycerine.

It is found that the glycerol is distributed between curd and lye approximately in proportion to the total water in each layer; and K_G is defined as concentration of glycerol in curd/concentration of glycerol in lye. The lower K_G the more effective the wash.

Alternatively, it can be said that the drier the curd, that is the higher its TFM%, and the less enmeshed lye it retains, the better.

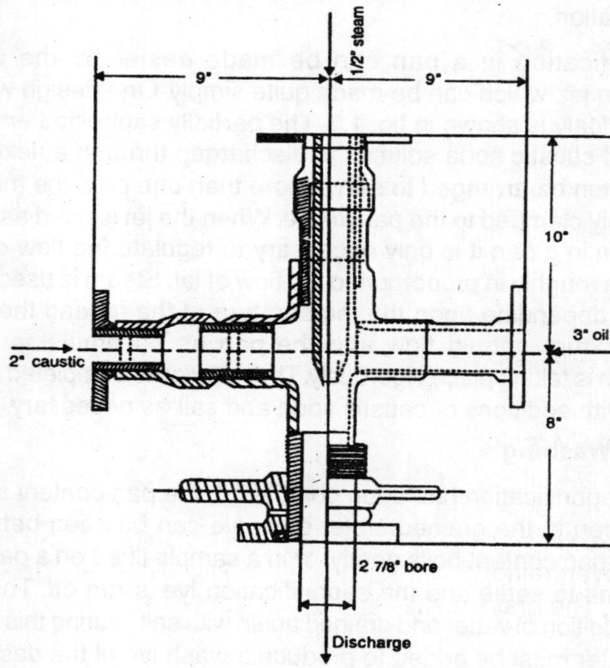

Fig. 1.3. Saponification jet.

This is analogous to the improved removal of dirty detergent solution from domestic washing which results if the articles are wrung, or spun, more effectively between rinses. This important point can be illustrated by some simple calculations. Assume that the lye contains 11.5% salt and 88.5% water plus glycerol. Consider first a very well settled curd at 60% TFM. Its anhydrous soap content is about 60.0 × 1.085 = 65.1% and, if it contains 1% salt (substantially in accord with the 66% rule), its content of Water plus glycerol is 100.0 – 65.1 – 1.0 = 33.9%. As water and glycerol occur in constant proportion in the layers.

$$K_G = \frac{\text{concentration of water in curd}}{\text{concentration of water in lye}}$$

$$= \frac{\text{concentration of glycerol plus water in curd}}{\text{concentration of glycerol plus water in lye}}$$

$$= 33.9/88.5 = 0.383.$$

Less well settled curds are equivalent to mixtures of the 60% TFM curd and additional lye. For a mixture of 1 part 60% TFM curd and 0.05 parts lye :

	Soap	*Salt*	*Water*	K_G		
from 1 part 60% curd	0.651	0.010	0.339	0.383		
from 0.05 parts lye	–	0.006	0.044	–		
in 1.05 parts new curd	0.651	0.016	0.383			
in 1 part new curd	0.620	0.015	0.365	0.365 / 0.885	=	0.412

= 57.1 TFM

Similar calculations and graphical interpolation provide the data for Table 1.4.

A carefully grained and well settled pan should result in a curd at about 58% TFM, giving a K_G of abut 0.4, but it is easy to produce less dry curds. It is particularly important to use the minimum concentration of electrolyte which is sufficient to produce lye substantially free from soap, as coarse, overgrained, curds occlude more lye than those which are only just grained. The graining details are given in table 1.5 of a 'washer' type soap.

Table 1.4. Variation in K_G with dryness of soap curd.

TMF% in curd	*Soap %*	*Salt %*	*Water + glycerol %*	*Partition coefficient K_G*
60	65.1	1.0	33.9	0.383
58	62.9	1.3	35.8	0.405
56	60.7	1.7	37.6	0.425
54	58.5	2.0	39.5	0.447
52	56.3	2.3	41.4	0.468
50	54.2	2.6	43.2	0.488

Table 1.5. Figures for graining of a washer type soap.

NaCl in free solution %	*TFM %*
10.5	4.15 (a thin nigre)
10.84	0.18
11.4	0.14
11.7	0.17
12.0	0.17
12.5	0.12

It will be seen that nothing is gained by using more salt than about 1.0% over that needed for a very rough fit giving a thin nigre. The actual concentration of salt required depends upon the fat blend. That used in Wigner's washer' soap is not quoted, but it may well have been something like 30% hard fat, 30% lauric oil, 30% soft oil and 10% rosin. Other factors equal, the quantity of lye needed to remove a given percentage of glycerol from the soap varies with the number of washes used. Wigner calculates the figures given in Table 1.6.

Table 1.6. Quantity of lye needed to obtain different percentage recoveries of glycerol with various numbers of washes (Wigner).

Number of washes	Parts of lye per part of curd for yield of	
	80%	85%
1	2.47	3.92
2	1.53	2.12
3	1.31	1.83
4	1.24	1.69
5	1.18	1.60
6	1.14	1.54
7	1.12	1.48

As might be expected :

(i) The quantity of lye which has to be produced with the traditional system of washing for a given percentage recovery is reduced very substantially by increasing the number of washes from one to three or four; but the benefit which accrues from more washes becomes increasingly small (also very large individual washes might well be impractical because of pan size).

(ii) With this system of washing yields of glycerol above about 80% become increasingly difficult to achieve.

Settling time is also very important, so that for a given total quantity of lye produced, it may be counter-productive to increase the number of washes further if this leads to an inadequate time to settle each wash.

A useful, but very simple arithmetical calculation shows that if each wash removes, say, 0.4 parts of the glycerol present in a curd when it is washed, so that 0.6 parts are left in the washed curd, *n* washes will leave 0.6^n in the final washed curd.

If the weakest lye which it is economical to process contains, say, 2% of glycerol, and K_G equal to 0.4 is achieved, the curd from which the last lye came contains 2 × 0.4 = 0.8% glycerol. It follows that soaps made from fat blends with a high glycerol content and those from fats with a low content, should both be washed down to 0.8% glycerol; so that more lye should be produced from the glycerol rich soaps.

When, as is usual, salt recovered in the process of glycerine lye evaporation is re-used in soapmaking its glycerol content has a considerable adverse effect upon the efficiency of glycerol recovery, or on the quantity of water which has to be evaporated to achieve a given recovery, particularly when the level of recovery is high. With regard to glycerol recovery, it is best to use in the final washes whatever new salt is needed to make up for losses. From the angle of soap quality the new salt is better used in the manufacture of the highest quality bases; but, for convenience, new and recovered salt are often used indiscriminately.

Fitting

The washed curd should be well settled, preferably overnight, before it is fitted, because the quantity of water in the fitted soap prior to settling affects the yield of neat soap, as can be shown by a simple materials balance. Let the total mass of material at the completion of the fit equal 1 and the mass of nigre produced equal *x*, so that the mass of neat soap equals (1 – *x*). Then if :

a = TFM% of the total pan contents

b = TFM% of the nigre, and

c = TFM% of the neat soap,

a TFM balance can be written

$$1 \times a/100 = bx/100 + c\,(1 - x)/100, \text{ or } r = \frac{c - a}{c - b}$$

In words this can be written, nigre produced (as a fraction of the whole mass) :

$$= \frac{\text{TFM\% of neat soap} - \text{TFM\% of pan contents}}{\text{TFM\% of neat soap} - \text{TFM\% of the nigre}}$$

Even more significant than the dryness of the curd, which affects *a*, is the nature of the fit used, which governs the TFM content of the nigre, *b*, as discussed earlier; but this has to be decided in relation to quality requirements, including removal of dirt. Table 1.7, shows examples of the influence of different pan drynesses with two types of fit. The significance of type of fit is illustrated further in Table 1.8, with some additional columns from. Recalculation suggests minor errors in some of the figures, but these do not affect the conclusions. The curd is assumed to contain 58% TFM and 1.45% salt, equivalent to 12% in lye. Columns 1–3 are taken from smoothed curves drawn from the data in Table 1.2. Column 4, the TFM% in the total mass after fitting, assumes that only water is added to the curd; and is calculated for the first line by saying that frees solution (occluded lye) in 100 parts of curd is (1.45 × 100)/12 = 12.08. This is diluted to (12.08 × 12)/9.65 = 15.02 to reduce its salt concentration from 12.0% to 9.65%. Hence water added = 15.02 – 12.08 = 2.94; and the TFM% in fitted soap is (58.0 × 100)/102.94 = 56.35%. Column 5 is obtained by application of the materials balance equation. Percentage nigre in total mass equals (63.0 – 56.35)/ (63.0 – 18.5) × 100 = 14.9% (compare 15.2% reported, as shown in the table). Column 6 equals (column 2 × column 5)/column 4 = (18.5 × 15.2)/56.35 = 5.0% (4.8% reported). Column 7 equals salt in curd recalculated as a percentage of the new total mass = 1.45 × 100/102.94 = 1.41%. Column 8 equals new free solution as a percentage of new total mass = (15.02 × 100)/102.94 = 14.6% (15.0% reported).

Table 1.7. Influence of dryness of pan contents and type of fit on loss of usable soap to nigre.

Average TFM% in pan	*Nigre, percentage of pan contents*		*Percentage of TFM in nigre*	
	Coarse fit yielding neat soap at 63% TFM and nigre at 18.5% TFM	*Fine fit yielding neat soap at 61% TFM and nigre at 38.5% TFM*	*Coarse fit*	*fine fit*
56	15.7	22.2	5.18	15.3
54	20.3	31.2	6.98	22.2
52	24.6	35.6	8.80	26.4
50	29.3	49.0	10.84	37.7
48	33.8	57.8	13.02	46.2

Table 1.8 Additional information concerning the fitting operation (the curd is assumed to contain 58% TFM and 1.45 salt, equivalent to 12% in lye).

Line	*Neat soap TFM% (1)*	*Nigre TFM% (2)*	*NaCl% in free solution (3)*	*TFM% on total mass (4)*	*%Nigre on total mass (5)*	*% of totalTFM in nigre (6)*	*NaCl% in total mass (7)*	*%Free soluation in total mass (8)*
a	63.0	18.5	9.65	56.35	15.2	4.8	1.41	15.0
b	62.5	28.5	8.75	55.52	20.6	9.9	1.39	16.6
c	62.0	33.5	8.15	54.88	25.2	14.6	1.37	17.8
d	61.5	36.5	7.70	54.34	28.8	18.1	1.35	18.85
e	61.0	38.5	7.35	53.89	32.0	21.3	1.34	19.75
f	60.5	40.3	7.10	53.65	34.4	24.0	1.33	20.4
g	60.0	41.5	6.85	53.18	36.8	26.4	1.33	21.2

The composition of the pan contents needed for any selected type of fit can be obtained either by adding water when the soap mass has too high an electrolyte content, or by adding electrolyte solution when it is too low. In addition, it is necessary to adjust the caustic soda content so that, after the electrolyte has been partitioned as indicated in Table 1.3, the neat soap will have the required alkalinity. Because of the large 'loss' (to reprocessing) of soap when a rather wet curd is given a fine fit, it is often advisable to use a rough fit prior to the finishing fine fit. This removes water and electrolyte, together with a relatively small mass of soap because of the low TFM content of the rough fit nigre. Hence, the quantity of the nigre from the final fit is small and its removal does not involve the rejection of very much soap despite its high TFM.

Fitting, as carried out in the traditional way, requires skill and experience; and is best learned by personal tuition by an experience soapboiler. The soap mass is boiled extensively; and the end point is judged by the look of the boiling soap and by the way it leaves a heated trowel. The soapboiler's trowel test is carried out using a bricklayer's trowel. The trowel is heated by immersion in the boiling soap, after which the adhering soap is scraped off. The trowel is then again immersed, drawn out edgewise and tilted to about 60° to see how the soap runs off. A soap which is too close for a typical medium/fine fit travels slowly, is apt to stick to the trowel, and the trailing edge tends to leave streaks of soap adhering to the blade. A soap which is too open slides off the trowel fairly rapidly and breaks into a number of small pieces. In the ideal condition the soap film should be transparent; and should slide slowly and steadily from the trowel, leaving the surface of the trowel clean and bright. It should break up into two, or three, large broad flakes. The trailing edge of the moving film should thin out gradually to an almost imperceptible transparent wafer of soap which may extend to ¼ inch behind the main body of soap.

The actual yield of usable neat soap is less than that which might be expected from the loss of nigre, because crusts of solid soap form on the soap surface and on the sides of a pan which has cooled during settling; and so cannot be cleansed with the liquid neat soap.

As mentioned earlier, soap given an open fit settles relatively rapidly, and neat soap suitable for soap powders, and for household soaps made using the modern chilling and extrusion processes, can commonly be cleansed after 1–2 nights settling, instead of the 3–4 nights needed after a medium/fine fit.

Wigner System of Quantitative Soapboiling

The data can be collected from experimental boils for the phase equilibria for the various fat blends used in a factory. If the composition of the pan contents is known, it is then possible to calculate what additions should be made to achieve a desired wash, or fit A problem in the application of this idea is that steam condenses as the soap is boiled with open steam, so that it is difficult to know how much water is present. Also, the density of the pan contents is influenced by the bubbles of steam and total mass cannot be determined by staffing to measure volume. These difficulties can be over come by the use of a pneumercator type of gauge shown diagrammatically in Fig. 1.4. When air has bubbled gently through the soap and the compressed air supply is shut off, the column in the manometer balances the soap above the air orifice; and the manometer can be calibrated directly in terms of the mass of material in the pan, regardless of its density. Allowance must be made for the material in the pan dish. Water content is determined by difference between the total mass and the known additions. The theory explains in detail how the quantitative method of control of the traditional process can be achieved, together with the use of nomographs to minimise calculations. Possible extended use of this system has been overtaken by other developments to be described, which have made the traditional process largely obsolete, although it is still used by many small, and/or, less technically developed, companies.

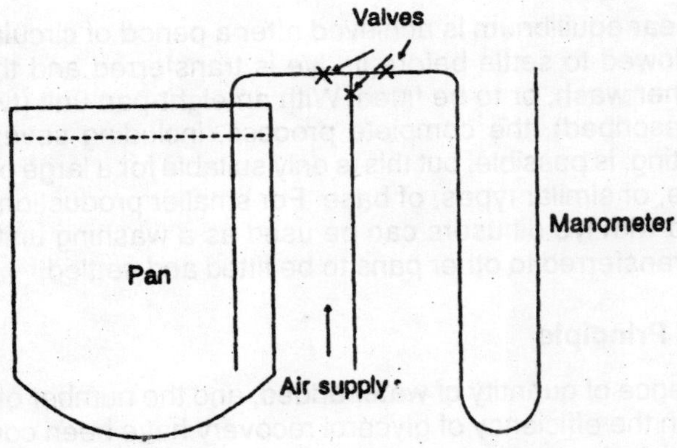

Fig. 1.4. Pneumercator gauge for measurement of pan contents.

Developments of the Traditional Process

One important weakness of the traditional process is the low glycerol content of the later washes. This results in the production of large quantities of weak lyes; and seriously limits the glycerol recovery which is economical, or even practical. Some weak liquors can be used to dilute the caustic soda, or to dissolve salt, but it has long been appreciated that counter current operation of the washing system is needed, as used in other extraction processes. Counter-current washing is complicated by the addition of water to close the soap and then of salt, or brine, to grain it in each washing stage; and a major advance, few years ago, was the discovery that soap can be washed quite satisfactorily by just mixing curd and lye, and allowing the mix to settle. All modern washing processes wash the soap in the grained condition in this way.

This principle was first applied in pans. Steam jets can be used to mix and transfer the pan contents; or a mechanical system can be used. Fig.1.5 shows diagrammatically a system which was used satisfactorily for a number of years. Fig. 1.5 (a) shows a fish-tail shaped nozzle, sometimes called a lye diffuser, through which lye is pumped into the upper part of the layer of soap curd in a pan. The nozzle is installed at the end of a jointed pipe system arranged so that the discharge is horizontal, which is also able to be adjusted to the level required just below the soap surface. Fig. 1.5(b) shows a group of four pans (diagrammatically in line, but, in practice, conveniently arranged in a square), with the essential pipe connections; and Fig. 1.5(c) shows the operation of one pan. Lye is transferred from one pan to the next by the pump through the lye diffuser; and is then circulated from the lye layer at the base of the pan into the curd layer. The action of the jet of liquid from the lye diffuser causes circulation and mixing of lye with curd, so that near equilibrium is achieved after a period of circulation. The pan is then allowed to settle before its lye is transferred and the curd is ready for another wash, or to be fitted. With an eight-pan unit (two sets of four as just described), the complete process, including several nights settling after fitting, is possible, but this is only suitable for a large production of a single type, or similar types, of base. For smaller productions a set of four pans fitted with lye diffusers can be used as a washing unit, and the washed curd transferred to other pans to be fitted and settled.

An Additional Principle

The influence of quantity of water added, and the number of washing stages used, on the efficiency of glycerol recovery have been considered. The way in which the water is added is also important. The principle is simple, it being that fresh water should, as far as possible, be added at the last washing stage. This is because water added at the saponification stage is used only once for the removal of glycerol from the soap; whereas water added at the end of a multi-stage process is used several times. It is also to be noted that although processes can be divided into saponification, washing, and fitting stages, glycerol is transferred from the soap in each stage. Various liquors containing some glycerol, such as those from nigres, or from the concentration of soapstock, often need to be introduced into the soapmaking process. The principle for the most effective return of such liquors is that they should, as far as possible, be introduced into the soapmaking system at the point where the concentration of glycerol in the system is the same as that in the liquor. This discussion explains the point made earlier that it is advantageous as regards recovery to concentrate a soapstock, so that a portion containing the fatty matter, but relatively little water, can be added at the saponification stage, and a liquor containing a small percentage of glycerol can be introduced at a later stage.

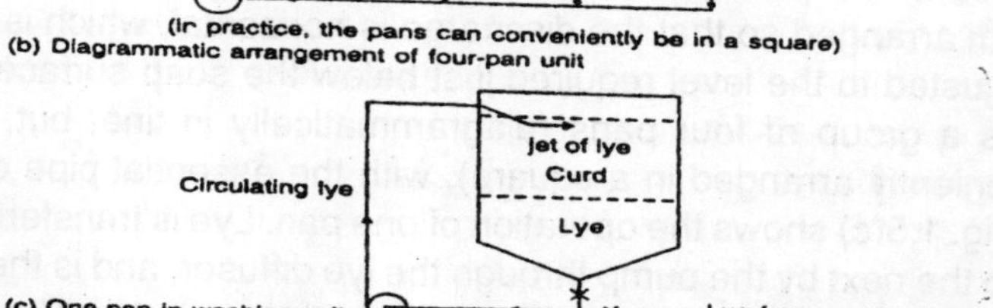

Fig. 1.5. Lye diffuser system of washing soap in pans.

The saponification of 1 tonne of a typical 80% tallow 20% coconut oil fat blend require about 0.118 tonnes Na_2O, allowing 2% excess. This is equivalent to 0.317 tonnes caustic soda liquor at 102°Tw, containing 48% NaOH or 37.2% Na_2O. The 1.317 tonnes reaction mixture which is produced from 1 tonne of fat plus 0.317 tonnes 102°Tw caustic soda contains about 0.95 tonnes fatty matter, or 72% TFM. When mixed with liquors and grained, this will produce lye plus a curd containing, say, 58% TFM. To convert the 72% TFM soap to 58% TFM soap the total mass has to be increased to 0.95/0.58 = 1.64 tonnes; that is 1.64-1.32 = 0.32 tonnes of material must be added. This could be, and sometimes is, salt plus water; but water introduced in this way is added at the wrong end of the process and is used inefficiently. It is better to use clean spent lye; a procedure sometimes known as use of the 'lye absorption principle'. It may seem peculiar to return to the fresh soap mass glycerol which has already been separated, but the procedure is analogous to what is done in a stage of a counter-current washing process; and it can be shown to be beneficial both by calculation and in practice. The best way to return lye to the saponification may vary with the soapmaking process in use and various soda liquor containing 0.48 × 0.317 = 0.152 tonnes of NaOH and 0.165 tonnes of water is diluted with 0.32 tonnes of spent lye containing, say, 11% NaCl, 11% glycerol and 78% water, the mixture will contain :

NaOH	0.152	+	–	=	0.152 tonnes
NaCl	–	+	0.035	=	0.035 tonnes
Glycerol	–	+	0.035	=	0.035 tonnes
Water	0.165	+	0.250	=	0.415 tonnes
					0.637 tonnes,

so that the diluted caustic soda solution contains 23.9% NaOH and 5.5% NaCl. In practice, it may be advisable to add rather less spent lye, to give a caustic soda solution for use in saponification containing about 30% NaOH and 4% NaCl. A small percentage of salt, of the order of 4%, is useful in the caustic soda solution to ensure that an adequate concentration of electrolyte is maintained. If sufficient final lye is re-cycled to the 48% NaOH liquor to give a saponified mass containing about 58% TFM and the lye from the next stage is added in the usual way, the saponification lye will be about the same size as the lye separated in the other washing stages. In some processes, the objective of not using fresh water to dilute the 48% caustic soda is achieved by adding lye from the second stage (that is the first wash if the saponification wash is not counted) instead of final lye. In this case, the volume of the saponification lye is less than that from subsequent washes by the volume needed to reduce the soap mass from 72% to 58% TFM.

THE COMPONENTS USED IN MODERN SOAPMAKING PROCESSES

Equipment for Saponification

Modern continuous saponification units use either :

(i) Devices to provide a very intimate mixture of fat and caustic soda solution, followed by completion of the reaction in a mass of soap.

(ii) Reaction in a mass of soap, which is usually recirculated, to which the reagents are added, and from which nearly completely saponified material is blend off.

Reaction in a circulating mass of soap is an application of what is called the dominant bath procedure. The soap may be circulated under atmospheric pressure, which limits the temperature to just over 100ºC; or the system may be closed to that higher pressure and temperature can be used.

The saponification unit is shown diagrammatically in Fig. 1.6, uses a colloid mill to bring the fat and caustic soda solution into intimate contact followed by flow through a reaction tube and mixer.

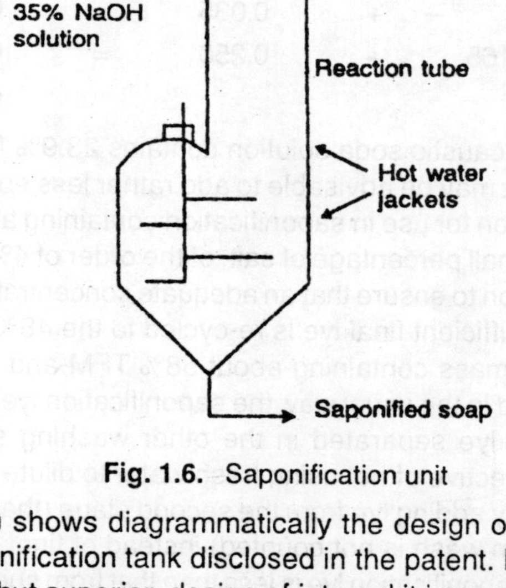

Fig. 1.6. Saponification unit

Fig. 1.7(a) shows diagrammatically the design of the jet and 1.7(b) that of the saponification tank disclosed in the patent. Fig. 1.7(c) shows a more complex, but superior, design of jet; and it is possible to use several designs of saponification tank with various numbers of baffles.

The solutions containing up to 15% of electrolyte favour the formation of an oil in water emulsion, 15-20% no emulsion, and above 20% a water in oil emulsion; a water in oil emulsion is preferred. Conditions, including design of jet, temperatures and electrolyte content (including caustic soda) must be adjusted to give a good emulsion. If the fat blend is nearly neutral, some free fatty acid, or soap, can be added if thought necessary. The Fig. 1.7 also discloses the following example; a jet with 1½ inch (38 mm) feed pipes and a ¼ inch (6.4 mm) steam jet fed with 70 psig steam is capable of emulsifying 7-8 tonnes of mixed fats containing 10-15% FFA per hour using a caustic soda solution containing 27-30% NaOH and 3% NaCl. of emulsifying 7-8 tonnes of mixed fats containing 10-15% FFA per hour using a caustic soda solution containing 27-30% NaOH and 3% NaCl. Temperatures should be arranged so that the emulsion only heats to just about 100°C when left in a small vessel to saponify. Table 1.8 from the patent gives results obtained with various fats containing a range of FFA contents. It will be noted that fats with a low FFA% required more time for self-saponification than other with a higher FFA%. To avoid risk of jet blockage the flow of fat should always be started before that of caustic soda. The principles can be combined with the idea of saponification in a circulating mass of soap. Two possible arrangements are shown in Fig. 1.9. The soap is recirculated at a high rate and the emulsion from the jet falls, or overflows, into it. The pressure is substantially atmospheric. The jet and tank system, preferably with recirculation, provides a sound, but inexpensive, saponification unit.

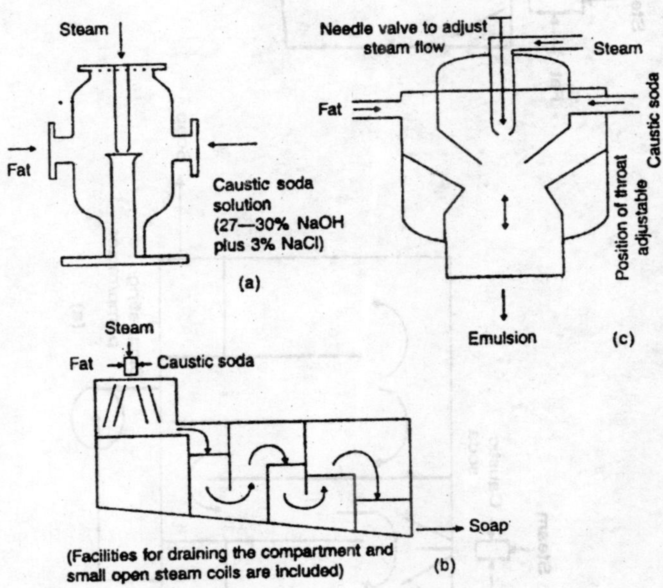

Fig. 1.7. Jet and tank system of saponification

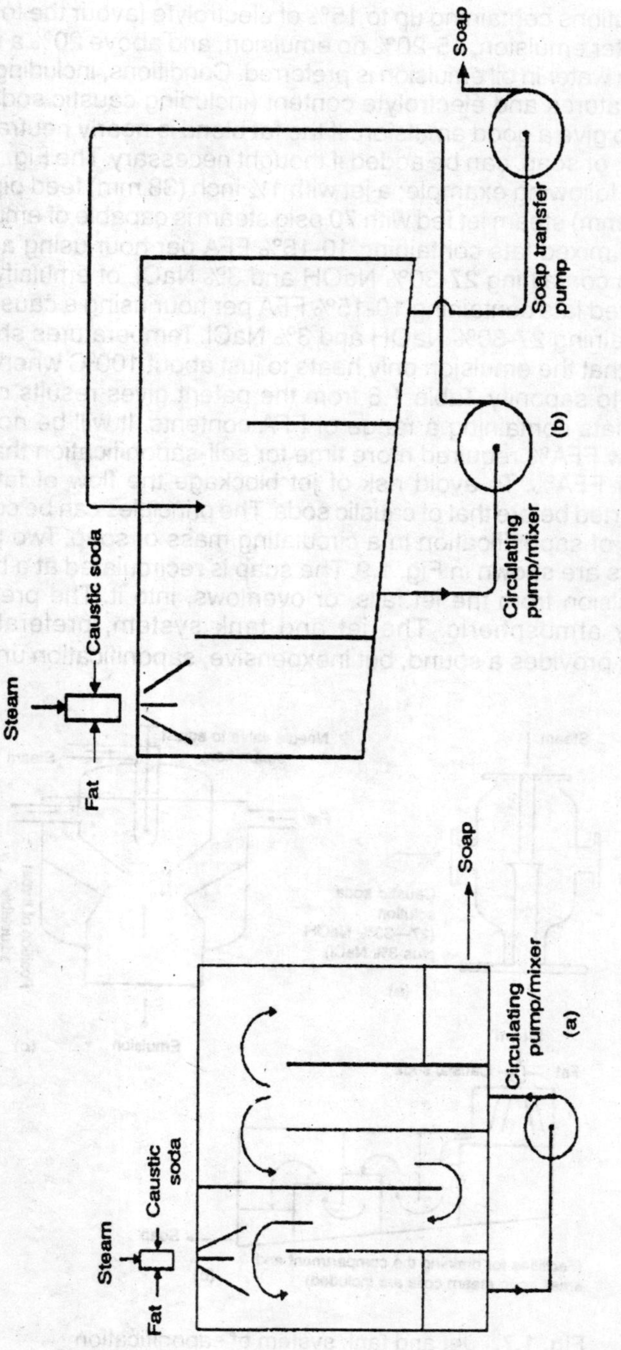

Fig. 1.8. Jet saponification using tank recirculation

Table 5.9 Data from continuous saponification unit.

Type of fat	*FFA%*	*Temperature of oil, °C*	*Temperature of emulsion, °C*	*Time for self-saponification 98-100% (mins)*
Neutral palm oil	0.6	54	61	23
Palm oil	46.2	52	85	2
Palm kernal oil	6.4	52	62	5
Groundnut oil	17.4	54	74	4
Mixed oils	1.7	46	59	3.5
mixed oils	20.0	43	70	1

The final temperature of the self saponified soap mass is approximately 100°C

As part of the *De Laval Centripure* process the saponification equipment shown diagrammatically in Fig. 1.9. The saponification unit comprises a lower tower divided into two sections *a* and *b*, and an upper tower *c*. Section *b* is further divided by a baffle which restricts flow from its lower to its upper part. Pump 1 circulates material from the top of section *b* back to the bottom of section *a*, *and the caustic soda solution is fed into its circulating line. Pump 2, which has several times the capacity of pump 1, draws material from both section a* and section *b;* and returns it to near the top of the lower part of section *b*.

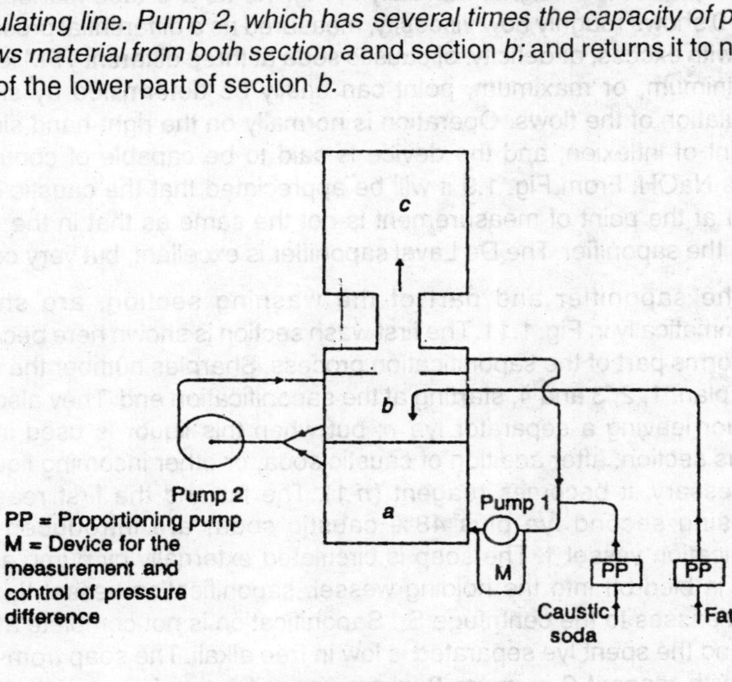

Fig. 1.9. Saponification unit.

The fat is introduced into section *b*. The whole Centripure plant is hermetically sealed; and the saponifier is understood to operate at up to about 125ºC under sufficient pressure to keep most of the water liquid. Contact parts are of stainless steel. After only a few minutes in section *b* the soap passes to the upper tower *c*, which is a holding vessel. Saponification is said to be about 99.8% complete on transfer from *b* to *c*, and over 99.95% complete when the soap leaves *c*, with only about 0.1% free alkali. Earlier designs used caustic soda solution at about 28% NaOH, giving a saponified mass at about 62% TFM, and with this design lye absorption can be practised by dilution of the strong caustic soda with spent lye.

A more robust unit which can produce soap at 72-73% TFM by the use of 48% NaOH caustic soda. Spent lye is then added to the mass leaving the saponifier to achieve both lye absorption and cooling. An important feature of saponifier is a control system based upon changes in viscosity which occur when the quantity of caustic soda added varies slightly from the stoichiometric quantity (that is the theoretical requirement for complete reaction). Pump 1 is of the positive rotary, gear, type which transfers soap at a constant rate, so that the pressure rise induced by the pump increases as viscosity increases. This is measured and controlled by a pneumatic controller, indicated diagrammatically in Fig. 1.9 as a U tube manometer. Fig. 1.10 shows roughly how viscosity, measured as a differential pressure, varies with excess, or deficity, of caustic soda at three different TFM levels. The minimum, or maximum, point can easily be determined by simple manipulation of the flows. Operation is normally on the right-hand side of the point of inflexion; and the device is said to be capable of control to ±0.01% NaOH. From Fig. 1.9 it will be appreciated that the caustic soda content at the point of measurement is not the same as that in the soap leaving the saponifier. The De Laval saponifier is excellent, but very costly.

The saponifier and part of the washing section, are shown diagrammatically in Fig. 1.11. The first wash section is shown here because it also forms part of the saponification process. Sharples number the units in their plant 1, 2, 3 and 4, starting at the saponification end. They also call the liquor leaving a separator lye *n*; but when this liquor is used in the previous section, after addition of caustic soda, or other incoming liquors, as necessary, it becomes reagent (*n*-1). The fat and the first reagent, comprising second lye plus 48% caustic soda, are introduced into saponification vessel 1. The soap is circulated externally by pump and a portion is bled-off into the holding wessel, saponification vessel II, from which it passes to the centrifuge S_1. Saponification is not complete at this stage and the spent lye separated is low in free alkali. The soap from S_1 is mixed with reagent 2 in mixer 2 where saponification is completed with liquor containing an adequate excess of caustic soda. Additional 48% caustic soda can be added to R_2 as indicated, but sufficient usually remains from additions later in the process and the provision for addition to R_2 is not normally included. It will be noted that the *Sharples process* uses two-stage saponification for the reasons. Actually provision is made for the completion of saponification in the washing stages of most processes, even though free fat may not be left deliberately after the main saponification. The *Sharples process* also includes the version of the lye absorption principle which uses second stage lye.

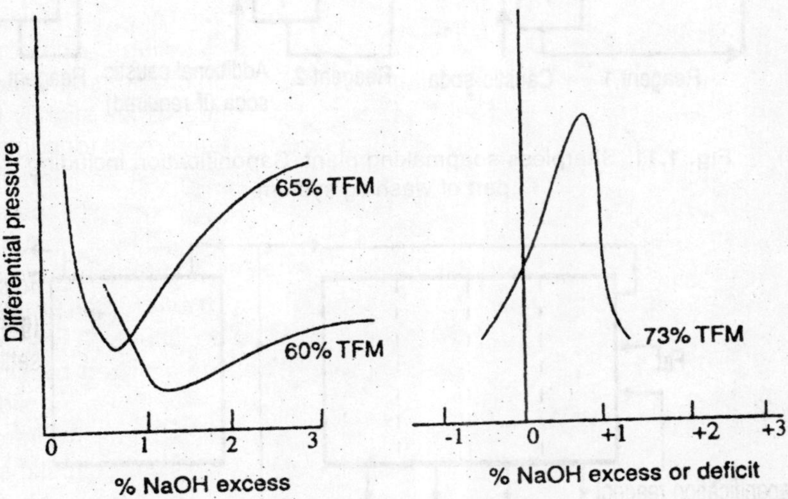

Fig. 1.10. Variation in viscosity, or differential pressure, with excess, or deficit, of caustic soda - De Laval saponifier.

Meccaniche Moderne and *Mazzoni* continuous soapmaking plants use very similar saponification systems shown diagrammatically in Fig. 1.12. Saponification takes place in a four compartment autoclave operating at about 120°C under two atmospheres pressure; and soap is re-cycled. The soap then moves to the mixer/cooler, which has four compartments with axial mixers. Saponification is substantially completed in this vessel. The first two compartments have water cooling coils and the temperature is reduced to about 90°C; this reduces solubility of soap in lye, and the two phases separate so that they can be parted in the static, gravity, separator to which the mixture is passed.

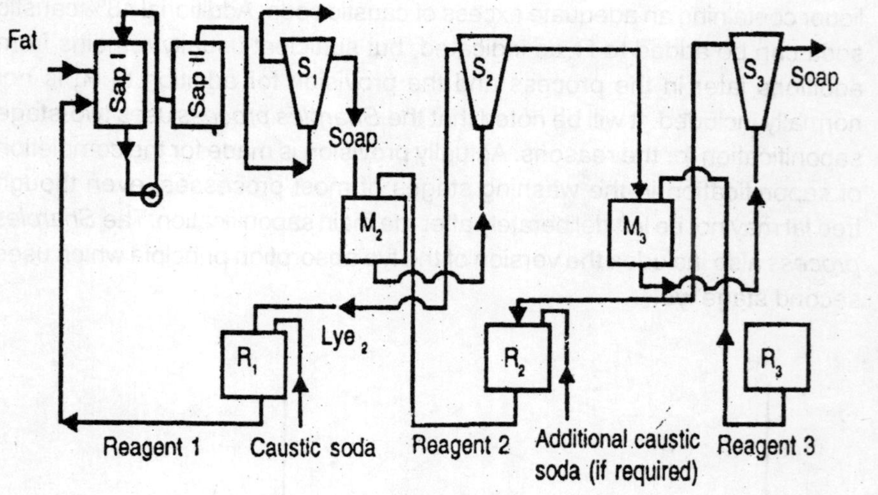

Fig. 1.11. Sharpless soapmaking plant. Saponification including part of washing system.

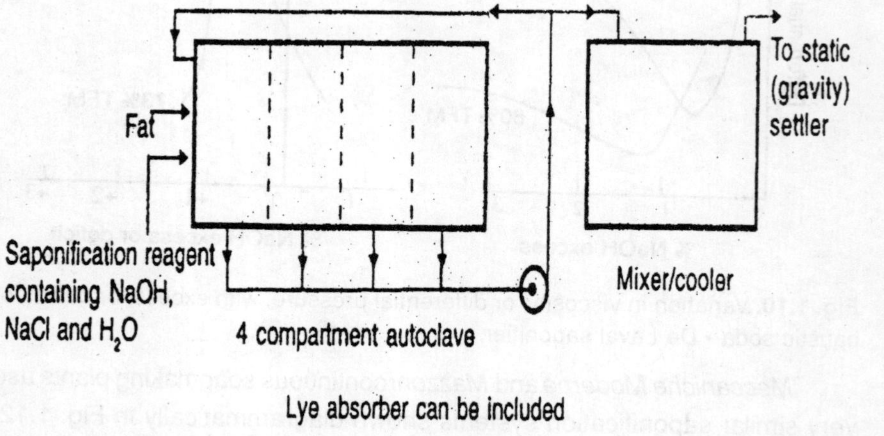

Fig. 1.12. Saponification system for Meccaniche moderne and mazzoni SCN plants.

Equipment for Washing

As mentioned earlier, all modern soapmaking plants wash the glycerol out of the soap by counter-current transfer of glycerol from soap in the grained condition to the lye. Many types of equipment can be used, but all fall into one of the following kinds :

(i) Mixers and static, or gravity, settlers.

(ii) Mixers and centrifugal separators.

(iii) Truly continuous counter-current contactors.

A tray-type multi-stage washer, somewhat similar to the washing tower is shown diagrammatically in Fig. 1.13. Six stages of mixer/settler washing are included in a single washing tower. Each stage comprises a settling section with inclined top and bottom, through which is inserted a tube with a mechanically rotated mixer. The soap rises through a tube from the top of a settler section into the next mixer; and lye joints it from the section above at a rate controlled by a positive displacement (Mono) pump.

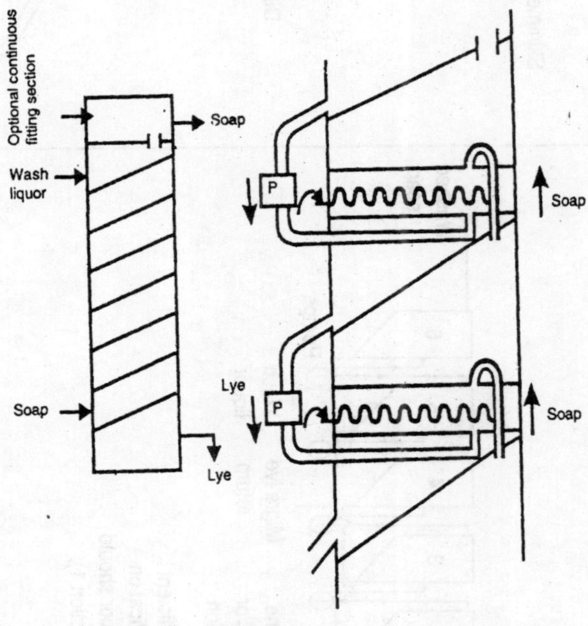

Fig. 1.13. Monsavon washing tower.

A continuous washing unit, known as a *DPU (divided pan unit)*. The main features are shown in Fig. 1.14. In the original unit a 14 foot (4.27 m) cube pan is divided into six sections, but a tank divided into any reasonable number of sections and arranged to suit a required layout can be used. The flows are those standard for a mixer/settler system. Open inpeller centrifugal pumps are used to mix lye and soap curd, and to return the mixture to the middle level in the next stage. Recirculation round the pumps to increase mixing to improve performance. Large floats designed to position themselves at the curd/lye interface control the outflow of lye by actuating gate, or treacle, type valves. To minimise the force needed to move the value disco,

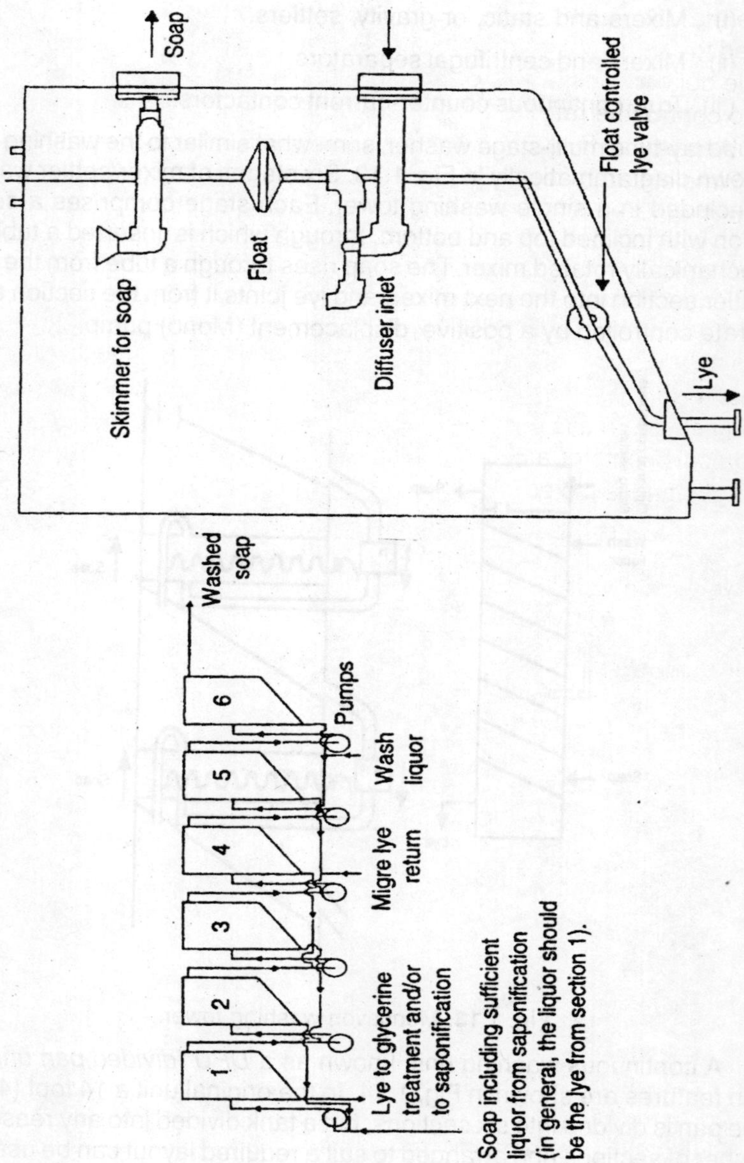

Fig. 1.14. Divided pan type washing unit.

a small clearance is left between the stationary and the moving plate; in consequence these valves will not stop the flow completely, but do all that is necessary for control. The float rods extend above the top of the unit, so that the operator can push them down momentarily from time to time to ensure that the valves are working properly. A simple basket type filter is installed to protect the crude soap feed pump. This pump is preferably of a variable delivery positive type, such as the Plenty pump, so that it can be used to control the rate at which the soap is fed. The unit made from a 14 foot cube pan was found capable of washing 4-15 tonnes/hour of 58% curd soap. Simple, flap-type, non-return valves are fitted in the lye lines near to the centrifugal pumps to prevent back-flow of soap. The unit should be well lagged; and fitted with a stainless steel cover, provided with inspection doors.

Meccaniche Moderne and *Mazzoni* use four stage mixer/settler washing units similar in principle to the DPU, but they differ in design from each other and from the DPU. Fig. 1.15 shows the main features of a Mazzoni washing stage. In this unit, the four washing stages are placed together in the compartments of a single tank. Soap curd overflows from the tops of the stages and is mixed with lye in the pumps.

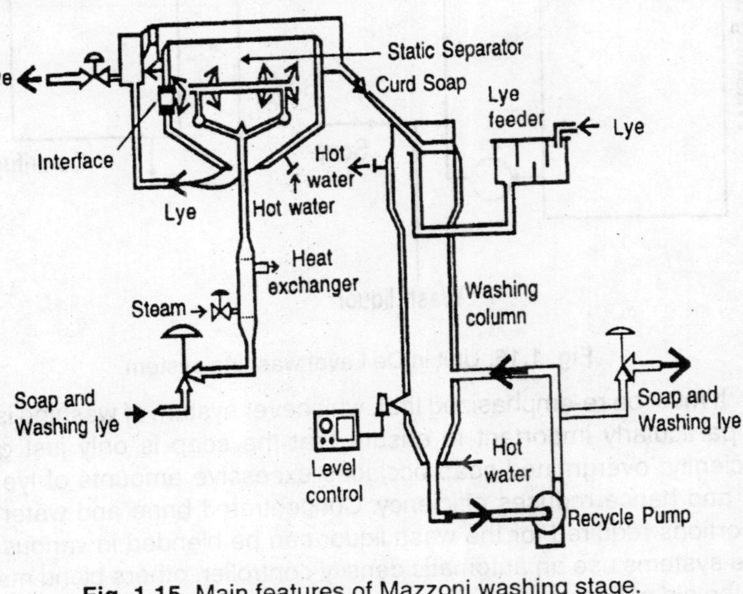

Fig. 1.15. Main features of Mazzoni washing stage.

Plants which use mixers and centrifugal separators use essentially the same flow sheet as those with gravity settlers, as shown in Fig. 1.11 for the *Sharples plant*. Some *De Laval plants* use a similar system, with a different type of centrifuge, as shown in Fig. 1.16. A viscosity recorder, is used to aid the control of the grain; the proportions of water and concentrated brine being varied manually. Because centrifuges normally separate more efficiently than gravity settlers, less washing stages are required; and often only two are included, apart from the centrifuges used in the saponification and fitting stages. Centrifuges also collect most of the particulate dirt in the material processed; and the bowls need to be cleaned when they become as full as is permissible.

The *rotating disc contactor,* shown diagrammatically in Fig. 1.17, can provide a particularly effective unit for the washing of soap. The shaft rotates at about 80 rpm; and the diameter of the rotating discs is slightly smaller than that of the holes in the fixed discs, so that the shaft can be withdrawn. Lye recirculation to use the lye absorption principle can be arranged in various ways to suit the saponification system employed

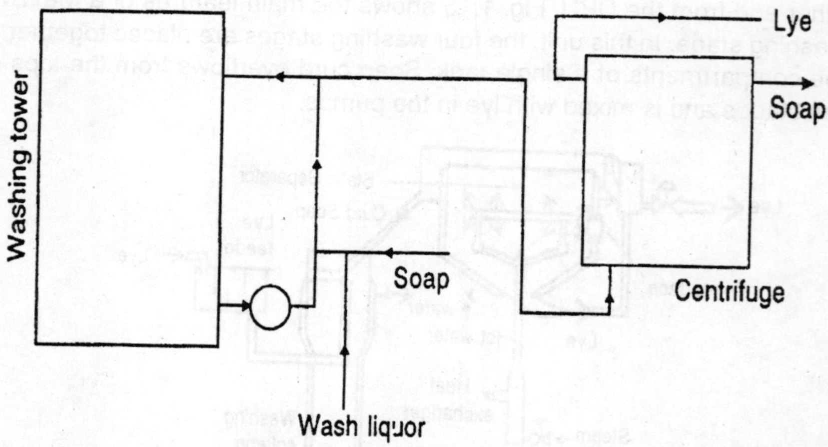

Fig. 1.16. Unit in De Laval washing system.

It must be re-emphasized that, whichever system of washing is used, it is particularly important to ensure that the soap is only just grained sufficiently; overgrained soap occludes excessive amounts of lye in the curd and hence reduces efficiency. Concentrated brine and water in the proportions required for the wash liquor can be blended in various ways; some systems use an automatic density controller, others blend manually with the aid of flow measurers, such as rotameters.

Equipment for Fitting and Final Separation

In the traditional process fitting was a complex operation involving much boiling, but it has been found that it is only necessary to mix the washed curd with the water and, if required, electrolyte needed to give the correct composition for the desired type of fit. An early example of mechanical fitting in a pan used the lye diffuser described, when it was found that soap fitted mechanically settled more quickly than soap which was boiled in the conventional way, probably because it was not filled with bubbles of steam

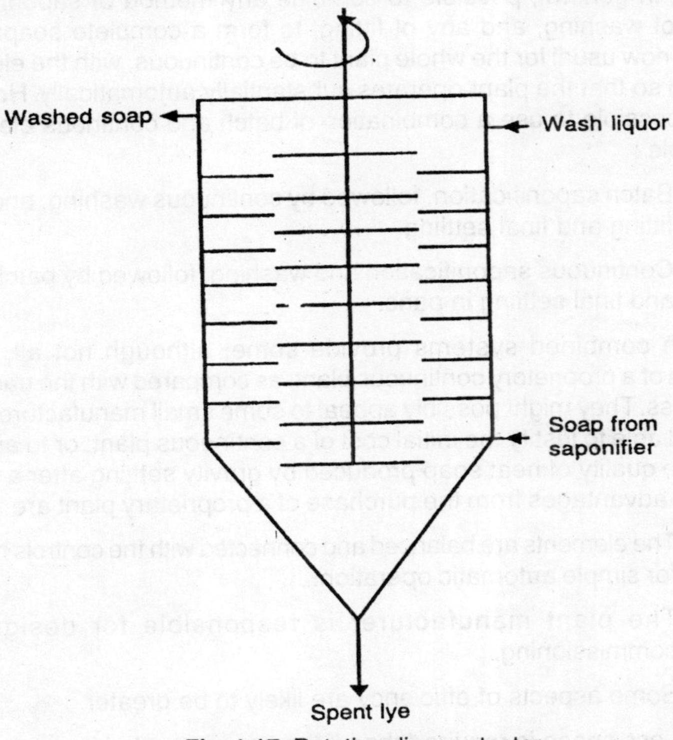

Fig. 1.17. Rotating disc contactor.

Some modern continuous processes use only a simple line mixer, or even just injection of fitting liquor into the pipeline through which the soap flows. Others use a holding and mixing column into which the fitting liquor is injected with recirculation of the soap. The De Laval process uses such a column with circulation and the addition of fitting liquor is again controlled by differential pressure measurement directly related to viscosity. The mixture passes to a second column intended to ensure full establishment of equilibrium.

Obviously, long settling under gravity is not practicable in a continuous process; and centrifuges are always used for the final separation. Open fits giving a thin nigre, or nigre lye, are also common; and arrangements are usually included for the continuous return of the nigre lye to the washing system.

Complete Soapmaking Plants

It is, in general, possible to combine any method of saponification with any of washing, and any of fitting, to form a complete soapmaking plant. It is now usual for the whole plant to be continuous, with the elements integrated so that the plant operates substantially automatically. However, it is also possible to use a combination of batch and continous elements, for example :

(i) Batch saponification, followed by continuous washing, and batch fitting and final settling.

(ii) Continuous saponification and washing, followed by batch fitting and final settling in pans.

Such combined systems provide some, although not all, of the advantges of a proprietory continuous plant, as compared with the traditional pan process. They might possibly appeal to some small manufacturers who do not feel able to justify the initial cost of a continuous plant; or to any who require the quality of neat soap produced by gravity settling after a fine fit. Additional advantages from the purchase of a proprietary plant are :

(i) The elements are balanced and connected with the controls needed for simple automatic operation.

(ii) The plant manufacturer is responsible for design and commissioning.

(iii) Some aspects of efficiency are likely to be greater.

(iv) Less space is required than if the soap is settled in pans.

Fig. 1.11 discussed in the section on saponification equipment also shows the arrangement of a Sharples washing stage. In a complete *Sharples* plant, the soap curd from centrifuge S_3 is mixed with fourth stage reagent (water, brine and 48% caustic soda) in a fitting mixer, equipped for recirculation by external pump, and the mixture is centrifuged to give neat soap and thin nigre which is returned to R_3 where it forms part of the third reagent. Two centrifuges in parallel may be used for the final stage, because a lower rate of throughput is needed for proper separation of neat soap than for curd.

Plant Performance

Apart from matters of quality and capacity, the performance of a soapmaking plant is judged by the efficiency with which it separates the glycerol using a given quantity of water. Both these important criteria can be expressed in various ways. The most direct way in which to express recovery is in terms of percentage yield, that is glycerol in spent lye as a percentage of glycerol in fats. It is also often reported in terms of the glycerol content of the soap produced (usually calculated at 63% TFM, or at 100% TFM). The relationship between the two measures depends upon the glycerol content of the fat blend used; and Table 1.10 gives figures calculated by simple arithmetic for (a) a high glycerol fat blend containing 10.5% glycerol, and (b) an acid oil type of blend containing 6% glycerol. The quantity of water used can be expressed as lye/fat ratio, lye/63% TFM soap ratio, or as the concentration of glycerol in the final spent lye. Some figures showing the relationship between these criteria for the two fat blends are given in Table 1.11. The relationship between percentage recover and lye/fat ratio depends upon the process used and is a measure of its efficiency. The glycerol content of the wash liquor used, which depends upon the glycerol added in recovered salt and in any weak liquors introduced at the final wash stage, affects recovery and becomes increasingly significant as the level of recovery increases and the glycerol in soap decreases. In general, it is possible to improve recovery at the expense of lye/fat ratio (or concentration of glycerol in lye) and vice versa. Just as with simple washing in pans, the efficiency of a mixer/separator washing stage is directly influenced by the dryness of the separated curd, as can be measured by determination of K_G. With gravity settlers, values of K_G around 0.4 have ben found which indicates that the mixing of lye and curd is as effective as washing by the traditional method of closing the soap and re-graining at each stage. Centrifuges usually produce curds containing less enmeshed lye than gravity settlers; and so provide more efficient washing stages with lower values of K_G. Operators can check the performance of a plant by estimation of K_G for the various stages, or even by just determination of the TFMs of the various curds from time to time. Inadequate settling time (that is too great a throughput for the particular plant) can result in wet curds; but, as indicated earlier, poor performance is often due to over-graining.

Glycerol cannot be separated until it has been liberated by the chemical reaction, so that it is important to ensure that saponification is as complete as possible at the earliest possible stage. Broadly, it can be said that around 95% recovery is common with a lye/fat ratio of, say 0.7; which, from Table 1.11, is equivalent to a lye containing about 14% glycerol from a fat blend containing 10.5% glycerol.

Table 1.10. Relationship between glycerol percentage in soap and percentage recovery from (a) fat containing 10.5% glycerol and (b) fat containing 6% glycerol.

Percentage glycerol in 63% TFM soap	*(a) Fat blend containing 10.5% glycerol*		*(b) Fat blend containing 6% glycerol*	
	Percentage of the glycerol in the fats left in the soap	*Percentage transferred to lyes*	*Percentage of the glycerol in the fats left in the soap*	*Percentage transferred to lyes*
0.1	1.4	98.6	2.5	97.5
0.2	2.9	97.1	5.0	95.0
0.3	4.3	95.7	7.5	92.5
0.4	5.7	94.3	10.0	90.0
0.5	7.1	92.9	12.5	87.5
0.75	10.7	89.3	18.8	81.2
1.0	14.3	85.7	25.0	75.0
1.5	21.4	78.6	37.5	62.5

No allowance for any losses is made in this table.
It is assumed that 1 tonne of fat produces 1.5 tonnes of 63% TFM soap.

Comparison between the modern and the traditional pan processes are :

(i) The old process took about 5 - 8 days, so that much space was required. Material passes through the modern processes in an hour or so; or even less.

(ii) The continuous process normally re-cycle the nigre, or nigre-lye, and are completely self-contained.

(iii) In addition to the large saving in steam, and in capacity needed for lye treatment and evaporation, which results from the higher concentration of glycerol in lyes, the modern processes use much less steam than the pan process itself.

(iv) The modern processes use more power than the old, but the cost per tonne of soap is not high.

(v) Comparison of quality is less clear. Advantages for the modern processes are that :

(a) There is little opportunity for airborne dirt to contaminate the soap; and centrifuges remove particulate dirt effectively.

(b) There may be less risk of damage by oxidation and prolonged heating, but it seems doubtful whether this difference is substantial.

Table 1.11. Relationships between criteria for quantity of water used in soapmaking under various circumstances.

Ratio lye/fat	*Ratio lye/63% TFM soap*	*Concentration of glycerol in lye*			
		Fat containing 10.5% glycerol		*Fat containing 6% glycerol*	
		Recovery = 95%	*Recovery = 85%*	*Recovery = 95%*	*Recovery = 85%*
0.4	0.27	25.0	22.3	14.3	12.8
0.5	0.33	20.0	17.9	11.4	10.2
0.6	0.40	16.6	14.9	9.5	8.5
0.7	0.47	14.3	12.8	8.1	7.3
0.8	0.53	12.5	11.2	7.1	6.4
0.9	0.60	11.1	9.9	6.3	5.7
1.0	0.67	10.0	8.9	5.7	5.1
1.1	0.73	9.1	8.1	5.2	4.6
1.2	0.80	8.3	7.4	4.8	4.3

On the other hand :

(i) Very thorough saponification is possible with the pan process.

(ii) Soap from properly operated continuous plants is entirely satisfactory for modrn finishing processes. The neat soap produced is also satisfactory for many purposes, but it showed nigre spots when frame cooled unless the centrifuge throughput was very low. Further work might show that any such problem can be avoided by adjustment of conditions.

Preliminary Tratment of Spent Lyes in the Soapmaking

Spent lyes contain variable quantities of free alkali and soap (particularly low molecular weight soaps), as well as colouring matter, particulate dirt and other impurities. The system of two-stage saponification, in which the final spent lye is separated from soap containing some free fat, produces lye with a low free alkali content; and in modern counter-current processes this is the only lye sent to the glycerine department. Some soapmakers prefer to saponify as completely as possible in the first stage, which, as well as having possible quality advantages, ensures that the glycerol is all liberated as early as possible. With the old process most lyes are transferred for recovery of crude glycerine and the traditional procedure was to leave the lyes in tanks below the pans where they cooled. Soap separated on the surface, was skimmed, and then returned to a suitable boil of probably low grade soap. The cooled and skimmed lyes are transferred to the glycerine department where they are acidified to a pH of about 4.6

with mineral acid, preferably hydrochloric to avoid unnecessary introduction of sulphate into the system. The tank contents was agitated with compressed air and allowed to settle. The lower layer of acidified lye is transferred to the first treatment process. When a sufficient layer of fatty material had collected from several acidifications, it is skimmed off and either discarded or returned to a low grade soap, possibly after filtration. The value of this scum fatty acid is doubtful. It is a poor soapmaking material and contained low molecular weight and hydroxy acids, both of which produce rather soluble soaps liable to be rejected to the next lyes; and so to build up in the system. The acidified lye is well suited to the rest of the lye treatment process. The process had important disadvantages :

(i) It involves a loss of alkali and the need to purchase additional mineral acid to neutralise this alkali.

(ii) It lead to a loss of heat which had to be replaced later, although some of this loss is liable to occur anyway, if a substantial buffer stock of lyes is held in the factory.

(iii) It is a messy procedure which occupies considerable space and labour.

(iv) Unless particular care is taken to keep the alkaline part of the system clean, and mud is generally deposited in the lye tanks, it could provide conditions favourable to the growth of the micro-organisms which destroy glycerol and produce rimethylene glycol (TMG, 1,3-propane diol), a substance which is troublesome in the glycerine refinery, as well as an indication that glycerol has been destroyed.

It has been found that lyes could with advantage be neutralised with fatty acids, or with fats containing a substantial proportion of free fatty acid. The operation, known as lye neutralisation, can be carried out in various ways, but it is necessary to ensure intimate contact between fatty acid and lye.

2

Solid, Household and Toilet Soaps Manufacture

Introduction

Genuine household type soaps can be made from soap base in various ways; that is by allowing the soap to cool in frames or water-coolers, or by extrusion, which is now almost universal, apart from some small traditional manufacturers who still use the old processes. Similar processes are used for filled household soaps.

Toilet soaps can also be made in several ways, but for very many years extrusion processes have been dominant. Extrusion processes for household soaps and for toilet soaps have features in common; and it is convenient to discuss some general aspects of the two processes after the older household soap processes have been considered, but before extrusion processes for household and toilet soaps are discussed more specifically.

The Older Processes for Household Soaps

Genuine soaps are produced by solidifying soap base without major additions; but minor additions of colour, perfume, preservative, etc., and of cresols in the case of carbolic soaps, are frequently made in simple mixing pots called crutchers. The oldest and simplest process is then to run the soap into moulds in which it is left to cool. Almost any containers can be used, but rectangular boxes with detachable sides, known as frames, are usual. Frames can be static, arranged in rows and fed with liquid soap by an arrangement of troughs and gates, or mobile, that is fitted with wheels, so that they can be put under the outlet from the crutcher and then moved elsewhere to cool. Solidification in production sized frames often takes about six days. Two operations should usually be carried out during the solidification of soap in a frame :

(i) hand crutching whilst the soap is still substantially liquid. This is mixing by a man who normally stands on the sides of the frame using a hand crutcher, which is a perforated steel plate with a shaft and handle at right angles to the plate, pushed up and down in the soap in the frame.

(ii) knocking out, in which the bolts which hold the sides of the frame are loosened and the still plastic, or partly liquid, soap is pressed down with a pummel. In this way the soap which has contracted on cooling is pressed out to fill the frame. Otherwise some bars from zones which have contracted will be short.

The frame joints are liable to leak; and gaps are caulked with paper pressed into the joints as necessary.

When the frame contents are completely solid, the sides of the frames are removed and the blocks are cut into slabs with a mobile cutter using a frame of wires drawn through the soap. The slabs are then cut into bars with another wire cutter. The bars are usually kept for some time in an 'open pile', that is, each layer of bars is placed with spaces between the bars, and each layer is laid at right angles to the one below. This allows air to penetrate the stack; and a slightly dried-skin is formed on most of each bar. The bars are trimmed and, usually, given a simple imprint with a stamper struck with a mallet (or a mechanical equivalent) before being packed in cases as bar soap. Alternatively, the bars are cut into billets and stamped into tablets using dies and shells as described later for toilet soaps.

Mechanical, or hand, stampers can be used; and the tablets may be wrapped and/or cartonned. A considerable quantity of unusable soap is produced in the frame process. In particular, the top and bottom slices and other off-cuts have to be re-boiled, or re-melted, before being returned to a crutching pot with new soap.

To reduce the tirne (and hence space) needed to convert liquid soap into the solid form, machines were devised in which cooling by water was used. Fig. 2.1 shows a slab cooler, sometimes known as a Jacobi cooler, although types were made by various firms. The liquid soap is run from the pan, or from a crutcher if additions are made, into a pressure vessel from which it is forced by compressed air into the cooler. The cooler is something like a filter-press, in which water-cooled plates alternate with frames in which the soap is solidified. The plates are faced with stainless steel, or other corrosion-resistant metal; and baffles are provided as shown inside the corrosion-resistant metal; and baffles are provided as shown inside the plates to cause the water to flow at a good velocity over the whole of the cooling area. Solidification occurs in a few hours, and the slabs of solid soap are handled like slabs from the frame cooling process.

Other water coolers produce bars directly. Tubes of non-rusting metal, with the cross-sections required to give bars of the desired dimensions, are arranged in a water-jacket (the unit being rather like a calandria). Each tube is fitted with a plunger which is moved downwards to draw in liquid soap from the header tank situated at the top of the unit immediately above the upper tube plate and the tube mouths. When the tube contents have ben solidified by the water flowing through the jacket, they are pushed out in the form of bars by upward movement of the plungers. Experiments have been carried out on the moulding of individual billets of the required shape and dimensions.

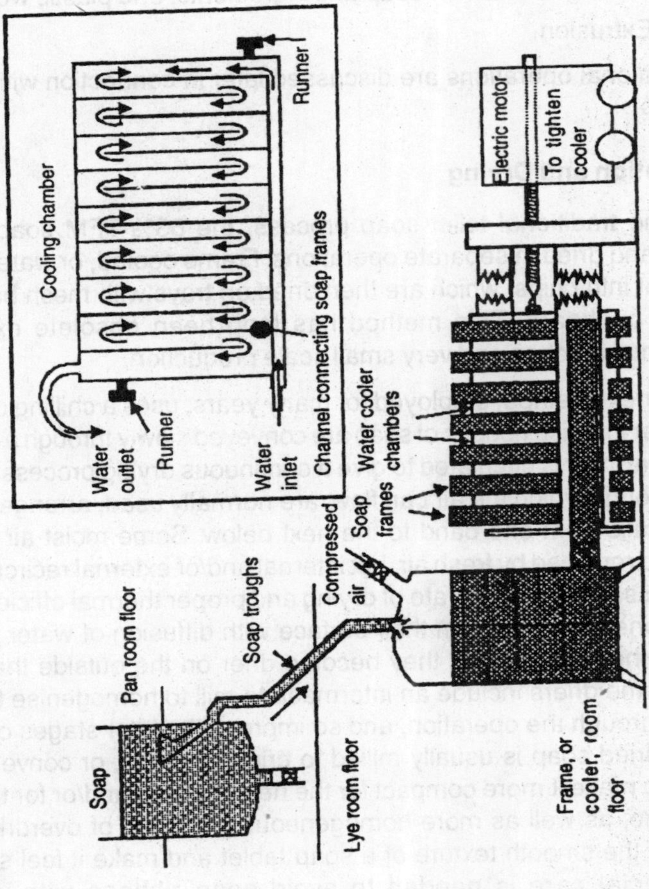

Fig.2.1. Water cooler - Slab type.

SOME PRINCIPLES RELATED TO THE PRODUCTION OF EXTRUDED SOAP

General

Soap base produced using a conventional fit normally leaves the settling pan, or final centrifuge, at about 62-64% TFM. Bureau of Indian specifications require a genuine household soap to contain not less than 62% TFM, and a toilet soap not less than 76.5, 78.0, or 79.0% TFM, depending upon type. Other specifications are possible, but the soap base needs to be dried in the production of all normal toilet soaps. The following operations involved :

(i) Solidification.

(ii) Drying, now often combined with solidification.

(iii) Homogenisation of soap and ingredients, and plastic working.

(iv) Extrusion.

Additional operations are discussed later in connection with specific processes.

Solidification and Drying

In the traditional toilet soap process, the 63% TFM soap base is solidified and dried in separate operations. Frame cooled, or water cooled, soap is cut into chips, which are then dried on trays with mesh bases in a warm air cupboard. This method has long been obsolete except for experimental batches and very small scale production.

The next method, employed for many years, uses a chilling drum and a band drier in which ribbons of soap are conveyed slowly through a chamber in which warm air is circulated to give a continuous drying process. Several bands, through which the air can flow, are normally used, arranged so that the soap falls from one band to the next below. Some moist air must be vented and replaced by fresh air, but internal and/or external recirculation of air is necessary for a good rate of drying and proper thermal efficiency. The soap ribbons are dried from their surface with diffusion of water from the interior to the surface; and they become drier on the outside than in the interior. Some driers include an intermediate mill to homogenise the soap part way through the operation, and so improve the later stages of drying. The fully dried soap is usually milled to crimped chips, or converted into noodles, to make it more compact for the next process and/or for transport and storage, as well as more homogeneous. Particles of overdried soap can impair the smooth texture of a soap tablet and make it feel sandy, or gritty. Special care is needed to avoid soap ribbons with irregular protruberances, or undue thinness, which can become overdried; and to remove dust whenever necessary. The removal of dust applies also to conveyors. The chilling drums used to convert liquid soap base to solid ribbons are large diameter water cooled drums on which the soap is spread in a thin layer. This is often done by providing a small roll to work close to the upper part of the drum. A small reservoir of liquid soap is held in the 'nip' between the two rolls and a layer of soap is formed on the cooled drum which is subsequently removed as ribbons by a serrated knife followed by a full-bladed knife. The large drum into which the cooling water is sprayed can operate half-full of water, or a discharge pipe introduced through the trunnion and bent downwards can keep the drum nearly empty.

Band driers have now largely been replaced by driers in which the liquid soap is heated in a heat exchanger, usually tubular or plate type, and then flashed by reduction in pressure. Three types are used which in principle differ only in the pressure to which the soap is flashed :

(i) Tubular, or plate, driers in which the liquid soap is heated and the pressure then reduced to atmospheric by passage of the fluid through a throttle. Vapour is discharged and the concentrated liquid soap is solidified on a chilling drum, or other device.

(ii) Vacuum flash driers in which the hot liquid soap is flashed into an evacuated chamber. Flashing to a vacuum also chills the soap and converts it to a solid form.

(iii) Driers in which partial drying by flash to atmospheric pressure is followed by a second stage in which the residual liquid soap is reheated and flashed to vacuum.

The simplified sketch for countercurrent flow in a spray-drying tower is shown in Fig. 2.2(a) and Fig. 2.2(b) shows vacuum drier chiller unit, is a key element in modern plants for the production of both household and toilet soaps.

When used to produce *household soap,* the heater is not needed, except as a pipe. The liquid soap enters the spray chamber at about 80-90^{0}C and sufficient evaporation occurs to cool and solidify the soap by conversion of sensible to latent heat of vapourisation.

The liquid soap is sprayed into the walls of the evacuated chamber and is scraped off by blades on the same shaft set at 180^0 to the nozzles. Water vapour is drawn through dust collectors by the vacuum system. The solidified soap falls to the base of the chamber and is removed continuously by the first worm extruder (refiner). The noodles of soap fall into the vacuum chest from which they are extruded in the form of a continuous bar by the second extruder (plodder). The two extruders are shown in Fig. 2.2(b), but only one in Fig. 2.2(a).

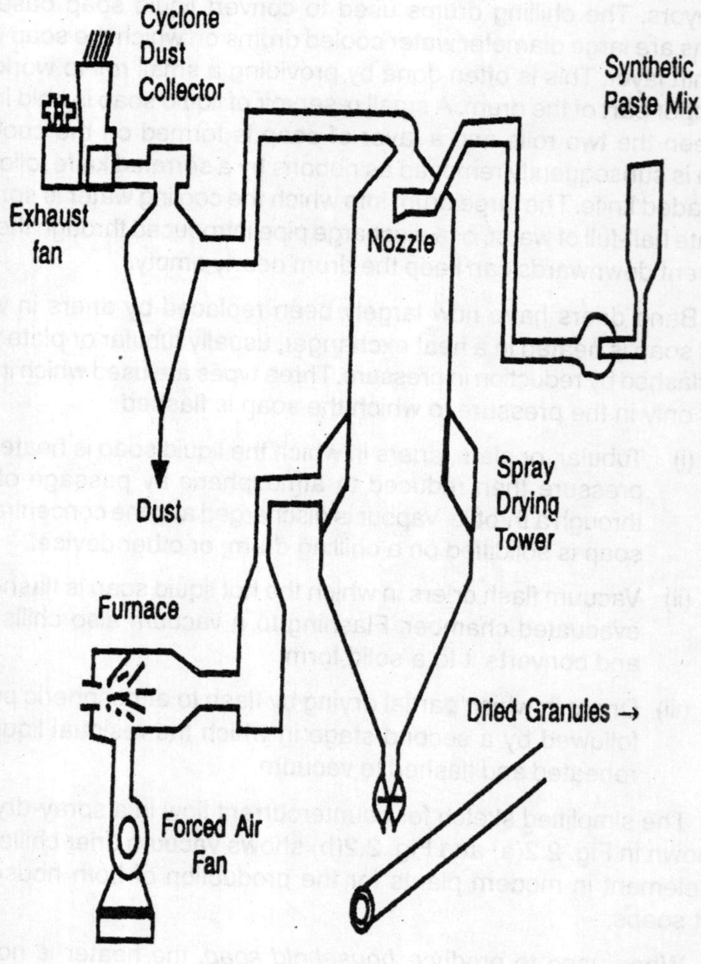

Fig. 2.2 (a). Simplified sketch for countercurrent flow in a spray drying tower.

The worm extruders, which are considered in detail later, also serve to seal the chambers so that vacuum can be maintained.

When the unit is used as a drier to produce *toilet soap noodles,* heat is supplied in the heat exchanger to increase the evaporation, and the second extruder is changed from a plodder to a refiner by removal of the cone and substitution of an end with a perforated plate and rotating knives to give noodles of dried soap.

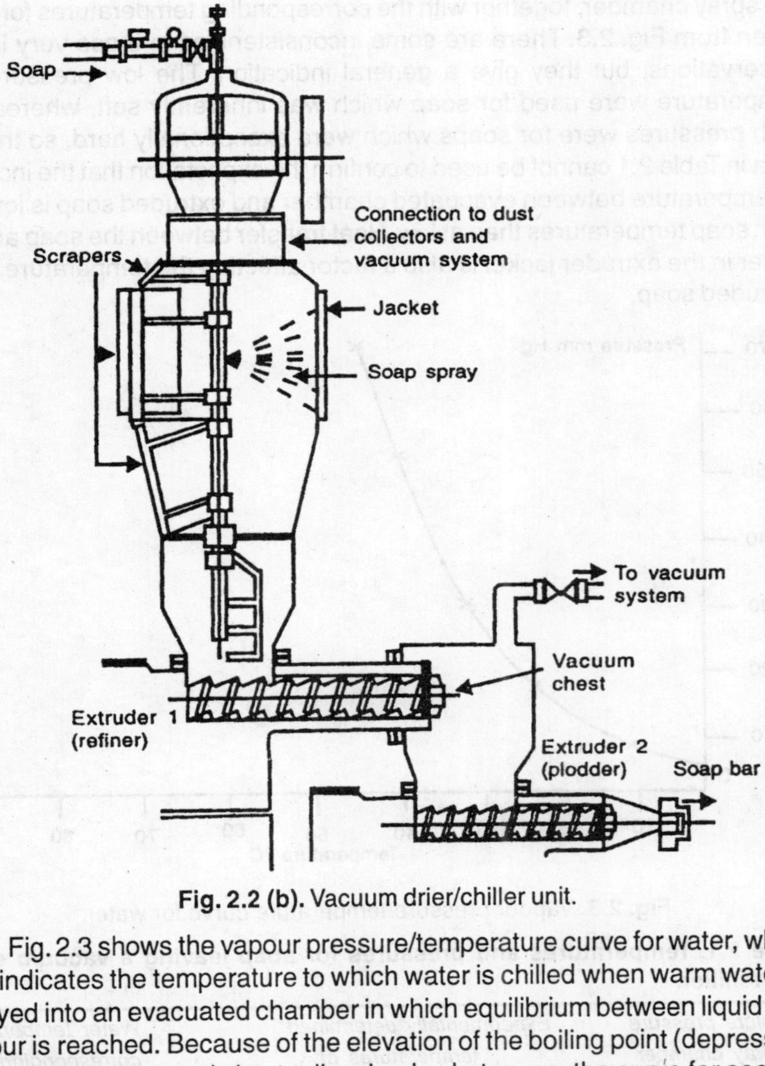

Fig. 2.2 (b). Vacuum drier/chiller unit.

Fig. 2.3 shows the vapour pressure/temperature curve for water, which also indicates the temperature to which water is chilled when warm water is sprayed into an evacuated chamber in which equilibrium between liquid and vapour is reached. Because of the elevation of the boiling point (depression of the vapour pressure) due to dissolved substances, the curve for soap of any given water content indicates a somewhat higher temperature than that for water at the same pressure; but the curve for water shows roughly how the temperature to which the soap is cooled varies with the absolute pressure in the evacuated chamber. Mechanical work done on the solid soap in the extruder, or extruders, raises the temperature to an extent which increases as the soap increases in hardness, that is as soap from a given fat blend becomes drier and/or colder. Table 2.1 shows some limited experimental figures for the temperature of the extruded soap with various pressures in the spray chamber, together with the corresponding temperatures for water taken from Fig. 2.3. There are some inconsistencies in these very limited observations, but they give a general indication. The low pressure and temperature were used for soap which was inherently soft, whereas the high pressures were for soaps which were exceptionally hard, so that the data in Table 2.1 cannot be used to confirm the expectation that the increase in temperature between evacuated chamber and extruded soap is lower at high soap temperatures than at low. Heat transfer between the soap and the water in the extruder jacket is also a factor affecting the temperature of the extruded soap.

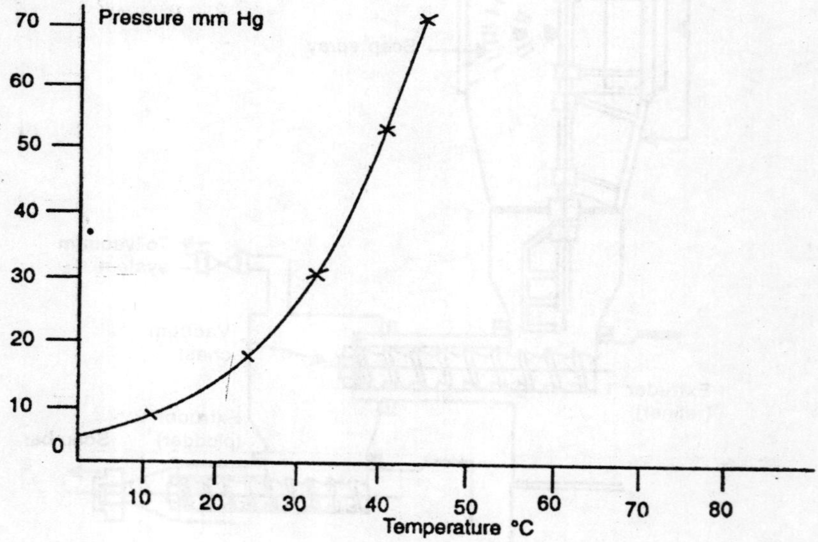

Fig. 2.3. Vapour pressure/temperature curve for water.

Table 2.1. Temperatures and pressures for soap leaving a vacuum spray drier/chiller.

Absolute pressure in spray chamber (mmHg)	*Experimentally determined temperatures of extruded soap (°C)*	*Water temperatures corresponding to pressures (°C)*
10	18-24	10
20-35	–	22-26
35	35	31
39	39	33
42	35	35

A vacuum system as shown in Fig. 2.2(a) with no booster jets, can only reduce the pressure to the vapour pressure of water at the temperature at which the cooling water leaves the main condenser. If cooling water at 15°C is used and the quantity is such that it leaves at 25°C, the pressure in the soap spray chamber will be 24 mmHg plus a few millimetres for the non-condensible gas present and the pressure drop through the vapour system; say 28-30 mmHg. This is sufficient for some reasonably firm soaps at about 63% TFM, but lower pressures of 10-20 mmHg are often better for household soaps. To obtain lower pressures than those which can be produced by a condenser and air pump (mechanical or jet) alone, it is necessary to include in the vacuum system a booster jet, or thermocompressor, to compress the vapours before they reach the main condenser. A booster jet is essential when the cooling water is warm, or only available in limited quantity; also when filled, or other soft, soaps are being processed. No steam need be used in the booster jet, if fitted, for the production of toilet soap noodles. If very hard soaps, such as those from 80-100% coconut oil, are to be processed it is usually necessary to use a higher pressure in the spray chamber but, often preferably, not in the vacuum chest. This can be achieved by a partially closed valve, or similar throttle, in the relevant vapour line. As well as necessary for the production of extrudable soap, this higher pressure and temperature avoids the inclusion of specks of extra hard soap. These specks can be removed by fine gauzes in the extruders; but frequent stoppages to clean the gauzes are then needed. The output with 80-100% coconut oil soaps is well below that with soaps of more normal composition. Chilled water for use in the jackets round the extruder worms is also sometimes provided by partial evaporation under vacuum, a process known as spray chilling. The use of chilled water is often desirable with soaps that are soft.

An approximate indication of the amount of drying which results from the use of various liquid and solid soap temperatures can be obtained by the same method as that used for flash evaporation in fatty acid distillation. Assume initially that no vapourisation occurs in the soap pipe prior to the spray nozzles. The specific heat of soap is about 0.75; and the latent heat of vapourisation of water is about 566 CHu/lb (1019 Btu/lb) for the range 90-20°C, 545 CHu/1b (981 Btu/1b) for the range 150-20°C, and 523 CHu/lb (941 Btu/lb) for the range 150-100°C. For 1 lb of liquid soap, let the evaporation be *y* 1b, so that the dried soap produced equals (1-*y*) lb. The heat balance for the case in which liquid soap at 90° C is chilled to solid soaps at the base of the chamber at 25°C is approximately $1 \times 0.75 \times (90\text{-}25) = y \times 566$ or $y = (0.75 \times 65)/566 = 0.086$, or 8.6%. If the liquid soap fed contains 63% TFM, the solid produced contains $(63 \times 100)/(100\text{-}8.6) = 68.9\%$ TFM.

Table 2.2 shows the results of similar calculations for various conditions. In the estimation of the temperature of the extruded bar (or noodles), experience has been used, with allowance for the heating effect of the mechanical work in the extruders and the influence of likely barrel cooling water temperatures. In the production of household soap (with no heat added by the heater) a feed at 63% TFM emerges at about 69% TFM in good agreement with the figures calculated in Table 2.2. As shown in Table 2.2, the feed must be reduced to about 57-58% TFM, if a bar at about 63% is to be produced, provided the liquid soap is sprayed at about 90^{0}C. This dilution of the feed with weak electrolyte (brine or sodium silicate) can be carried out in a crutching pot, or, more conveniently, by direct injection into the soap feed pipeline. The evaporations, and hence final TFMs, estimated in Table 2.2 for toilet soap base are low, this is doubtless primarily because some vapourisation occurs in the heater, so that additional heat is added without a further increase in soap temperature.

In one series of experiments, the dust collected from the vapours when making soap at about 63% TFM was 0.08% of the throughput, whereas it rose to 1.0-1.2% when toilet soap noodles were being produced. Soap lost in the cooling water for the vacuum system was negligible.

Steam and water requirements of flash driers/chillers, can vary considerably. The sensible heat in the liquid soap is utilised in vacuum units, as compared with processes in which the soap is solidified on chilling drums, but steam and/or power is required for vacuum maintenance, particularly when booster jets are needed to achieve the required soap temperature.

Table 2.2. Evaporation and TFM of chilled soap under various conditions of flash drying (no vapourisation prior to nozzle assumed).

TFM	*Feed temperature (^{0}C)*	*Pressure in spray chamber (mmHg)*	*Temperature of water equivalent to pressure (^{0}C)*	*Evaporation (%)*	*Extruded soap (^{0}C) (est.)*	*Extruded soap TFM(1) (%)*
63.0	90	30	29	8.1	34	68.6
63.0	90	25	26	8.6	32	68.9
63.0	90	20	22	9.0	28	69.2
63.0	90	10	11	10.4	23	70.3
62.0	90	20	22	9.0	28	68.1
57.0	90	25	26	8.6	30	62.4
63.0	125	25	26	13.6	31	72.9
63.0	140	25	26	15.6	31	74.6
63.0	150	25	26	17.0	32	75.9
63.0	160	25	26	18.4	32	77.2
63.0	140	atmospheric	100	5.7	-	66.8
63.0	160	atmospheric	100	8.6	-	68.9

Reasons why flash drier/chiller units have largely replaced other types of plant for both household and toilet soaps are :

(i) they are versatile, although, as explained later, some different ancillary equipment is needed for toilet and for household soaps.

(ii) they take up much less floor space, and involve much less soap in process, than the frame, or water cooling, processes for household soaps; or band driers plus the necessary finishing equipment for toilet soaps.

(iii) relatively little labour is needed.

(iv) more steam, power and cooling water are needed than for some of the older alternatives; but the overall cost comparison is normally favourable.

(v) as discussed later, there are commonly quality advantages, although house-hold soap is softer and more readily dissolved than that made from the same fat blend, and at the same TFM%, by the older processes. This may be an advantage with tallow now usually the cheapest good quality fat.

Extrusion, Homogenisation and Plastic Working

Worm type extruders are used for two purposes :

(1) To homogenize and work soap in order to get it into the required plastic condition. Such machines are often called refiners. They push the soap through gauzes backed by perforated plates; and it emerges in the form of rods which are cut into noodles by knives which rotate with the worms. Refiners are also used to convert soap ribbons into noodles for pneumatic, and other, transport.

(2) To form the soap into bars of the required cross-section which can be cut into bars for sale, or into billets to be stamped into tablets. Machines which carry out this task are called plodders.

The quality of an extruded soap is considerably affected by plodder performance which will now be considered in some detail. Fig. 2.4 shows diagrammatically the main features of the most common type of non-vacuum plodder, with a single worm and single orifice. Small pieces of homogenised and worked soap, in the form of noodles, or crimped chips, are fed into the hopper and then pushed along the barrel by the worm. Air is squeezed out; and the cylinder of soap is forced along like a nut on a screw, arranged so that the screw can only rotate and the nut only move longitudinally. The soap is pushed through the holes in the perforated plate in the form of rods which are welded togetheı in the cone; nad a bar of the required cross-section emerges continuously from the eye plate. A gauze, say 16 mesh BS (0.385 mm holes), in front of the perforated plate is often advantageous, but is not always used, and it does tend to reduce throughput.

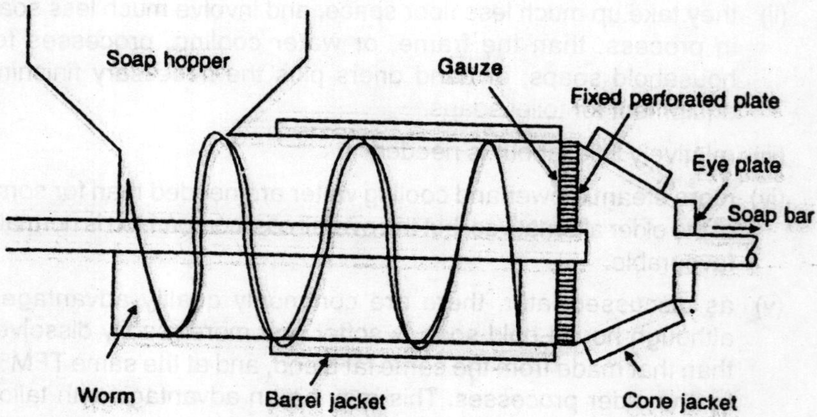

Fig. 2.4. Non-vacuum plodder.

An important advance during the last few years is the vacuum plodder. The soap hopper which feeds the plodder is enclosed and soap is fed into it by a refiner, roughly as shown in the lower part of Fig. 2.2(b). The hopper, or vacuum chest, is connected to a vacuum system, so that the air between the pieces of soap taken into the plodder worm is at a pressure much below atmospheric and the mass of air is much lower than when an open hopper is used.

Under some circumstances it is possible to use an eye-plate with two holes, so that two bars are extruded simultaneously. Plodders, called duplex or twin-worm, are also available in which two worms and cones are fitted in a single casing.

Cold, or cool, water is usually used in the jacket to cool the plodder barrel; and warm water or other heating medium in the jacket on the cone. When collar, or shell, type dies without cutting, or shaping, boxes are used to stamp tablets, the mass (weight) of the tablets is controlled by the cross-section of the billet, the length to which the billets are cut, and the density of the soap. It is often convenient to use an eye plate in which small adjustments can be made to one dimension of the hole with a slide, as shown diagrammatically in Fig. 2.5. In order to obtain smooth surfaced bars and tablets, it is normally necessary to use a heated eye-plate and a small electrical heater, of about 100 watts power, is a convenient way to achieve this. It is important to ensure that the edges of the eye plate are free from defects as lines on extruded bars do not usually stamp out.

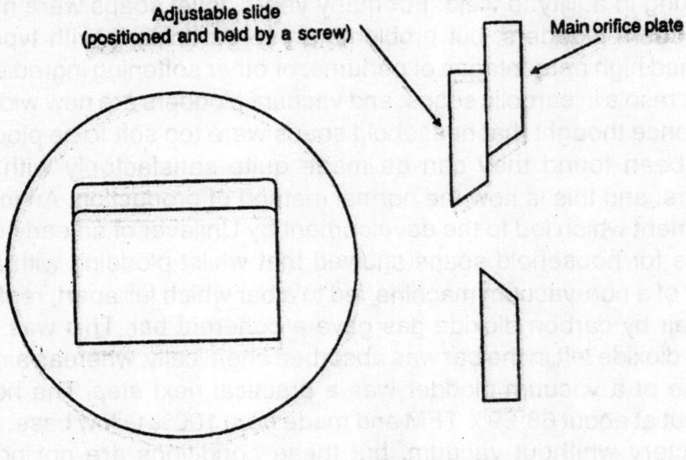

Fig. 2.5. Eye plate with adjustable slide.

Worm extrusion is an apparently simple operation, but results can be influenced by a number of factors in a rather complex way. One variable tends to interact with others, and it is helpful to consider first some general principles. As already described, the noodles, or crimped chips, are fed into the worm with air between the pieces (much less in mass when the hopper is under vacuum than when it is open to atmosphere). This air should be forced back as the soap is compacted by the worm in the barrel; and the effectiveness with which this is done is influenced by the pressure developed in the plodder. The presence of undue air in the bars, or tablets, shows up in the form of blisters when the pieces of soap are allowed to stand for a few hours. Two convenient tests for this defect, sometimes known as blister, or thumbnail, cracking are (1) to cut tablets longitudinally with a sharp knife, or wire, and to leave the halves cut face upwards for a period, after which thumbnail-shaped cracks develop in faulty soap; and (2) to determine the density of the soap, which will be lower than normal if air is present.

The rods of soap formed by the perforated plate must well properly in the cone to produce as substantially homogeneous bar. All plodded bars are weaker in the direction of extrusion than in the cross-direction, but the difference should be relatively small. A useful test is to take a length of plodded bar and to twist it backwards and forwards in the hands to ascertain how well the rods have welded together and how brittle the soap is. The aim is to produce a bar which is uniform; and free from streakiness and tendencies to blister and crack. This requires conditions under which sufficient pressure is developed, but the soap is also sufficiently plastic for the rods to weld together well. To some extent these requirements are opposed, but tends to be lacking in ability to weld. For many years, toilet soaps were made with non-vacuum plodders, but problems arose particularly with types which contained high percentages of perfume, or other softening ingredients such as the cresols in carbolic soaps; and vacuum plodders are now widely used. It was once thought that household soaps were too soft to be plodded; but it has been found they can be made quite satisfactorily with vacuum plodders; and this is now the normal method of production. An interesting experiment which led to the development by Unilever of an early extrusion process for household soaps showed that whilst plodding with air in the hopper of a non-vacuum machine led to a bar which fell apart, replacement of the air by carbon dioxide gas gave a coherent bar. This was because carbon dioxide left in the bar was absorbed chemically, whereas air was not. The use of a vacuum plodder was a practical next step. The household soap, but at about 68-69% TFM and made from 100% tallow base, extruded satisfactory whithout vacuum, but these conditions are not normal for household soap.

When non-vacuum plodders are used to produce toilet soaps it is particularly important to ensure that the worm is kept well covered with properly compacted soap.

Apart from the additional cost, the only disadvantage of vacuum compared with non-vacuum ploders is that there can be some additional loss of the more volatile components of a perfume.

Plodding is affected by soap factors and by machine factors :

Soap factors include :

(i) Composition of the fat blend.

(ii) Moisture, or TFM, content.

(iii) Salt content.

(iv) Soap temperature.

(v) Nature and quantity of added ingredients. As already mentioned, high contents of perfume, cresols, and some superfatting agents, soften the soap and can cause problems even with toilet soaps at around 79% TFM.

Machine factors include :

(i) Use, or non-use, of vacuum.

(ii) Worm (and barrel) dimensions.

(iii) Clearance between worm and barrel, which increases with time due to wear, until the machine has to be reconditioned.
(iv) Worm speed.
(v) Temperature of barrel cooling water.
(vi) Use of gauzes behind the perforated pressure plate.

It is important to balance various factors so as to achieve the best results. For example, if the soap is of an inherently soft composition, it may be advisable to dry it to a lower moisture content, to cool the noodles to a lower temperature, or, in the case of household soaps, to include a higher content of salt. Conditions in the layer of material adjacent to the plodder barrel wall are important. Plodder performance tends to fall when the clearance between worm and barrel increase, but it may be possible to mitigate this to some extent by the use of very cold water in the barrel jacket which hardens the layer of soap adjacent to the barrel wall.

Before a further discussion of machine factors, it is convenient to present some design and performance data for a number of plodders tested some years ago. Most of these plodders are no longer available; and new machines are now usually obtained from the main producers of soap finishing plants.

Experiments have shown that small diameter plodders are much more sensitive to the temperature of the cooling water in the barrel jackets than those of large diameter. When this temperature is found to be important, it is best to arrange a circulating system to which cold water is added as required to maintain the required temperature and the surplus water is allowed to overflow. The normal pattern is for output to increase as barrel jacket water temperature increases up to near the point at which churning starts with a fall in output. This again emphasises the significance of the soap layer near to the barrel wall. Even when the required output can be obtained from a small diameter plodder, it is usually found desirable for quality reasons to use a large diameter machine when bars of large cross-section are to be made.

Special perforated pressure plates which rotate with the worm, or are fitted in the final flight of the worm, have ben described, but it is doubtful whether they are beneficial.

Plodder worms are often made with the pitch greater at the hopper than at the discharge end in order to allow for the increase in bulk density and consequent decrease in volume as the noodles are compacted and the air squeezed out. This seems logical, but limited tests failed to show an advantage.

It is possible to gain some insight into the working of a plodder by stopping the machine, removing soap from the hopper, filling up again with similar soap of a different colour, and running the machine for a short time until the second coloured soap has reached a point in the cone. The cone of soap is then removed as a whole and cut longitudinally, or into a series of slices. The boundaries between the two soaps provide interesting information as to the flow of soap through the machine.

When ingredients, such as perfume, pigments and colour solutions, are added in appropriate proportions to dried toilet soap noodles the ingredients are spread on the surface of the soap. It is then necessary to homogenise the mixture, and to work the material; this can be done with either refiners or mills, or a combination of the two.

As already indicated, refiners are worm extruders, basically similar to plodders, except that the cone is omitted and a multibladed knife is fitted to rotate with the worm and to cut off the rods of soap as they emerge from the perforated plate in the form of short pieces called noodles. In continuous production lines units of three refiners in series are often used. The three barrels are usually arranged in a stopped horizontal fashion, or inclined. In either case, this saves space and the soap which emerges from one barrel drops into the hopper of the next stage. Refiners use gauzes behind the perforated plates, to improve the homogenisation and working of the soap; and to strain out any particles, such as hard soap, dirt, or fibres. The gauze in one stage may be finer than the gauze in the preceding stage because the soap is warmed and made more plastic as the operation proceeds. To fine a gauze in the first stage would tend to result in excessive pressure and power consumption; and/or reduced throughput. The percentage of hole area in a gauze depends upon the wire diameter, as well as the number of holes per inch (mesh size), but the wire must be sufficiently strong to withstand the pressure on the unsupported areas over the holes in the perforated plate. A 52 mesh gauze (0.3 mm hole) is about the finest likely to be used. In some cases the fine gauze can be supported by a coarse gauze, say 12 or 16 mesh (1.4 or 1.0 mm hold), between it and the pressure plate. The higher temperature induced by a fine gauze may be compensated by increased barrel cooling, that is by the use of more, or colder, water.

It should be noted that vacuum flash driers provide one, or two, stages of refining (before some important ingredients have been added); and a vacuum plodder one additional stage of refining.

Throughput 2.25-2.5 tonnes/h depending upon the build-up of debris on the meshes, which are usually cleaned about every two hours. The total power consumption is about 26 kwh per tonne of soap at 78% TFM. The soap enters the first stage at 30-35°C and leaves the last at 38-42°C.

The barrels are water cooled in series using 4800-6000 1bs/hr. Water temperature rises from 13-14°C to 21-28°C.

Mills can be used as an alternative to refiners; and they were so used many years before refiners were developed. Mills can have 3, 4 or 5 rolls. For continuous toilet soap line: sets of three three-roll mills in series are often used, but large new installations now more often select refiners. At one time, granite rolls were common, but now cast iron rolls (often with a chilled skin), at least some of which are water cooled, are almost universal. Granite rolls are sometimes considered desirable if medicated soaps containing corrosive ingredients, particularly mercuric iodide, are to be processed. Roll arrangements for 3, 4 and 5 roll mills are shown diagrammatically in Fig. 2.6. Each roll rotates at a substantially higher speed than the proceeding one, so that :

(i) The soap transfers from roll to roll, and so moves through the mill as indicated in the diagram.

(ii) There is a shearing action at each nip which homogenizes the mix and tends to break down any particles of hard soap.

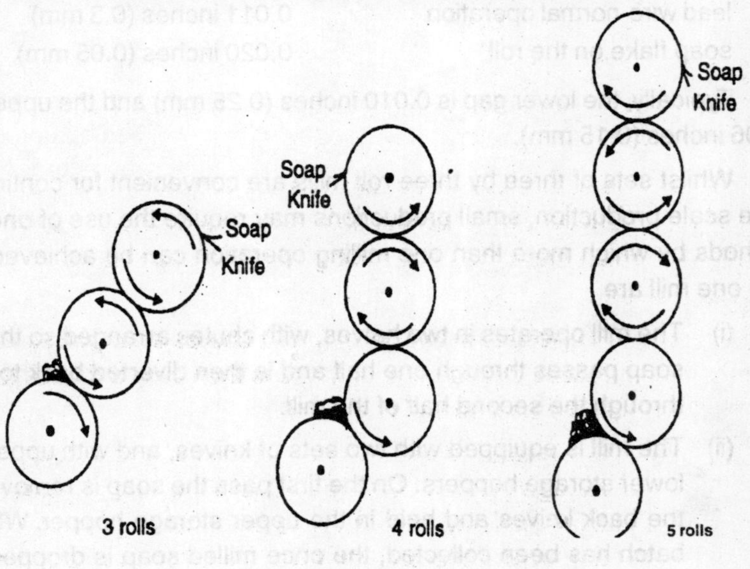

Fig. 2.6. Roll arrangements in mills.

Traditionally, the final roll was fitted with two knives. The first was serrated and removed alternate ribbons of soap; and the second was a complete blade which removed the remaining ribbons. These knives were often followed by crimping bars arranged to impede the flow of the ribbons and so to produce compact, crimped, pieces of soap. The more modern procedure is to use a comb-like knife which produces conveniently crimped pieces of soap directly. With some mills the knife, or knives, is/are positioned mechanically; in others, pressure is maintained hydraulically. The position of the middle roll is fixed and the top and bottom rolls are adjusted to give the required clearances. In the mill this is done manually with hand wheels; in some more modern mills, the gaps are set and held hydraulically. Because of the increase in roll speed upwards, the gap must decrease from nip to nip in order to maintain a full ribbon on the rolls.

The most satisfactory way to measure the true running clearance between a pair of rolls is to insert a piece of lead wire whilst the mill is running normally and to measure it after it emerges. Neither the thickness of the soap flake produced, or that of a piece of lead wire passed through the mill when it is empty, gives the correct answer. One test showed :

lead wire-rolls empty	0.004 inches (0.1 mm)
lead wire-normal operation	0.011 inches (0.3 mm)
soap flake on the roll	0.020 inches (0.05 mm)

Typically, the lower gap is 0.010 inches (0.25 mm) and the upper gap 0.006 inches (0.15 mm).

Whilst sets of three by three roll mills are convenient for continuous large scale production, small productions may require the use of one mill. Methods by which more than one milling operation can be achieved with only one mill are :

(i) The mill operates in two halves, with chutes arranged so that the soap passes through one half and is then diverted back to pass through the second half of the mill.

(ii) The mill is equipped with two sets of knives, and with upper and lower storage hoppers. On the first pass the soap is removed by the back knives and held in the upper storage hopper. When a batch has been collected, the once milled soap is dropped into the lower hopper and is given a second milling. This process is repeated if a third milling is required. When the soap has been milled sufficiently, it is taken off by the front knives and leaves the machine.

Points in comparison between milling and refining of toilet soap are :

(i) with proper operation soap quality is similar; but mills have an advantage if overdried soap has to be incorporated.

(ii) studies some years ago showed little difference in cost.

(iii) mills are more easily cleaned for a change from one soap to another; and so have an advantage when the plant is to be used for short runs of different varieties of soap. Mills are also preferable if the plant is only operated intermittently, as the soap in refiner worms cools and hardens (and hence has to be removed) on standing for several hours.

(iv) refiner systems can be substantially enclosed to minimise loss of perfume by vapourisation and pick-up of air-borne dust.

(v) it is sometimes claimed that the noodles from a refiner pack into the plodder worm better than crimped chips from a mill. This is of little significance if a vacuum plodder is used, because the actual plodder worm is fed with noddles from the refiner part of the machine.

The use of three refiners, plus refining in a flash vacuum chiller/drier and in a vacuum plodder, is typical modern practice, but some plants use less working and a few more. Some operators still consider the inclusion of a milling stage desirable. If mills and refiners are used in series, it seems sensible to refine first, in order to strain out unwanted particles, before any such particles are broken by the shearing action in a mill. The converse arrangement, in which the mill comes first, might impede effective straining in the refiner by breaking down the particles.

So as to avoid damage, mills, refiners and plodders are usually provided with a replaceable link which will break if the machine is overloaded.

Properties of Solid Soaps

Important properties of a piece of solid soap are :

(1) hardness, including sufficient firmness to avoid damage to the tablet whilst it is being handles in the factory, in transit and in use. Soaps dry out and become harder on storage.

(2) lathering properties, which are closely related to the rate at which soap is removed from the tablet surface when it is rubbed, for example, with a damp cloth or the hand. This rate is more important than the true solubility of the soap.

(3) freedom from undue tendency to form mush when the tablet is left damp, particularly when it is left on a damp surface. Much formation seems to be related to tendency to swell in water and to disintegrate; that is to crack in use.

(4) tendency to crack on storage, or, more particularly, in use.

(5) smoothness to the touch in use; that is freedom from grit, or sandiness.

(6) freedom from deterioration of odour and of colour, including the development of spots or patches. Also freedom from undue distortion.

(7) detergent properties. Differences between one soap and another can be significant when bar soaps are used for laundry purposes, but they are largely unnoticed when tablets are used for personal washing, which is now the major application in the more developed countries.

An experienced person can assess the hardness of a piece of soap by pressing it with a thumb, but an instrument is desirable to provide more reliable and comparative data. One type is a penetrometer, in which the force necessary to push a sphere (or hemisphere) of given size a set distance into a soap surface is measured. The method used determines the quantity of water which has to be run into a can on a lever arm, as shown diagrammatically in Fig. 2.7(a). Another type of instrument sometimes called a sectilometer measures the force needed to cut a piece of soap of known width with a wire of given diameter drawn through it at a steady speed. In one version the wire is held on a structure connected to the frame of the instrument by springs, and the extension of the springs, that is the position taken up by the wire, is a measure of the force being exerted A trace as shown in Fig. 2.7(b) is obtained, and the height is an arbitrary measure of hardness. The initial peak, due to the extra hardness of the outer skin, can normally be disregarded. The cutting wire, attached to a spring balance, was drawn through the soap and the reading of the balance was a measure of hardness.

Apart from the influence of chemical composition, the properties of a piece of soap can be affected by its physical state. There is an extensive literature relating to phase differences, crystal compositions, crystal size,

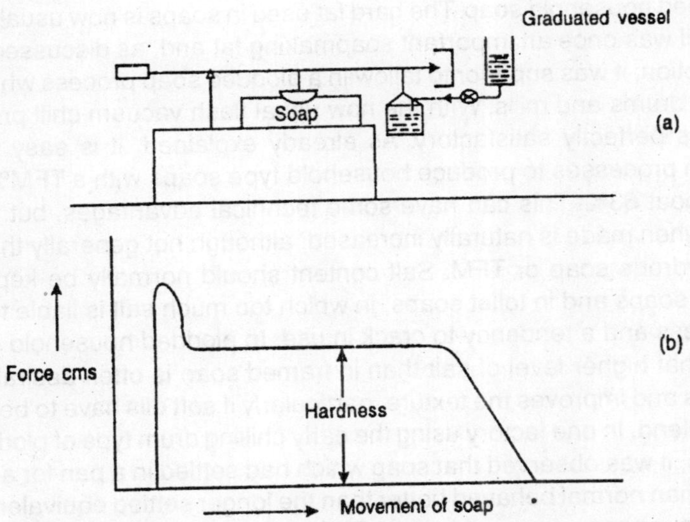

Fig. 2.7. Measurement of hardness. (a) Penetrometer (an electrical contact in a circuit with flashlamp bulb and battery, can be used to indicate the end-point). (b) Sectilometer trace.

and crystal orientation. It is, however, conflicting; and published information is not readily applied to practical situations. Many operators find an empirical approach more useful, although observations concerning factors such as temperatures and conditions under which the soap is worked may apply only to specific soaps under a limited range of circumstances.

There are major differences between soaps produced by slow cooling in a frame, and to a lesser extent in water coolers, and those made by the modern chill, work and extrude methods. Fractional crystallisation, with solidification of sodium stearate and sodium palmitate before that of the unsaturated and lower molecular mass soaps, can occur when soap cools slowly in a frame, to give a very different structure from that in an extruded bar. Framed soaps are much harder and slower lathering than plodded household soaps of similar composition. Unless filled, they also have a rough surface, showing what is called 'feather', and they tend to distort as they dry out. Plodded soaps show a smooth surface, provided a properly shaped and heated eye plate is used. When dried out, plodded soaps may become wedge-shaped if the moisture loss is mainly from one side of the case, but they retain a more pleasing shape than framed tablets. The softer and freer lathering characteristics of plodded soaps make desirable the use of a harder fat blend than in best quality framed soaps. The so-called 'washer' type of framed soap used substantial proportions of lauric and soft oils with the hard fat, whereas hard fat with 10-15% lauric oils is often found ideal for a plodded household soap. The hard fat used in soaps is now usually tallow. Palm oil was once an important soapmaking fat and, as discussed later in this section, it was superior to tallow in a plodded soap process which used chilling drums and mills. With the now usual flash vacuum chill processes tallow is perfectly satisfactory. As already explained, it is easy with the modern processes to produce household type soaps with a TFM% higher than about 63%. This can have some technical advantages, but the cost per lb when made is naturally increased, although not generally that per lb of anhydrous soap or TFM. Salt content should normally be kept low in framed soaps and in toilet soaps, in which too much salt is liable to cause brittleness and a tendency to crack in use. In plodded household soaps a somewhat higher level of salt than in framed soap is often desirable as it hardens and improves the texture, particularly if soft oils have to be used in the fat blend. In one factory using the early chilling drum type of plodded bar process, it was observed that soap which had settled in a pan for a shorter period than normal behaved better than the longer settled equivalent which would have been superior if framed. This was particularly the case when the hard fat was tallow rather than palm oil. It was later found that the same advantage could be achieved by an addition of an appropriate quantity of brine to well settled soap. Genuine Hard Soaps, allow up to 1.25% salt in extruded soap, but only upto 0.75% in batch (that is framed or water cooled) soaps. It has been found that, within the range of compositions tested, hardness, swelling and cracking after immersion in water did not vary greatly. Mechanical tests on rate of foam generation in hard water with sebum present showed a definite peak at 85/15; but subjective assessments by panels of users carried out under controlled conditions showed that preference increased with increase in coconut oil content up to the maximum tessted. The panel members used more soap with the higher coconut oil soaps; 0.5 g per use with the 95/5 soap and 0.8 g with 75/25. Slushing (much formation) also increased linearly with coconut oil content.

When it is required to estimate the composition when made of competitive, or other stored, soaps it is important to allow for the fact that salt and caustic soda migrate into the core of the tablet as drying takes place from the outside. As already explained, an average sample for analysis can be obtained by taking an aliquot portion of a solution of the whole tablet, or of an eighth cut to represent the whole tablet. Sodium carbonate concentration tends first to increase and then to decrease on moving inwards from the outside of a tablet. This may be associated with carbonation of caustic soda by carbon dioxide absorbed from the atmosphere.

INGREDIENTS ADDED TO HOUSEHOLD AND TOILET SOAPS

General

Many types of ingredient are added to soaps, particularly toilet soaps. The main classes of additives are :

(1) preservatives.
(2) perfumes.
(3) colours, opacifiers and optical brighteners.
(4) germicides and other medicinal ingredients.
(5) superfatting agents.
(6) scum dispersants, leading to NSD tablets and bars.
(7) alkaline fillers.
(8) miscellaneous.

Preservatives

Following points should be considered for the stability of a soap :

(1) selection of a fat blend without substantial proportions of highly unsaturated fatty acids. At one time 2-3% of rosin was included in toilet soap and other bases to improve keeping properties, but rosin is little used now.

(2) preservation of fats by natural and artificial antioxidants.

(3) the need for thorough saponification, although much less drastic treatment with caustic soda than was once common is now usual.

(4) the need to minimise the presence in the soap base of heavy metals, particularly iron and copper, and perhaps, nickel.

The most important soap preservatives are substances which negate the adverse catalytic effects of heavy metals which often cause brown spots, or patches, as well as more general deterioration :

(5) organic sequestrants, such as EDTA and, less usually NTA. Too much EDTA can form coloured (yellow) complexes with iron; and it is often better to use EHDP (ethane hydroxydiphosphonic acid) to sequester the iron, plus a small concentration of EDTA to deal with the copper. Concentrations of these preservatives should be determined by experiment to suit local conditions.

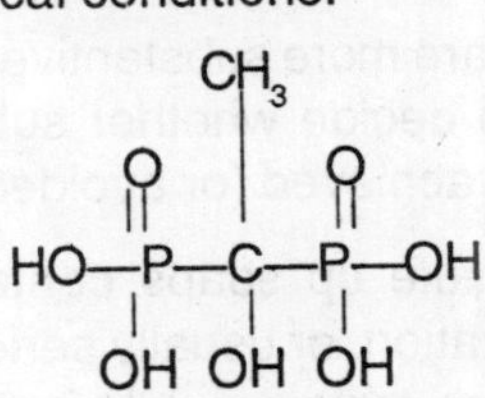

(6) Magnesium silicates which can also be used to inactivate heavy metals in soaps other than those superfatted with fatty acids; presumably they work by adsorption. Magnesium silicate can be made separately and added as such, but it is usual to add the ingredients magnesium sulphate and sodium silicate solutions to the soap so as to form magnesium silicate *in situ.* When modern driers which include tubular or plate heaters are used, it is advisable to inject the silicate after the soap has passed through the heater; otherwise scale is liable to form on the heating surfaces.

Typical additions are :

For toilet soaps :

0.33% of a 50% solution of $MgSO_4.7H_2O$ (equals 0.027% of Mgo) plus 0.6% of 57°Tw (1.285 specific gravity) neutral sodium silicate (equals about 0.12% SiO_2).

for household soaps, say, 0.004% magnesium sulphate expressed as MgO plus 0.006% sodium silicate expressed as SiO_2.

Magnesium silicate preservative is not used in soaps superfatted with fatty acids because it causes grittiness. Some technologists consider that it may suffer this defect with conventional toilet soaps; but it has been widely used for many years and has the merit of cheapness and ready availability of the ingredients. Antioxidants of the BHT type are sometimes used in soaps as well as in fats.

Perfumes

Between 0.5% and 2.0% of perfume is usual in toilet soaps although higher concentrations are sometimes used, with about 0.8-1.0% common in the mass produced popular brands. Great care is necessary in the selection of a perfume, both as regards appeal to users and technical factors. It is usually advisable to approach one, or more, companies with experience in the field of soap perfumery and to give them as much information as possible regarding requirements :

(i) The perfume should accord with the general image possessed by, or desired for, the brand.

(ii) Some perfumes are more substantive to the skin than others; and it is important to decide whether substantivity is desirable and how far it can be achieved (or avoided).

It is necessary to make up soaps containing the perfumes to be considered at the concentration, or usually series of concentrations, which seems appropriate. Storage tests, usually including accelerated tests at temperatures higher than ambient, should be carried out; and these should include exposure to strong light both naked and in the proposed packaging. Consumer tests should be carried out on soaps which have been matured for an adequate time. Perfumes for toilet soaps are normally blends made from a large number of ingredients many of which contain a large number of different chemical compounds. Perfumers with adequate experience in the soap-field should only submit blends which are sufficiently stable to the alkalinity of soap, light, etc; and which will not deteriorate excessively in colour and/or odour on storage. Additives such as EDTA can affect the alkalinity of a soap and proposed perfumes should be checked by the soap manufacturer under conditions relevant to his particular product and market. Vacuum plodders are more liable than simple plodders to remove very volatile components from a perfume. In addition to possible deterioration of the soap, it is important to ensure that the soap containing deterioration of the soap. It is important to ensure that the soap containing a perfume under consideration is substantially free from allergic, or irritant, reactions by potential users. This requires extensive tests but, again, experienced perfume houses have built up knowledge and should be able to provide blends for which they can give adequate assurances. The small soap manufacturer is not normally in a position to carry out adequate tests.

Household soaps are often made without perfume. When perfume is added, it is usually a relatively cheap but powerful type, such as citronella, at a low concentration. Many years ago oil of myrbrane, nitro-benzene, was also popular, particularly for tropical markets, despite its toxic nature.

Colours, Opacifiers and Optical Brighteners

Colours used in soaps of two types, dyes soluble in water or in an organic solvent, commonly the perfume, and pigments which are added as suspensions. As for perfumes, various checks are necessary in addition to an assessment of aesthetic appeal before a colour system is accepted as satisfactory :

1. *adequate stability :* When the soap is stored and/or exposed to light (naked and packaged). Some colours have been used which are not very stable to alkali and which could only be used with dried soap base exceptionally low in free caustic soda; such dyes should be avoided if possible.
2. *safety for the user :* Some dyestuffs, or impurities they contain, have carcinogenetic properties; and many countries have strict regulations concerning colouring matters which are used in cosmetics, as well as in foods and drugs.

Opacifying agents are also added to soaps to obtain the desired appearance. Titanium dioxide (of which there are two major types, rutile and anastase) is now the normal material used; and 0.2% is a typical addition to give an opaque toilet soap. Zinc oxide has also been used. but is less effective than titanium dioxide. At one time magnesium carbonate was employed as an opacifier in filled household soaps. Extruded soaps, particularly household types, are liable to show a pattern of relatively translucent soap on the surfaces cut at right angles to the direction of extrusion, known as end marks. If the end marks cannot be eliminated by adjustment of the conditions of plodding, a small addition of titanium dioxide will largely obscure the pattern and make the soap more attractive in appearance. A little opacifier also helps to minimise changes in colour as a soap dries out and becomes more translucent.

As already mentioned special types of optical brightener, such as Tinopal are used to improve the colour and brightness of white soaps. It is also possible to use a low concentration of cotton substantive optical brightener to improve slightly the performance of household soaps in laundry work; but care is necessary to avoid risk of patchy effects when the soap is rubbed on extra dirty parts of articles.

Germicides and Other Medicinal Ingredients

Many brands of soap have been sold on the basis of germicidal, or freshness, claims; and a number of different bacteriostatic, or bacteriocidal, ingredients have been and/or are used to justify such claims. The traditional ingredient was a mixture of cresols and related phenols, often known as cresylic acid, which give 'carbolic' soaps. Carbolic soaps, commonly, but not necessarily, coloured red, usually contain about 2% of phenols when intended for the domestic market. It is necessary to select cresylic acid which is reasonably free from pyridine, and other nitrogenous bodies, which can lead to unpleasant smells when the cresylic acid is included in alkaline soap. Naphthalene is often dissolved in the cresylic acid to improve the odour of the soap. Phenols tend to be held in the soap micelles when the soap is dissolved, so that domestic type carbolic soaps do not show much greater anti-germ properties than soap alone. Special soaps with much higher concentrations of phenols have been made for hospital and similar duties.

More recently various more potent ingredients have been used; and antigerms properties have been demonstrated on human skin. Freshness claims require the further step that use of the soap can reduce the odour from body areas such as the armpits by reducing, or preventing, the decay of stale perspiration to produce unpleasant odours. Unfortunately, many of these ingredients have been found liable to have undesirable side effects on some users; and great care is necessary to select one which is permitted and fully safe. Apart from straightforward toxicity (mainly where a gross excess has been included in the product in error), and sensitisation, or allergic reaction, problems have arisen through :

(1) the presence of impurities in the germicide as bought.

(2) breakdown to produce damaging compounds when the soap is stored for long periods at relatively high temperatures, and, particularly, when scrap is re-boiled and returned to the product.

(3) photosensitisation, that is skin, and possibly more general, reaction when a person who has washed with the soap is exposed to bright light.

Superfatting Agents

Many superfatting agents, including lanolin, petroleum jelly, coconut oil, and stearin (commercial stearic acid), are used in soaps; they are intended to increase mildness in use. As mentioned earlier, an important type of superfatted soap uses a fat blend with a high proportion of coconut oil to tallow; and is superfatted with 5-10% of fatty acids similar to the main fat blend. The maximum effect upon the lather is obtained with about 8% FFA. An unsuperfatted soap made with 30 - 60% of coconut, or palm kernel, oil tends to be more irritant (less mild) than a conventional toilet soap, but the inclusion of the free fatty acid, and consequent elimination of the free alkali, brings mildness back to about that of a 20% CNO 80% tallows soap.

Scum Dispersants, Leading to NSD Tablets and Bars

Much technical and marketing effort has been expended on the development of toilet tablets in which soap is replaced partially, or completely, by non-soapy surfactants and other ingredients. Objectives are :

(1) to eliminate scum and 'bath-tub ring'.

(2) to produce an immediate lather on bath, or wash basin, water.

(3) with some formulations, to produce a personal washing tablet which is slightly acidic rather than slightly alkaline.

Problems are :

(1) cost, with many consumers not prepared to pay the higher price relative to soap.

(2) to produce tablets which are not too dense and which do not absorb excessive water and become soft.

Many formulations have been patented and/or tried. Some are more, or less, soap-free, but others contain substantial proportions of soap. Stearin is an important constituent of some tablets.

NSD bars for use instead of household soap bars have been successful in some countries. Typical ingredients are sodium alkylbenzene sulphonate, sodium tripolyphosphate, sodium silicate, and sodium sulphate; plus a plasticiser. Waxes and starch may be included to improve texture and feel. The blends are milled and plodded.

Miscellaneous Ingredients

Many other ingredients are, or have been, added to toilet soaps to improve texture, feel, lather, and benefits to the skin of the user; the real merits of some are dubious. Recent developments which include the use of citroellylsenecioate (also known as the citronellyl ester of 3,3-dimenthyl acrylic, or 3-methyl crotonic acid), as a non-germicidal deodourant.

Efflorescence

After storage some soaps develop a surface deposit known as efflorescence. This can be of several types, in particular :

(1) A heavy white deposit, often fibrous in appearance, which comprises inorganic salts, probably mainly sodium sesquicarbonate, and which develops on soaps run with alkaline fillers. Changes in the fillings used may help to reduce this efflorescence. Glued-up soaps are said to be particularly prone to the defect, with fillings based on neutral silicate worse than those using alkaline silicate.

(2) A white fibrous deposit which can form on extruded genuine household soaps. This deposit comprises filaments of soap which are pushed out through weak spots in the tablet surface; that is the filaments grow from the base like hairs. This type of efflorescence develops when there is a fairly rapid rate of drying from the soap surface; and it can usually be avoided by the use of well sealed wrappers of a material with a low moisture vapour permeability. A useful accelerated test for proneness to develop soap hair efflorescence is to cause a rapid flow of water through a relatively thin piece of the soap. This can be done by closing the end of a large test-tube which contains some water with a small piece of soap and storing the tube in a vertical position in a dry atmosphere. In this way, the upper surface dries cut in the low humidity atmosphere, whilst the lower surface picks up water from the nearly saturated air below it. Traces of heavy metals on the soap surface, from stamping lubricant or contact with materials such as carton board, can tend to induce the efflioresence.

(3) A thin white film which can arise on toilet and other soaps. One cause is the use of excessive quantities of stamping lubricant containing

salt; and some versions of magnesium silicate preservative are also sometimes thought to have an adverse tendency.

MODERN PROCESSES FOR THE PRODUCTION OF HOUSEHOLD SOAPS

The main unit of the now standard plant for the production of household soap is the vacuum chiller/extruder shown in Fig. 2.2(b). Broadly in similar plants suitable lengths can be cut from the continuous bar extruded by the vacuum plodder using either a wire cutter swung backwards and forwards at the plodder nozzle, or a simple device shown in Fig. 2.8, sometimes known as a 'hacker-off. This comprises a cutting wire on a small frame which is connected by a rod of the required bar length to a small plate; the cutter and the plate being at right angles to the rod. The operator holds the plate against the moving end of the bar which is supported on a short piece of narrow wooden roller conveyor, and when sufficient has been extruded, pushes the cutter through the soap. Bars cut in one of these ways can be handled like bars produced from framed soap. Fully mechanised lines, including billet cutter, conditioning tunnel, stamper, wrapping and/or cartoning machine, case packer and case sealer, are now common; variations to suit individual needs are possible.

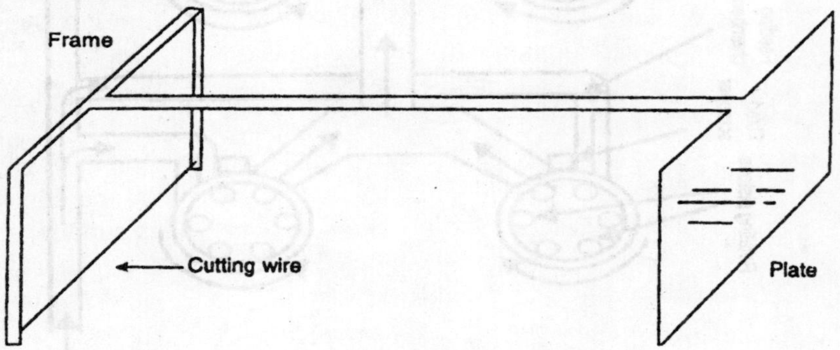

Fig. 2.8. Hacker-off.

Unilever developed independently a process for the production of household soaps which also used a vacuum plodder, but in which the soap was solidified on chilling drums and worked in mills. This process performed well with high palm oil fat blends, but was less satisfactory when the hard fat was tallow. A rather high salt content was important; and it was found that a tubular heater to give about 1% evaporation prior to the chilling drum was markedly beneficial with high tallow blends. It is not clear whether this was due to the small reduction in moisture content of the soap, or whether the temperature from which the liquid soap was chilled was the major factor. The more versatile vacuum chilling units are now preferred; and these do involve rapid chilling over a fairly large temperature range.

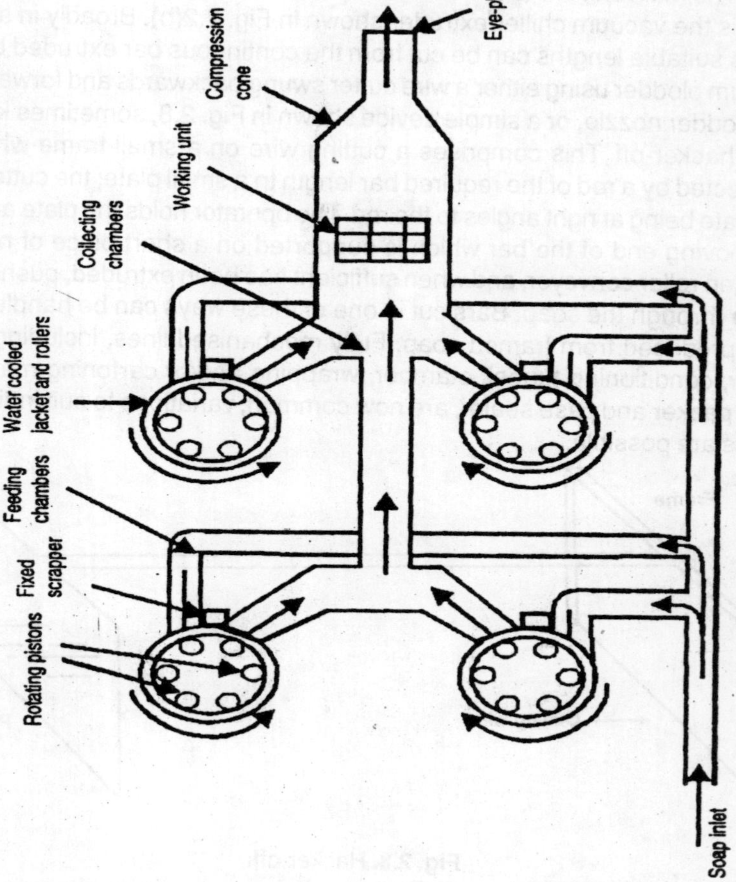

Fig. 2.9. Meccaniche extrusion/chiller for household

An extrusion unit shown diagrammatically in Fig. 2.9. In this the liquid soap is cooled and forced cut through a barrel, cone and eye plate by rotors which acted as pumps as well as coolers. This plant has also been supersceded by the vacuum chilling system.

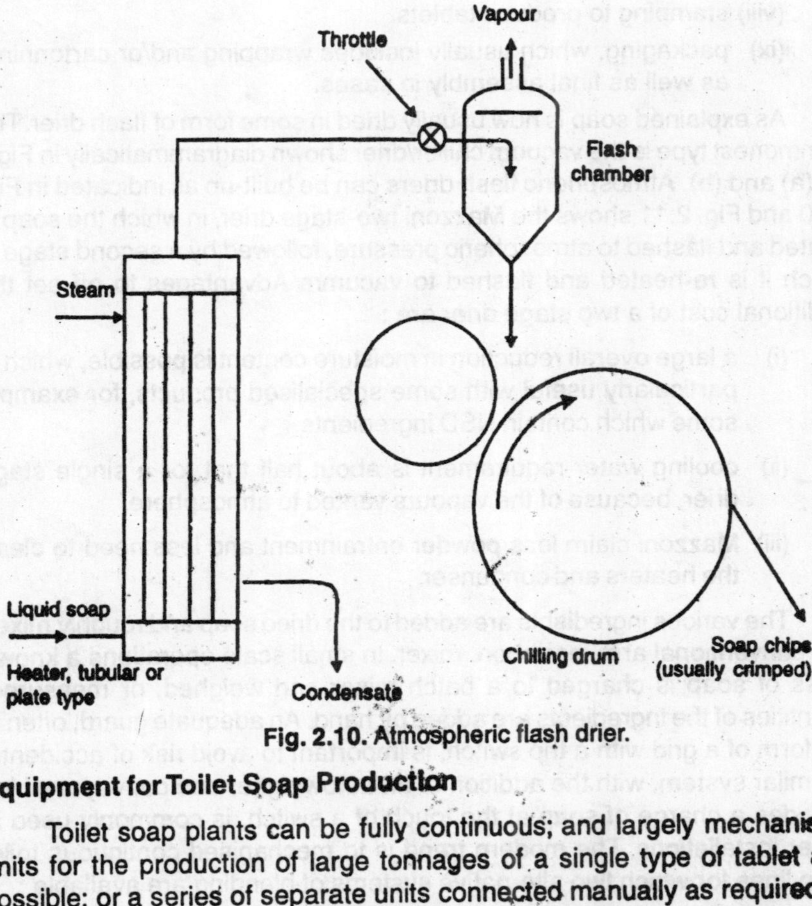

Fig. 2.10. Atmospheric flash drier.

Equipment for Toilet Soap Production

Toilet soap plants can be fully continuous; and largely mechanised units for the production of large tonnages of a single type of tablet are possible; or a series of separate units connected manually as required to make a range of products can be used. As already indicated, there are a number of possible ways in which the main operations can be carried out; but a line will include equipment for most, but not necessarily all, of the following operations :

(i) chilling and drying.

(ii) Rough mixing of dried base with perfume and other ingredients.

(iii) homogenisation and plastic working.

(iv) cooling of homogensied chips or noodles.

(v) extrusion of a continuous bar by a vacuum, or non-vacuum plodder.

(vi) cutting into billets.

(vii) cooling and conditioning of billets.

(viii) stamping to produce tablets.

(ix) packaging, which usually includes wrapping and/or cartonning, as well as final assembly in cases.

As explained soap is now usually dried in some form of flash drier. The commonest type is the vacuum chiller/drier shown diagrammatically in Figs. 2.2(a) and (b). Atmospheric flash driers can be built-up as indicated in Fig. 2.10 and Fig. 2.11 shows the Mazzoni two-stage drier, in which the soap is heated and flashed to atmospheric pressure, followed by a second stage in which it is re-heated and flashed to vacumm Advantages to off set the additional cost of a two stage drier are :

(i) a large overall reduction in moisture content is possible, which is particularly useful with some specialised products, for example some which contain NSD ingredients.

(ii) cooling water requirement is about half that for a single stage drier, because of the vapours vented to atmosphere.

(iii) Mazzoni claim less powder entrainment and less need to clean the heaters and condenser.

The various ingredients are added to the dried soap and roughly mixed in a conventional arm, or ribbon, mixer. In small scale operations a known mass of soap is charged to a batch mixer and weighed, or measured, quantities of the ingredients are added by hand. An adequate guard, often in the form of a grid with a trip switch, is important to avoid risk of accidents. A similar system, with the addition of an autoweigher and conveyor which provides a charge of soap at the touch of a switch, is commonly used in larger installations. The modern trend is to mechanised continuous toilet soap lines for which two alternative systems of blending are available :

(i) the automatic batch system in which increments of soap, liquids and solids are measured by weight or volume, mixed, and passed on to a hopper.

(ii) Relatively long worm type mixers through which the soap is passed continuously at a predetermined rate and to which streams of the various ingredients are added by dosing pumps for the liquids and weigh band feeders for the solids.

The automatic batch system is more accurate and has advantages when critical ingredients, such as germicidal slurries which are difficult to dose continuously at the required low rate, are included. The continuous system is probably rather simpler. To produce good toilet soap, it is particularly important to ensure complete homogeneity; and this includes the incorporation of returned scrap which may be drier and cooler than the rest of the material.

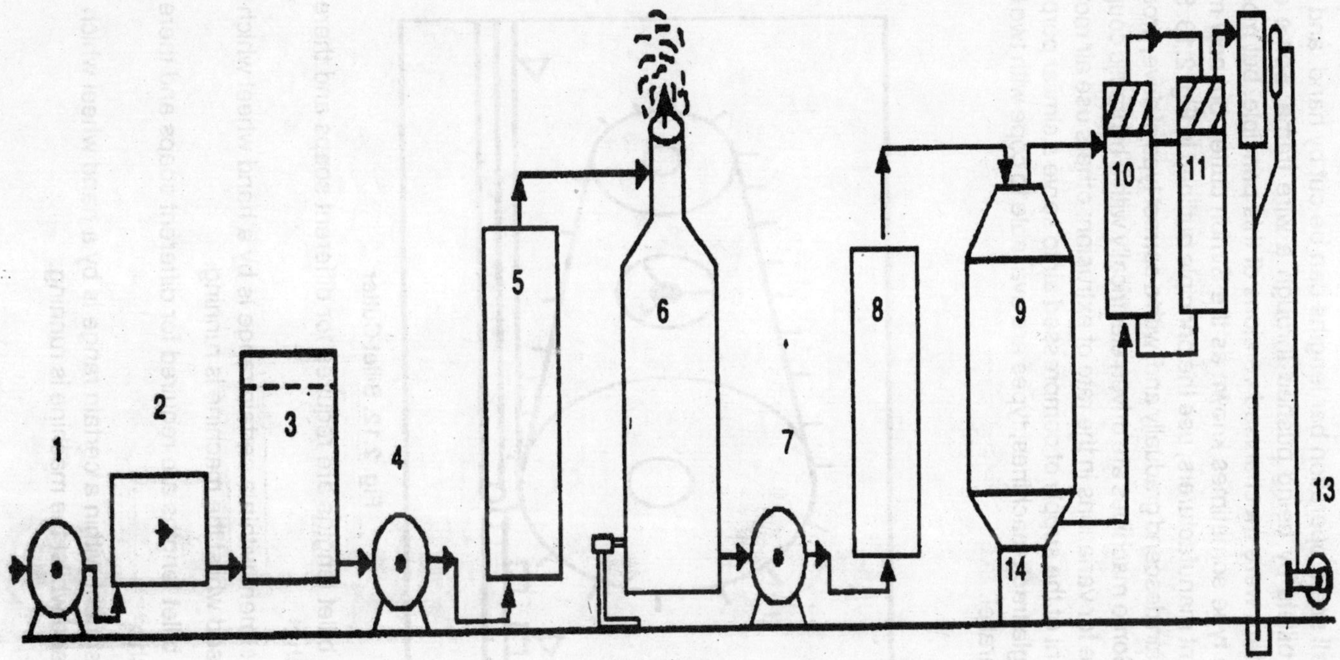

Fig. 2.11. Mazzoni multistage drier ; 1. Fitrate a pump; 2. Feed tank; 4. Stage feed pump; 5. First stage heat exchange; 6. Flash chamber; 7. Second stage feed pump; 8. Second stage heat exchanger; 9. Vacuum spray chamber; 10. First stage separator; 11. Second stage separator; 12. Barometic hotwell; 13. Soap base extrusion.

The next operation is to cut the extruded bar into billets of the required length. In small scale operation bar lengths can be cut by hand, and then converted to billets by being pushed through a wire frame. Some early automatic cutters were mechanised versions of this principle, but modern cutters, of the type sometimes known as the Simon cutter, but now made by several plant manufacturers, use the principle outlined in Fig. 2.13. Solid knives on a chain descend gradually and, with a correct type of drive, produce vertical cuts. Some machines are driven electrically with a hydraulic coupling to compensate for variations in the rate of extrusion; others use air motors, with adjustment of the supply of compressed air to serve a similar purpose. As well as single track machines, types are available to cope with two bars extruded in parallel.

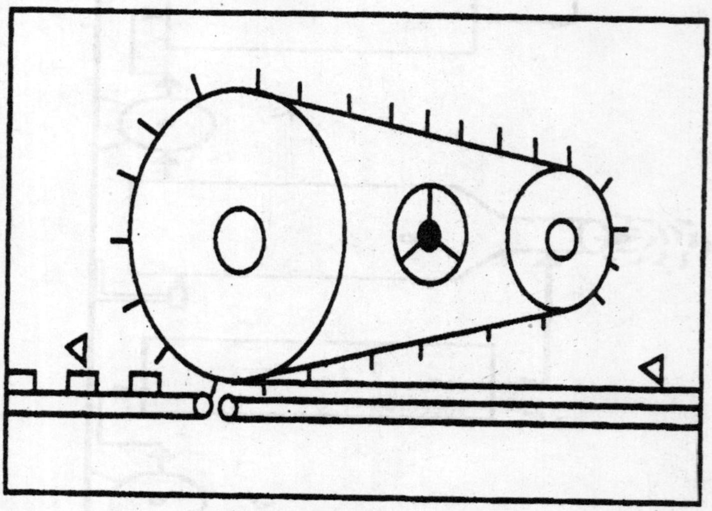

Fig. 2.12. Billet Cutter

Different billet lengths are required for different soaps and there are cutters in which :

(i) Adjustment within a certain range is by a hand wheel which can be used whilst the machine is running.

Different billet lengths are required for different soaps and there are cutters in which :

(i) adjustment within a certain range is by a hand wheel which can be used whilst the machine is running.

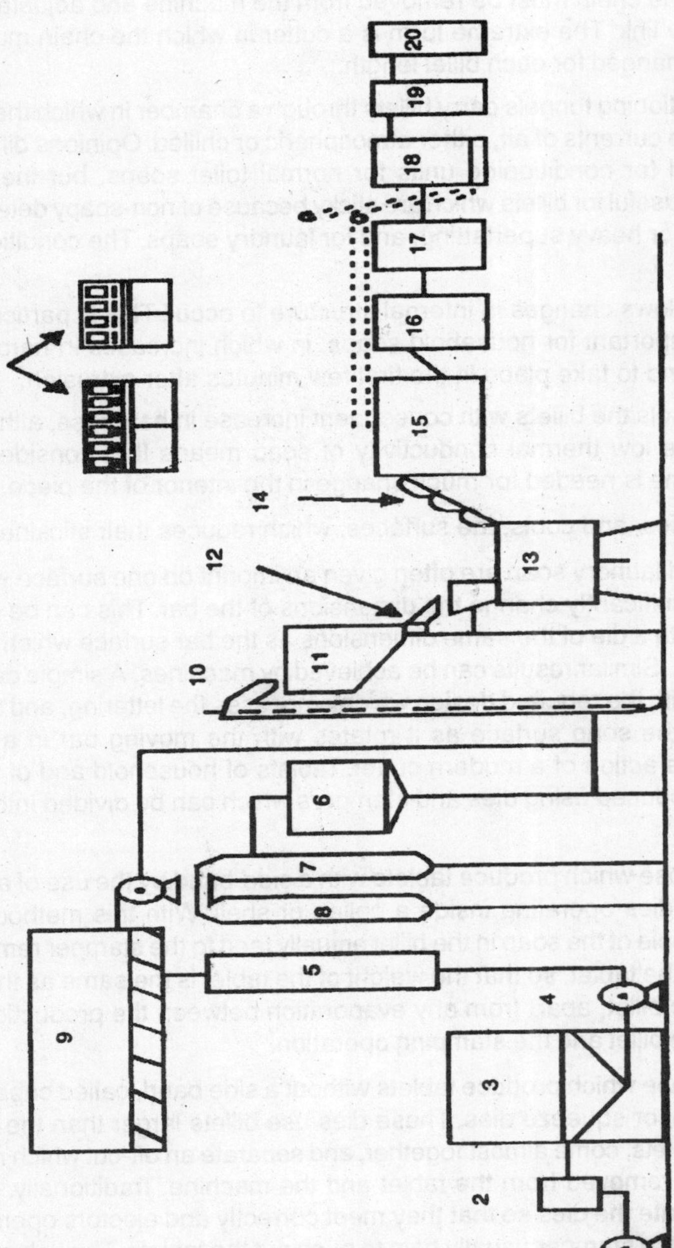

Fig. 2.13. Meccaniche Moderne toilet soap line. 1. Filtration pump; 2. Soap filter; 3. Feeding tank; 4. Feed pump; 5. Heat exchanger; 6. Vacuum drying chamber; 7. Main separator; 8. Auxiliary separator; 9. Water cooling unit; 10. Bucket elevator; 11. Storage equipment; 12. Vibrating dosing unit; 13. Mixer refiner; 14. Conveying belt; 15. Milling machine; 16. Vacuum plodder; 17. Cutting machine; 18. Stamping machine; 19. Refrigeration unit; 20. Wrapping machine; 21. Control panels.

(ii) The chain must be removed from the machine and adjusted link by link. The extreme form is a cutter in which the chain must be changed for each billet length.

Conditioning tunnels carry billets through a chamber in which they are subjected to currents of air, either atmospheric or chilled. Opinions differ as to the need for conditioning units for normal toilet soaps, but they are particularly useful for billets which are sticky because of non-soapy detergent ingredients or heavy superfatting, and for laundry soaps. The conditioning process :

(i) Allows changes in internal structure to occur. This is particularly important for household soaps, in which increases in hardness tend to take place in the first few minutes after extrusion.

(ii) cools the billets with consequent increase in hardness, although the low thermal conductivity of soap means that considerable time is needed for much change in the interior of the piece.

(iii) dries, and cools, the surfaces, which reduces their stickiness.

Bars of laundry soap are often given an imprint on one surface which does not significantly change the dimensions of the bar. This can be done manually with a die of the same dimensions as the bar surface which is hit with a mallet. Similar results can be achieved by machines. A simple device is a wheel with the required design which embosses the lettering, and other imprint, on the soap surface as it rotates with the moving bar in a way similar to the action of a modern cutter. Tablets of household and of toilet soap are produced using dies and stampers which can be divided into two major types :

(i) those which produce tablets with a side-band by the use of a pair of dies operating inside a collar, or shell. With this method the whole of the soap in the billet actually feed to the stamper remains in the tablet, so that the weight of the tablet is the same as that of the billet, apart from any evaporation between the production of the billet and the stamping operation.

(ii) those which produce tablets without a side band, called capacity, pin, or squeeze dies. These dies use billets larger than the final tablets, come almost together, and separate an off-cut which must be removed from the tablet and the machine. Traditionally, pins locate the dies so that they meet correctly and ejectors operated by the stamper usually help to push out the tablets. The volume of the tablet is controlled by the capacity of the cavity enclosed by the two dies when they come together; and its weight is determined by this volume and the density of the soap. The gap between the dies in the closed position is about 0.002 inches (0.05 mm); and this can be varied a little for weight control purposes. Larger changes in weight normally require re-sinking of the dies, although it may be possible to make a small reduction by grinding the die edges. So far as is known capacity dies are not used for household soaps.

A wide range of stamping machines, or stampers, is available, ranging from hand stampers to high speed automatic machines. For many years machines known to those in the industry as the Jones 'K' type were almost universal for mechanised stamping of both household and toilet tablets. This type, and similar ones now made by various manufacturers, uses a shell with four pockets which rotates in the vertical plane in steps of a quarter turn. The billet is pushed into a pocket and is transferred to the next station where it is shaped by a pair of dies which move in horizontally. Modern machines normally give a double blow, that is the dies come together, move a little apart, and then come together again. This helps the escape of air and improves the quality of stamping. The double blow is quite different from the fault of double stamping in which a second billet enters a pocket from which the stamped tablet has not been removed. After it has been moved to the third station, the stamped tablet is pushed out onto the discharge conveyor. The last station may be used for cleaning. The dies are loaded with powerful springs; and should fit reasonably closely into the pockets in the shell. In this way the soap is squeezed out to fill the cavity formed by the two dies and part of the pocket wall. If the fit between dies and shell pocket is not good an unattractive fringe will appear on the tablets. With expensive soaps any fringe, and more particularly, than which is liable to be produced with capacity dies, may be trimmed by hand, but this is not possible with popular brands produced by high speed, does not permit the escape of trapped air, unless other arrangements are made for its release. An escape route can be made by the provision of a small gap between die and shell, on the central part of the long side. Alternatively, the part of the shell through which the dies move, that is not the central part which acually shapes the tablet, can be provided with escape grooves. Some operators drill fine holes (vents) in parts of the dies where air could be trapped, such as lettering which is raise on the tablet and hence recessed in the die. Small threads of soap are squeezed out of the vents, but the amount should be small and the 'pimples' which are left insignificant. Venting in this way increases the sharpness of the lettering. It is important to keep dies clean.

A lubricant, commonly a weak brine, or a solution of glycerine and salt, may be used to reduce any tendency for the soap to stick to the dies, but it should only be applied sparingly to the billets. Excess salt bearing lubricant is liable to cause surface cracking and a type of efflorescence mentioned earlier. A 10% solution of sodium lactate in water is said to be effective and to avoid risk of surface cracking. Modern stampers now usually have facilities for the circulation of refrigerated fluid through the dies; and this cooling, with billet conditioning if required, often makes the use of lubricant unnecessary. Dilute acetic acid was once used as a stamping lubricant for household soaps.

At one time it was thought necessary to select a nearly brick-shaped tablet for production with 'K' type stampers, and this type of tablet is the easiest to handle, but it has been found possible to widen the range of shapes provided they have a side band.

Until fairly recently, capacity dies could only be used with hand, or certain slow speed machine, stampers. Now fully automatic, high speed, machines are available for this duty. They often work vertically and very important features are effective mechanisms for the discharge of the tablets and the removal of the 'flash' or off-cut. The scrap may amount to some 30% of the billet, and it has to be returned to the plodder, usually via a refiner, for re-processing. The development of these machines has enabled cushion shaped tablets, without any side-band, to be handled on high speed mechanised lines and so facilitated the selection of such shapes for mass produced popular brands. Hand, pedal operated, or pneumatic stampers are still used for small production lines and for very fancy, novelty, shapes.

Bronzes, such as gun metal or silicon bronze, are used for dies and shells, often quite satisfactorily, but with high copper alloys there is some risk of slight contamination of the soap surface with copper which is a powerful catalyst for degradation reactions. Stainless steel dies in monel shells are often considered the best materials for the duty. They are expensive initially, but have a long life. Stainless steel dies in stainless steel shells have been avoided by some companies because of the risk of 'galling', or chafing, when one piece of stainless steel is rubbed on another, but it is understood that the combination has been used successfully. Some authorities favour the use of die surfaces which are slightly matt, and like to 'condition' dies by a period of contact with soap. Others prefer to use highly polished stainless steel surfaces.

The best shape of billet to produce a given design of tablet is controversial and a matter for experiment. One school of thought favours the use of a billet as near as possible in shape to the final tablet, others prefer to use billets which have to be completely re-shaped in the stamping operation. The latter may select a cylindrical billet, or, preferably, an oval with flat areas on the long sides. Some factories feed the cut billets into the stamper directly, but others use cutting, or shaping, boxes through which the billets are pushed on their way into the stamper shell. The use of a shaping box permits the use of final billets which fit closely into the shell pocket. This avoids the development of the flow lines which are often seen when straight ended billets directly from a cutter are stamped to tablets with bowed ends, or rounded corners, for which such billets must be shorter than the final tablet. Shaping boxes are also said to improve substantially the uniformity of weight of tablets from 'K' type stampers, but they produce a trim which has to be removed and reprocessed.

As already mentioned, toilet soap plants range from small units with the minimum amount of equipment to large departments including mechanised lines devised to suit particular requirements. A small unit, for which dried soap is purchased, may comprise a mixer, mill, plodder, stamper, and wrapping machine; or a small number of some, or all, these items. Chips, or noodles, are stored between operations in bins. Trays are used for the transfer of billets and tablets from stage to stage; and to deal with fluctuations in the throughputs of the various units. All the major plant manufacturers supply complete mechanised toilet soap units, tailored to suit individual needs; and many variations are possible, including the duplication of some items in parallel when necessary to balance throughputs. An important requirement is a facility for the diversion of billets, or tablets, which are surplus to the immediate needs of the next machine; and to return this material, plus any offcuts, for reprocessing. Fig. 2.13.

Transparent and Translucent Soaps

Transparent soaps have been known in many countries for a long time; indeed, in outline, the traditional Pears process uses the following stages :

(i) all-in saponification of a tallow, rosin and lauric oil blend in industrial alcohol with caustic soda.

(ii) solidification to bars of the required shape (oval for Pears) in water cooled bar coolers.

(iii) cutting into billets, often after the bars have been grooved to provide chamfers on the billect edges, followed by partial removal of alcohol and water in stoves, prior to stamping to tablets with flat faces.

(iv) prolonged maturing in stoves, with continued evaporation of alcohol and water. During this process the tablets develop the traditional concave shape of Pears soap.

Alcohol is removed from the air extracted from the various drying stages in activated carbon adsorbers; and the weak alcohol liquor stripped from the carbon is rectified in a normal type of still for re-use. Some ingredients included are : castor oil in the fat blend; and sugar solution and other ingredients are included in some final mixes. Cooling is in frames in which the soap is left for long periods, but more alcohol appears to be left in the soaps than in Pears. This is also the case with saddle soaps.

Translucent, and ever transparent, soaps can also be made from a toilet soap base by extensive working under the right conditions on mills, or in machines somewhat similar to refiners. Transparent soaps made by a heavy working and extrusion processes may have a tendency to produce an opaque mush in use which can be unslightly, particularly with concave tablets such as Pears on which it has been called the 'fried-egg' effect.

Floating Soaps

Several methods have been used to produce floating soaps :

1. The level of soap in a crutcher is arranged so that air is whipped in; and in the case of a crutcher with a central worm, the direction of rotation of the worm may be reversed.
2. In a process, partly dried soap is heated and flashed into a chamber from which it is pumped to a Votator after air has been injected into the pipe line. The Votator is a brine cooled, scraped wall, chilling unit, from which the aerated soap is discharged as a continuous bar.
3. In a process, soap pellets at about 70°C are worked and aerated in a 'converter' with intermeshed screws from which the mass is discharged continuously to a moulding machine.
4. A process in which hollow capsules containing air are inserted into normal soap bars plodded with a central hollow.
5. A process in which aluminium powder is mixed with the soap to form hydrogen by reaction with alkali.

Filled, or Run, Soaps

Low-priced bar soaps can be made by addition to neat soap of water containing a suitable concentration of sodium silicate, or other electrolyte. The required concentration varies with the fat blend and with the nature of the fit used; and for frame or water-cooled soaps it is common practice to make up a few small-scale mixes from each boil, although simple graphs can be produced for each type of soap which at least give a good approximation.

The filled soaps can be classified as :

1. *Liquored soaps containing more than about 50% TFM.* These products are essentially homogeneous neat soaps. For example, to produce a 61% TFM soap from base at 63% TFM of the composition. 100 parts of 63% base yield 100 x (63/61) = 103.28 parts of 61% TFM soap. Neat soap produced by a fit which gives 61% TFM contains 0.545% NaCl, so that 103.28 parts contain 0.545 x (103.28/100) = 0.563 parts NaCl. Hence salt to be added = 0.563 - 0.434 = 0.129, and liqour to be added = 103.28 - 100.00 = 3.28, so that concentration of salt solution to be added = 0.129/ 3.28 x 100 = 3.9%. Such soaps can be produced either by a suitable fit, or by addition of the appropriate salt solution to base at, say, 63% TFM. The direct fitting method can be used down to about 60% TFM, but the mixing method is possible down to around 50% TFM. The figures quoted as an example are for a soluble, washer-type, base and much weaker salt solutions are needed for a less soluble, high tallow or palm oil, base. If alkaline sodium silicate is used instead of salt, 1 part of Na_2O in the silicate is roughly equivalent to 1.3 parts of NaC1.

2. *Liquored soaps containing less than about 50% TFM, usually 28 - 42%.* Liquored soaps run to less than about 50% TFM are not homogeneous, but on setting for a few hours at crutcher temperature separate into layers equivalent to neat soap and snigre. When the correct concentration of sodium silicate is used there is only a small neat soap layer which can be dispersed satisfactorily in the bulk of the saturated solution (nigre). Adequate hand crutching in the frames is required to minimise separation. Sodium silicate, which has colliodal properties, appears to stabilise this dispersion; and this type of run soap cannot be made with salt. If too high a concentration of silicate is used, unacceptable separation will occur in the frames and/or the soap will be rough in texture; whereas with too low a concentration the soap will be soft and pasty. In other words, just sufficient electrolyte is needed to ensure that the nigre phase is saturated with soap. Tallow/rosin, or palm oil/ rosin soap bases are particularly suitable for the manufacture of this class of soap. More concentrated silicate solutions are required than for the higher TFM class.

Glued-up soaps

These soaps are made from fat blends containing a high proportion of rosin (say 35% rosin, 65% tallow), often at about 56-58% TFM. Strong alkaline, or neutral, silicate, together with soda ash (anhydrous sodium carbonate) and sometimes sugar, form the fillings. The mixture becomes very viscous and special facilities, such as portable frames which can be placed to be filled directly under the crutcher, may be required. The soap is not homogenous and crutching down to a fairly low temperature is necessary. As mentioned earlier these soaps are liable to effloresce.

Laundry Soap

Though bar laundry soap is rapidly disappearing, it is still manufactured. The procedure is the same as described above for toilet soap, but the raw materials are, for example, 4 parts tallow and grease, and 2-3 parts rosin. The latter is added, after the grease has been saponified, in the form of sodium resinate, which is made in a separate kettle by the action of soda ash on the rosin, which consists chiefly of abietic acid rather than glycerides, the formation of sodium resinate is a neutralising reaction.

The kettle mixture for laundry soap is pumped from the kettle to a crutcher which is a smaller tank fitted with a special agitator and with a steam jacket; one of the following materials is added : silicate of soda, upto 30 per cent; soda ash 2 to 5 per cent, either alone or with borax, 1 per cent; or trisodium phosphate, upto 5 per cent. The mixture is crutched until homogenous, and then run off at the bottom of the crutcher into a frame. The contents of such a frame, of which there may be hundreds, is 1000-1200 lbs of soap. The contents of frames hardens to a solid block in 3 days, the sides of the box may then be removed. The block is dried some what and then cut into slabs which are, in turn out into bars and pieces. The water content of the finished soap is 8-10 per cent.

Improvements in Laundry Soap

Many small and medium scale laundry soap producers manufacture the soap from soap stock or acid oil available from vegetable oil refineries. Due to the different properties of vegetable oils and their fatty acid composition attention is drawn to several minor seed oils/fats, which can be used in combination with the by-product soap stock/acid oil to produce good quality laundry soap.

Some Principles of Soap Formulation

For obtaining consistent quality of laundry soap, it is necessary to blend various oils and fats in appropriate proportions. Depending upon their availability to do this successfully, the soap manufacturer must have thorough knowledge of the properties and fatty acid compositions of all the available oils and fats. The properties i.e., saponification value (S.V.), Iodine value (I.V.) and Titre of various oils and fats are given in Table 2.3.

Table 2.3. Properties of oils and fats.

Oil/Fat	*S.V.*	*I.V.*	*Titre °C*
Coconut	251 - 264	7 - 10	20-24
Palm kernel	244 - 254	14 - 20	20-28
Palm	196 - 202	48 - 56	43-47
Groundnut	188 - 195	84 - 102	26-32
Cottonseed	189 - 198	99 - 113	30-37
Til (Sesame)	188 - 195	103 - 116	20-25
Mustard/Rapeseed	170 - 180	97 - 108	11-15
Soyabean.	189 - 195	120 - 141	23-27
Ricebran	181 - 189	99 - 108	24-28
Mahua	188 - 200	53 - 70	36-15

The saponification value of oil/fat is related to its molecular weight. The iodine value indicates the unsaturation, i.e., double bonds present in the fatty acid molecules. Titre gives the melting characteristics of fatty acid mixture obtained from the respective oils/fats. The unsaturation in fatty acids decide the 'softness' or hardness' of the oils/fats. The higher the iodine value of an oil/fat the lower is the titre and melting point. In other words oils/fats with high iodine values are 'soft' and those with low iodine values are 'hard' oils/fats.

The average fatty acid compositions of major oils/fats are given in Table 2.4.

Table 2.4. Fatty acid composition.

	Fatty Acids (wt %)							
Oil/Fat	*Caprylic*	*Capric*	*Lauric*	*Myristic*	*Palmitic*	*Stearic*	*Oleic*	*Linoleic*
Coconut	5-9	4-9	45-52	13-19	7-10	-	5-8	-
Palm Kernel			46-52	14-17	7-9		13-19	
Palm					40-60		39-45	7-11
Groundnut					6-11		52-71	13-26
Cottonseed					20-23		23-35	42-54
Til (seasame)					7-12		35-50	35-50
Mustard/Rapeseed			(Erucid	40-50)			10-20	10-20
Soyabean					7-12	2-6	19-30	48-58
Ricebran					12-18		40-50	29-42
Mahua					20-25	16-21	40-50	10-15

Only major fatty acid contents are listed here. Out of the fatty acids mentioned in the Table 2.4, oleic and linoleic are unsaturated fatty acids and they give the iodine value and hence 'softness' to the oil/fat. All other fatty acids are saturated ones with zero iodine value and give 'hardness' to oils/ fats. Thus, the oil charge for soap making should contain appropriate quantities of these fatty acids so as to attain desired hardness of soap. The 'hardness' of a given oil/fat may be increased to desired level by hydrogenation. If natural 'hard' oils are not available, the soap manufacturer can hydrogenate available 'soft' oils and use them in required proportion. Ideally, the oil/fat charge for soap manufacture contains a mixture of nut oils, hard oils and soft oils, Generally the percentages of these components do not exceed the following values: Nut oils 30%, Hard oils 50% and Soft oils 30%.

However, for small and medium scale soap producer's, it is not economical to use costly nut oils in laundry soap. Therefore, they have to use formulations based on hard and soft oils/fats only.

Use of Minor Oils/Fats

Minor oils/fats available in the neighbouring region can be used in soap. They should have high melting points and low iodine values. Several such 'hard' oils are suggested which are available from nearby oil extraction units. Their characteristics and fatty acid compositions are also given. The major hard oils/fats which can be used for soap making are: Dhupa, khakan, kokum, pisa, mango kernel, salt dharambe. Out of these, khakan fat contains major quantities of lauric and myristic acids, while, pisa fat contains more than 90% of lauric acid and is even better than Coconut oil and palm kernel oil. The characteristics and fatty acid compositions of these minor oils are given in Table 2.5 and 2.6 respectively.

Table 2.5. Characteristics of minor oils.

Oil/fat	*S.V.*	*I.V.*	*M.P., °C*
Kokum	189	34-36	41-42
Dhupa	187-192	36-43	30-40
Khakan	233	6	41
Pisa	256	11	43-44
Mango kernel	190-195	32-61	34-43
Sal	182-195	31-44	34-37
Dharambe	198-200	48-54	33-37

Table 2.6. Fatty acid composition of minor oils.

Oil/fat	Lauric	Myristic	Palmitic	Stearic	Oleic
Kokum	–	–	–	52-56	39-42
Dhupa	–	–	10	41	42
Khakan	21	53	19	–	–
Pisa	96	–	–	–	4
Mango kernel	–	–	6-18	24-49	33-53
Sal	–	–	2-10	32-55	36-53
Dharambe	–	–	–	35-40	55-60

However, this list is not exhaustive. Many other fats are available from nature which can be used in soap making without much pretreatment. The quantity of these 'hard' fats to be added will depend on their own as well as the properties of the acid oil taken for saponification. Detailed descriptions of these minor oils and fats are presented here.

There are large number of such minor oils and fats available throughout India. They have varying but useful properties and fatty acid compositions. Depending on the availability of these oils and fats near the laundry soap manufacturers, appropriate selection should be done to include these oils and fats in the laundry soap formulation. In the long term, it will be definitely beneficial to develop these oils and fats since they are of free-origin and are locally available every year. If required, a backward integration into production of these minor oils and fats will be profitable for the small or medium scale laundry soap producer in the long run.

Mowrah (Mahua)

Mowrah is also called as Mahua or butter tree. Its botanical names are *Madhuca indica, M. latifolia*, and *Bassia latifolia*. It is a medium sized to large tree usually with short bole and large rounded crown. Its berries are ovoid, upto 5 cm long greenish turning reddish yellow to orange when ripe. There are 1 to 4 seeds that are ovoid and brown coloured. It is a tree of dry tropics and is found throughout greater parts of India. It is common throughout Central India, Maharashtra, Andhra Pradesh and Madhya Pradesh. The seeds yield yellow oil (20-60%) with an unpleasant taste. The oil has following characteristics :

Specific gravity	0.856-0.875
Refractive Index at 40^{0}C	1.458-1.462
Saponification value	187-200
Iodine value	53-70
Acid value	5-50

RM value	0.7-3.6
Unsaponifiable matter	1-3%

Major fatty acids (%) : Oleic 44.6, stearic 24.5, palmitic 17.4, linoleic 9.3, arachidic 3 and myristic 1.2.

The oils is used for edible and cooking purposes in some rural areas. Refining and hydrogenation yield on edible fat. It is sometimes used as an adulterant for ghee. The oil is also used for soap making. Refined oil is used in the manufacture of lubricating greases and fatty alcohols. It is also used for candles, as batching oil in jute industry and as a raw material for the production of stearic acid. It has emollient and emetic properties. Both expelled and solvent extracted oils are available commercially.

Kokum

Kokum is a slender tree having drooping branches. It is also called as Mangosteen oil tree, or Brindonia tallow tree. Its botanical name is *Garcinia Indica*. Kokum fruits are globular or spherical enclosing seeds.

Kokum trees are found in the forests of Western Ghats, in Southern Maharashtra and slopes of Nilgiri hills. Kokum kernels contain about 44% fat. The fat has following characteristics :

Melting point	40-43°C
Titre	60°C
Refractive index	1.4565-1.4575
Saponification value	187-191.7
Iodine value	25-36
RM value	0.1-1.0
Unsaponifiable matter	2.3%

Major fatty acids (%) : Stearic 56.4, oleic 39.4, palmitic 2.5, linoleic 1.7%.

Kokum fat is mainly used for edible purpose, adulterant of ghee. It is considered nutritive, demulcent and emollient. Alongwith Mowrah (Mahua) butter, it is used in chocolate and confectioneries. Kokum fat is also suitable for ointment, suppositories and other pharmaceutical preparations. It is used in Ulcers, dry lips and hands etc. It is also suitable for candle and soap making, sizing of cotton yarn and lighting. Presently the production of kokum fat is about 200 to 300 tonnes and much of it finds a ready export market for use in coco a butter substitutes.

Dhupa

Dhupa is also called as White dammer or Indian copal tree. Its botanical name is *Vateria indica.* It is a large, evergren tree. Its capsules (fruits) are ovoid, pale brown, fleshy and are single seeded. The seeds are reddish white or creamy. Dhupa tree is indigenous to forests of Western Ghats from North-Kanara to Kerala. It is also planted in Karnataka as avenue tree. The average fruit yield per tree is 500 kg. The seeds of Dhupa yield a greenish yellow to white, semi-solid fat to the extent of 22 to 27% by weight. The fat is fairly soft and has a slightly pleasant odour. It can be easily bleached by exposure to sunlight. Dhupa fat has following characteristics :

Melting point	30-40^{0}C
Specific gravity at 25^{0}C	0.9120
Refractive index at 40^{0}C	1.456-1.459
Saponification value	187-192
Iodine value	36-43
Acid value	1.4-13.0
Unsaponifiable matter	0.6-2.5%

Major fatty acids (%) : Oleic 42.2-47.8. stearic 38.9-45.1, palmitic 9.7-13.0, linoleic 0.2-2.3, arachidic 0.4-4.6.

Dhupa fat after refining is used for edible purposes. It is used in confectionry and as an adulterant of ghee. In other applications, it is used in candle and soap making. Medicinally, it is applied in rheumatism and allied problems.

Pisa

The botanical name of pisa is *Actinodaphne augustifolia* or *A. Hookeri.* It is a shrub or medium sized tree. The berries are globular or eliptic red when ripe and are pungently aromatic. Pisa is found in the evergreen forests of Eastern and Western Ghats, Karnataka, Orissa, Sikkim and North East India upto an altitude of 1500 m. It is particularly abundant in Ahmednagar, Nasik and Satara districts of Maharashtra. The seed contains 63% kernel and 31% shell. Both these parts-shell and kernel contain oil, kernel contains 32 to 75% fat called as 'Pisa fat'. It has the following characteristics :

Specific gravity at 40^{0}C	0.9209
Refractive index at 40^{0}C	1.4403
Saponification value	249.5-255.5
Iodine value	7.1-12.3

Acid value	4.0-25.9
Unsaponifiable matter 1.2-7.3%	

Major fatty acids (%) : Lauric (C_{12}) 88.6-96.0; capric 1.8-4.9, myristic 0-0.8 and oleic 0-5.7.

Pisa fat is used for lighting lamps and as an external application in sprains of joints. It is an excellent source of lauric acid, better than coconut or palm kernel oils. The soaps prepared from lauric acid-rich fat have excellent detergency, hardness and solubility. Pisa fat produces soap with excellent wetting and lather formation and detergent qualities. The fat can be used for commercial production of lauryl alcohol which at present is imported to meet the requirements of cosmetic, textile, pharmaceutical, perfumery and syndet industries. The oil can also be used in the manufacture of confectionery, agarbattis and candles. It can be used as lubricating agent for watches and other delicate machines, and as wetting agent for insecticidal preparations. The seed shell gives about 20 to 25% oil. It has following characteristics :

Refractive index at 40°C	1.4590
Saponification value	209.7
Iodine value	62.4
Acid value	33.2
Unsaponifiable matter	7.6%

Major fatty acids (%) : Oleic 54.5, palmitic 25.5-25.7, Lauric 12.2-13.3, linoleic 6-7.4.

One survey estimated a potential of 10,000 tonnes of pisa seeds. However, the present collection of fat is estimated to be around 100 tonnes.

Mango Kernel

The mango tree i.e., *Mangifera indica* occurs throughout India and the high density areas are Andhra Pradesh, Uttar Pradesh, Maharashtra, Orissa, Bihar and West Bengal. The area under cultivation is around one million hectares. The seed (stone) inside the fruit consists of a hard fibrous outer shell and an inner kernel-the source of mango kernel fat. The dry stone accounts for 10% of the fruit. The dry kernel constitutes 75% of the stone and oil content of the kernel is about 10% to 12%. After removing the outer shell the kernels are recovered and are subjected to solvent extraction for recovery of fat.

Mango kernel fat is pale yellow or cream in colour. The characteristics of Mango kernel fat are as follows :

Acid value	6.4-12
Iodine value	32-60.7
Saponification value	190.1-195.1
Unsaponifiable matter, %	0.75-2.4
Specific gravity at 30°C	0.901
Refractive index at 40°C	1.455-1.457
Titre °C	51
Melting point °C	34-43

Major fatty acids (%) : Palmitic 6-18, stearic 24-49, oleic 33-53, linoleic 1-13, arachidic 1-2.6.

The refining of mango kernel fat can be easily carried out by using conventional processes. The main application of mango kernel fat is as a raw material for making cocoa butter substitutes. It can also be used as ointment bases.

The biggest hurdle in the mango kernel fat production is the procurement of stones. Therefore, the current yearly production of mango kernel fat is too low compared to the potential.

Sal

The botanical name of sal tree is *Shorea robusta.* The total area of sal forests in India is estimated at 111,500 sq. km. The forests occur in two principal regions-Central Indian belt and at the foot of the Himalayas. Sal bears a profusion of fruit about the size of a pea with five segments of fruiting calyx enveloping it and forming three wings (2 inches each) and two narrower smaller segments around the fruit. In the mature fruit the enclosed nut remains green but gradually turms brown at storage. The typically dry fruit is composed of 23% wing, 30% pod and 47% kernel. The size of the kernel is small, on an average 4 to 4.5 g. The oil content of sal kernel is about 14%. Therefore, the preferred method of recovering this oil is solvent extraction.

The characteristics of sal fat are :

Refractive index at 40°C	1.4560-1.4619
Titre °C	48-53.4
Melting point °C	34.5-37.0
Acid value and saponification value	182-195
Iodine value	31-44.3
Unsaponifiable matter, %	0.9-2.2

Major fatty acids (%) : Palmitic 1.7-10.4, stearic 32.6-55, oleic 36.5-52.5, linoleic 0.3-2, arachidic 1-8.6.

Degumming and neutralisation of sal fat can be carried out by conventional methods, sal fat is dark green and requires slightly higher proportions of bleaching earth (4-6%) for effective bleaching. (Pretreatment with phosphoric acid in conjunction with aqueous sodium chlorite, followed by neutralisation and bleaching (3% earth, 0.3% carbon), yield light coloured oils without a greenish tinge). The bleached fat can be deodorised by usual methods. Sal fat is widely used in preparation of cocoa butter substitutes, large quantities of sal fat are exported to UK, Japan and other countries. It is believed that the sal tree bears a good crop every alternate year.

Dharambe

Dharambe is a small to medium sized tree with horizontal or dropping branches. Its botanical name is *Garcinia Camboqia.* The family is same as that of kokum tree. The fruit of Dharambe is ovoid and seeds are surrounded by a succulent aril. It is common tree in the evergreen forests of Western Ghats, from Konkan to Travancore. It also grows in Shola forests of Nilgiris. Dharambe seeds yield a white granular fat to the extent of about 31 to 50%. The characteristics of the fat are :

Melting point	36.60C
Titre	51.20C
Specific gravity at 400C	0.9003
Refractive index at 400C	1.4583
Saponification value	203.5
Iodine value	52.5
Acid value	5.0
Hydroxyl value	11.1
Unsaponifiable matter	1.0%

Major fatty acids (%) : Oleic 56.2, stearic 38.4, palmitic 1.6, arachidic 1.5 and linoleic 1.1.

Dharambe oil is used for edible purposes. It may be exploited as a good source of oleic acid.

Driers and Metallic Soaps

Metallic soaps are a group of water-insoluble compounds containing alkaline-earth or heavy metals combined with monobasic carboxylic acids of 7 to 22 carbon atoms. They can be represented by the general formula $(RCOO)_xM$ (neutral soap), where R is an aliphatic or alicyclic radical and M is a metal with valence *x*. They differ from ordinary soap by composition and their insolubility in water. Their solubility or solvation in a variety of organic solvents accounts for their many and varied uses (See Table 2.7). Driers are the most important group of metallic soaps promoting or accelerating the drying, curing, or hardening of oxidisable coating vehicles such as paints.

Composition and Properties

The acid or anion portion of a metal soap can be varied. Typical anions currently used are rosin and tall-oil fatty acids, saturated and unsaturated naturally occurring long-chain monocarboxylic fatty acids with 7 to 22 carbon atoms, and naphthenic, 2-ethylhexanoic, and the newer synthetic tertiary acids.

Acid soaps contain free acid (positive acid number), whereas neutral (normal) soaps contain no free acid (zero acid number). The basic soap is characterised by a higher metal-to-acid equivalent ratio than the normal metal soap. Particular properties are obtained by adjusting the basicity.

Properties are furthermore determined by the nature of the organic acid, the type of metal and its concentration, the presence of solvents and additives, and the method of manufacture. Generally, metals of low atomic weight form soaps with higher melting points (e.g., lithium). Higher melting points are also characteristic of soaps made of high molecular weight, straight-chain, saturated fatty acids. Branched-chain, unsaturated fatty acids form soaps with lower melting points. Light powders are characteristic of precipitated soaps, whereas soaps made by fusion are usually hard solids. Liquids and pastes are mixtures or solutions of soaps in hydrocarbon and/or nonvolatile solvents. Liquid soaps are manufactured as fluid as possible compatible with maximum metal content. Newer techniques are available in which liquid soaps of very high metal content (18-24%) are obtained which still posses excellent fluidity. Both liquid and paste soaps are manufactured to strict viscosity and flow specifications.

The odour of a soap is determined by its organic constituents. Colour, another important property of metal soaps, is determined by the type and amount of metal used, the colour and quality of the organic raw materials, the method of manufacture, and the care in processing.

Table 2.7. Applications of metal soaps.

Application	*Metal*
Stabilisers for plastics	Ba, Cd, Sn, Sr
Fungicides	Cu, Hg, Zn
Catalysts	Co, Cu, Mo, Mn, Cr, Ni
Driers	Bi, Ca, Co, Fe, Pb, Mn, Zn, Zr
Fuel additives	Ba, Fe, Mg, Mn, Pb

Manufacture

Metallic soaps are manufactured by three methods; the precipitation or double-decomposition process; the fusion process; and the direct metal reaction (DMR) process. The choice of process and variation depends upon the metal, the desired form of the product, the desired purity, raw material availability and cost, metal content, etc. The desired final composition determines the stoichiometry of the starting materials, i.e., whether an acid, neutral, or basic soap is obtained.

In the case of metallic soap solutions, the metal is assumed to be the active part and the acid portion serves as carrier for the metal, conferring oil solubility; water insolubility, and compatibility with other components of the system in which it is to be used. Therefore, it is economically advantageous to incorporate as much metal per unit of acid as possible, providing the resulting soap is oil soluble and fulfills the requirements of the application.

Health and Safety, Factors

The hazards encountered in the manufacture, processing, handing, and use of metal soaps are associated for the most part with the inherent toxicity of the metals and solvents present. In general, the acid portion of the metal soap is low in toxicity. However, naphthenic acid is highly irritating to the skin on prolonged contact. High concentrations have a narcotic effect.

Metallic soaps are used in driers, waterproofing agents, fuel additives, rubber, greases, lubricants, and chemical thickeners, plastics, catalysts, fungicides, and cosmetics and pharmaceuticals.

DRYCLEANING AND LAUNDERING

Drycleaning

Drycleaning can be defined as the cleaning of fabrics in a substantially nonaqueous, liquid medium. This process has evolved during the last 60-70 years into a highly effective, low cost, safe method of removing soils from all types of textiles. The industry enjoyed steady growth until the introduction of wash-and-wear garments, and after a period of adjustment, again started to expand and diversify. Recent growth has been aided by the development of new equipment, cleaning techniques, and applications.

The important distinction between dry and wet solvents is that the latter (principally water, glycols, and other hydroxylic compounds) swell the hydrophilic textile fibres, but the drycleaning solvents do not. Dimensional changes that fibres undergo as they swell in water are transmitted throughout the textile structure and can cause serious fabric damage. These changes can be local distortions (wrinkles) or more extensive, causing shrinkage. Drycleaning solvents do not swell the textile fibres and thus do not cause wrinkles or shrinkage. This is one of the principal advantages of drycleaning processes over laundering. Another advantage is that drycleaning solvents remove oily soils at low tempera-tures, whereas a high temperature, colloidal suspension mechanism is needed in wet laundering processes.

The main difference between drycleaning and laundering processes in the solvent used. Since both methods remove soil by the same mechanisms, similar operations are used. Garments are tumbled in the cleaning liquid in horizontal washers to separate soil and fabric as thoroughly as possible without damage. Detergents are used in both cases to emulsify or solubilise the soil insoluble in the cleaning liquid. Special detergent ingredients peptise and suspend insoluble soils.

The Drycleaning Operation

The following sequence of operations is used in the normal drycleaning process :

1. Soiled garments are marked and sorted.
2. Prespotting is performed when required.
3. Garments are rotated in a tumble-type washer containing the drycleaning solvent.
4. Solvent is drained from the tumbler and most of the residual solvent removed by centrifugal extraction.
5. The small amount of remaining solvent is removed in heated dryers.
6. Dirty solvent from the wash cycles is continuously passed through diatomaceous earth and activated carbon or disposable cartridge filters to remove as much of the fugitive dyes and insoluble soils as possible.
7. Soils not removed by filters, diatomaceous earth, or activated carbon can be removed from the solvent by distillation.

8. Dry, solvent-free garments are inspected and spot cleaned a second time, if necessary.
9. A garment may be "wet cleaned" at this point, but this is usually omitted when operating a charged-solvent system.
10. After a final inspection, the garments are assembled according to customer's order.
11. Garments are bagged and placed on racks ready to be picked up. Mechanical conveyors aid in fast recovery of a customer's garments.

Many drycleaning operations provide special services, such as garment repair, dyeing, and moth-and waterproofing treatments. Many operators add optical brighteners, antistatic agents, and sizing to improve the brightness and feel (hand) of a garment.

Materials

Drycleaning solvents remove oily soils easily by simple solution, and hence detergents are not required. However, detergent addition greatly enhances the removal of the many other soils that are generally present. Detergents probably inhibit redeposition of soil by being adsorbed on the soil particles to cause a lowering of the interfacial energy between them and the solvents, at the same time increasing the interfacial energy between particle and fibre surface.

A modern procedure called the charged system uses a detergent that forms a stable colloidal solution in the solvent. The term colloidal solution, as used here, means a solution containing disperse aggregates called micelles. The key to the success of the charged system is the reduced effective vapour pressure of water dissolved in detergent micelles. This prevents the solubilised water from being completely removed from solution by the garment.

Sulphonates of mixed petroleum hydrocarbons, system detergents, have now been replaced by purer synthetic detergents, particularly the amine and sodium salts of alkylarenesulphonic acids. Drycleaning detergents are not formulated products similar to household laundry detergents but principally surfactants or a mixture of surfactants, with concentrations of active ingredients ranging from 40-90%.

Water control

Sensitive and reliable control systems are required to maintain the 70% rh in a drycleaning unit. These controls are designed to measure the moisture, inject water into the system, and close the injection valve at optimum rh. Some water also enters the unit with the garments.

Two types of water-control systems are widely used. The direct type uses an electric hygrometer to measure relative humidity in the atmosphere above the solution. An indirect method based on the electrical conductivity of the solution has proved the most successful.

Solvents

An acceptable drycleaning solvent must be an effective solvent for fats and oils, sufficiently volatile to permit easy drying, easily purified, and of low toxicity. Solvents should not weaken, dissolve, or shrink the ordinary textile fibres or cause bleeding of dyes. They must be noncorrosive to metals commonly used in drycleaning machinery and have a flash point above 37.7^{0}C or be nonflammable.

The main advantages of chlorinated hydrocarbon solvents over the petroleum solvents are their nonflammability, permitting their use in many areas where zoning laws prohibit the use of a flammable solvent. Perchloroethylene (tetrachloroethylene) is the most widely used drycleaning solvent.

Solvent Purification, Distillation

The principal method of purifying drycleaning solvents is distillation, which has displaced the caustic clarification process. There has been an unfortunate tendency in recent years for cleaners to omit distillation and depend entirely upon activated charcoal and fatty acid-adsorbing sweetener powders for solvent purification. Lower quality cleaning results from this cost-cutting practive.

Carbon recovery

Devices called sniffers should be an essential part of any drycleaning operation to protect workers from exposure to drycleaning solvents and increase operating life.

Industrial drycleaning

In the last decade a new service, known as industrial drycleaning, has become significant in the drycleaning industry. With improvement in fabric appearance, colour retention, hand, odour, and moisture penetration, customer resistance to fabrics of synthetic fibres has disappeared. Rental and maintenance service of career apparel, industrial garments, and linen supply items became economically feasible. In the most successful processes, high concentrations of water were added to the cleaning solvent or a 100% water cycley incorporated.

Laundering

Laundering is the process in which soils and stains are removed from textiles in an aqueous medium. Together with drycleaning, which accomplishes a similar result in nonaqueous solvents, commercial laundering constitutes a multi-billion dollar (10^9) industry. However, the largest portion of consumer textiles is laundered in the home.

Commercial laundering

Commercial laundry practice differs in many ways from home laundering. For example, in the commercial and industrial laundry plant, ion exchange is always used as water softener. Caustic and silicated alkalies are usually employed as detergent builders, and tallow soap is much more widely used than in home laundering. Classification of articles is generally by soil intensity.

Home laundering

The laundry is first sorted, primarily by colour. Further sorting by type of fabric and garment construction is advisable. Pretreatment is often effective, loosening stains that might be firmly set at the higher temperatures employed in the regular washing cycle. The regular washing cycle for white and coloured fabrics, from heavily soiled work clothes to lightly soiled lingerie, normally employs a heavy-duty detergent. Water softening agents are added in areas where water supplies are unusually hard, in addition to bleaches such as liquid sodium hypochlorite, dry chlorine bleach, or oxygen bleach. Fabric softeners impart softness and fluffiness to finished fabrics and reduce static cling, especially in synthetic fabrics. Some household detergents include a fabric softener, combining both laundering and softening in a single application.

Materials

Textiles are either from natural or synthetic fibres. More than 90% of the natural fibres encountered in laundering are cotton; the only other natural fibre laundered of any importance is wool. The chemical constitution of these fibres is quite different, and therefore they must be handled differently in laundering.

Water is the most important material used in laundering, assisted by detergents. Water provides the medium through which mechanical action is transmitted to the fabrics to be cleansed and serves as a wetting agent to penetrated the soil-fibre interface and displace the soil from fibres. It carries chemicals to the soiled area and removes suspended soil. The quality of the water used for washing is crucial to the quality of the finished product.

Chemicals

Chemicals used in laundering are classified as follows : alkalies, detergents, bleaches, sours and finishing specialities.

3
Raw Materials for Soap Industry

Introduction

Although some cleaning operations can be carried out with organic solvents and other materials, most are done with water; and the detergents (cleaning agents) discussed in this book are intended to improve the cleaning performance of water.

Fats from domestic animals which had been killed for food, and olive oil (which could be obtained more readily than other vegetable oils), were used for the manufacture of soap. until caustic alkalis became available, saponification must have been difficult and probably incomplete. The fats may have been allowed to deteriorate with the development of free fatty acids which react readily with alkali carbonates; and the soap so formed would have helped the reaction. The process has been said to have been one in which the fats and alkali carbonate solution were boiled to dryness in a pot over an open fire. More water was added, and the mixture boiled down again; this process being repeated as many times as necessary. The first reaction may have been slow hydrolysis of the fat to give free fatty acid which was then neutralised by the alkali carbonate to give soap. If sodium carbonate was used, a 'hard soap' was produced, but with potassium carbonate the product would have been some sort of 'soft soap', unless a further stage of salting out with common salt (sodium chloride) was employed to convert the potassium soap to sodium soap.

As the chemical industry developed, alkalis (sodium carbonate and sodium hydroxide) made from salt have largely replaced the sources mentioned earlier. Soap cannot be used in acid solution (because it is decomposed with the liberation of fatty acids); and it forms a precipitate with the calcium and magnesium in hard water. Hence, although soap is a good all-round detergent, it has limitations, particularly for some industrial purposes in the textile field.

RAW MATERIALS

Surfactants, Builders and Fillers

Soaps, and the alternative non-soapy detergents, have a number of the important properties and one such property is the reduction of the surface energy, or surface tension (more strictly interfacial tension), of solutions which contain them, so that they are called surface active agents. This is commonly contracted to *surfactants.* Surfactants contain a hydrophobic (water hating, or repelling) and a hydrophilic (water loving, or attracting) end. Alternatively, this can be expressed as a lipophilic (fat loving, equals hydrophobic) and a lipophobic (fat hating, equals hydrophilic) end. Such chemical compounds are having amphipathic properties. Non-soapy surfactants are also sometimes called *syndets.*

Solutions of acids, bases (alkalis) and salts contain charged particles called ions. Ions which carry positive electrical charges are called cations and others which carry negative charges are called anions. Ions can carry one unit of charge (called monovalent or univalent), two units (divalent), and so on. Examples are :

Hydrochloric acid which ionizes $HCl = H^+ + Cl^-$

Sulphuric acid which ionizes $H_2SO_4 = H^+ + HSO^-_4 HSO^-_4 = H^+ + SO_4^{2-}$

Sodium hydroxide which ionizes $NaOH = Na^+ + OH^-$

Ammonium hydroxide which ionizes $NH_4OH = NH_4^+ + OH^-$

Sodium carbonate which ionizes $Na_2CO_3 = 2Na^+ + CO_3^{2-}$

Magnesium sulphate which ionizes $MgSO_4 = Mg^{2+} + SO_4^{2-}$

Trisodium orthophosphate which ionizes $Na_3PO_4 = 3Na^+ + PO_4^{3-}$

All normal chemical compounds are electrically neutral, so that the charges on the positive and negative ions which they contain, or produce in aqueous solution, balance. That is sodium chloride and magnesium sulphate are $Na^+ Cl^-$ and $Mg^{2+} SO_4^{2-}$ respectively, but sodium sulphate is $Na_2^+ SP_4^{2-}$.

It should be noted that chloride ions (Cl^-) have completely different properties from those of chlorine gas (Cl_2). Similarly, the sodium ion (Na^+) differs from metallic sodium (Na).

Many surfactants ionise; and those with the hydrophobic-hydrophilic portion in the anion are called anionic surfactants. Examples are :

(i) Soap, which is a mixture of salts (usually sodium) of long chain fatty acids, $R.COO^-Na^+$, where R represents a long hydrocarbon chain.

(ii) Alkyl benzene sulphonates, $R - C_6H_4 - SO_3^-N_a^+$

Similarly, surfactants with the hydrophobic-hydrophilic portion in the cation are described as cationic. Examples are :

(i) Quaternary ammonium salts, such as alkyl trimethyl ammonium chloride, $R—N(CH_3)_3^+.Cl^-$.

(ii) Alkyl pyridinium salts, such as cetyl pyridinium bromide, $C_{16}H_{33}—C_5H_4N^+Br^-$.

The balancing ions, such as Na^+ or Cl^-, in anionic and cationic surfactants respectively, are sometimes called *gengenions.* Unlike the anionics, which are the most important group of surfactants used in detergent products, the cationics are used mainly in fabric softeners and as germicides.

A third group of surfactants, which is becoming increasingly important in the detergents field is the *nonionic* type. By definition, these compounds do not ionise, but they contain a hydrophobic and a hydrophilic end to make them surfactants. There are naturally occurring nonionic surfactants, such as saponin, but those of importance in the detergents industry are synthetic. The hydrophobic portion is normally an alkyl chain, or an alkyl substituted aromatic hydrocarbon. The hydrophilic portion is usually a polyglycol chain produced by the condensation of ethylene oxide with itself and with an active hydrogen atom in the hydrophobe molecule. In the most important sub-group, the active hydrogen atom is in an hydroxyl group of a long chain alcohol, or an alkyl phenol. The reactions can be illustrated by reference to a long chain alcohol, R—OH.

$$R — OH + \underbrace{CH_2 — CH_2}_{O} \rightarrow R — O — CH_2 — CH_2 — OH$$

This compound, in which one molecule of ethylene oxide has been attached, is itself an alcohol; and more ethylene oxides can be added similarly to form a polyglycol chain containing *n*—O—CH_2—CH_2—groups.

$$R—O—CH_2—CH_2—OH + n(CH_2)_2O \rightarrow R—O—CH_2—CH_2—$$
$$(O—CH_2—CH_2)_{n-1}—O—CH_2—CH_2—OH$$

Other compounds to which ethylene oxide can be added to form nonionic surfactants are fatty acids (in which the carboxyl group,—COOH, contains an—OH), long chain amines and long chain amides, in which there is an active hydrogen atom in the—NH_2 group.

The ethylene oxide condensates just considered end with an alcohol group; and this can be sulphated to produce another type of anionic surfactant.

Certain nonionic surfactants are made with propylene oxide in conjunction with ethylene oxide. There is also a fourth group of surfactants known as the *amphoterics.* These can ionise as either anionic or cationic substances, depending upon the alkalinity, or acidity, of the solution in which they are present. Amphoteric surfactants are generally expensive and used only in rather specialised products. A very large number of surfactants have been developed and the more important types, with their properties and uses, are discussed in Chapter 2.

It will be appreciated that soap is a detergent, but the word 'detergent' is frequently confined to the non-soapy surfactants and products based upon them. In this book the term 'detergent' will be taken to include soap; and non-soapy types will be called non-soapy detergents (abbreviated to NSDs). NSDs are also called soapless detergents, or synthetic detergents. The latter term is not very appropriate, as soaps can also be made from fatty acids produced by the oxidation of petroleum-based hydrocarbons.

Soaps and non-soapy surfactants may require the addition of other substances to make them perform well. This is particularly so with the NDSs, which need additives to make them effective heavy duty fabric washing products capable of dealing with really dirty clothes and other articles. Such additives are called *builders.* The overall cleaning effect of a detergent solution is the net result of soil removal and soil redeposition; and some authors say that only substances which perform both functions should be called builders. *Fillers* are substances added to a detergent to cheapen the product. In some cases the distinction between fillers and builders is blurred. For example, sodium silicate and sodium carbonate which are, or were, added to household soaps to reduce cost also have some beneficial effects.

Types of Soaps and Soapmaking Terms

The oils and fats used in the manufacture of soap are essential triglycerides, that is esters of the trihydric alcohol, glycerol. Here the common, but not universal, convention which reserves the word 'glycerol' for the pure compound, $CH_2OH–CHOH–CH_2OH$ (1,2,3 trihydroxypropane or 1,2,3 propanetriol), and calls the actual materials *'glycerines'*, is followed. For example, a soap lye crude glycerine may be found to contain 83.5% glycerol and a distilled glycerine 99.1% glycerol. The fatty acids which are combined with the glycerol in a fat are almost exclusively straight chain monocarboxylic acids with an even number of carbon atoms, including the one in the carboxylic group. For example :

Stearic acid $C_{17}H_{35}.COOH$
Oleic acid $C_{17}H_{33}.COOH$
Lauric acid $C_{11}H_{23}.COOH$

The triglycerides, which comprise the bulk of an oil or fat which is fresh, have the formula $CH_2–O–OCR_1–CH–O–OCR_2–CH_2–O–OC–R_3$ where R_1, R_2 and R_3 are long chain alkyl groups which may be the same, or different. Here it is only necessary to add that an oil is a fat which is liquid under the prevailing conditions, but the distinction is somewhat arbitrary and a matter of convention. Coconut oil is normally solid in temperate areas, but it is called an oil because it is liquid in its tropical countries of origin. Tallow, which is a typical fat, is now commonly transported as an oil in heated road and ships/ tanks.

The soaps used as detergents are the soluble salts of mixtures of fatty acids. The cation is usually sodium, but potassium, or a mixture of sodium and potassium, is used in soft and shaving soaps. Ammonia (giving ammonium soaps) and various organic nitrogenous bases are sometimes used to neutralise the fatty acids in specialist products. The fatty acid salts of other metals are substantially insoluble. Those of calcium and magnesium are formed as undesirable precipitates when soap is used in hard water, but they, and some other insoluble soaps, are used for various industrial purposes.

Household sodium soaps are called *'hard soaps'* to distinguish them from jelly-like *'soft soaps'*, which were at one time used extensively in the textile industry and the home. As already mentioned, *soft soaps* are commonly made with potassium as the cation; and from liquid oils. The term hard soap can be confusing in that these soaps are normally softer when made than the other main group of *solid soaps* and the *toilet soaps.* Sodium soaps can be made by :

(i) *Direct saponification,* almost always with caustic soda :

$$\underset{\text{fat}}{CH_2.O.OCR.CH.O.OCR.CH_2.O.OCR} + \underset{\text{caustic soda}}{3NaOH} \rightarrow$$

$$\underset{\text{glycerol}}{CH_2OH–CHOH–CH_2OH} + \underset{\text{soap}}{3R.COO\,Na}$$

(ii) *Splitting,* or *hydrolysis,* of the fat with water to fatty acids plus glycerol; followed by separation of the glycerol, and neutralisation of the fatty acids with caustic soda, or sodium carbonate, to form soaps.

(iii) *Neutralisation of fatty acids produced in other ways,* particularly by the oxidation of a petroleum hydrocarbon.

A major distinction is between soaps made by an *'all-in'* process and soaps made by the *'fully-boiled'* process. All-in soaps are so-called because the fat (or fatty acid) and the alkali are just mixed, so that everything put into the pot goes into the product. Glycerol is not separated; and it is important to avoid any undue excess of alkali. All-in processes are divided into *'semi-boiled'*, in which external heat is applied, and *'cold-process'* in which it is not, the only heat coming from the heat of the saponification reaction. All-in processes can be carried out very simply; and they are still used by some small local manufacturers in some of the less-developed countries, where these manufacturers in some of the less-developed countries, where these manufacturers are sometimes known as traditional soapmakers. Soaps which include potassium are made by an all-in process, because graining with salt, which is an inherent part of the fully-boiled process, would displace potassium by sodium.

Most soap made by direct saponification of fats is produced by some version of the fully-boiled process. This process includes three main stages, although other operations are sometimes added :

(i) *Saponification,* the chemical reaction which forms soap and liberates glycerol. This is sometimes called *killing* the fat.

(ii) *Washing,* in which the soap mass is *grained,* or *salted-out,* with salt (or other electrolyte) and, on standing, separates into a lower aqueous layer called *lye,* and an upper layer of *soap curd,* also called *kettle wax.* The soap curd contains a proportion of enmeshed lye. A washing operation transfers part of the glycerol to the lye; and also removes dirt from the soap.

(iii) *Fitting or finishing.* In this operation the electrolyte content of the soap mass is adjusted so that on prolonged standing (or passage through a cêntrifuge) an upper layer of *neat soap,* or *soap base,* and a lower layer of *nigre,* or *nigre lye,* is obtained. The nigre is reprocessed. Fitting achieves a further purification of the soap and produces the neat soap in a desirable physico-chemical state.

Removal of the neat soap from a vessel in which it is settled is called cleansing. Soapmakers use the term *closing* to describe a reduction in electrolyte content (with consequent reduction in tendency to separate) and *opening* for the converse operation. Those terms, however, have rather electrolyte content (with consequent reduction in tendency to separate) and *opening* for the converse operation. Those terms, however, have rather different connotations in relation to the washing and the fitting stages.

The large vessels in which soap is made in the traditional form of the process are often called *pans* or *kettles.*

Bar soaps, known as *curd soaps*, were made at one time by an elaboration of the washing stage just described; but neat soap is the normal starting material for the production of most soap products (hence the name 'soap base'). If the fitting stage is carried out properly, and the soap is well-settled, the neat soap has a fairly constant composition, although this can be varied somewhat. Usually neat soap contains about 61-64% *TFM (total fatty matter)*, equivalent to about 67-69% anhydrous soap and 30-32% water.

When neat soap is cooled with no more than minor additions (if any), a *genuine soap* is produced. It is also possible to reduce the soap content of the product by addition of suitable alkaline solutions (or dilute brine) to give what are called *filled*, or run, soaps. A special type of filled soap is described as *glued-up.*

Genuine soaps made by the older processes using frames, or water coolers, have substantially the same composition as the base from which they are produced. With the modern spray-chilling and extrusion processes, the distinction between genuine and filled soaps is obscured by the fact that evaporation occurs during the process and dilute electrolyte has to be added if it is required to bring the TFM back to 62-64%. Genuine and filled soaps can be sold as *bars,* or cut into *billets* and stamped into *tablets.* These soaps are known by various names: *laundry, common,* or *household*, as well as *hard* or *bar.*

To a soapmaker a *lye* is an aqueous liquor which normally contains only a negligible concentration of soap, the exception being a *thick,* or *nigre lye* which may carry about 1-3% soap. The term lye is used in several ways. It came originally from the alkali industry, where it means a solution of caustic soda (or possibly other alkali); and it is sometimes used in this sense in the soap industry, particularly by older soapmakers. The lye separated from soap curd in the washing stage of soapmaking is called *spent lye* provided it contains little caustic soda. If it contains a substantial concentration of caustic soda (and hence requires to be processed further in the soapmaking department), it is called *half-spent lye.* The glycerol concentration in the spent lye produced is very important; but when a soapmaker speaks of the strength of a lye (or a soap mass), the reference is normally to caustic soda rather than glycerol content.

When fats are hydrolysed with water, with or without a catalyst, the process is often called *splitting,* and the aqueous glycerine separated *sweet water.* In some countries, soap lyes are called sweet water, and some glycerine distillers use the term sweet water for the dilute liquor produced in some types of still, which is otherwise called *weaks.*

The term *lye* is used for any liquor separated after soap has been grained, and *sweet water* for the glycerol bearing liquor from a splitting operation.

Acids, Alkalis, Buffers, pH and Indicators

Acids and bases are now defined as proton donors and proton receivers respectively, but for present purposes, the older and narrower definition of an acid as a substance which yields hydrogen ions in solution and a base (alkali) as one which yields hydroxyl ions is adequate. Actually, all aqueous solutions contain both hydrogen and hydroxyl ions, and the definitions should be in terms of an excess of either hydrogen or hydroxyl ions.

Pure water itself ionises reversibly to a very small extent, $H_2O \rightleftarrows H^+ + OH$,

and the equilibrium constant is equal to $\frac{[H^+] + [OH^-]}{[H_2O]}$,

where = concentration of hydrogen ions in gram equivalents (moles) per litre.

= concentration of hydroxyl ions in gram equivalents (moles) per litre.

and $[H_2O]$ = concentration of molecular water in gram equivalents (moles) per litre.

As the extent of the ionisation is very slight, the concentration of molecular water is constant, and $[H^+] \times [OH^-] = K$, the ionic product for water. At 25^{0}C, $K = 10^{-14}$, so that $[H^+] \times [OH^-] = 10^{-14}$. To avoid the need to consider concentrations in terms of 10 raised to various negative powers, the pH and pOH scales have been devised. pH is defined as $-\log_{10}[H^+]$ and pOH as $-\log_{10}[OH^-]$. The ionic product equation can then be rewritten pH + pOH = 14. From the definitions of pH and pOH it follows :

(i) The lower the pH the higher the concentration of hydrogen ions, that is the more acidic the solution; and similarly for pOH.

(ii) Because the scales are logarithmic, a solution with a pH of 3 contains ten times the hydrogen ion concentration of one with a pH of 4.

From the relationship pH + pOH = 14, pOH = 14 – pH, and for most purposes the pOH scale is unnecessary, as the whole range of acidity and alkalinity can be expressed in terms of pH.

In solutions which are neutral (neither acidic nor alkaline) pH = pOH = 7; and those with a pH below 7 are acidic and those with a pH above 7 are alkaline, or basic.

A decinormal (N/10) solution of any strong acid, assumed to be fully ionised, contains 0.1 gram equivalents, or moles, of hydrogen ions per litre, that is $[H^+] = 0.1$; and its $pH = -\log_{10}[0.1] = 1$. More concentrated solutions of strong acids can have a negative pH, as well as one between 1 and 0. Similarly, an N/10 solution of a strong base, say caustic soda, has $[OH^-] = 0.1$ and a pOH of 1. Its pH is, therefore, 14 – 1 = 13. Again, more concentrated solutions of caustic soda have a pH above 13.

To set N/10 caustic soda in context with other alkalis to be discussed later, it contains 4 g/l of NaOH, or 0.4% m/m as its specific gravity is approximately 1.

Strong lavatory cleaners are commonly acids, but most other cleaning with aqueous solutions requires alkaline conditions. Both pH (alkaline potential) and quantity of alkali present are important, but should be distinguished. From the previous discussion it will be noted that an N/10 solution of caustic soda has a high alkaline potential, but only a small alkaline capacity (that is, it will only neutralise a small quantity of acid).

Classes of Salts

Four classes of salts, those from strong acid-strong base, weak acid-strong base, strong acid-weak base, and weak acid-weak base are now considered.

Salts of a strong acid and a strong base

Solutions of salts of strong acids and strong bases, such as sodium chloride and sodium sulphate, are substantially neutral. The alkylbenzene sulphonic acids are strong, so that the sodium alkylbenzene sulphonates are neutral.

Salts of a weak acid and a strong base

The alkalis used in detergent products are nearly always salts of this type, so that their properties are important to the detergents technologist.

Consider the addition to pure water of sodium acetate, $CH_3.COONa$, a substance similar in many ways to a soap, although acetic acid is soluble in water and stronger than the fatty acids in soap (but still weak compared with hydrochloric acid). The anion of the weak acid, the acetate ion in this example, reacts with water to form molecular acetic acid and hydroxyl ions $CH_3.COO^- + H_2O \rightarrow CH_3.COOH + OH^-$ so that the solution becomes alkaline. A more complete way to consider the situation is to say that the solution contains sodium ions (Na^+) and that all the following reactions must reach and maintain equilibrium :

$$CH_3.CO\bar{O} + H_2O \rightleftarrows CH_3.COOH + O\bar{H} \quad (a)$$

$$H_2O \rightleftarrows \overset{+}{H} + OH^- \quad (b)$$

$$CH_3.COOH \rightleftarrows \overset{+}{H} + CH3CO\bar{O} \quad (c)$$

The sequence of events can be indicated as follows :

1. Reaction (a) forward increases [OH^-].
2. The increase in [OH^-] from (1) causes a decrease in [H^+] from (b) in reverse.
3. The decrease in [H^+] from (2) leads to an increase in [$CH_3.COO^-$] from (c) forward.
4. The increase in [$CH_3.COO^-$] from (3) causes further increase in [OH^-] from (1) above, and so on until all the equilibria are established.

The sodium ion in the sodium acetate solution does not react significantly with water, $Na^+ + H_2O \rightarrow NaOH + H^+$ because NaOH is a strong base which ionises $NaOH \rightarrow Na^+ OH^-$, followed by $H^+ + OH^- \rightarrow H_2O$, which returns the situation to $Na^+ + H_2O$.

The weaker the acid, the higher the concentration of unionised acid and the lower that of its ions; hence the higher the concentration of hydroxyl ions produced and the more alkaline the solution. A solution of a pure soap develops a pH around 9, depending upon the type of soap and its concentration. Carbonic acid and the silicic acids are very weak, so that their sodium salts give more alkaline solutions than soap. Sodium carbonate is strongly alkaline and sodium bicarbonate (which can be regarded as carbonic acid half neutralise with caustic soda) is mildly alkaline.

The hydrolysis reaction for the bicarbonate ion is $HCO_3^- + H_2O \rightleftarrows$ H2CO3 + OH. That for the carbonate ion takes place in two stages

$$CO_3^{2-} + H_2O \rightleftarrows HCO_3^- + OH^-$$

$$HCO_3^- + H_2O \rightleftarrows H_2CO_3 + OH^-$$

Salts of a strong acid and a weak base

In this case the cation of the weak base reacts with water leaving the solution acidic. For example with ammonium chloride $NH_4^+ + H_2O \rightleftarrows NH_4OH + H^+$.

Salts of a weak acid and a weak base

In a solution of a salt of a weak acid and a weak base both cation and anion react with water. For ammonium acetate

$$NH_4^+ + CH_3.COO^- + H_2O \rightleftarrows NH_4OH + CH_3.COOH$$

The pH of the solution then depends upon the relative stregths of the acid and base.

The different strengths of sulphuric and carbonic acids cause sodium bisulphate ($NaHSO_4$) to be a strong acid whereas sodium bicarbonate ($NaHCO_3$) is a weak alkali, although both are their respective acids half neutralise with caustic soda.

Since the pH of some important alkalis varies with concentration. It will be noted that the pH of solutions of the less strong alkalis tends to level off as concentration increases and never reaches the levels produced by caustic soda and the very alkaline silicates. In some cases it even falls with an increase in concentration. Table 3.1 gives information concerning the pH of 1% m/m solutions of various alkalis.

A buffer, or buffer solution, is one in which the pH changes relatively little when an acid or alkali is added to it. Many 'soils' (i.e. the matter to be removed by the washing process) particularly those which contain sweat) include acidic constituents, and it is important that detergent solutions should remain at near the selected pH throughout the washing process; this requires a buffering effect. Buffers are also used to produce solutions of known pH, for example, in the preparation of a set of comparator tubes which show the colours developed by an indicator at a series of known pH values.

Table 3.1. Approximate pH values for 1% m/m solutions of various alkalis.

Alkali	*pH 1% m/m solution*
Caustic soda	13.2
Sodium orthosilicate, anhydrous	12.9
Sodium sequisilicate, anhydrous	12.6
Sodium metasilicate, anhydrous	12.3
Trisodium orthophosphate, anhydrous	12.0
Ammonium hydroxide	11.4
Sodium carbonate, anhydrous	11.4
Alkaline sodium silicate, anhydrous	11.2
Sodium percarbonate	10.6
Neutral sodium silicate, anhydrous	10.5

Contd....

Sodium pyrophosphate, anhydrous	10.5
Sodium perborate, $NaBO_2.H_2O_2.3H_2O$	10.2
Sodium sesquicarbonate, $Na_2CO_3.NaHCO_3.2H_2O$	10.0
Sodium tripolyphosphate, anhydrous	9.5
Borax, $Na_2B_4O_7.1OH_2O$	9.2
Disodium hydrogen phosphate, anhydrous	8.8
Sodium bicarbonate	8.4
Graham's salt (Calgon), sometimes called sodium hexametaphosphate	6.9

Unless there are other differences in composition, as may occur in commercial materials, a hydrate should show the same pH as its anhydrous salt after adjustment of concentration to the same level of anhydrous salt in the two solutions.

Effective buffers are produced by a combination of a weak acid and its salt, or a weak base and its salt. Examples are :

Boric acid (HBO_2) and borax ($Na_4B_2O_7.1OH_2O$),

Sodium bicarbonate ($NaHCO_3$) and sodium carbonate (Na_2CO_3), and

sodium dihydrogen orthophosphate (NaH_2PO_4), and

disodium hydrogen phosphate (Na_2HPO_4).

In the second and third examples, the sodium bicarbonate and the sodium dihydrogen phosphate act as weak acids. The sodium silicates work in a similar way and are very effective buffers.

The buffering action of a weak acid (HA) and its sodium salt (NaA) can be explained as follows,

The solution contains Na^+ and A^- ions from the salt, together with the unionised acid, its ions and water. The equilibria

$$HA \rightleftarrows H^+ + A^- \quad (a)$$

and

$$H_2O \rightleftarrows H^+ + OH^- \quad (b)$$

Have to remain satisfied.

If acid is added to the system $[H^+]$ is increased, but it is then reduced nearly to its original value by reaction (a) in reverse. If alkali is added, OH^- is temporarily increased, but is reduced by reaction (b) in reverse, leaving less $[H^+]$. HA then ionises according to (a) to restore equilibrium at near its original value.

The changes in pH as an alkali is added to an acid, as in an analytical titration, depend upon the strengths of the acid and the alkali. The end point in a titration can be determined using an electrical pH meter, or from conductivity measurements, but indicators which change colour at certain values of pH are commonly used, particularly in factory practice. many indicators are available and their colour changes occur at different pH ranges; this makes the proper selection of indicator important in many cases. Some common indicators with the pH range over which the colour change occurs are shown in Table 3.2. In order to obtain the correct end point in a volumetric analysis it is necessary to select an indicator which changes colour at near the equivalence point. Suitable indicators can be selected as shown in Table 3.3 by combining the information in Table 3.2.

Table 3.2. Some common indicators.

Indicator	*Colour change*	*pH range*
Methyl orange	red - yellow orange	3.1 – 4.5
Bromcresol green	yellow - blue	3.8 – 5.4
Methyl red	red - yellow	4.7 – 6.4
Litmus	red - blue	5.0 – 7.0
Cresol red	yellow - red	7.2 – 8.8
Thymol blue	yellow - blue	8.0 – 9.6
Phenolphthalein	colourless - purple	8.5 – 10.5
Thymolphthalein	colourless - blue	9.4 – 10.6

Table 3.3. Indicator selection.

Titration	*Approx. pH range At equivalence point*	*Suitable indicator*
Strong acid - strong base	4 - 10	Almost any
Weak acid - strong base	7 - 10	Phenolphthalein
Strong acid - weak base	4 - 7	Methyl orange, methyl red
Weak acid - weak base	very narrow	No indicator satisfactory

Some important applications in the detergents industry are :

(i) The estimation of *free fatty acid (FFA)* in a fat is carried out in alcoholic solution (FFA is soluble in alcohol), by titration with standard caustic soda, or caustic potash, to the phenolphthalein end point (estimation of a weak acid with a strong base).

(ii) To estimate *free caustic alkali in a soap,* the sample is dissolved in hot alcohol (neutralised if necessary), barium chloride solution is added to precipitate any sodium carbonate present, and the caustic soda is titrated with standard sulphuric acid to the phenolphthalein end point. Phenolphthalein is chosen because it is required to estimate only the strong alkali, caustic soda, and not to include mild alkalis such as soap. It is necessary to remove sodium carbonate from solution because it is alkaline to phenolphthalein (in the titration of a sodium carbonate solution the phenolphthalein end point is at the bicarbonate stage).

Soaps are often checked for caustic soda content by 'spotting' a freshly cut surface with phenolphthalein solution, noting whether a purple colour develops, and, if so, how quickly. With experience it is possible to judge roughly the free caustic soda content of the sample. Soapmakers now use this test, instead of the traditional testing on the tongue, at relatively high levels of caustic soda. For the routine examination of production samples of toilet soap, which should contain little, or no, free caustic soda, spotting is useful to decide whether, or not, a quantitative estimation is necessary.

(iii) If it is required to estimate the *total free alkali* (hydroxide plus carbonate) in a soap, an excess of standard sulphuric acid is added to the sample in alcoholic solution, the mixture is boiled to remove carbon dioxide liberated from the carbonate, and the excess acid (actually fatty acid liberated from the soap by the stronger sulphuric acid) is back titrated with standard caustic soda to the phenolphthalein end point.

(iv) An important sequence of tests is used to determine *total fatty matter (TFM), total alkali* and *'soda as soap'*. The sample of soap is decomposed by the addition of a known quantity of standard acid, the fatty matter liberated is separated (by ether extraction) and weighed. The excess acid is back titrated with standard alkali to the methyl orange end point. Methyl orange is selected for this estimation, because it is required to include alkali combined with weak acids, such as silicic and boric. Hence weak acids left in the aqueous liquid from which the fatty matter has been separated should not be allowed to act as acids in the analysis. The alkali which is combined with the fatty acids to form soap, known as 'soda as soap', is determined by dissolving the extracted fatty matter in neutral alcohol and titrating to the phenolphthalein end point with standard caustic soda. In many routine tests, it is only required to estimate TFM. It is then not necessary to use standard acid, and it is possible in many cases to add a weighed piece of beeswax and to separate the fatty matter which has been liberated from the soap in the form of a wax cake. The weight of TFM is found by the deduction of the weight of the added beeswax from that of the cake. Some sample calculations using the results of tests such as those just outlined are given later, after various materials have been discussed.

INORGANIC MATERIALS IMPORTANT IN THE DETERGENTS INDUSTRY

Common Salt, or Sodium chloride (NaCl)

Salt is used mainly to grain soap. It can be purchased in crystalline form, but it is now often bought as a saturated brine containing about 25% NaCl. When crude glycerine is being recovered from soap lyes, a major part of the salt in the lyes is recovered in the evaporation process and is returned to soapmaking as either solid salt, or brine. Salt is now often recovered directly as brine. In any case some new salt has to be purchased to make up for losses.

Solid salt is used in some soapmaking procedures, but modern processes usually require saturated brine, made by dissolving salt in water, or in a liquor containing a small concentration of glycerol. A convenient system for the preparation of brine on the large scale is shown diagrammatically in Fig. 3.1. The salt is fed in a stream (usually by a worm conveyor) to the top of a small tower to the base of which water is introduced at the required rate. The slurry overflows to one of a group of tanks in which dissolution is completed by compressed air introduced through a perforated pipe. With experience, the flows of water and salt can be adjusted so that saturated brine is produced, leaving only a small excess of salt in the tanks. This has to be dissolved occasionally by addition of water to the tank and blowing with air. If the salt is slightly dirty, or if it contains calcium or magnesium, it is often useful to make the brine slightly alkaline and to filter it before it is sent to the soapmaking department. This also reduces the content of heavy metals, such as copper and iron.

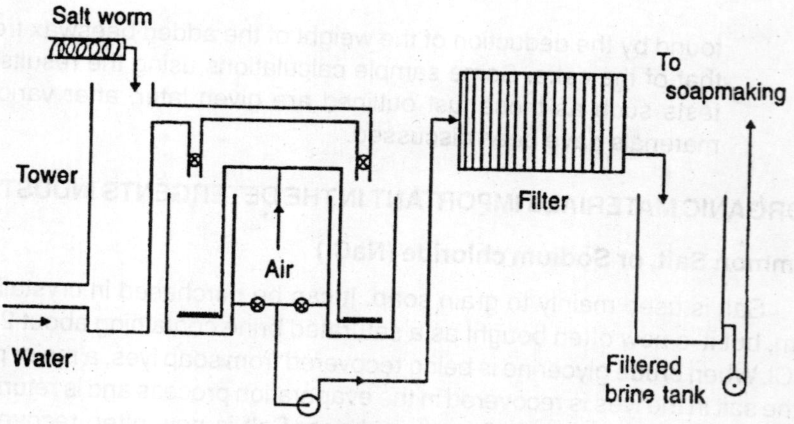

Fig. 3.1. Brine preparation.

Caustic Soda or Sodium Hydroxide (NaOH)

Caustic soda is sold as powder, flake, solid blocks produced by running molten, anhydrous, material into lightweight steel drums, and also as a concentrated solution containing 45-50% NaOH. Detergent manufacturers normally need to dissolve solid to produce a concentrated solution before use and, when possible, there are considerable advantages in buying solution, provided transport costs are not excessive. Caustic soda is a dangerous chemical and adequate precautions, including the wearing of goggles and other protective clothing, are important when it is being handled. Efficient soapmaking normally requires the use of a concentrated solution containing 45-50% NaOH which is subsequently diluted with lyes. The heat evolved when solid caustic soda is dissolved to produce these concentrated solutions is sufficient to raise the temperature to near boiling point. Solid blocks in steel drums are normally the cheapest form of solid, and they can be dissolved by cutting off the ends of the drums with hammer and chisel (and sometimes perforating the cylinders with a pick) before placing the material in the dissolving tank with suitable lifting tackle. The tank should be sized so that the rather small quantity of water needed to produce a solution of the required concentration covers the drum, or drums. Some operators use a tank with a perforated plate, or grid, near the base. The rise in temperature and density gradients provide circulation and reasonably rapid solution. The empty drum shells must be rinsed with a little water from a hose to prevent loss of alkali and to make the metal safe to handle.

It is often convenient to express quantities and concentrations of alkaline materials in terms of Na_2O. The conversion factors can be calculated by the usual methods of elementary chemistry. Using a table of atomic masses, and considering caustic soda as an example.

$$2\ NaOH = Na_2O + H_2O$$

$$2 \times (23 + 16 + 1) = (46 + 16) + (2 + 16)$$

$$\text{or } 2 \times 40 = 80 \quad 62 \quad 18$$

The equivalent mass of Na_2O = 62/2 = 31; and x% of NaOH is equivalent to $x \times 31/40 = 0.775x$% Na_2O.

The concentration of a caustic soda solution is often expressed, and determined approximately, from its density measured at a known temperature around ambient. Density is mass per unit volume (that is g/ml, or 1b/ft^3), but it is often expressed in terms of specific gravity, or relative density, which is density relative to that of water. Table 3.4 gives approximate relationships between concentration and density for some caustic soda solutions.

Caustic potash or Potassium Hydroxide (KOH)

Considerations similar to those for caustic soda apply to caustic potash. In most factories much less caustic potash than caustic soda is used, and somewhat less concentrated solutions are usually adequate. The heat of solution is even greater than that for caustic soda and solutions are not normally produced at more than about 40% KOH. The equivalent mass of caustic potash is 39.1 + 16 + 1 = 56.1 and that of K_2O is [(2 × 39.1) + 16]/ 2 = 47.1 so that y% KOH is equivalent to $y \times (47.1/56.1) = 0.84y$% K_2O, $y \times (40/56.1) = 0.713y$% NaOH, or $y \times (31/56.1) = 0.553y$% Na_2O.

Table 3.4. Approximate concentrations and densities of caustic soda solutions at 15.6°C (60°F).

% NaOH	*% Na_2O*	*S.G.*	*°Tw*	*°Be*
1	0.78	1.01	2	1.4
2	1.55	1.02	4	2.8
4	3.10	1.04	8	5.6
8	6.20	1.09	18	12.0
10	7.75	1.11	22	14.4
20	15.5	1.22	44	26.1
25	19.4	1.28	56	31.7
30	23.3	1.33	66	36.0
35	27.1	1.38	76	39.9
40	31.0	1.43	86	43.6
45	34.9	1.48	96	47.0
50	38.8	1.53	106	50.2

The concentrated solution containing 45-50% NaOH is commonly called 100°Tw liquor.

Sodium Carbonate (Na_2CO_3)

Anhydrous sodium carbonate, commonly known as soda ash, is available in light and heavy forms, which essentially differ only in bulk density. Most sodium carbonate is produced from salt. Care is necessary in selecting natural sodium carbonate for use in detergent products because it is liable to contain iron and organic dirt.

Sodium carbonate forms hydrates, the decahydrate, $Na_2CO_3.1OH_2O$, being traditional washing soda once widely found in households. Other hydrates are $Na_2CO_3.H_2O$ and $Na_2CO_3.7H_2O$. Detergent manufacturers seldom need to buy hydrated sodium carbonate, but the formation of these hydrates is very important in the manufacture of certain types of soap and NSD powders.

Sodium Bicarbonate ($NaHCO_3$)

Sodium bicarbonate is a fine white powder which is only mildly alkaline, so that it is little used in detergent formulations. Mixtures of pure soap powder and sodium bicarbonate have been made for special purposes, and the buffering action of sodium bicarbonate may be useful in reducing the pH of certain high carbonate formulations.

Sodium Sesquicarbonate ($Na_2CO_3.NaHCO_3.2H_2O$)

Sodium sesquicarbonate, also known as 'modified alkali', exists in the form of needle-shaped crystals. It is intermediate in alkalinity between sodium carbonate and sodium bicarbonate, and has a number of uses. In particular:

(i) As a mild alkali in commercial laundries, although this use is declining.

(ii) As a major constituent of certain floor and other hard surface cleaners.

The Sodium Silicates

A number of different types of sodium silicate are available and are important in many industries including detergents. They can be regarded as combinations of SiO_2 (silicon dioxide), Na_2O and, in some cases, H_2O. There are two major types :

(i) *Crystalline silicates* which are definite chemical compounds.

sodium orthosilicate, $SiO_2.2Na_2O$ (Na_4Sio_4),

sodium sesquisilicate, $2SiO_2.3Na_2O$ ($Na_6Si_2O_7$),
and, sodium metasilicate, $SiO_2.Na_2O$ (Na_2SiO_3).

(ii) *Colloidal silicates* which are not definite compounds and which can have any ratio of SiO_2/Na_2O between about 1.6 and 3.85. The ratio is normally expressed by mass, but as the molecular mass of SiO_2 (60) is nearly the same as that of Na_2O (62), the composition by mass is nearly the same as that on a molar basis (mass ratio $SiO_2/Na_2O \times (62/60)$ = molar ratio). In the detergents industry, the usual ratios, by mass, are about 3.2 known as 'neutral silicate', and 2.0, known as 'alkaline silicate'. Despite these names, all the sodium silicates are alkaline, as shown in Table 3.1, but the higher the ratio the less alkaline the material. The alkalinity of a sodium silicate solution is directly related to its Na_2O content, the SiO_2 having little, if any, effect.

Orthosilicate and sesquisilicate are very alkaline and are used for specially difficult jobs in some commercial laundries. Metasilicate, sometimes known by the proprietary *brand* name 'Metso', is widely used in laundries and as an ingredient in some detergent formulations. It is available anhydrous and as the pentahydrate $Na_2O.SiO_2.5H_2O$. Both are white solids, and various granularities are commonly sold. Both materials are delivered in paper sacks.

Sodium silicates are normally made by fusing together pure quartz sand (more than 99% SiO_2) and soda ash which provides the Na_2O; carbon dioxide is evolved. The colloidal types leave the cooler which follows the furnace as a 'soluble glass'. This glass is not readily soluble and has to be dissolved in a digester under pressure. The solution is settled to remove impurities and concentrated by evaporation. This is normally done by the silicate manufacturer, but some large users may find it economical to instal the equipment needed to handle soluble glass, particularly if the silicate has to be transported long distances. The silicate solutions produced from soluble glass are sometimes called 'water glass', an old name for sodium silicate solutions.

Concentrated sodium silicate solutions are viscous, and the viscosity is greater for those with a high $SiO_2.Na_2O$ ratio than for those with a lower ratio (above about 1.7 where a minimum is found). For this reason, alkaline silicate (ratio 2) is commonly purchased at 100°Tw or 120°Tw (120°Tw alkaline silicate contains 32.15% SiO_2 plus 16.07% Na_2O giving a total solids content of 48.2%), whereas neutral silicate (ratio 3.2) is usually bought at around 80°Tw (28.9% SiO_2 plus 9.0% Na_2O giving 37.9% total solids).

Sodium silicate solutions can be handled in mild steel, or cast iron, equipment. Thaks should be covered to avoid formation of hard skins by evaporation of water from the surface. Suitable heating facilities are necessary in tanks subject to cold, or temperate, climates to avoid excessive viscosity at low temperatures.

Sodium silicate solutions can be drum dried to produce soluble powders containing 15-20% of water. Cross-fields sell 'C' soluble powder (an alkaline silicate of ratio 2.0, containing 56.0% SiO_2, 28.0% Na_2O and 16.0% H_2O) and 'M' soluble powder (a neutral silicate of ratio 3.3, containing 64.5% SiO_2, 19.5% Na_2O and 16.0% H_2O). Other silicate manufacturers produce similar products. 'C' soluble powder will dissolve readily in cold water, but 'M' soluble requires water at 75-80°C for easy dissolution.

Potassium Silicates

Potassium silicates are sometimes used in soft soaps, liquid soaps and heavy duty liquid NSD products.

Borax

Borax is available as the decahydrate, $Na_2B_4O_7.10H_2O$, and as the pentahydrate, $Na_2B_4O_7.5H_2O$. It is a white powder which is a weak alkali used in some mild soap and NSD products.

Sodium Phosphates

Sodium phosphates are very important constituents of detergent products, although now sometimes restricted for environmental reasons. A number of different types of sodium phosphates are, or have been, used in detergent products, and it is important to distinguish between them.

All the sodium salts of the chain polyphosphoric acids are sequestering, complexing, or chelating, agents, that is they take alkaline earth and heavy metal ions into complexes which leave only a very low concentration of the ions of the complexed metal free in the solution. For example, sodium pyrophosphate complexes calcium from a solution of calcium chloride by the reaction.

$$4Na^+ + P_2O_7^{4-} + Ca^{2+} + 2\,Cl^- \rightarrow 4\,Na^+ + [CaP_2O_7]^{2-} + 2Cl^-$$

There are also a number of ring sodium phosphates with the general formula $(NaPO_3)n$, of which the only one significant in the detergent industry is sodium trimetaphosphate, $Na_3P_3O_9$. Unlike the chain polyphosphates, this compound is not a chelating agent, but, it can be used as precursor of sodium tripolyphosphate.

The various condensed phosphates can be produced by elimination of H_2O from a phosphate containing a higher ratio of H_2O (or Na_2O) to P_2O_5, or by addition of H_2O (or a base such as NaOH) to one with a lower ratio. The most important condensed phosphates are tetrasodium pyrophosphate and penta-sodium tripolyphosphate. The pyrophosphate is formed by heating disodium hydrogen orthophosphate

$$2\,Na_2HPO_4 = Na_4P_2O_7 + H_2O,$$

and the tripolyphosphate by heating a mixture of disodium hydrogen orthophosphate and sodium dihydrogen orthophosphate

$$2Na_2HPO_4 + NaH_2PO_4 = Na_5P_3O_{10} + 2H_2O.$$

In both cases small proportions of other sodium phosphates are found in the product.

The very important pentasodium tripolyphosphate, often called polyphosphate or TPP, exists in two forms or phases. Form 1 is the form stable at high temperatures and it hydrates rapidly to the hexahydrate, $Na_5P_3O_{10}.6H_2O$. Form 2, the low temperature form, hydrates more slowly. In practice, the sodium tripolyphosphate of commerce is a mixture of the two forms, but manufacturers can produce grades with various form 1 contents. The approximate Form 1 content is commonly measured by the Temperature Rise Test; this is carried out by measuring the rise in temperature when water is added to the sample of tripolyphosphate in glycerine under standard conditions. Under the test conditions about 90% of the potentially available heat of hydration is released by Form 1 and 10% by Form 2. From this, Form 1 content = (TR – 6) × 4%. Three grades produced are as under :

T.R. °C	Form 1 from formula %	Description
16.4	42	Fast hydrating
12.8	27	Fast hydrating
6.5	2	Slow hydrating

Particle size also influences rate of hydration; fine powders hydrating more rapidly than coarser powders of the same Form 1 content. The material with TR = 16.4°C just mentioned is a granular grade, whereas the other two are relatively fine powders. Some practical implications of rate of hydration are considered later.

The condensed phosphates hydrolyse slowly in solution, and tripolyphosphate changes to ortho and pyrophosphate. The rate of hydrolysis increases with temperature and under acidic conditions. If the hydrate $Na_5P_3O_{10}.6H_2O$ is heated sufficiently to remove water, decomposition to ortho and pyrophosphate occurs and little, or no, tripolyphosphate remains.

The various sodium phosphates are white powders which can be handled in bags, or in bulk.

Potassium Phosphates

Potassium phosphates corresponding to the sodium salts can be produced; as in the case of the silicates, potassium pyrophosphate is sometimes selected for use in liquid detergents because of its superior solubility.

BLEACHES, INORGANIC AND ORGANIC

General

Chemical bleaching (as distinct from adsorption bleaching with activated earths or activated carbon) is used to improve the colour of ingredients in the manufacture of detergent products, and chemical bleaches are also used in formulations to improve performance by the removal of organic colour from fabrics or other articles. Chemical bleaching is usually carried out with oxidising agents, but reducing agents have sometimes been employed.

Sodium and other Hypochlorites

These so-called chlorine bleaches are made by reacting chlorine gas with an alkali, or alkaline earth. At one time slaked lime was used to give bleaching powder (also called 'chloride of lime', a misnomer); but the alkali is now usually caustic soda wich gives sodium hypochlorite, or 'bleach'.

$$2\ NaOH + Cl_2 = NaOCl + NaCl + H_2O$$

To achieve adequate stability it is necessary to leave an excess of 1 or 2% of caustic soda, so that bleach liquor is strongly alkaline (hypochlorous acid is also weak, so that its sodium salt is itself alkaline).

It will be noted that sodium chloride equivalent to the hypochlorite is formed and is left in the bleach liquor. This is significant in that the chloride ion, Cl^-, as well as the hypochlorite ion, OCl^-, is necessary for the production of chlorine gas when bleach liquor is made acidic. Hydrochloric acid provides its own chloride ion, but with other acids, such as sulphuric, the sodium chloride plays an essential part in the reaction

$$NaOCl + 2\ HCl = NaCl + Cl_2 + H_2O$$

$$NaOCl + NaCl + H_2SO_4 = Na_2SO_4 + Cl_2 + H_2O$$

or, ionically, $OCl^- + Cl^- + 2H^+ = Cl_2 + H_2O$

Because of the toxic nature of chlorine gas it is important to avoid its evolution into the atmosphere, particularly in buildings. Accidents have occurred where acid has been used to adjust the pH when sodium hypochlorite is employed to sterilise water in swimming baths, etc., and too much has been added. Similarly, when sodium hypochlorite and acidic lavatory cleaners have been mixed in error. The same type of situation could occur in the detergents factory unless proper precautions are taken. A subtle variation of the problem can arise with lavatory cleaners which include trichlorcyanuric acid, and the acid, sodium bisulphate. Hypochlorous acid is generated from the trichlorcyanuric acid, but no significant evolution of chlorine occurs when normal supplies of water are used to flush the lavatory. If, however, the products are used with sea, or other salt, water an unpleasant amount of chlorine can be produced.

In the treatment of fabrics (and in the factory), hypochlorite bleach is normally used in alkaline solution. The active agent is then really active, or nascent, oxygen (O). If oxidisable materials, such as most organic coloured compounds, are present, the active oxygen will react; if not, the atoms may combine slowly to produce gaseous oxygen (O_2), which is gradually released. Although the effective bleaching agent is active oxygen, it is usual to determine the concentration of hypochlorite present in terms of available chlorine, that is the quantity of chlorine liberated when the solution is made acidic. One method is to add potassium iodide, acidify, and titrate the iodine liberated with standard sodium thiosulphate.

$$NaOCl + NaCl + H_2SO_4 \rightarrow Na_2SO_4 + Cl_2 + H_2O$$

$$\downarrow$$

$$NaCl + O$$

Hence one atom of active oxygen, atomic mass 16, is equivalent to two atoms of chlorine, atomic mass 2 × 35.5 = 71 (or to one molecule of chlorine, molecular mass 71). The molecular mass of sodium hypochlorite, NaOCl, is 74.5. Therefore, 74.5 parts of NaOCl are equivalent to 71 parts of available chlorine; so that a solution containing 10.0% of NaOCl contains 10.0 × (71/74.5) = 9.53% available chlorine. This close numerical similarity may seem surprising.

When used to bleach fabrics in a washing process, sodium hypochlorite is normally added to a rinse in a separate operation after the main wash, otherwise part of the available chlorine would be mopped up by oxidisable matter in the soil. Another very important use of sodium hypochlorite is as a disinfectant. It is effective agent all types of micro-organisms, but some types, such as bacterial spores, require longer times and higher concentrations than more delicate types of organism. The active chemical species is understood to be hypochlorous acid and disinfectant performance increases with fall in pH. The main limitation of sodium, and other, hypochlorites is again that they can be used up by other oxidisable matter often present with the organisms; this means that sufficient must be used to maintain the necessary concentration of active bacteriocide for the required time.

Sodium hypochlorite solution is produced with about 13-14% available chlorine content, and it is commonly received in factories at this strength. Even with strongly alkaline it tends to decompose slowly on storage. Decomposition can be with evolution of oxygen gas as explained earlier, but it also occurs by the formation of sodium chlorate,

$$3NaOCl = NaClO_3 + 2NaCl$$

Loss of available chlorine is greater when the concentration of sodium hypochlorite is high than when it is low.

Substances which produce available Chlorine when dissolved

When it is desired to add a substance to a dry detergent product which will produce available chlorine when water is added for use, there are two major types of compound available :

(i) Chlorinated trisodium orthophosphate, or sodium phosphate hypochlorite (SPH), described as $(Na_3PO_4.12H_2O)_5$ NaOCl or $(Na_3PO_4.11H_2O)_4$ NaOCl approximately. This contains about 3.5% available chlorine.

(ii) An extensive range of organic compounds which contain N–Cl groups in which the chlorine is 'available'. The most important are probably trichlorcyanuric acid (TCCA), with about 90% available chlorine, and potassium dichlorcyanurate, with 59% available chlorine.

An important practical difference between the two groups of compounds is their behaviour in relation to the water content of the product. With SPH, the water shown in the formula is necessary for stability, and if the product dries out on storage available chlorine is likely to be lost. On the other hand, the chlorcyanurates and similar compounds are readily decomposed with loss of available chlorine if the product picks up water. Scouring powders containing TCCA, etc. usually need an ingredient, such as anhydrous trisodium orthophosphate, which will mop up water vapour which leaks into the pack, and so protects the TCCA. These products also commonly include a stabilising olefine, usually as a perfume ingredient.

Sodium chloride, $NaClO_2$

Commercial sodium chloride containing about 80% of $NaClO_2.2H_2O$, with sodium chloride, sodium hydroxide and sodium carbonate (of which the alkalis are stabilisers) is available. A material is also sold which contains about 48% $NaClO_2.2H_2O$, plus 48% sodium nitrate which is added as a corrosion inhibitor. Sodium chlorite is used in some processes for the chemical bleaching of fats.

Hydrogen Peroxide and the per-salts

These compounds liberate active, or nascent, oxygen which is the bleaching agent. They are often considered milder on dyes and fabrics than sodium hypochlorite, but at concentrations which give equal stain removal this is not necessarily true.

Hydrogen peroxide solution is sometimes used in industry, but it cannot be included in detergent products, as can certain 'per-salts' which are widely included in detergent powders sold in many countries. The most important per-salt is sodium perborate, $NaBO_3.4H_2O$, or $NaBO_2.H_2O_2.3H_2O$, containing about 10% available oxygen. The monohydrate, containing about 16% available oxygen is also sometimes used. As shown in Table 3.1, sodium perborate is also an alkali. Sodium perborate is generally considerd ineffective at temperatures below 60°C and it works best at higher temperatures of 80-100°C, although some benefits from the inclusion of sodium perborate at temperatures as low as 35°C have been claimed. A number of compounds described as *bleach activators* have been found which react with perborate in the wash liquor to form peracetic acid (or its salt) which bleaches at lower temperatures than perborate. The most important of these activators is TAED, tetra-acetyl ethylene diamine. Others are TAGU, tetra-acetyl glycol uril, tetra-acetyl methylene diamine, and p-acetoxy-benzene sulphonate.

The principal other per-salt used in detergent formulations is sodium percarbonate, $2Na_2CO_3.3H_2O_2$. This compound is less stable than sodium perborate in detergent powders, but it may have some advantage in products to be used at relatively low temperatures, and it avoids the inclusion of boron to which there are some environmental objections when the waste water containing it may be used for irrigation.

Reducing Bleaches

Reducing bleaches are of little importance in the detergent industry, but sodium hyposulphite, $Na_2S_2O_4$ (also known as sodium hydrosulphite or blankite), is sometimes used to improve the colour of soap during the boiling process.

ANALYSIS OF SOAP PRODUCTS

General

Some analytical tests used for soap products are outlined. Calculations using the results of such tests, and other information presented in subsequent sections, will now be given for two typical examples, a household soap and a soap powder. First some additional tests will be outlined.

Chlorides (Salt)

Chlorides (salt) can be determined as follows. A 10 g sample of soap is dissolved in hot distilled water and transferred to a 250 ml narrow necked graduated flask. Sufficient calcium nitrate is added to precipitate the soap (about 15 ml of a 20% solution), and the flask is filled to the 250 ml mark with distilled water. The mixture is filtered and 100 ml taken in a porcelain bowl where it is titrated with standard silver nitrate solution using a little potassium chromate as indicator. The reactions are :

$$NaCl + AgNO_3 \rightarrow AgCl + NaNO_3$$

Silver chloride
(insoluble white)

$$K_2CrO_4 + 2AgNO_3 \rightarrow Ag_2CrO_4 + 2KNO_3$$

Silver chromate
(insoluble brick red)

Because silver chloride is less soluble than silver chromate, there is no permanent change of colour from the yellow due to potassium chromate to brick red until all the chloride has been precipitated. A blank estimation, without soap, should be carried out and the figure deducted from the test titration. If 0.1 N silver nitrate solution is used, 1 ml is equivalent to (58.5/10) ÷ 1000 = 0.00585 g NaCl, or 0.00355 g chloride expressed as Cl. With the quantities just specified, the salt found came from 10 × (100/250) = 4 g soap, and, if the titration after deduction of the blank is *y* ml, the salt content of the soap is *y* × 0.00585 × (100/4) = 0.146 *y*% as NaCl.

Silica, SiO_2

To separate silica, a sample of the soap, or soap powder, is ashed in a platinum dish with fusion mixture (potassium carbonate plus sodium carbonate) and the mix is heated to melting point. When cool, the melt is dissolved in distilled water, transferred to a porcelain basin and carefully acidified with hydrochloric acid. It is then evaporated to dryness, moistened with hydrochloric acid and again evaporated to dryness after any large lumps have been broken with a glass rod. The basin and contents are baked in an oven at 135°C, or gently on a sand bath, cooled, and then a little hydrochloric acid and water added. This process renders the silica insoluble, so that it can be filtered and weighed after the filter paper has been ashed. If insolubles other than silica may be present, the silica can be vaporised as silicon tetrafluride, SiF_4, by evaporating two or three times after additions of hydrofluoric acid and a few drops of sulphuric acid. This second residue is not silica and should be deducted from the crude residue first obtained.

Available Oxygen

Available oxygen can be estimated by acidification of a solution of a weighed sample with sulphuric acid and titration with standard potassium permanganate.

Household Soap

The main constituents of a genuine household soap are :

(i) Soap, comprising fatty matter (mainly fatty acids) and the alkali ombined with it.

(ii) Free caustic soda.

(iii) Sodium carbonate.

(iv) Sodium chloride.

(v) Glycerol.

(vi) Water, possibly plus colour and perfume.

Soap powder

If a powder contains phosphates, the P_2O_5 content can be determined by a gravimetric method, and various more complicated procedures are available for the estimation of different types of phosphate. If only a figure for P_2O_5% is available, it is necessary to make assumptions as to the type of phosphate, and/or to use trial and error methods to make the figures balance in a way which seems reasonable. There are also complications with regard to the determination of the total alkali.

WATER HARDNESS AND WATER SOFTENING

Water used for washing, and other purposes, in home and factory contains impurities to a degree which varies with its source. In the detergent field, the most important impurities are the calcium and magnesium salts which constitute water hardness. Traces of iron can lead to iron stains (sometimes known as iron mould), but this is more common in laundries than in the home.

The effect of water hardness is abvious with soap in that precipitates are formed; and no lather is produced until the calcium and magnesium in the water have been removed as insoluble soaps. Although it does not prevent lather, hardness, particularly calcium hardness, does have an adverse effect upon the performance of NSD products, at least in the washing of textiles, unless builders are also present in sufficient quantity. Unbuilt non-soapy surfactants are used successfully for dishwashing in hard as well as soft water.

Water Hardness

Water hardness is divided into :

(i) Temporary, or alkaline, hardness due to bicarbonates. This hardness was called temporary because it is largely removed by boiling (or heating to near boiling point), when the bicarbonates are converted to relatively insoluble carbonates which precipitate on kettles and other heating surfaces. Actually, the alkaline earth carbonates are slightly soluble, so that the hardness originally due to bicarbonates is not completely removed by boiling. The modern term is alkaline hardness, so called because this hardness can be determined by titration with standard acid to the methyl orange end point.

(ii) *Permanent hardness,* due to other salts, such as sulphate, chloride and nitrate.

(iii) *Total hardness* can be estimated by :

(a) Titration with Wanklyn's (standard soap) solution to a permanent lather (that is one which persists after the bottle in which the estimation is carried out has rested on its side for five minutes). Particularly with water high in magnesium, a false end point can occur when the calcium, but not the magnesium, has been precipitated. This lather does not last for five minutes.

(b) Titration with standard EDTA (ethylene diamine tetra-acetic acid) solution, using as indicator a black dye, known variously as Eriochrome, Solochrome, etc. EDTA is a sequestering agent which, like the condensed phosphates, complexes the calcium and magnesium in the water.

Permanent hardness is not estimated directly, but is found as the difference between total and alkaline hardness.

Hardness, calcium plus magnesium, is usually expressed in terms of $CaCO_3$, although CaO has been used in some countries.

The demarcations between waters classed as soft, moderately hard, etc., are necessarily arbitrary. Laundries usually soften the water to be used in washing operations.

Methods of Softening Water

There are three main methods to soften water :

(ii) The *lime-soda Process* in which calcium hydroxide (slaked lime) and sodium carbonate are added to the raw water. The main reactions are :

$$Ca(HCO_3)_2 + Ca(OH)_2 \rightarrow 2CaCO_3\downarrow + 2H_2O$$

$$Mg(HCO_3)_2 + 2Ca(OH)_2 \rightarrow Mg(OH)_2\downarrow + 2CaCO_3\downarrow + 2H_2O$$

(magnesium hydroxide is considerably less soluble than magnesium carbonate).

$$CaSO_4 + Na_2CO_3 \rightarrow CaCO_3\downarrow + Na_2SO_4$$

$CaCO_3$ and $Mg(OH)_2$ are relatively insoluble, and are separated by settling and decantation, followed, if necessary, by filtration. Because of the slight solubility of $CaCO_3$ and $Mg(OH)_2$, the water retains a little hardness.

(ii) *Base exchange.* Various materials, including natural zeolites (types of silicate minerals), synthetic zeolites, and certain synthetic resins, are capable of softening water by an exchange of sodium for calcium and magnesium. The bed of base exchange granules is then regenerated by the action of a sodium chloride (salt) solution which reverses the softening reaction. Calling any base exchange material NaZ, the reactions are roughly :

Softening $2NaZ + Ca \text{ salt} \rightarrow CaZ_2 + 2Na \text{ salt}$

Regeneration $CaZ_2 + 2NaCl \rightarrow 2NaZ + CaCl_2$

The excess brine (or other sodium salt used for regeneration), carrying with it the soluble calcium and magnesium salts (usually chlorides), is run to waste, and the regenerated bed is rinsed before being used for the next cycle. Alkaline hardness is converted to sodium bicarbonate in the softened water. This is a disadvantage in some situations, for example, it can reduce the pH of a wash system comprising soap and sodium sesquicarbonate. A suitable addition of caustic soda converts the bicarbonate to sodium carbonate. Water softened by base exchange may not be suitable for boiler feed, particularly if the raw water is high in alkaline hardness. One procedure is to mix a little raw water with the softened water. A base exchange bed filters out any particulate dirt from the water. It also removes any soluble iron, but the treatment of raw water high in iron content can lead to problems in regeneration.

4

Oils, Fats and Their Pretreatment

Introduction

Oils and fats, belong to the class of compounds called lipids, which are insoluble in water, but soluble in ether and other organic solvents. The lipids have long been considered important as one of the three major classes of food material. They differ from the other two, proteins and carbohydrates, in that they provide more than twice the number of calories per unit weight when converted to carbon dioxide and water. Oils and fats are usually distinguished from one another by their melting point and, to some extent, by their sources. Oils are generally liquid at ordinary temperatures while fats are solid or semisolid. The fats are usually of animal origin while oils are extracted from plant tissue, fish, or marine animals. Both fats and oils are composed largely of glycerol esters of fatty acids.

The Fatty Acids

The soapmaking oils and fats are essentially glycerides, that is fatty acid esters of the trihydric alcohol glycerol. Recent investigations, have shown that natural oils and fats may contain a wide variety of fatty acids, including some with odd numbers of carbon atoms, branched chains, ketonic groups, or ring structures. Apart from ricinoleic acid, an hydroxy acid which is the major constituent of castor oil, it can be assumed that the important fatty acids all have a straight, unsubstituted, hydrocarbon chain with an even number of carbon atoms, including the one in the carboxyl group. That is, the alkyl groups contain an odd number of carbon atoms. The fatty acids can be divided into several groups. The first series comprises the saturated acids C_nH_{2n+1}–COOH; and members with various chain lengths are listed in Table 4.1. The other series are unsaturated; that is, they contain less hydrogen than the saturated series and what are known as double bonds. The unsaturated acids have lower melting points than the saturated acids with the same numbers of carbon atoms. The main groups of unsaturated fatty acids are :

(i) The mono-unsaturated series, C_nH_{2n-1}–COOH, with one double bond.

(ii) The di-unsaturated series, C_nH_{2n-3}–COOH, with two double bonds.

(iii) The tri-unsaturated series, C_nH_{2n-5}–COOH, with three double bonds.

(iv) Acids with four, or more, double bonds.

Table 4.1. The saturated fatty acids C_nH_{2n+1}–COOH.

Number of carbon atoms	*Popular name*	*Melting point, °C*
4 (i.e., n = 3)	butyric	-8
6	caproic	-3
8	caprylic	17
10	capric	32
12	lauric	44
14	myristic	54
16	palmitic	63
18	stearic	70
20	arachidic	75
22	behenic	80
24	lignoceric	84

Two types of isomers (that is, compounds with the same empirical formula, such as $C_xH_yO_z$, but with different structures and hence different properties) exist amongst the unsaturated fatty acids :

(i) Positional isomers, in which the difference is in the position of the double bond, or bonds, in the carbon chain.

(ii) Geometric isomers.

The two carbon atoms, which form the double bonds, each have attached to them a hydrogen atom and a carbon chain. The double bond prevents free rotation; and if the like groups are attached on the same side of the molecule the compounds is called the *cis*-isomer; if they are on the opposite sides it is the *trans*-isomer. For example, with the very important $C_{17}H_{33}$COOH acids, possible isomers include :

CH_3—$(CH_2)_7$—CH
‖
HOOC—$(CH_2)_7$—CH

oleic acid (*cis* form)

mp 15°C

CH_3—$(CH_2)_7$—CH
‖
HC—$(CH_2)_7$—COOH

iso-oleic, or elaidic acid

(*trans* form), mp 44°C

Many other isomers are possible with the double bond in other positions in the chain.

Natural acids are usually, but not invariably, *cis.* The higher melting *trans* forms are produced when fats are hydrogenated, or otherwise heated, particularly in the presence of certain catalysts.

It will be appreciated that with variations in chain length, the numbers and positions of the double bonds, and *cis/trans*-isomerism at each double bond, there are a very large number of possible unsaturated fatty acids.

A systematic way of identifying a fatty acid is :

(i) the number of carbon atoms is indicated by a Greek prefix, for example dodeca = 12, tetradeca = 14, hexadeca = 16, and octadeca = 18.

(ii) the name of a saturated acid ends in -anoic, so that stearic acid is octadecanoic acid.

(iii) the number of double bonds is indicated by a suffix, so that the name of a fatty acid with one double bond ends in -enoic, one with two double bonds in -dienoic, one with three double bonds in -trienoic, and so on.

(iv) the position of a double bond is given by the number of the first carbon in the double bond, starting from the carbon in the carboxyl group (or, alternatively, by the numbers of the carbon atoms between which the double bond occurs).

Thus, oleic acid is,

$$CH_3(CH_2)_7—CH=CH—CH_2—CH_2—CH_2—CH_2—CH_2—CH_2—CH_2—COOH$$

10 9 8 7 6 5 4 3 2 1

cis 9-octadecenoic acid, or *cis*-9, 10-octadecenoic acid. The position of a substituent group is numbered similarly.

A few of the more important unsaturated fatty acids are listed in Table 4.2.

The oils from fishes and marine mammals, such as whales and seals, contain fatty acids with a wide range of chain lengths, some of which include three to six double bonds.

In polyunsaturated fatty acids, a special arrangement of the double bonds, known as a conjugated system, —CH=CH—CH=CH—, is possible. This gives oils such as tung, which contains eleostearic acid, 9, 11, 13-octadecatrienoic acid (an isomer of linolenic acid), specially strong drying

Table 4.2. Some important unsaturated fatty acids.

Formula	Scientific name	Popular name	Melting Point °C
One double bond			
$C_{15}H_{29}COOH$	*cis*-9-hexadecenoic	palmitoleic	–
$C_{17}H_{33}COOH$	*cis*-9-octadecenoic	oleic	15
$C_{17}H_{33}COOH$	*trans*-9-octadecenoic	elaidic or iso-oleic	44
$C_{19}H_{37}COOH$	*cis*-eicosenoic	–	–
$C_{21}H_{41}COOH$	*cis*-13-docosenoic	erucic	34
$CH_3—(CH_2)_5—CH—CH_2—CH{=}CH—(CH_2)_7COOH$	12-hydroxy-cis-9-octadenoic	ricinoleic	–
Two double bonds			
$C_{17}H_{31}COOH$	*cis*,cis-9,12-octadecadienoic	linoleic	–5
Three double bonds			
$C_{17}H_{29}COOH$	*cis,cis,cis-9,12,15-*octadecatrienoic	linolenic	–15

properties; that is they can form hard paint, or varnish, films. Such oils are unsuitable for soap.

The Fatty Acid Compositions of Oils and Fats

One fat (or oil) can differ from another in several ways, but the most fundamental is in fatty acid composition. Oils and fats are obtained from a wide range of animal and vegetable sources; and it is to be noted that even those from nominally the same kind of source can vary considerably. In the case of animal fats, this can be related to the part of the animal from which the fat came, the food which the beast ate, and the particular breed of sheep or cattle. Similarly, vegetable oils vary with factors such as plant variety and climate. A striking example is the oil known as rape, or colza, obtained from the seeds of certain varieties of *brassica*. Traditionally, this oil contained some 50% of *erucie* (including also eicosenoic) acid, but varieties of seed giving what is sometimes called canbra oil has now been developed which contains only 0–5% erucic acid. Rape oil is widely used for edible purposes, but doubts have arisen regarding the advisability of ingesting much *erucic* acid; and the new types of rape oil meet this requirement. High erucic oils are still valuable for some industrial purposes.

Table 4.3 gives some approximate compositions of important oils and fats, grouped into categories often used by soapmakers. The *hard fats* contain some 45-55% of palmitic plus stearic acids and about 35-50% oleic plus palmitoleic acids. They give firm sodium soaps with excellent detergent properties, particularly at temperatures approaching the boil. Their sodium soaps are not very readily soluble, so that lather is obtained only slowly when a piece of the soap is rubbed in cool water.

The *lauric,* or *nut oils* are characterised by a very high proportion, about 70-80%, of C_{10}–C_{14} saturated acids, hence the name lauric oils. They give hard, freely soluble, sodium soaps.

The *soft oils* (liquid vegetable oils) contain low proportions of saturated acids and high proportions of unsaturated acids, particularly oleic and linoleic. They give sodium soaps which are softer and more freely soluble than those from the hard fats. It will be noted that there are appreciable variations in the compositions of the oils included in this class.

The oils classed here as *soft/drying oils* are more unsaturated than those in the soft class. They include appreciable proportions of acids containing three, or more, double bonds: and are not generally suitable for use in solid sodium soaps, unless the unsaturation is reduced by hydrogenation or, sometimes, polymerisation. Some kinds are used directly in soft soaps.

Rosin, or *colophony*, is not a glyceride, but it was at one time used extensively as a fat in the manufacture of soap. Various grades were available which differed in colour and odour. The better grades were gum rosins, the residue after turpentine has been distilled from the exudate from pine trees.

Other Differences Between Various Fats

Fats can differ from one another in ways other than differences in fatty acid composition :

(i) In glyceride structure, that is the way the various (fatty acids are combined with the three hydroxyl groups in the molecules of glycerol. This is of great importance in some uses of fats, but it is irrelevant when the fats are to be saponified, or hydrolysed, to soaps or fatty acids.

(ii) In the nature and proportions of the non-glyceride substances they contain. These ingredients can loosely be classified into three groups :

(a) Inherent constituents, such as vitamins A, D and E (tocopherol); pigments such as carotene, gossypol and chlorophyll; and various sterols. Some of these which are significant to the soapmaker are pigments which need to be removed and natural antioxidants, including tocopherol.

(b) Free fatty acids which develop when fats are stored under poor conditions, or extracted from materials which have been allowed to deteriorate. Examples are palm oil and rice bran oil. Palm oil produced under good conditions from plantation fruit should have an FFA (free fatty acid) content of 2-5%. Oil recovered from the fruit of wild palms by villagers may containers 20-30% of FFA, or even more. The oil in rice bran deteriorates seriously in even a few hours if steps are not taken to inactivate enzymes present in the bran.

(c) Miscellaneous impurities which are found in all soapmaking fats, but particularly in lower grade materials, such as those recovered from wastes. Proteinaceous materials, and coloured and odorous constituents of many kinds, can be present as well as particulate dirt. Deterioration leading to development of a high FFA% commonly also results in the presence in the fat of brownish olouring matter and other undesirable impurities. A relatively odern problem results from the presence in tallows and greases of traces of polythene, which come from plastic

Table 4.3. Approximate fatty acid compositions of some oils and fats.

	Saturated acids					Unsaturated acids				Others
	C_{10} and below	C_{12}	C_{14}	C_{16}	C_{18}	C_{20} and above	oleic	C_{18} linoleic	linolenic	
Hard fats										
Beef tallow	-	1	5	27	16	1	42	3	-	5 palmitoleic
Mutton tallow	-	1	4	24	27	-	37	4	-	3 palmitoleic
Palm oil	-	-	1	44	5	-	40	10	-	-
Chinese vegetable tallow	-	1	4	61	6	-	28	-	-	-
Lard	-	-	2	28	14	-	44	-	-	3 palmitoleic
Bone grease	-	-	-	-	-	-	-	-	-	1 C_{20} unsaturated
Goat tallow	-	4	2	26	28	2	38	-	-	-
Lauric or nut oils										
Coconut oil	13	48	19	8	3	-	8	1	-	-
Palm kernel oil	7	52	15	7	2	-	16	1	-	-
Babassu oil	11	45	16	7	5	-	14	2	-	-
Soft oils										
Olive oil	-	-	-	10	2	-	82	6	-	-
Groundnut oil	-	-	-	10	3	3	50	34	-	-
Cotton seed oil	-	-	-	25	2	-	21	51	1	-

	Saturated acids					Unsaturated acids				Others
	C_{10} and below	C_{12}	C_{14}	C_{16}	C_{18}	C_{20} and above	oleic	C_{18} linoleic	linolenic	
Maize (corn) oil	-	-	-	13	3	-	36	48	-	-
Soyabean oil	-	-	-	13	4	-	23	52	7	1
Sunflower oil	-	-	-	7	3	1	23	65	1	-
Sesame oil	-	-	-	9	4	-	45	42	-	-
Rapeseed I	-	-	-	3	1	1	15	15	10	55 erucic and similar
Rapeseed II	-	-	-	5	2	1	52	28	12	-
Soft/drying oils										
Linseed oil	-	-	-	6	4	-	22	16	52	
Tung oil	-	-	-	4	1	-	8	4	3	80 eleostearic
Whale (baleen) oil	-	-	8	17	2	-(73% unsaturated C14-C22, 1-6 bouble bonds)				
Herring oil	-	-	5	18	2	-(75% Various unsaturated)				
Menhaden oil	-	-	12	22	3	-(63% various unsaturated)				
Miscellaneous										
Castor oil	-	-	-	1	2	1	4	5	1	86 ricinoleic

film included in fatty materials collected from butchers and other sources.

Additional points in relation to the general quality of fats are discussed later.

SOME ANALYTICAL CHARACTERISTICS OF OILS AND FATS

General

Well equipped modern laboratories now usually characterise mixtures of fatty acids by GLC (gas liquid chromatography), or similar techniques, using methyl esters formed from the fat or soap. This gives composition in terms of the percentages of individual fatty acids, from which, if required, deductions can be made as to the blend of fats from which the fatty acids probably came. The older tests outlined in the following subsections are still used for various purposes, including specifications. Before the common availability of GLC, analysts deduced approximate fat compositions from these figures and from certain tests for specific oils or fats, but in a routine laboratory it was often only possible to reach fairly generalised conclusions.

Moisture and Dirt

For routine purposes, moisture can be determined by loss of weight at 105°C. This can conveniently be estimated by heating a sample in a flat porcelain dish over a small flame, using a very short thermometer to stir and to indicate the temperature. This gives total volatile matter; and moisture can be determined more accurately by the Karl Fischer method. Dirt is determined by filtration of a hot dry sample of the oil through a dry filter paper and weighing the residue after fatty matter has been removed with a solvent such as light petroleum (40 - 60°C) boiling range).

Titre

Dry fatty acids are first prepared from the fat or soap. The liquid fatty acids are cooled under standardised conditions; and the titre of the sample is the highest temperature reached when a rise occurs due to the latent heat of solidification. It is, thus, a measure of the melting point of the mixture of fatty acids.

FFA (free faty acid) Content, Acid Value, Saponification Value, and Ester Value

Estimation of the free fatty acid content of a fat can be expressed in terms of Na_2O%; or it can be converted to percentage of a notional fatty acid. For many fats, FFA is quoted in terms of oleic acid which has an equivalent mass of 282, so that per cent. FFA as oleic equals FFA as Na_2O

× 282/31, or Na_2O × 9.10. In the case of palm oil it is sometimes expressed in terms of palmitic acid (factor 8.26); and for lauric oils in terms of lauric acid (factor 6.45). FFA content can also be expressed in terms of mg KOH required to neutralise the FFA in one gram of fat; this figure is known as the acid value (AV), or acid number. If n = FFA% as Na_2O, the FFA in lg fat is equivalent to $n \times 1000/100 = 10\,n$ mg Na_2O, or $10 \times 56.1/31 = n \times 18.1$ mg KOH.

Saponification value (SV), or saponification number, is similarly expressed as the number of milligrams of KOH required to saponify completely one gram of fat. The test is carried out by heating under reflux a suitable weight of fat with a known volume of standard alcoholic potash and back titration of the excess potash with standard acid to the phenolphthalein end point. The net quantity of KOH used has reacted with both FFA and glyceride and gives the SV.

Ester value (EV), or ester number, equals SV-AV; that is it a measure of the glyceride present in the sample.

Saponification value (or, more strictly, the acid value of the fatty acids), and the fatty acid ratio are both measures of the average equivalent mass, and hence average chain length, of the mixture of fatty acids in the fat.

Content of Unsaponifiable Matter

The percentage of *unsaponifiable matter* in a fat is determined by extraction with ether after complete saponification with caustic potash. A soap may also contain a proportion of free fat, which should normally be very small except when saponifiable superfatting materials are added deliberately. A sample of soap is extracted and, after the extract has been weighed, it is boiled under reflux with caustic potash to complete saponification, and the unsaponifiable is extracted. The first extract gives total unsaponified and the second unsaponifiable. Unsaponified fat equals total unsaponified minus unsaponifiable.

Iodine Value

The average degree of unsaturation of a fatty material is measured by determination of its *iodine value,* or iodine number. Several methods are available, but the Wijs method, using iodine monochloride in glacial acetic acid as the reagent is usual. The weighed sample of fat is dissolved in carbon tetrachloride and a measured volume of reagent added. After the appropriate time for addition of iodine to the double bonds has elapsed, water and potassium iodide are added and the excess iodine is titrated with standard sodium thiosulphate. The difference between the titration of a blank without fat and that of the sample represents the iodine absorbed, from which the iodine value is calculated as the number of grams of iodine absorbed by 100g of fat. The weight of fat used in the test must give an excess within narrow limits and a repeat test may be needed after an approximate value has been found. Care is needed in interpreting the results with highly unsaturated materials; in particular, oils containing fatty acids with conjugated double bonds do not take up the stoichiometric quantity of iodine, but these do not normally concern the soapmaker. Iodine values can be determined on dry fats, or on dry fatty acids (normally plus the unsaponifiable matter, that is on total fatty matter), but, with a given fatty acid composition, the value will obviously be lower with the fat than with the fatty acids, because of the diluting effect of the combined glycerol.

Reichert-Meissl, Polenske and Kirschner Values

The *Reichert-Meissl, Polenske* and *Kirschner* values of a mixture of fatty acids (derived from a fat or a soap) are determined by distillation under standardised conditions; and are measured in terms of the ml 0.1/V NaOH needed to neutralise the fatty acids in the distillates. The Reichert-Meissl value is determined on the water soluble fraction, and is a measure of the milk, or butter, fats present. The Kirschner value measures butyric acid more specifically. The Polenske value, of particular interest to soapmakers, determines the water insoluble volatile acids; and is a measure of the lauric oil included, with some indication whether it is coconut of palm kernel.

Specific Gravity or Relative Density

The *specific gravity* of the fatty acids is also useful, particularly when rosin may be present.

Rosin Content and Tests for Specific Oils

Tests are available to show the presence of *rosin* (Leibermann-Storch) and to determine its percentage (McNichol or Wolff). There are also tests to indicate specific fats; for example, the Halphen test for cottonseed, or kapok, oils, although a positive may also be obtained from the fats of animals fed on cotton seed cake.

Specifications Qualities of Tallows and Greases

The most important for soapmakers are those concerned with tallows and greases, because these fats are the major constituent of most soaps; and because they can vary widely in quality. Now tallows are often of mixed origin and are commonly sold on the basis of specification related to analytical characteristics, including colour and/or colour after a standard bleach. Soapmaker often find that a colour of soap, rather than a colour of fat, test is particularly relevant, although it does not appear in the usual specifications.

A convenient colour of soap test for routine purposes is to take a sample of the tallow, or other fat, bleached if appropriate, in a white enamel cup, add a slight excess of alcoholic caustic soda and boil with constant stirring. The fatty is saponified and the alcohol boiled off; this leaves granules of soap which are assessed by eye by an experienced observer. Other colour of soap tests used instrumental measurements of the colour of a solutions of the soaps.

Tallows are defined as fats with a titre of 40°C, or above; and an iodine value below 60 calculated on the fatty acids from a determination on the fat (Wijs method). Greases are defined a having a titre between 36°C and 40°C; and an iodine value below 63 calculated on the fatty acids. Tallows and greases produced by solvent extraction must be so described. (Ref. BIS 887:1977 for Animal Tallow and BIS 1780:1961 for Vegetable Tallow).

THE PRE-TREATMENT OF OILS AND FATS; AND THE PRODUCTION OF BY-PRODUCTS USED IN SOAPS

General

Most fats are pre-treated prior to use in edible products, as are many intended to be used in soaps, although large quantities of the better grade fats are made into soap without any pre-treatment. Some of the pre-treatments mentioned below are important to the soapmaker mainly because they produce by-products which can be used in soaps.

Types of Pre-treatment

The main types of pre-treatment are :

(i) *De-gumming* or *de-sliming*. This is usually used with soyabean and other oils with a high content of phosphatides and other unsaponifiables. Warm water, sometimes with about 0.1% of phosphoric acid, is added to hydrate some of the impurities which are then separated in a centrifuge to leave a relatively dry, clean oil. Commercial lecithin is recovered from the other fraction, particularly in the case of soyabean oil. These gums, known generally as 'break' material, can also be separated by heat.

(ii) *Acid refining,* is carried out with concentrated sulphuric acid in the pre-treatment of linseed, and other drying oils, for use in paints. The strong acid chars the phosphatides and related materials. Treatment with sulphuric acid is also used to clean up low grade materials prior to splitting with water (particularly by the Twitchell process).

(iii) *Alkali,* or *soda, refining* is normally included in the preparation of fats for edible purposes. It is not commonly employed in the pre-treatment of soapmaking fats, but it can be useful to upgrade certain tallows for use in high quality soap bases. An excess of caustic soda (or sometimes sodium carbonate) solution is used to neutralise the FFA in the fat and to carry away in the lower aqueous soapstock layer other impurities, plus some neutral fat. Careful attention is necessary to avoid an undue loss to the soapstock of good neutral fat.

(iv) *Steam distillation* can be used to reduce the free fatty acid content of a fat; a process which has been employed particularly with fairly high FFA palm oil. The fatty acids separated are used in soap. The relatively high temperatures involved bleach some fats, particularly palm oil; but some colouring matter tends to be 'set', and so more difficult to remove after the treatment.

(v) *Deodourisation* is a steam distillation process carried out under fairly high vacuum to remove odiferous and taste producing impurities from fats. Deodourisation of edible fats is normally carried out on materials which have been soda refined and bleached; otherwise FFA would be removed in this process with other volatile constituents and this is better done by soda refining. The process is sometimes used to remove highly odorous constituents from coconut and palm kernel oils to be included in high proportions in certain toilet soaps. Metal scavengers, such as citric, tartaric and phosphoric acids are often added to fats prior to deodourisation.

(vi) *Bleaching,* widely used for soapmaking as well as edible fats, can be by adsorption or by chemical means.

(vii) *Hydrolysis,* or *splitting,* often followed by distillation of the fatty acids, is, with the manufacture of soaps from fatty acids.

(viii) *Hydrogenation,* or *hardening,* in which the unsaturation of a fat is reduced by catalytic hydrogenation. This process is used extensively in the edible fat industry. At one time, particularly when whale oil was plentiful and cheap, it was also used to produce soapmaking hard fats from oils which were too unsaturated for direct use in most soap products. With current prices it is now little used in the soapmaking field, but it may be useful in countries which produce large quantities of unsaturated oils and, for politico-economic reasons, need to use these materials for the production of soap. The hydrogenation process decolourises oils such as palm by converting carotionid pigments into colourless compounds.

The chemistry of hydrogenation is complex and the product obtained depends upon processing conditions as well as upon the starting material. This is because in the production of fats which retain a substantial degree of unsaturation, as is normally required, the hydrogenation can be more, or less, selective; and isomerisation can occur.

Soapstocks and Acid Oils, or Acidulated Soapstocks

Soapstocks, the by-products from the soda refining of fats, are an important source of fatty matter for soapmaking. They can be used in several ways :

(i) Directly as the soapstocks.

(ii) After concentration with additional fat.

(iii) After acidification with sulphuric acid to produce acid oils, sometimes known as acidulated soapstocks.

Advantages of using soapstocks directly in soapmaking are :

(i) The alkali used in the soda refining process is transferred to soapmaking so that caustic soda is saved.

(ii) Sulphuric acid does not have to be used to convert the soapstocks to acid oil.

(iii) Glycerol liberated by saponification of glycerides in the soda refining process is transferred to soapmaking and not lost as when acid oil is produced.

Advantages of transfer to soapmaking via an acid oil are :

(i) Transport costs are saved, unless the refinery producing the soapstock is adjacent to the soap factory. Soapstocks should usually contain 30-50% TFM, but may be weaker, particularly when washings are included.

(ii) The water content of the soapstock can have an adverse effect on the efficiency of the soapmaking process which is avoided by the use of acid oil.

(iii) The acidification, and disposal to waste of the aqueous layer, followed by washing of the acid oil, removes various impurities which are not then transferred to soapmaking. If required, the quality of the acid oil can be improved by bleaching, or if necessary, by splitting and distillation. Alternatively, certain chemical bleaching processes can be used with soapstocks. Soapstocks can also be purified by completion of saponification, followed by graining with salt and the discard of the lye. This will result in the loss of some of the free glycerol in the soapstock.

Concentration of soapstock is achieved by mixing the soapstock with a carefully controlled quantity of additional fat at a temperature above 70°C. The quantity of fat needed should be determined by experiment, but it is often found that about 3.8 parts of new fat should be added to soapstock containing perhaps 0.5-1.0% glycerol, which can be introduced in an appropriate manner into the soapmaking system. The upper fatty layer, containing the soap, can be handled as an oil. If conditions, particularly temperatures, are not right an emulsion may be formed and no proper separation achieved. Such emulsions can often be broken by addition of brine, or treated soap lye. Benefits which can accrue from the concentration of soapstock are mainly improvements in soapmaking efficiency.

Acidification of soapstocks is usually carried out with sulphuric acid in wooden, plastic, or lead-lined vas. After sufficient acid has been added to leave free mineral acid, the mixture is boiled with steam until the soap is split and the emulsion broken. After the mass has been settled, the aqueous layer containing various impurities is run to waste; and the acid oil is washed with hot water as many times as necessary.

Crude cottonseed oil is often soda refined twice. The first treatment, plus alkali and water washes, gives washed cottonseed oil and a very dark soapstock, sometimes known as black cottonseed grease. This black grease, which contains substantial proportions of gossypol and phospholipids, is not normally suitable for incorporation in soaps directly, or as an acid oil. Usable, but rather dark, fatty acids can be recovered from it by splitting and distillation. The washed cottonseed oil is soda refined again to yield a soapstock, or acid oil, of reasonable quality for soapmaking.

The fatty matter in soapstocks, and acid oils, has a very similar fatty acid composition to the parent oil, or fat, but the colour and general quality are inferior.

Bleaching of Oils and Fats

Methods used to bleach oils and fats can be divided into adsorption bleaching, used for both edible and soapmaking fats, and chemical bleaching used only for soapmaking fats.

In *adsorption bleaching*, the molten fat, or oil, is brought into contact with a powdered solid adsorbent, which can be natural fullers earth, or activated earth or clay, or, to a iimited extent, activated carbon used in conjunction with activated earth. Activated earths are made by the action of mineral acids on suitable mineral substances, such as bentonite or montmorillonite. The adsorbent removes colouring matter from the oil which is then separated by filtration. Sulphuric acid markedly improves the performance of natural fullers earth and may also be useful with activated earths. An addition to the bleaching vessel of about 10% of the weight of natural earth used is often found suitable for soapmaking oils.

The use of 2-3% sulphuric acid, followed by 3-5% earth, in the bleaching of certain dark liver oils is recommended.

Only about half the ratio of earth to oil is required with a good activated earth to give the same result as that obtained with natural earth. Various grades of activated earth are available, some acidic and some more nearly neutral. Acidic earths are usually more effective than neutral types and are commonly used with soapmaking oils. They may cause a very slight increase in the FFA of a soda refined oil and, for this reason, they may not be desirable with some edible oils. The proportion of earth needed to achieve the desired bleach should be determined by experiment. It varies widely from one oil to another, and with the colour of bleached oil required. 2-6% of activated earth, or 4-10% of natural earth, is common for soapmaking oils; the highest proportions often being needed with palm oil.

Batchwise bleaching in single vessels is usual for soapmaking oils, but continuous bleaching processes are sometimes used in edible fat refineries operating on a large scale. Batchwise bleaching can be carried out in open vessels, fitted with closed steam coils and with an agitator to keep the earth in suspension in the oil and to promote heat transfer without local overheating; but closed vessels working under vacuum (50-70 mmHg absolute pressure) are usually used and are better because :

(i) Moisture is removed more effectively.

(ii) There is less risk of undesirable oxidation of the oil by air, particularly if steps are taken to deaerate the oil as much as possible before it reaches bleaching temperature.

Vacuum bleachers can be of various designs, but vertical, cylindrical, vessels with dished base and top are common. Various types of agitator, including paddles or tubines are possible. Heating is usually by internal steam coils, but in the case of very large bleaching vessels, external circulation through a tubular or similar heater is sometimes used, and is preferable. Coolers may be fitted to cool the oil before it is filtered. In the case of edible oils, this is to minimise risk of oxidation whilst the oil is exposed to air, with soapmaking tallows and greases it is primarily to remove polythene, for which purpose the oil should be filtered at below about 70°C. Bleaching temperature is not very critical; typically, good quality tallows and other oils and fats are bleached at 90-95°C, poorer qualities at about 110°C, and palm oil at 120-130°C. About 15 minutes is said to be sufficient for equilibrium to be reached, but the complete bleaching cycle takes several hours.

The role of water is important. Complete drying of the bleaching earth will destroy its efficiency; and water in the oil charged to the bleacher does no harm as regards final quality. It has been reported that an addition of water can improve the performance of activated earths when bleaching tallow; other experience shows that sufficient water is important when palm oil is being bleached with activated earth, or with natural earth plus 10% acid; and if necessary, water is added to bring the level to about 2%. On the other hand, it is usually found necessary to adjust temperature, pressure and time, so that the oil is substantially dry before the bleaching stage is completed in order to achieve proper adsorption of colouring matter.

Mild steel, or cast iron, is normally used for the vessels and coils of bleachers, even when sulphuric acid is added, but a splash plate near the acid inlet is desirable to direct the acid to the oil rather than the vessel wall. The earth is commonly sucked in from a hopper by the vacuum.

It is necessary to separate the earth from the oil completely and in such a way that the quantity of oil left in the filter cake is minimised. This requires a substantial pressure, so that vacuum filters are not suitable, and facilities are needed to permit the cake to be air blow and/or steamed. Filter presses, manual or, more recently, mechanised, are traditional; but some types of leaf-filter can be convenient and require little labour. The oil discharge arrangements should minimise the risk of fume being dispersed in the work area, particularly during steaming or blowing. Filters are normally cast iron. Various filter cloths, of different weights, weaves and materials are now available; and the following table, provides useful information concerning the main fabric materials :

Material	*pH range*	*Maximm temperature °C*
Cotton	6-10	100
Polyamide	7-12	110
Polypropylene	2-12	100
Polyester	2-7	160
Polyvinylidene chloride	2-11	80

Cotton cloths were traditional for bleaching earths and are still widely used; but synthetics, particularly polyester, withstand acidic conditions better and may have several times the life of cotton, which can outweigh the higher initial cost.

Cotton cloths seal the joints between the plates well, but synthetic cloths do not; and special treatment of the areas of the cloths which form the seal, or special mechanical devices, may be needed. Fine weave metal gauzes are used in some mechanised filters. As in other filtrations, the cloth, or other primary medium, must retain most of the solids, but the initial layer of earth residue on the cloths forms the true filter medium, and it is usually necessary to retum the first runnings for re-filtration.

A second filtration through a polishing filter is sometimes used to remove traces of fines which pass through the first filter. Paper may be used over the cloths, particularly in polishing filters, to improve the clarity of the filtered oil. When filter-presses are to be used, there is a choice between the plate and frame type and the recessed plate type. Either can be satisfactory for the main filtration; but, contrary to what might be expected, a plate and frame press should be chosen for polishing. This is because in a polishing filter a thin layer of very fine earth builds up, and becomes impervious, before the chamber is nearly full. It is then necessary to drain the oil and to remove the paper and residue. This can be done with a plate and frame press, but not satisfactorily with a recessed plate press having a central feed inlet.

The proportion of oil left in the filter cake after it has been steamed and/or blown with air as effectively as possible, varies considerably with the type of earth used. With natural earth it is often possible to achieve about 30% on the weight of residue, but with activated earths it is usually higher and 40-50% is common; up to 70% has been mentioned with edible oils. The loss of oil per tonne of crude fat treated is controlled by the percentage of bleaching earth used, as well as by the percentage of oil left in the residue, so that it is frequently less with an activated than with a natural earth, despite the higher retention of activated types. This loss of oil is a major item in the cost of bleaching, often exceeding the actual cost of the earth. Even a small percentage of activated carbon can greatly increase the oil retention of an earth.

One reason why plant bleaches may be more effective than laboratory bleaches lies in the bleaching which occurs whilst the mix is being passed through the cake in the filter. Multi-stage counter-current operation has theoretical advantages, but is not often practised. It is, however, sometimes useful to clean up, and bleach slightly, an oil for a relatively low grade soap by pumping it through full presses. The oily residue discharged from the filters can sometimes by sold for use in animal feedstuffs (in which substantial percentages of some kind of fat are often included). Processes for recovery of oil from these residues include :

(i) Wet extraction with a solution of alkali, which is not very efficient.

(ii) Extraction with a hydrocarbon solvent. This gives a rather low yield of oil of moderate quality, but requires all the precautions for a process with a flammable solvent.

(iii) Extraction using a mix and settle process with a chlorinated solvent, such as trichloroethylene. This gives a higher yield of a poorer quality fat, because the chlorinated solvent extracts more coloured and oxidised material than the hydrocarbon solvent. Better settling, and an even higher yield, but of a very dark brown oil, can be achieved by steaming the solvent residue mixture. It is often found that it is not worthwhile to recover oil from bleaching earth residues. Disposal of earth residues, extracted or not extracted, can be difficult; particularly if residues from the bleaching of highly unsaturated oils, which can be subject to spontaneous combustion, are involved.

Chemical bleaching normally involves the oxidation of the colouring matter in the oil or fat. The result varies greatly with the kind of fat; and palm oil, and by-products containing palm oil residues, are particularly responsive to oxidation bleaching. In some cases, an undesirable odour develops; and chemical bleaching is not used with edible fats, or, usually, with fats to be made into the better quality toilet soaps.

The oxidation can be carried out with air (or oxygen), with alkali dichromate (plus acid), with sources of available chlorine, or of chlorine dioxide, or with other reagents. Air can be blown through hot palm oil to produce air bleached palm oil. Soap made from this oil has a slight brownish shade and a characteristic odour. These qualities limit its use, but it has been employed in orange/red carbolic toilet soaps. Bleaching of palm oil with chromic acid is very effective. The oil is agitated with air for several hours after addition of sodium dichromate, salt, and hydrochloric acid. After the mix has settled, the aqueous layer is run to waste and the oil is washed several times with water. More recently, most chemical bleaching processes have used chlorine compounds.

Oils and fats, particularly acid oils, can be bleached under acid conditions. Sodium chlorite is usually employed, activated with acid; and the active species is thought to be chlorine dioxide (ClO_2). The bleaching of tallows and greases by using sodium chlorite plus sufficient sulphuric acid reduces the pH to 4, or below. It has been found that no additional activator is necessary if the fatty matter contains sufficient FFA (usually above about 20%); and when the fat is not sufficiently acidic, the preferred activator is phosphoric acid. About 0.5-1.0% of sodium chlorite is used. The process can be caried out in a simple vessel in which agitation is provided by compressed air from a perforated pipe. The vessel can be constructed of mild steel, but stainless steel is preferred. Alternatively, continuous bleaching plants can be designed for use if the scale of operation is sufficiently large. When phosphoric, or other mineral, acid is used, particular care must be taken to avoid addition of reagents when no fat is present; otherwise an explosion is liable to occur. The bleached fat should be saponified as soon as possible. Soaps made from chemically bleached fats tend to deteriorate more than those made from adsorption bleached materials.

Chlorine compounds can also be used under alkaline conditions to bleach soaps, including soapstocks. Soapstocks should be completely saponified, and soaps should preferably be washed to remove the glycerol before the bleaching operation. Sodium hypochlorite has long been used to bleach soap in the pan, but, particularly for soaps containing some palm material, there are advantages in using :

(i) Sodium hypochlorite activated with hydrogen peroxide.

(ii) Sodium chlorite activated with sodium hypochlorite, although various other activators are possible.

The sodium hypochlorite/hydrogen peroxide process can conveniently be carried out in a continuous reactor in the form of a vertical cylinder with two turbo impellers; one near the base and the other part way up. The soap flows upwards, is mixed with the sodium hypochlorite in the lower impeller, and the hydrogen peroxide is fed to the eye of the upper impeller. Sufficient hot water must be introduced to avoid the grained condition in the reactor, it being remembered that sodium hypochlorite with its associated salt and caustic soda is a strong electrolyte. Hypochlorite to give about 2% available chlorine plus 0.1% hydrogen peroxide, both expressed on TFM, may be found suitable.

As already mentioned, sodium hydrosulphite has been used in the pan as a reduction bleach to improve the colour of good coloured soaps; it is not very effective and is now seldom employed. The hydrosulphite powder is sprinkled onto the surface of the soap when in a 'closed' condition, and the pan contents are boiled for about ten minutes.

Selection of Fat Blends for Various Soaps

Soaps can be made from a wide range of fats; and unusual fats, or blends, are used in some countries for politico-economic reasons.

For many purposes, including conventional toilet soaps and household soaps made by the modern vacuum chilling/extrusion processes, a blend of about 15-25% lauric oil (coconut or palm kernel) and 75-85% hard fat (usually tallow or palm oil) gives a soap base with an excellent combination of properties. The hard fat gives a firm texture and good detergency at high washing temperatures; the lauric oil also gives a firm soap, but improves the rate of solution and freedom of lather. Particularly for household soaps, but also for cheaper toilet soaps, less than 15% lauric oil is sometimes used because of cost. To high a content of lauric oil tends to give a soap which is rather harsh (irritant) to the skin, unless superfatting is employed. High lauric oil soaps are sometimes used for certain textile operations and when the soap is to be used in sea, or brackish, water; but tablets containing non-soapy detergents may now provide a better answer to the salt water problem.

Assuming that tyre and iodine value for blends are additive, values for a mixture of 80% tallow, of titre 41°C and IV of fatty acids 45, with 20% coconut oil, titre 22°C and IV 10, can easily be calculated :

Item	*Titre °C*	*Iodine value*
80% Tallow	0.8 × 41 = 32.8	0.8 × 45 = 36.0
20% Coconut oil	0.2 × 22 = 4.4	0.2 × 10 = 2.0
Blend	37.2	38.0

A titre of 36-38°C and an iodine value of about 37 are often considered ideal for a conventional toilet soap. If a rather hard, high titre, tallow is to be used, a proportion of good quality soft material, such as lard (choice white grease) or groundnut oil, will adjust the titre and iodine value of the blend; and produce a soap with an improved balance of plastic properties. Oils with significant proportions of highly unsaturated acids are liable to give soaps with tendencies to deteriorate through oxidation on long storage, particularly at relatively elevated temperatures. Care must, therefore, be exercised in the choice of soft material for high quality soaps and minor ingredients in the fats can be important. Some years ago an example occurred in which inclusion of a proportion of distilled bone grease fatty acids to soften the blend resulted in abnormal deterioration of the colour of a white toilet soap after some months storage. Olive oil, which has a very high content of oleic acid and little polyunsaturated acids, is a particularly good soft oil. It was a traditional soapmaking material in Mediterranean countries, but, apart possibly from some exceptionally poor, inedible, grades it is now much too expensive for use in soap. The use of preservatives, primarily but not exclusively, to minimise the adverse affects of heavy metal catalysts in producing deterioration on storage.

Tallow and palm oil are the main hard fats. Apart from some difficulty in the production of very white soap, palm oil is an excellent soapmaking material, but it is now normally too expensive compared with tallow. Few years ago, whale oil was relatively cheap and much was hardened (hydrogenated) for use in soap. Special attention needed to be paid to the hardening conditions to produce an acceptable tallow substitute, but hardened whale oil was generally less good than tallow. Little whale oil is now available and the soft vegetable oils are normally more expensive than tallow.

Hardening may be useful in countries where there are pressures to use soft oils in soapmaking; and, although not very good technically, hardened fish oils may be economically attractive for low grade soaps under some circumstances.

For household soaps made by the old frame, or water-cooling, processes, a substantial proportion of soft oil is advisable to produce a good lathering soap. Although soft oils can be, and are, used with the modern household soap processes, they are not genearlly desirable.

Rosin was used extensively in soaps at one time, primarily because it was cheap; but it does also have useful properties. To some extent, it is an alternative to lauric oils as a means by which the solubility and lather of a frame-cooled household soap made from hard fats can be improved; and tallow/rosin soaps were popular. A good quality rosin also gives the soap a characteristic odour which was generally thought pleasant and preferable to that of a tallow soap. At one time, 2-3% of good quality rosin was included in toilet, and other soap blends as a preservative. Soaps with a high rosin content tend to be sticky, which makes them unsuitable for some purposes, including soap powders.

Particularly for household soaps, the fat is the predo-minant item in the cost of the product, so that it is very important commercially to use as effectively as possible any relatively cheap materials, such as by-products, which can be obtained. These by-products are often of somewhat uncertain composition, although described as 'soft acid oil', etc. A preliminary assessment of their suitability can be made from an analysis giving fatty acid compostion by GLC; or, less precisely, from fatty acid constants, such as titre and iodine value. Colour, odour and stability on storage must also be considered.

Fatty Acid and Glycerol Contents of Fats, and Related Matters, Glycerine Credit

Initially, it will be assumed that the fat contains only triglycerides and fatty acids; complications due to the possible presence of di-and monoglycerides will be considered subsequently. Also, the calculations will be based on 100% fatty matter; but the small corrections for the 1-2% of moisture and dirt commonly found in crude fats can readily be made.

As already explained in the saponification value, acid value and ester value of a fat are all expressed in terms of mg KOH per g of fat.

The quantity of coaustic soda needed theoretically to saponify the fat is thus equivalent to SV mg of KOH per g fat. This is equal to

$$\frac{SV}{1000} \times \frac{31}{56.1} = SV \times 0.000533 \text{ g } Na_2O\text{/g fat (or t/t fat)}$$

The glycerol content of the fat is proportional to the ester value; and EV = SV − AV.

Glyceride + 3 KOH → $C_3H_5(OH)_3$ + 3 potassium soap.

$$3 \times 56.1$$
$$= 168.3 = 92$$

EV = mg KOH equivalent to the glyceride in lg fat

Hence, percentage glycerol in fat

$$= \frac{EV}{1000} \times \frac{92}{168.3} \times 100$$
$$= EV \times 0.0547$$

Estimation of the fatty acid content of a fat is more complicated, but the formula in terms of SV, EV and AV can be derived as follows :

Consider first a pure triglyceride with no FFA and let M = the average equivalent (= molecular) mass of the *fatty acids* it contains.

$$C_3H_5(OOC\text{—}R)_3 + 3H_2O \rightarrow C_3H_5(OH)_3 + 3R.COOH$$
$$3 \times 18$$
$$= 54 \qquad\qquad 92 \qquad\qquad 3M$$

To make the equation balance, the molecular mass of the glyceride = $3M$ + 92–54 = $3M$ + 38, that is the equivalent mass of the glyceride is

$$\frac{3M+38}{3} = M + 12.67$$

lg of fat is equivalent to (56.1 × 1000)/(M + 12.67) mg KOH, and, by definition to SV mg KOH. Hence,

$$\frac{56.1 \times 1000}{(M + 12.67)} = SV, \text{ or } M = \frac{56100 - 12.67SV}{SV}$$

Considering now pure fatty acids, the equivalent mass is M, instead of (M + 12.67) and SV = AV; so that M = 56.100/SV, or 56100/AV. In actual fat containing both triglycerides and free fatty acids, the ratio of combined to total fatty acid is EV/SV (assuming, as is usually approximately the case, that the composition of the free is similar to that of the combined fatty acids). The addition of 12.67 to the equivalent mass of the fatty acids applies only to the combined portion so that, from the equation for pure glycerides,

$$M = \frac{56100 - 12.67\,\text{SV} \times \dfrac{\text{EV}}{\text{SV}}}{\text{SV}}$$

$$M = \frac{56100 - 12.67\,\text{EV}}{\text{SV}}$$

The total mass of fatty acids in 1000 mg of fat equals the quantity of KO required to saponify it × M/56.1 = SV × M/56.1 Hence, from the expression just derived for M, the total fatty acids in 1000 mg fat.

$$= \frac{\text{SV}}{56.1} \times \frac{56100 - 12.67\,\text{EV}}{\text{SV}}$$

$$= 1000 - \frac{12.67\,\text{EV}}{56.1} = (1000 - 0.226\,\text{EV})\ \text{mg}$$

Hence, 100 parts of fat contain (100 – 0.0226 EV) parts total FA.

$$\text{FFA\%} = \frac{\text{AV}}{\text{SV}} \times \text{total FAs in 100 parts fat}$$

or,

$$\frac{\text{AV}}{\text{SV}} \times (100 - 0.0226\,\text{EV})$$

If it is required to use a determination of FFA% rather than of AV, the figure in terms of Na_2O% should be converted to FFA% using an estimated molecular mass for the actual fatty acid blend, rather than a notional one, such as that for oleic acid. In many cases the difference is not great.

It may also be helpful to note that

M = fatty acid ratio × 31

As an example, consider a tallow with SV = 195 and AV = 15, EV = 195 – 15 = 180

$$\%\text{FFA} = \frac{\text{AV}}{\text{SV}}(100 - 0.0226\,\text{EV}) = \frac{15}{195}\{100 - (0.0226 \times 180)\}$$

Theoretical requirement of caustic soda for saponification

$$= \text{SV} \times 0.000553$$

$$= 195 \times 0.000553 = 0.108\text{g } Na_2O/\text{g fat}$$

or = 0.139 NaOH/g fat.

glycerol content = EV × 0.0547

= 180 × 0.0547 = 9.85%

fatty acid content = (100 – 0.0226 EV)

= 100 – (0.0226 × 180) = 95.9%

As mentioned previously, all these figures are calculated for pure fatty matter in the fat, and strictly they should be corrected for its moisture and dirt content. This correction is usually only significant for the fatty acid content.

Table 4.4 shows figures calculated in this way for a number of typical soapmaking fats. It will be seen that :

(i) The theoretical caustic soda requirements fall into two groups, one for coconut (and other lauric) oils, and one for other fats.

(ii) The glycerol content varies widely with both the equivalent, or molecular, mass of the fatty acids and the percentage of free fatty acids.

(iii) The total fatty acid content does not vary much, although it is a little lower for the lauric oils, and a little higher when the FFA is high. After allowance for moisture and dirt, fatty acid content is about 94-96% for most fats.

As fats contain about 95% TFM, 1 tonne of fat yields about 95/63 = 1.51 tonnes of 63% TFM soap. This supports the common approximation that 1 tonne of fat should yield around 1½ tonnes of soap base at 62-64% TFM.

Saponification almost certainly occurs in stages; but mono- and diglycerides are not normally found in partly saponified fat, probably because they react with caustic soda more rapidly than triglycerides. In the case of hydrolysis of fats with water, substantial proportions of mono- and diglycerides are found during the process; and some are likely to be present in fats which have deteriorated with development of FFA, although presumably not in acid oils, unless they have deteriorated after production. The following calculations show that this can be important in the estimation of the glycerol content of a fat from its SV and AV.

Consider a low grade tallow, or grease, having an equivalent mass of its fatty acids of 279 (fatty acid ratio 9.0), so that the group (O.CO.R) is equal to 279-1 = 278. The molecular mass of the triglyceride, $C_3H_5(O.CO.R)_3$ is (3 × 12) + 5 + 3 (278) = 875; and it yields (92 × 100)/875 = 10.5% glycerol

Table 4.4. Contents of glycerol and fatty acids, and caustic soda requirements for saponification, of some typical fats (no allowance for possible presence of mono- and di-glycerides)

Fat	*SV*	*AV*	*EV*	*FFA% (calc)*	*Theoretical caustic soda requirement Na_2O% on fat*	*Glycerol content %*	*FA content %*
Tallow	195	5	190	2.5	10.8	10.4	95.7
Tallow	195	15	180	7.4	10.8	9.9	95.9
Grease	192	90	102	45.8	10.6	5.6	97.7
Coconut oil	257	5	252	1.8	14.2	13.8	94.3
Coconut oil	257	12	245	4.4	14.2	13.4	94.5
Coconut acid oil	257	150	107	57.0	14.2	5.9	97.6
Cottonseed oil	194	4	190	2.0	10.7	10.4	95.7

and (3 × 279 × 100)/875 = 95.4% FA. Similarly, the diglyceride, $C_3H_5(OH)(O.CO.R)_2$, has a molecular mass of 614; and yields 15.0% glycerol and 90.9% FA.

Again, the monoglyceride, $C_3H_5(OH)_2$ (O.CO.R), has a molecular mass of 353; and yields 26.1% glycerol and 79.0% FA.

Table 4.5 shows that glycerol and FA contents of various hypothetical fats build up from these components. It will be seen that glycerol content varies considerably between three compositions, all with 10% FFA, but that is before, the fatty acid contents do not vary very much.

Table 4.5. Compositions of hypothetical fats with varying proportions of the different glycerides and free fatty acid.

Composition of fat	*Glycerol* %	*Fatty acid* %
100% triglyceride	10.5	95.4
90% triglyceride + 10% FA	9.5	95.9
80% triglyceride + 5% diglyceride + 5% monoglyceride + 10% FA	10.5	94.8
70% triglyceride + 10% diglyceride + 10% monoglyceride + 10% FA	11.5	93.8
100% FA	–	100

Glycerol and fatty acid contents of the fats used in a soap factory are required for process control and for costing. For many fats the methods described in this section give satisfactory figures, but if substantial quantities of fats likely to contain mono- or di-glycerides are used, it is better to have actual analytical estimations of glycerol and fatty acid contents. A useful compromise is to have a sufficient number of analyses of low grade materials made to permit the compilation of tables, or graphs, relating glycerol and fatty acid contents to AV, or FFA%, for the various materials. Values can then be read off when similar materials are used again.

When a quantity of fat is used to make soap it contains both fatty acids and glycerol; and there is no absolute way in which to decide how much has been paid for each. The lyes from lauric oils and from low grade fats are more difficult to purify than those from a good grade tallow; and, if the lyes were worked-up separately, they would tend to produce a poorer quality crude glycerine. In practice, lyes from the various types of fat are usually treated and evaporated together. On this basis the glycerol in one fat has the same value as that in another; and crude glycerine normally has a reasonably well-defined price.

Handling and Storage of Oils and Fats, Deterioration of Fatty Materials

As mentioned earlier, the quality of oils such as palm and rice bran can be poor unless the source materials are treated carefully and promptly to minimise the action of air, water, enzymes and micro-organisms.

Oils and fats, particularly those containing the more highly unsaturated fatty acids, are subject to oxidation and development of rancidity. This, and the associated topic of flavour deterioration, is of major importance in relation to fatty foods. Care is also important with soapmaking fats, but the problem is somewhat less critical. The chemistry of rancidity development is complex, and only a few broad generalisations are discussed below :

(i) Initially oxidation occurs at a double bond with the formation of peroxides. As the process proceeds, the peroxides break down to aldehydes, ketones, hydroxy-acids and other compounds; in consequence the content of peroxides (often determined as a measure of rancidity) passes through a maximum and then tends to fall. The Kreis test for rancidity depends upon the red colour which develops when the fat is reacted with phloroglucinol in ether solution; and is some measure of the aldehyde and ketone content.

(ii) The oxidation starts slowly but, after an induction period of varying length, it accelerates markedly. Pro-oxidants and antioxidants can be present. Pro-oxidants are maily heavy metal catalysts, such as copper and iron; and one type of antioxidant sequesters, and so inactivates, these metallic catalysts. Other types of antioxidant interfere with the oxidation mechanisms. They can be natural, such as the tocopheraols (vitamin E), or artificial. Sequestrant antioxidants are widely used in soaps, as discussed later, but also with fats, as in the addition of citric acid before deodorisation. Natural antioxidants are more general in vegetable than in animal fats, so that the former tend to keep better than the latter with similar unsaturation. Antioxidants are usually partially removed when an oil is refined; and crude oils often keep better than refined. Beef tallow also tends to deteriorate less than some other animal fats. Various organic compounds can be added to a fat to imporove its keeping properties, but some, such as hydroquinone, can lead to the development of undesirable colour if the fat is made into soap. Edible fats at not more than certain specified concentrations, are :

(i) BHA (butylated hydroxyanisole).

(ii) BHT (butylated hydroxytoluene).

(iii) THBP (2,4,5-trihydroxybutyrophenone).

These compounds can also have some adverse affects on the colour of the soap after storage.

(iii) Oxidation bleaching naturally affects unsaturated fatty acids, but such chemically bleached fats are, or at least have been, widely used in soaps, although generally not in the higher grades. Care should be taken not to continue air bleaching of palm oil beyond the optimum point, after which colour deteriorates and undesirable reactions may occur. The high peroxide value of an air bleached palm oil can be reduced by soda refining, adsorption bleaching, or deodorisation, but, apart perhaps from passage through a filter press loaded with spent bleaching earth, these additional processes are unlikely to be commercially attractive.

(iv) Complete saponification is generally considered important to ensure good stability of a soap. It is also commonly considered desirable to leave a small percentage of free alkali in a soap; but superfatting with fatty acids, which eliminates the free alkali in the base, is not unsual.

(v) When solid fats are received at a factory in drums, or barrels, a melting out stage is required; this normally comprises a tank, or tanks, covered with a staging onto which the drums can be put. Steam jets discharge into the bung holes of the drums, which face downwards, and the molten fat and condensed water drip into the tank below. The mixture in the tank is settled, the water run off, and molten fat pumped away.

5

Manufacture, Purification of Fatty Acids and Production of Soap Base

Introduction

Fatty acids have been produced, purified and separated into fractions for very many years. The solid fraction, known as stearin (which actually usually contains a substantial of palmitic as well as stearic acid),was used particularly in candles; and the liquid fraction, known as red oil or olein, in the processing of wool, although there were, and are, other uses for both materials. Relatively minor quantities of various fatty acids were used in soap; and high quality stearin was, and is, used in shaving soaps.

The purchase of fatty acids simplifies the soapmaking process and obviates the need for lye, or sweet water, treatment and evaporation equipment. It also transfers to the fatty acid maker the problems of economical purchase and pre-treatment of crude fats. Many small producer of toilet soaps, the so-called remillers, have for many years gone even further and have bought dried soap base to which they add perfume and other ingredients, and just complete the processing and packaging.

Fatty acids can be produced for special purpose by the acidification of soap with mineral acid, usually sulphuric; and this process can be used to recover fatty acids from soapstocks after saponification has been completed and, if required, the soap has been grained and/or fitted to purify it. This procedure is used in the laboratory, but, on the plant scale, it is expensive and obviously does not provide and alternative method for the manufacture of soap. All important methods for the production of fatty acids from natural fats involve hydrolysis, or spitting, with water, with, or without, a catalyst. Processes can be divided into those carried out at atmospheric pressure and those which use high pressures and temperatures. The processes at atmospheric pressure are :

(i) Acid splitting.

(ii) Twitchell type splitting.

(iii) Splitting with lipases, the fat splitting enzymes.

The high pressure processes use water acided by a basic catalyst, usually zinc oxide. Higher temperatures, and/or longer times, are needed when no catalyst is employed, but processes without catalyst avoid the expense of the catalyst and of removing it from hydrolysis products,and are now usual in morden installations. When a zinc oxide catalyst is used, most of it reaches the fatty acid still residues. High temperature and pressure processes can be batch or continuous. As explained later, the normal high temperature processes require the presence of a liquid aqueous phase and this makes high pressure also necessary to avoid vapourisationof the water.

FAT SPLITTING

Principles of Fat splitting

The hydrolysis of fats takes place in stages and the reactions are reversible:

$$\underset{\text{triglyceride}}{C_3H_5(OOCR)_3} + \underset{\text{water}}{H_2O} \rightleftarrows \underset{\text{diglyceride}}{C_3H_5(OH)(OOCR)_2} + \underset{\text{fatty acid}}{R—COOH}$$

$$\underset{\text{diglyceride}}{C_3H_5(OH)(OOCR)_2} + H_2O \rightleftarrows \underset{\text{monoglyceride}}{C_3H_5(OH)_2(OOCR)} + \underset{\text{fatty acid}}{R—COOH}$$

$$\underset{\text{monoglyceride}}{C_3H_5(OH)_2(OOCR)} + H_2O \rightleftarrows \underset{\text{glycerol}}{C_3H_5(OH)_3} + \underset{\text{fatty acid}}{R—COOH}$$

By the usual principles of mass-action, the degree of split can be increased by the removal of a product from the reaction zone; and in practice this is the glycerol. Batch processes use two or more stages, in which the sweet is removed and replaced by fresh water, or by a sweet water with a concentration of glycerol lower than that in the sweet water removed. This is analogous to the way in which soap is washed in a number of stages; and, for the same reasons as in soapmaking, countercurrent contact is desirable in order to reach as a high a degree of split as possible with the minimum quantity of water. In the case of splitting, however, the need to recover the maximum yield of glycerol in as concentrated a form as possible is augmented by the need to liberate the maximum percentage of fatty acid from the fat.

The solubility of water in fatty acids and fats increases with rise in temperature. At temperatures up to 100°C it is slight, between 100°C and 200°C it increases slowly, and then, at temperatures above 200°C the rise is rapid. Ittner and Mills, in patents concerned with continuous splitting, report that at 235°C coconut fatty acids disolve about 17% of their weight of water when excess water is present, and the pressure is sufficiently high to keep it liquid. At 245°C coconut fatty acids dissolve about 20% of water and tallow fatty acids about 11%. At 287°C (with a pressure in excess of about 1050 psig) coconut fatty acids blend freely with more than their own weight of water to form a single clear liquid phase. Fatty acids of low molecular mass dissolve more water than those of higher molecular mass, and fatty acids more than the corresponding fats, possibly greatly so. In the high pressure processes, the main reactions occur almost entirely in the fatty phase. Free glycerol is partitioned betwen the fatty and aqueous phases, and, as already explained, two or more changes of water are normally used to achieve a high degree of split in batchwise processes. Each replacement of sweet water by fresh water (or by a sweet water low in glycerol content) causes a transfer of glycerol from the fatty to the aqueous phase and so disturbs the hydrolysis reaction in the fatty phase in the required direction. In a counter-current splitting tower, a similar effect is achieved by a transfer of glycerol from the fatty to the aqueous phase, as discussed in more detail later.

In the Eisenlohr process, fat and water, without catalyst, are pumped through Inconel tubes at 3,500 psig and heated to 330°C. These conditions with concurrent contact give repid reaction, presumably in a single phase, but the equilibrium is not very favourable, because there is no removal of liberated glycerol from the reaction zone. So far as is known, this process is not used commercially.

The data rate of splitting at various temperatures is shown in Table 5.1. Temperature and catalyst have very substantial effects, but there is little difference between the various fats tested. Fig.5.1 shows that the reaction between a neutral fat and water at 240°C starts slowly, accelerates and then slows down as equilibrium is approached; the curve being very similar to that for saponification of a fat with caustic soda. The shape of the curve, and the fact that the hydrolysis starts more rapidly if the fat contains more than about 4% FFA, confirms that the reactions are autocatalytic and suggest that the slow early stage with a neutral fat is because the reaction is then mainly at the fat/water interface. Fig. 5.2 shows how the degree of split at which the reaction rate becomes negligible (that is, equilibrium is nearly reached) varies with the percentage of glycerol in the water phase. These facts show that a fat which contains more FFA than about 4% starts to react more rapidly than one with less. Also, that to maintain an adequate reaction rate whilst producing a reasonably sweet water, the water must be changed at least before the split is 85 - 90% complete. The actual figures varies with the glycerol content of the fats being split and the ratio of fat water which is used.

Table 5.1. Influence of temperature on splitting time.

Temp °C	*Time to reach equilibrium (mins.)*			*Half-life time (mins.)*		
	Beef tallow	*Coconut oil*	*Groundnut oil*	*Beef tallow*	*Coconut oil*	*Groundnut oil*
225	156	158	156	62	58	50
240	82	85	85	34	33	25
260	47	46	53	18	23	16
280	34	33	33	8	10	10
260 (with 0.2% ZnO catalyst)	21	–	–	4	–	–

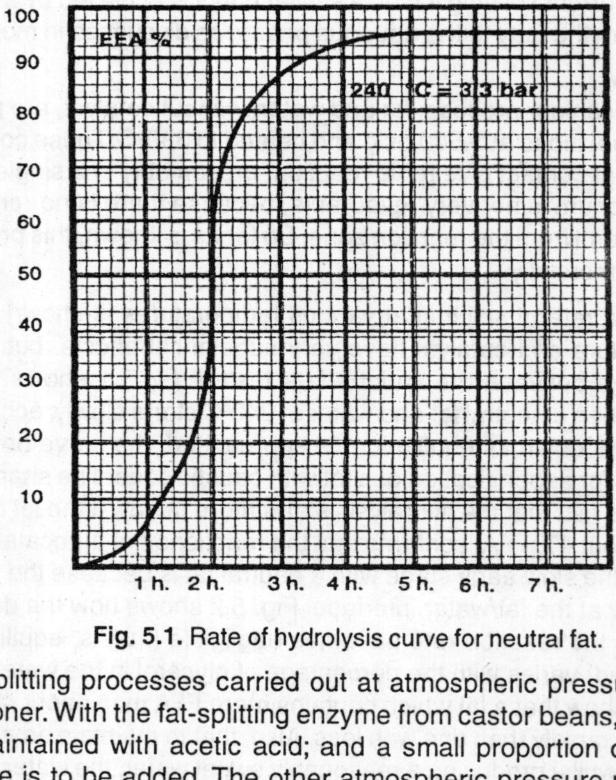

Fig. 5.1. Rate of hydrolysis curve for neutral fat.

Splitting processes carried out at atmospheric pressure use acidic conditioner. With the fat-splitting enzyme from castor beans, a pH of about 5 is maintained with acetic acid; and a small proportion of manganese sulphate is to be added. The other atmospheric pressure processes are carried out with addition of sulphuric acid to give strongly acidic conditions. The earliest process, used concentrated sulphuric acid (around 80%H_2SO_4) at 110 -120°C, which previously had been washed and and dried. Severe discolouration occurred; and organic sulphuric or sulphonic acids formed may have helped the acid catalyst by aiding emulsification. A modification in which a sulphuric acid was used in conjunction with water and sulphuric acid; and the mixture was boiled for considerable periods. The original Twitchell reagent, or catalyst, was made by reacting a fatty acid (usually oleric), and naphthalene, and/or benzene, with concentrated sulphuric acid. Most reagents used more recently, such as the 'Kontakt' type, are complex sulphonates, which are by-products from petroleum industry.

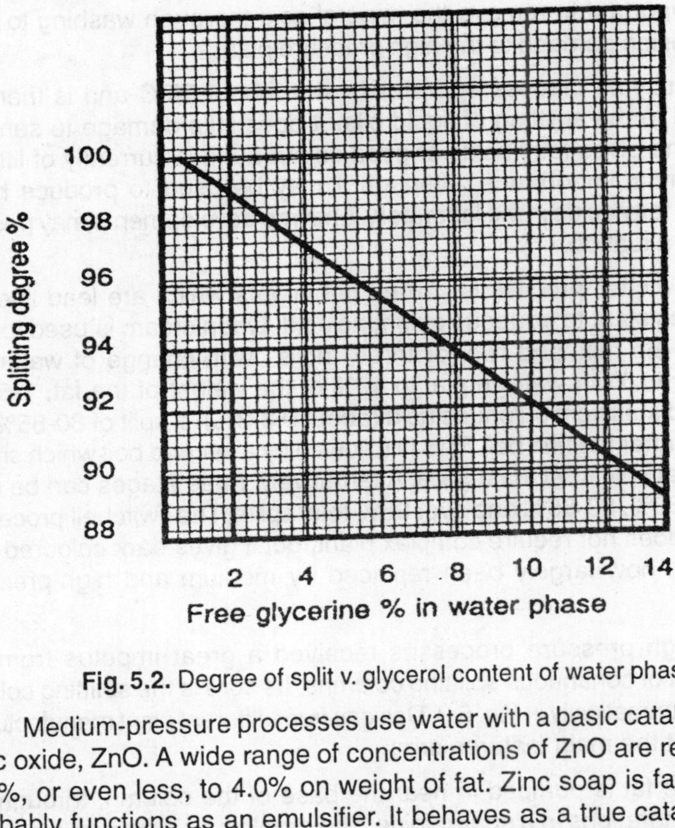

Fig. 5.2. Degree of split v. glycerol content of water phase.

Medium-pressure processes use water with a basic catalyst, normally zinc oxide, ZnO. A wide range of concentrations of ZnO are reported, from 0.2%, or even less, to 4.0% on weight of fat. Zinc soap is fat soluble and probably functions as an emulsifier. It behaves as a true catalyst in that it increases the rate of reaction under given conditions, but does not affect the equilibrium significantly. Zinc powder is sometimes also added and is said to improve the colour of the fatty acids. Other catalysts are magnesium oxide, calcium oxide, caustic soda alkalis; but zinc oxide has been found to be far the most effective. Despite the catalytic effect of calcium and magnesium oxides, it is usually considered advisable to use soft, or even demineralised, water in the pressure splitting, as well as the Twitchell, process. Water hardness can affect emulsification in the Twitchell process, and cause problems with insoluble soap scums in the high pressure processes.

Splitting Plant and Processes

Unless the fats to be split are of high quality. pre-treatment is usually necessary, or at least desirable. Break material can cause emulsification in tower which may interfere with the counter-current operation. Polythene in tallow is converted into black plastic masses in tower, or other autoclaves, which can block pipes and other plant items. As already mentioned polythene can be removed by the use of bleaching earth with filtration at below about 70°C. If a dilute sulphuric acid treatment is used prior to high pressure splitting, it is very important to remove the mineral acid thorough washing to avoid risk of corrosion damage to the high pressure plant.

The enzyme process operates best at about 35°C and is therefore most suited to the splitting of liquid oils. It does little damage to sensitive materials and gives fatty acids of good colour but it is currently of little, or no, commercial importance, although it may be used to produce highly unsaturated fatty acids in the laboratory. Enzyme developments may possibly change this situation.

The Twitchell process is carried out in vats which are lead lined, or otherwise resistant to aqueous sulphuric acid. Open steam is used to heat and agitate the mix; and two, or three, 'boils', with change of water, are normally given. With water equal to 40% of the weight of the fat, 1-5% of catalyst, and sufficient sulphuric acid (about 0.3-3%), a split of 80-85% can be obtained after the first boil. This is followed by a second boil which should raise the total split to at least 95%. Alternatively, three stages can be used giving, say, 60%, 80-85% and over 98% total splits. The Twitchell process is simple and does not require complex plant, but it gives dark coloured fatty acids. It has now largely been replaced by medium and high-pressure systems.

The high pressure processes received a great impetus from the development of continuous splitting columns. Its core is the splitting column shown diagrammatically in Fig. 5.3. Designs from different plant manufacturers may vary, but the main features are :

(i) The fat is pumped in near the base of the column, through the perforations in a sparge pipe. The droplets rise through the sweet water zone; and the sweet water, substantially free from fat, leaves from the bottom of the setting section.

(ii) Similarly, the water is introduced near the top of column and is suitably distributed into droplets which fall through the fatty matter phase. The fatty acids leave after passage through a settling zone.

(iii) Fairly low down in the column there is an interface above which the continuous phase is fatty, and below which it is aqueous.

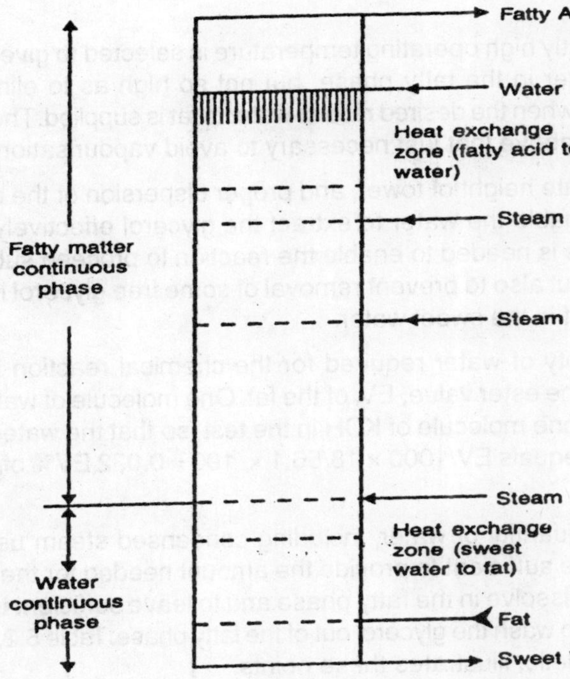

Fig. 5.3. High pressure splitting column.

(iv) Internal heat exchange, from fatty acid to incoming water near the top and from sweet water to incoming fat near the bottom, is important, to the discharge of the fatty acids at high temperature to a neutralisation mixer for production of soap powders. At least in some designs, special heat transfer devices are included in parts of the column.

(v) High pressure steam is introduced at suitable levels to establish and maintain the required reaction temperature. As an alternative to a sufficiently high pressure boiler it is possible to use a steam compressor to increase the pressure of the available steam.

(vi) The fatty acids are further cooled and dried by a reduction in pressure which allow dissolved (and suspended, if any) water to 'flash' off. Similarly, the sweet water is partially concentrated by allowing it to flash. In some installations, the flashed vapour is used in multiple effect to continue the concentration of sweet water; and other heat exchange may be possible to improve thermal efficiency. Condensate is collected for re-use as process water, made up with demineralised water.

A sufficiently high operating temperature is selected to give adequate solubility of water in the fatty phase, but not so high as to eliminate the aqeuous phase when the desired ratio of water to fat is supplied. The pressure is substantially above that just necessary to avoid vapourisation.

An adequate height of tower, and proper dispersion of the phases, is necessary to enable the water to extract the glycerol effectively from the fatty phase. This is needed to enable the reaction to proceed substantially to completion, but also to prevent removal of some free glycerol in the fatty phase instead of in the sweet water.

The quantity of water required for the chemical reaction is directly proportional to the ester value, EV, of the fat. One molecule of water (HOH) is equivalent to one molecule of KOH in the test, so that the water required for the reaction equals EV/1000 × 18/56.1 × 100 = 0.032 EV% of the mass of fat.

The total quantity of water, including condensed steam used in the process, must be sufficient to provide the amount needed for the reaction, plus enough to dissolve in the fatty phase and to leave sufficient to form an aqueous phase to wash the glycerol out of the fatty phase. Table 5.2, obtained by simple arithmetic, illustrates these points.

The first figures for the glycerol content of the sweet water assume that the fatty acids leave the column saturated with water at the reaction temperature, but that the glycerol is all transferred to the aqueous phase. The second set assume that the fatty acids are cooled in the heat exchange zone to a temperature at which they contain a negligible percentage of dissolved water and that the separated water joins the new water descending the column.

In practice, the glycerol content of the sweet water leaving a tower seems commonly to be about 12-18%, depending upon the type of fat and the conditions used. Provided the sweet water leaves the tower at a temperature sufficiently high for it to flash when the pressure is reduced, further concentration then occurs; and the flashed vapours may be used to produce additional evaporation.

The main manufacturers of fat-splitting plants, Lurgi, Gianazza, Mazzoni, and Wurster and Sanger, each make several types of plant. plants based upon counter-current splitting columns are now usual for large-scale operations, but batch, or multistage, types may be more suitable when the production required is small. High temperature process lead to a reduction in iodine value when highly unsaturated oils are handled, and milder methods may need to be selected if this is important. The choice of diagram is somewhat arbitrary; and it should be noted that plants similar in flow sheet, although doubtless different in engineering detail, are often offered by the other makers.

Table 5.2. Water requirements of fat-splitting columns and glycerol concentrations in sweet waters produced.

(Basis 1 tonne fat)

	80% tallow plus 20% coconut oil. 50% water on fat	*Grease 50% water on fat*	*Grease 40% water on fat*
Fatty acid content	0.954t	0.977t	0.977t
Glycerol content	0.111t	0.056t	0.056t
Water required for reaction	0.064t	0.033t	0.033t
Water dissolved in the fatty phase at 245°C (from solubilities given earlier and mass of (FA)	0.122t	0.107t	0.107t
Total water	0.500t	0.500t	0.400t
Water in aqueous phase in reaction zone (by difference)	0.314t	0.360t	0.260t
Percentage glycerol in sweet water, if water dissolved in fatty acids leaves with FA at reaction temperature	35	15.5	21.5
Percentage glycerol in sweet water if FA is cooled before leaving the tower to a temperature at which solubility of water in it is negligible	25.5	12	15

Fig. 5.4 shows the Lurgi batch-splitting plant. A feature is the continuous circulation of sweet water by external pump from the base to the top autoclave. Standard operating conditions are 230°C and 28 bar (406 psi); and it is stated that 95-96% split should be achieved with two changes of water (the split will also be influenced by the quantities of water and fat used, and the glycerol content of the fat). In the past, Lurgi has made continuous plants comprising three autoclaves of this general type linked in series for counter-current flows of fatty matter and water, but this equipment is no longer offered.

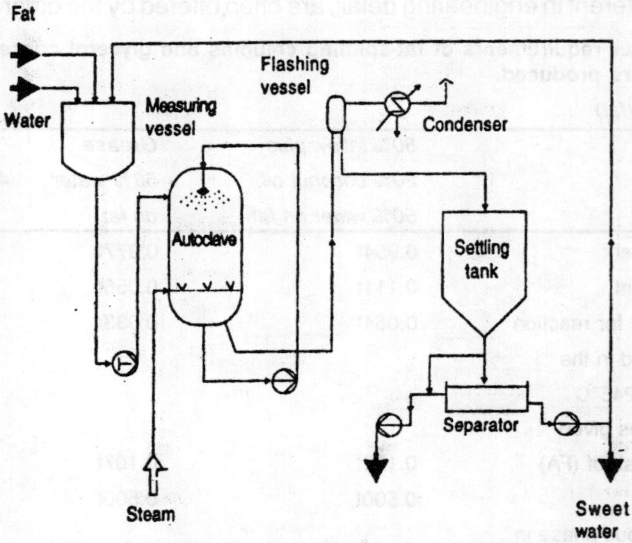

Fig. 5.4. Lurgi batch-splitting plant.

DISTILLATION OF FATTY ACIDS

General

Fatty acids directly from splitting plant can be, and sometimes are, made into soap, but it is often necessary to improve their quality by distillation. Apart from the requirements of high grade soap bases, this is because one of the merits of the fatty acid route to soap is the possibility of using lower quality, and hence cheaper, raw materials than would otherwise be possible, by taking advantage of the upgrading which can be achieved by distillation of the fatty acids. Simple distillation of fatty acids using direct fired stills initially operated at atmospheric pressure, but later under vacuum, with considerable open steam, has been used for over a hundred years. These stills caused considerable damage to the fatty acids and are largely obsolete.

Distillation separates the volatile fatty acids from non-volatile glycerides and other compounds. If justified, the residue can be re-split with the liberation of more fatty acids, from which a low grade distillate may be obtained (or the re-split material may be returned to the main steam of crude fatty acids, although a residue of non-volatile, non-hydrolysable material must eventually be discarded). A high degree of split in the main hydrolysis process minimises the amount of residue left on distillation and is important. The ultimate pitch left after as much fatty acid has been vapourised as is economically possible is a low value material which may have to be burnt. It is also usually desirable to separate the very low molecular weight acids (C_8 or C_{10} and below), together with other very volatile constituents, to improve odour; and to remove acids from luric oils which give somewhat irritant sodium salts. Mixtures of fatty acids, as produced from the natural oils and fats, can be separated into fractions useful for specialised applications, but this is not normally for use in soaps.

The glycerides are not significantly volatile under the conditions used for fatty acid distillation, but they can be distilled in 'molecular' or 'short-path' stills; and this process is sometimes used to produce mono-glycerides and similar products.

Distillation Principles

Fatty acids, particularly hydroxy and highly unsaturated types, are heat sensitive and are liable to be dehydrated, polymerised and/or isomerised. These, usually, but not invariably, undesirable, reactions are minimised by the use of the lowest possible temperature for the shortest possible time. Time and temperature are interdependent, so that a very short time at a relatively high temperature may be better than a longer time at a lower temperature; and vice versa.

Vapour pressure/boiling temperature data for some important fatty acids are given in Table 5.3 and for the region of greatest interest in Fig. 5.5. Little information appears to have been published for unsaturated acids other than oleic.

The compositions of vapour and liquid equilibrium at various temperatures for a binary (two component) mixture are shown diagrammatically in Fig. 5.6, drawn for a fixed total pressure. If a liquid of composition *x* is heated, boiling commences at temperature t_1 and the composition of the first vapour given off is *y*, that is it is richer in the lower boiling component *A* than the liquid from which it comes. This means that the liquid residue left is slightly richer in *B*, the higher boiling component. As vapourisation proceeds, the boiling temperature rises and compositions change along the liquid and vapour curves as indicated by the arrows marked *b* (boiling). At temperature t_2 the whole of the liquid is vapourised and the mixed vapours have the original composition *x*. At intermediate temperatures, such as t_3, a vapour of composition v is in equilibrium with liquid of composition *l*; and the quantities are inversely proportional to the distances from composition *x*.

Table 5.3. Vapour pressure boiling temperatures for some fatty acids.

Fatty acid	*Vapour Pressure mm Hg*						
	0.01	*0.1*	*1.0*	*2.0*	*5.0*	*10.0*	*100.0*
	Boiling temperatures °C						
Saturated C_4	–	–	26.0	35.5	50.0	61.5	107.5
Saturated C_6	11.5	34.0	62.0	72.0	86.5	98.5	146.5
Saturated C_8	33.5	57.5	87.5	98.5	113.5	126.5	177.0
Saturated C_{10}	55.0	79.0	110.0	121.5	137.0	150.5	202.5
Saturated C_{12}	73.0	98.5	131.0	142.0	158.0	172.5	226.5
Saturated C_{14}	89.0	116.0	149.5	161.0	177.5	192.5	249.0
Saturated C_{16}	105.0	132.5	167.0	179.0	197.0	211.5	–
Saturated C_{18}	119.5	147.5	183.5	196.0	213.0	–	–
Oleic	–	–	198	204	215	225	–

This is the basis upon which fractional distillation is founded. The separation in one stage cannot be more than that for equilibrium at the relevant temperature; and a number of stages are required to effect more than a limited degree of separation. This is usually carried out in a continuous fractionating still shown diagrammatically in Fig. 5.7. The column comprises a number of plates on each of which rising vapour and descending into contact, so that of component *A* is transferred from the liquid to the vapour in an approach to the new equilibrium relevant to the plate in question. Instead of plates, which give a stepwise, stage, separation, various types of packed columns are often used in which counter-current contact is continuous. Reverting to Fig. 5.6, if vapour of composition **x** is cooled,condensation will start at temperature t_2 and the first drop of liquid will have composition *z*. As cooling is continued, the composition of vapour moves along the vapour curve and that of the liquid along the liquid curve, as indicated by the arrows marked c(condensation). At temperature t_3 the last drop of liquid condensed under equilibrium has composition *l* and leaves a residual vapour of composition *v*, to be condensed separately; this is the basis of fractionation by partial condensation.

Theoretical analysis of the fractionation of multi-component mixtures is complex, or even impossible, but some useful generalisations can be deduced from imformation concerning binary systems:

(i) The function of the part of the column above the feed point, called the rectifying section, is to remove less volatile components from the rising vapours which become the distillate.

(ii) The function of the part of the column below the feed point, called the stripping section, is to strip more volatile components from the descending liquid which becomes the residue.

(iii) A fractionating column can only work if liquid reflux is returned to the top, and a reboiler heat and vapour to the bottom.

(iv) In general, only one substantially pure component can be separated from a single column. Hence an *n*-component mixture requires (*n*-1) columns to separate it into its *n* individual compounds. More than one complete unit, each with column, reflux and reboiler, can sometimes be included in one shell. In the case of fatty acids, it is seldom required to separate the mixture into individual compounds.

Fractionating columns can be fed with liquid or vapour, or a mixture of liquid and vapour. Liquid feed increases the flow down the stripping section of the column, whereas vapour feed increases the flow vapour up the rectifying section.

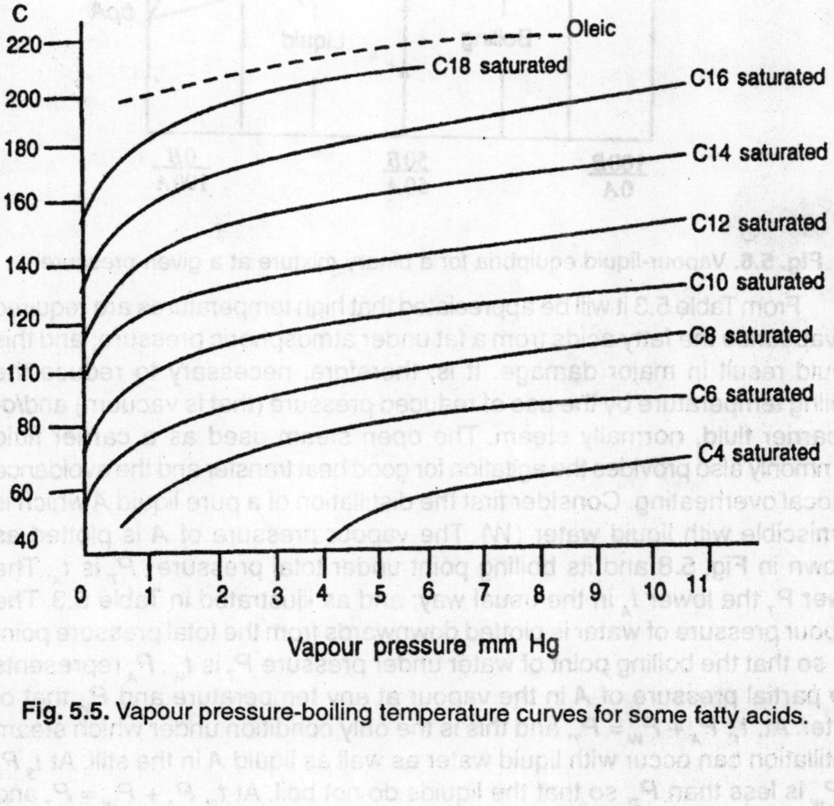

Fig. 5.5. Vapour pressure-boiling temperature curves for some fatty acids.

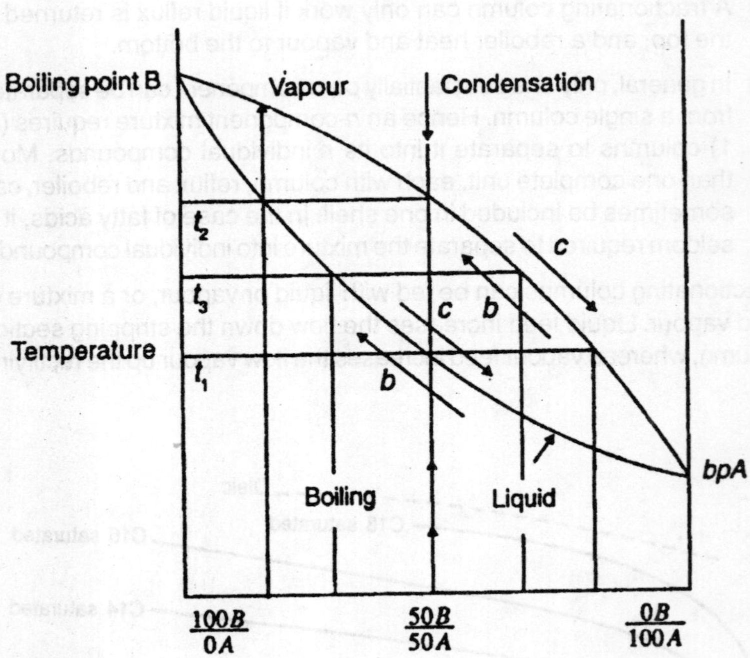

Fig. 5.6. Vapour-liquid equipbria for a binary mixture at a given pressure.

From Table 5.3 it will be appreciated that high temperatures are required to vapourise the fatty acids from a fat under atmospheric pressure; and this would result in major damage. It is, therefore, necessary to reduce the boiling temperature by the use of reduced pressure (that is vacuum) and/or a carrier fluid, normally steam. The open steam used as a carrier fluid commonly also provides the agitation for good heat transfer and the avoidance of local overheating. Consider first the distillation of a pure liquid *A* which is immiscible with liquid water (*W*). The vapour pressure of *A* is plotted as shown in Fig. 5.8 and its boiling point under total pressure P_T is t_A. The lower P_T the lower t_A in the usual way; and as illustrated in Table 5.3. The vapour pressure of water is plotted downwards from the total pressure point P_T, so that the boiling point of water under pressure P_T is t_W. P_A represents the partial pressure of *A* in the vapour at any temperature and P_W that of water. At, t_1, $P_A + P_W = P_T$, and this is the only condition under which steam distillation can occur with liquid water as well as liquid *A* in the still. At t_3 $P_A + P_W$ is less than P_T, so that the liquids do not boil. At t_2, $P_A + P_W = P_T$ and liquid *A* boils, but there is no liquid water in the still. From Dalton's law of partial pressure

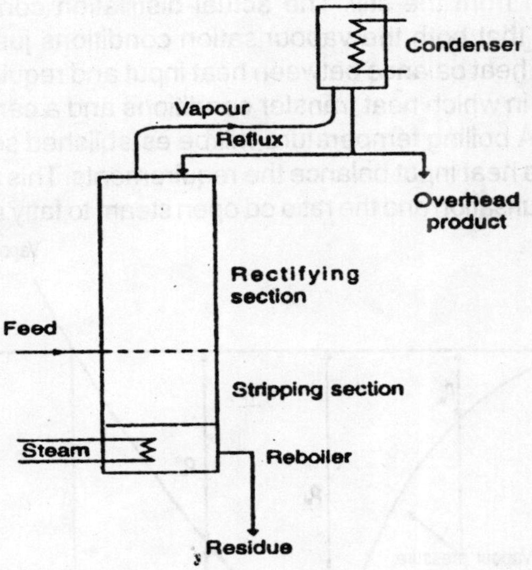

Fig. 5.7. Fractionating still for a binary mixture.

$$\frac{P_W}{P_A} = \frac{moles\ W}{moles\ A}, \text{ so that } \frac{mass\ W}{mass\ A} = \frac{P_W \times M_W}{P_A \times M_A}$$

where

M_A = molecular mass of water = 18

and

M_A = molecular mass of *A*.

Since $P_W = (P_T - P_A)$, this equation can be rewritten, mass in lb of open steam/lb distilled

$$= \frac{(P_T - P_A)^{18}}{P_A \times M_A}$$

When *A* is substantially a single compound, as in the case of glycerine distillation, useful quantitative results can be obtained from this equation. For complex mixture such as fatty acids, the equation provides qualitative indications of the significance of changes in total pressure, use of open steam and supply of indirect heat. The indirect heat provides the latent heat of vapourisation plus other requirements, such as sensible heat to raise the temperature of the feed to its boiling point and to replace heat lost by radiation and convection from the still. The actual distillation conditions establish themselves so that both the vapourisation conditions just discussed and the condition of heat balance between heat input and requirements are met. Consider a still in which heat transfer conditions and a certain flow of open steam are set. A boiling temperature will be established so that (a) $P_A + P_W = P_T$, and (b) the heat input balance the requirements. This also determiners the rate of vapourisation and the ratio od open steam to fatty acids vapourised.

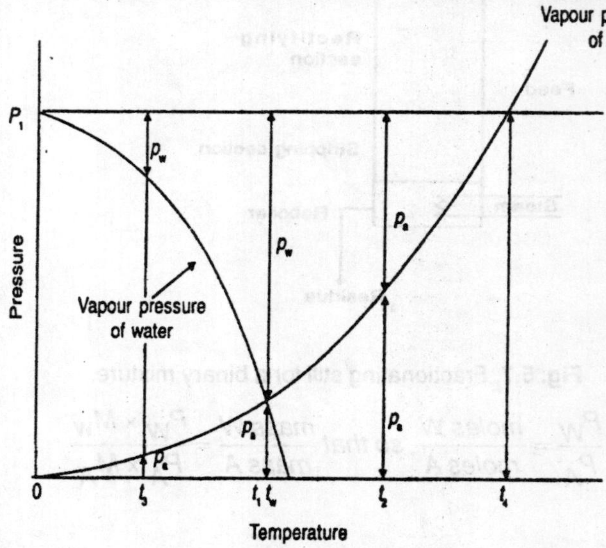

Fig. 5.8. Steam distillation of a pure liquid.

In the discussion so far, it is assumed that the partial pressure of *A* in the vapours equals the vapour pressure at the distillation temperature; that is the vapourisation efficiency, defined as P_A actual/P_A theoretical, is 1. If contact between open steam and boiling liquid is good, so that the steam is nearly saturated with organic vapour, this is often approximately true. It has been found that vapourisation efficiency, *E*, varies with the substance being distilled as well as with physical conditions in the still.

With the steam dispensed through small holes at an adequate depth below the surface of the liquid, he quotes 0.9 - 0.95 organic compounds of molecular mass below 100, but only about 0.5 for the steam distillation of lubricating oils of molecular mass greater than 250. Data for fatty acid distillation are not available. If a figure for *E* is known, or assumed, Ep_A should be substituted for P_A in the expressions in this section.

It will be noted that the usage of open steam per lb fatty acids distilled is reduced by :

(i) Reduction in the operating pressure at the point of vapourisation. This depends upon the pressure drop through the system as well as the absolute pressure induced by the vacuum maintenance system. In the limit, no open steam is used and the boils at t_A.

(ii) An increase in the boiling temperature which increase P_A. This results from higher indirect heat input relative to the flow of open steam.

(iii) An improvement in the contact between open steam and boiling liquid if *E* is initially low.

Conversely, boiling temperature can be reduced by an increased usage of open steam, as well as by a reduction in total pressure. If open steam usage is increased, care must be taken to avoid an undue rise in P_T due to the increased flow of open steam through the system to the vacuum equipment, and consequent increase in pressure drop.

As well as volatile material, mainly fatty acids, the crude fatty acids fed to a still non-volatile components, such as glycerides, unsaponifiables and proteinaceous matter . For convenience, the volatile part of the mixture is called *V* and the non-volatile *R* (residue), but both include compounds of varying volatility. By the laws of physical chemistry concerning solutions, the vapour pressure of *V* in equilibrium with a mixture of *V* and *R* is given by

$$pv\,\text{mix} = pv \times \frac{Mv}{M_V + M_R}, \text{ where}$$

$$M_V = \text{moles of } V \text{ present in the mixture}$$

and

$$M_R = \text{moles of } R \text{ present in the mixture}$$

Hence, as *V* is removed from the liquid by vapourisation, *pv* mix at a given temperature falls. In a batch, or semi-batch, still the more volatile components are vapourised first; and the residue in the pot becomes increasingly rich in the higher boiling and non-volatile components. The boiling temperature and the ratio of open steam to material vapourised rise until it is not economical to proceed further. In a continuous still, as now normally used, it is necessary to design the vapouriser so that the residue discharged is as free as possible from volatile matter.

The direct heat can be supplied in two ways :

(i) By transfer through a surface to the liquid at its boiling point under still conditions; or approximately so.

(ii) In an external heater in which the material is heated under a relatively high pressure so that the temperature rises, after which the hot liquid is discharged into the still where the lower pressure results in flash evaporation by conversion of sensible into latent heat. Under still conditions, the specific heat of fatty acids appears to be about 0.7 (0.5 at 25 - 100° C) and latent heat of vapourisation about 100 CHu/lb.Hence, roughly, $1 \times \Delta t \times 0.7 = x \times 100$ where Δt°C is the fall in temperature when the mixture is flashed and *x* is the fraction vapourised.

From this :

Δt°C	*x*
50	0.35
100	0.70
143	1.0

DISTILLATION EQUIPMENT

Vapourisers

In addition to points just elaborated, the requirements for a good vapouriser can be summarised as follows :

(i) The best combination of time and temperature, with both as low as possible, should be achieved. This means that any reservoir of boiling liquid should be as small as possible.

(ii) The pressure under which the liquid boils should be as low as possible. This is primarily controlled by the vacuum equipment, and by the pressure drop through the condensing system and connecting ducts, but it can also be affected by the vapouriser. In particular, the hydrostatic head under which the liquid is heated is important. One foot of liquid of specific gravity 0.8 produces an additional pressure of about 19 mmHg which is very significant when the pressure in the vapour space is only, say, 4 mmHg.

(iii) If open steam is used, the contact between steam and liquid should be intimate, so that *E* is as 1 as possible.

(iv) Volatile over the heating surface should be sufficient to avoid local over heating and to promote good heat transfer.

Semi-batch stills commonly use *simple pot vapourisers,* with open to agitate the boiling liquid and to act as carrier fluid; and direct heat supplied from a furnace, or via a carrier such as Dowtherm. A simple still of this type is shown in Fig. 5.9. As the initial charge of crude fatty acids is distilled more feed is introduced. The concentration of non-volatile matter in the still liquid increases until it is necessary to stop the feed and to work down the residue as completely as is economically possible. This type of still fails to meet the criterion time and temperature. It is possible to collect the distillate in separate fractions, and an impure first fraction (and possible also last fraction) may be separated. Otherwise, the only fractionation is by slight partial condensation; and distillate quality and yield tend to be poor because of thermal damage. The design is obsolete, but may still be used in some small capacity plants.

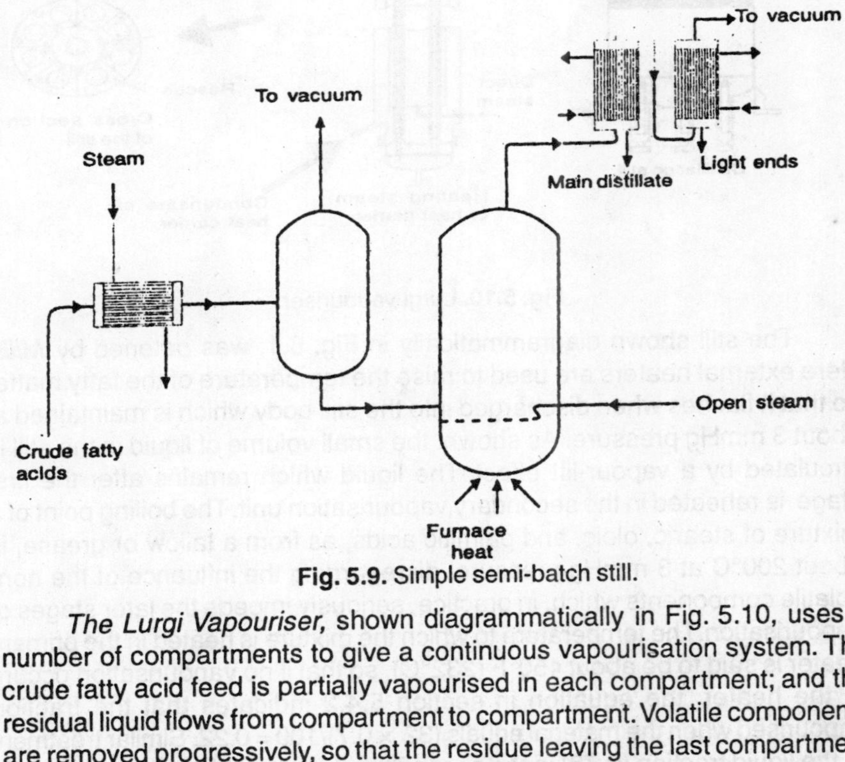

Fig. 5.9. Simple semi-batch still.

The Lurgi Vapouriser, shown diagrammatically in Fig. 5.10, uses a number of compartments to give a continuous vapourisation system. The crude fatty acid feed is partially vapourised in each compartment; and the residual liquid flows from compartment to compartment. Volatile components are removed progressively, so that the residue leaving the last compartment is substantially free of volatile. In addition, the boiling temperature rises gradually from compartment to compartment as the concentration of non-volatile increases, so that the bulk of the vapourisation occurs at the lowest possible temperature. The annular heating elements ensure a positive flow of high pressure steam, or other heating medium. The open steam produces a 'Vapour-lift' effect, similar to that in an air-lift pump, which causes a good flow of the fatty matter over the heating elements and minimizes the adverse influence of hydrostatic head. As shown, the mixture of steam and fatty matter impinges on a baffle, the vapours separate, and the liquid drop back to be recirculated, or to pass on to the next compartment. 5-10 compartments are used, depending upon the capacity of the plant. Some other plant manufacturers use a broadly similar type of vapouriser.

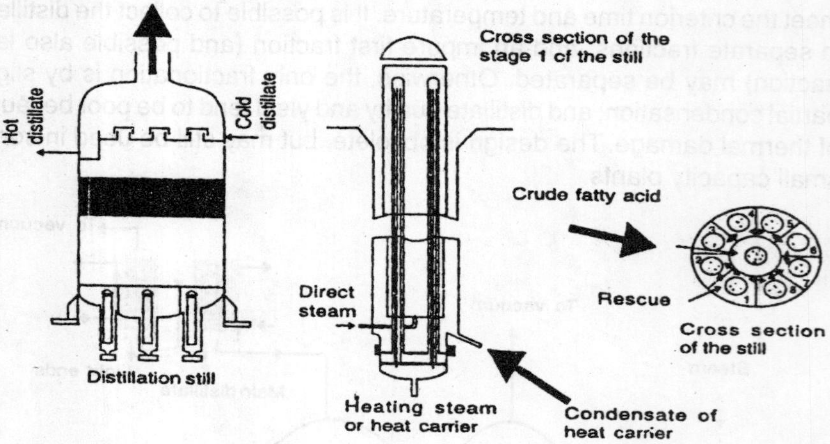

Fig. 5.10. Lurgi vapouriser.

The still shown diagrammatically in Fig. 5.1, was patened by *Mills*. Here external heaters are used to raise the temperature of the fatty matter so that it flashes when discharged into the still body which is maintained at about 3 mmHg pressure. As shown, the small volume of liquid in the still is circulated by a vapour-lift effect. The liquid which remains after the first stage is reheated in the secondary vapourisation unit. The boiling point of a mixture of stearic, oleic, and palmitic acids, as from a tallow or grease, is about 200°C at 3 mmHg pressure, disregarding the influence of the non-volatile components which, in practice, seriously impede the later stages of vapourisation. The temperature to which the mixture is heated in the primary heater is said to be about 450°F (232°C), so that if no vapourisation occurs in the heater, the equation in section 5.4.2 indicates that the fraction vapourised when the material equals $(32 \times 0.7)/100 = 0.22$. Similar treatment of the liquid fraction (0.78) in the secondary stage would vapourise another 0.17, making a total of 0.39 (39% of the feed). This may have been increased by substantial vapourisation in the heater, but facilities are also provided for recirculation round each stage, as shown dotted. As discussed earlier, the vapour pressure falls to a very low level as the residue is stripped nearly free from volatile; and this makes flash distillation alone difficult.

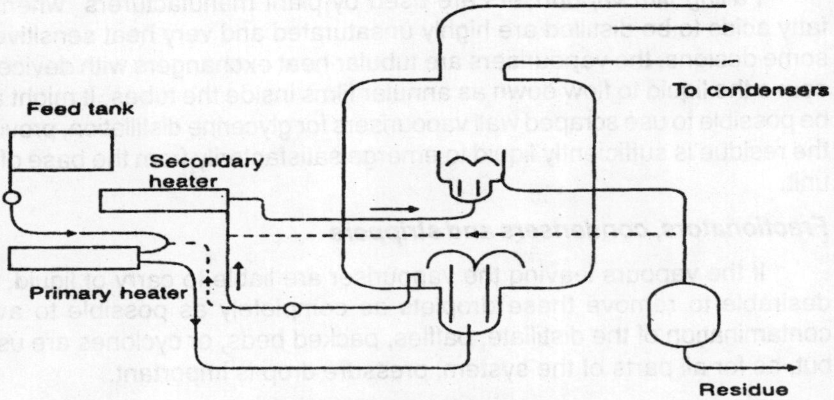

Fig. 5.11. Victor Mills still.

A vapourising column comperising bubble cap trays heated by Dowtherm vapour as shown in Fig. 5.12. The liquid flows across the trays and the unvapourised portion passes through the downcomers to the next tray below. Just as in a fractionating column, the vapour through the slots in the bubble caps produces violent agitation and good contact between liquid and vapour. A separate vapour outlet is provided above each pair of trays to minimise pressure drop. Open steam is injected into the liquid in the reservoir at the base of the column, and below the lower tray in each higher pair.

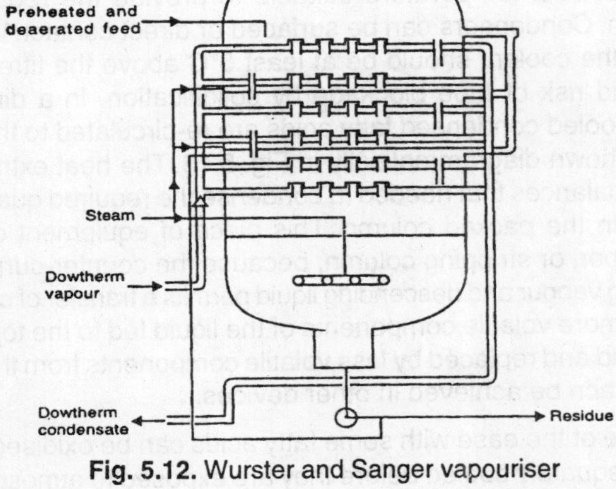

Fig. 5.12. Wurster and Sanger vapouriser

Falling film vapourisers are used by plant manufacturers when the fatty acids to be distilled are highly unsaturated and very heat sensitive. In some designs, the vapourisers are tubular heat exchangers with devices to cause the liquid to flow down as annular films inside the tubes. It might also be possible to use scraped wall vapourisers for glycerine distillation, provided the residue is sufficiently liquid to emerge satisfactorily from the base of the unit.

Fractionators, condensers and strippers

If the vapours leaving the vapouriser are liable to carry of liquid, it is desirable to remove these droplets as completely as possible to avoid contamination of the distillate; baffles, packed beds, or cyclones are used, but, as for all parts of the system, pressure drop is important.

To achieve a major separation of the components in a mixed vapour, as in the production of nearly pure lauric acid from coconut, or palm kernel, fatty acids, fractionating columns with substantial numbers of plates (or equivalent heights of packing), and using reflex and reboilers, are necessary. This exposes the liquid to increase time and temperature despite efforts which are usually made to hold as little as possible in the reboiler. Lauric oil fatty acids can withstand more drastic thermal conditions than the more unsaturated types (and they also have lower boiling points), so that more efficient fractionating columns can be used.

Simple columns may be used to separate good quality distillate from a relatively small low boiling fraction containing low molecular mass acids and volatile impurities; but these are usually stripping devices rather than columns with reboilers. This separation of an impure, low boiling, fraction is often achieved by the use of two separate condensers, arranged so that the vapours leave the first at a temperature suitable to provide the required partial condensation. Condensers can be surfaced or direct contact. With surface condensers the coolent should be at least 5°C above the titre of the fatty acids to avoid risk of tube blockage by solidification. In a direct contact condenser, cooled condensed fatty acids are re-circulated to the top of the column as shown diagrammatically in Fig. 5.13. The heat extracted in the liquid cooler balances that needed to condense the required quantity of fatty acid vapour in the packed column. This piece of equipment can also be called a stripper, or stripping column, because the counter-current contact between rising vapour and descending liquid permits a transfer of components. Some of the more volatile components of the liquid fed to the top of column are vapourised and replaced by less volatile components from the vapour. A similar effect acn be achieved in other devices.

Because of the ease with some fatty acids can be oxidised, distillates should be adequately cooled before they are exposed to atmospheric air.

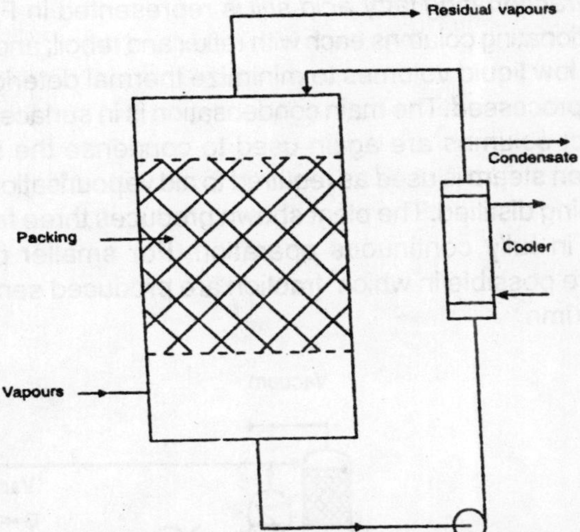

Fig. 5.13. Direct contact condenser/stripping column.

Complete stills

Many different types of fatty acid still have been, or still are, made and used.

Fig. 5.14 shows the *Lurgi simple distillation plant*. This uses the multi-compartment vapouriser (Fig. 5.10), A surface condenser for the main distillate, and a direct contact tower to strip the most volatile fraction from the steam. A special feature is the bubble cap tray in the top of the vapouriser on which the volatile components are stripped from the main distillate by the rising vapours.

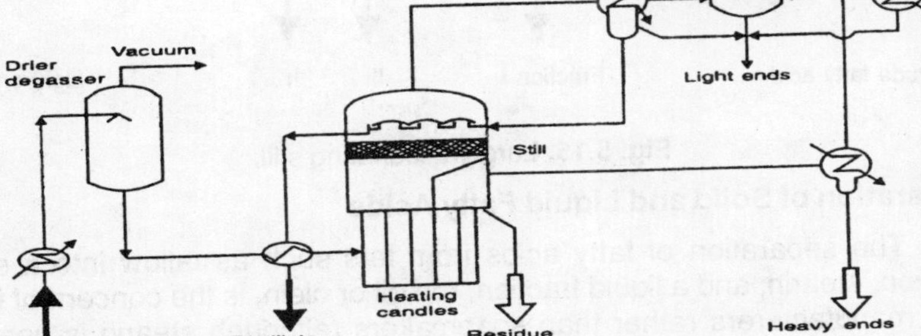

Fig. 5.14. Lurgi simple distillation unit.

The Lurgi fractionating fatty *acid still* is represented in Fig. 5.15. This includes two fractionating columns each with reflux and reboil; and the reboilers are said to have low liquid volumes to minimize thermal deterioration of the fatty acids being processed. The main condensation is in surface condensers, but direct contact columns are again used to condense the most volatile components. Open steam is used as required to aid vapourisation, depending upon material being distilled. The plant shown produces three fractions, plus the light ends, in fully continuous operation. For smaller plants, other arrangements are possible in which fraction are produced semi-batchwise from a single column.

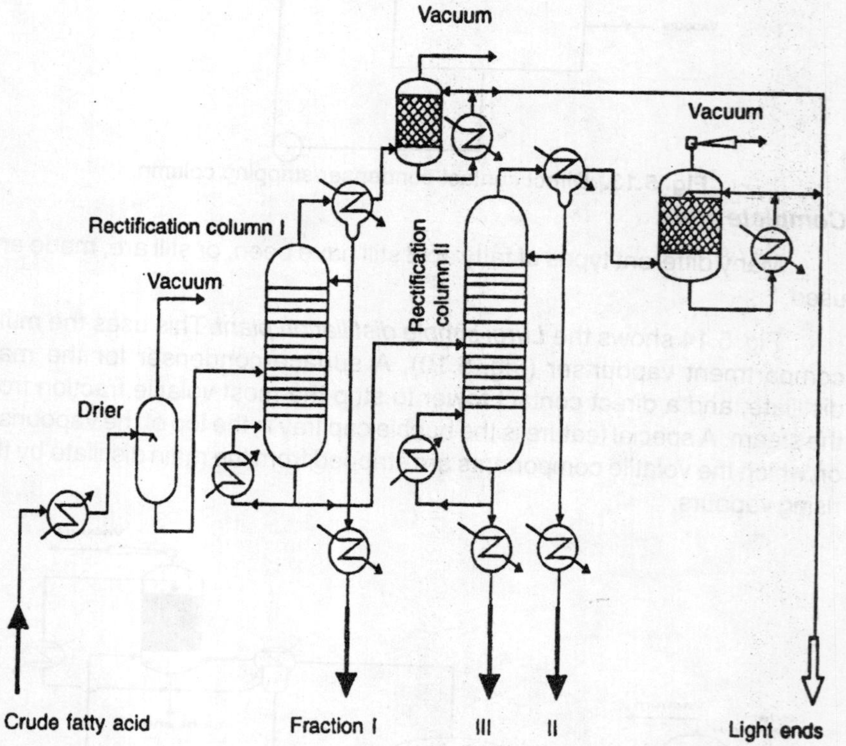

Fig. 5.15. Lurgi fractionating still.

Separation of Solid and Liquid Fatty Acids

The separation of fatty acids from fats such as tallow into a solid fraction, stearin, and a liquid fraction, red oil or olein, is the concern of fatty acid manufacturers rather than soapmakers (although stearin is used in shaving soaps); and the processes will only be mentioned briefly. The traditional method is to crystallise the fatty acids in trays, wrap the blocks in cloth and press. This gives single pressed stearin, and reprocessing with heated presses gives double and triple pressed stearin, which contain less unsaturated material than the single pressed grade. A more recent method involves crystallisation from a solvent; which is methanol in the Emersol process. Lurgi has a third of process in which stearin crystals wetted with a solution of wetting agent to give an aqueous dispersion which can be separated centrifugally from the non-dispersed olein phase

PRODUCTION OF SOAP BASE FROM FATTY ACIDS

Points to be considered in the selection of a process for the production of soap base from fatty include :

(i) As there is no glycerol to be recovered and, at least if distilled, the fatty acids should be clean, 'all-in' processes are attractive and are normally used. Alternatively, it is possible to follow neutralisation of the fatty acids by soapmaking operations including removal of a lye and/or a nigre; this makes the correct proportionation of fatty acids and alkali somewhat less critical, and removes dirt if the fatty acids are crude.

(ii) Sodium carbonate (soda ash) may be cheaper than caustic soda per unit of Na_2O and it can be used to neutralise fatty acids, although the operation is normally completed with caustic soda. Problems arise with the use of sodium carbonate because of the evolution of carbon dioxide gas, which needs to be separated and removed, and because of the formation of sodium bicarbinate. When neutralisation with sodium carbonate (to, say, 80%) is completed with caustic soda, any sodium bicarbonate reverts to sodium carbonate. The caustic soda can also saponify any glyceride in the fatty acids. Relevant reactions are :

$$2R.COOH + Na_2CO_3 \rightarrow 2R.COONa + H_2O + CO_2$$

$$R.COOH + Na_2CO_3 \rightarrow R.COONa + NaHCO_3$$

$$NaHCO_3 + NaOH \rightarrow Na_2CO_3 + H_2O$$

(iii) Neutralisation of fatty acids with concentrated (48% NaOH) caustic soda gives a soap at well above 63% TFM unless additional water is used and, if the soap is to be dried for the production of toilet soaps, it appears attractive to save heat in the drying process by neutralisation at a high TFM. Consider a blend of 80% tallow and 20% coconut oil (fatty acid ratio of blend about 8.55) neutralised with caustic soda solution containing 48% NaOH, or 37.2% Na_2O. Assume also an addition of 20% brine sufficient to give a salt content 0.5% NaCl and of refined glycerine to give 0.4%, both calculated on TFM. Salt is normally added, and glycerine sometimes, to give a composition similar to that of neat soap.

1 tonne fatty acid requires 1/8.55 tonnes Na_2O, or 1/8.55 ×100/37.2 = 0.314 tonnes of 48% caustic soda solution. Add 0.4/100 tonnes glycerine and 0.5/100 × 100/20 = 0.025 tonnes of brine, to give a total mass of 1.000 + 0.314 + 0.004 + 0/025 = 1.343 tonnes of soap with a TFM of 100/1.343 = 74.5%. If is desired to produce soap at 63% TFM, the total mass must be increased to 1.343 × 74.5/63 = 1.588 tonnes which requires additional water equal to 0.245 tonnes, or a dilution of the caustic soda solution to about 48 × 0.314/0.559 = 27%.

The simplest way to neutralise fatty acids with sodium carbonate is in a pan. An approximately saturated sodium carbonate solution is brought nearly to the boil and the fatty acids are added gradually. Sufficient time must be allowed between additions to permit the carbon dioxide to escape without the pan contents boiling or effervescing over. The saponification is completed with caustic soda.

COMPARISON BETWEEN SOAP MANUFACTURE BY DIRECT SAPONIFICATION AND BY THE FATTY ACID ROUTE

The comparison depends upon a number of circumstances which vary from factory to factory; and some important points are:

(i) The cost of the fatty raw materials, Splitting and distillation often permits the use of lower grade materials than are needed to produce soap of required quality by the direct saponification process, which may lead to substantial saving. The availability of suitable low cost by-products from edible oil plants may be important.

(ii) Possible use of sodium carbonate with the fatty acid route.

(iii) The yields of fatty acid converted into soap and of glycerol, taking into account material downgraded into lower quality soaps and to pitch discharged from fatty acid stills. Losses in pre-treatments, such as earth bleaching.

(iv) Initial capital costs; and capital and maintenance chages. High pressure splitting plants and fatty acid still are expensive. Some continuous direct soapmaking plants are costly, but efficient direct soapmaking plants can probably cost substantially less than modern splitting and distillation equipment.

(v) Cost of glycerine recovery. One of the factors which led to the development of the fatty acid route is the low concentration of glycerol in soap lyes then common; but, this difference has now been eliminated or greatly reduced. The fact that sweet waters do not contain salt is significant.

(vi) Other operating costs, including that for the high pressure steam, or other heating medium, used in the fatty acid route.

In addition to the cost comparison between the two routes as the major method of soap manufacture :

(i) Fatty acids may be needed for some products, such as certain modern soap powders

(ii) Companies which produce low grade by products, such as black cotton grease, may find it worthwhile to split and distil such materials,even if their main soapmaking is by direct saponification.

6

Recovery and Refining of Glycerine

Introduction

As explained in earlier chapters, the glycerol in fats is usually recovered in either soap lyes or sweet waters. Normally, these materials are purified and most of the water they contain is evaporated under conditions which do not vapourise any significant quantity of glycerol to give respectively soap lye crude glycerine or saponification, or hydrolyser, crude glycerine. Crude glycerine is normally purified by distillation is sometimes followed by bleaching and other treatments. Alternative processes which use ion exclusion and/or ion exchange instead of distillations are discussed in this chapter.

Some Analytical Tests And Specifications

It is convenient at this point to outline the main analytical tests used for glycerines and to consider some implications of the results which they give.

Glycerol Content

Glycerol content can be estimated by several methods. The standard method is now oxidation with periodic acid *(sodium periodate in acidic solution)* Glycerol is oxidised to formic acid according to the equation :

$$\underset{\text{glycerol}}{\begin{matrix} CH_2 & - & CH & - & CH_2 \\ | & & | & & | \\ OH & & OH & & OH \end{matrix}} + \underset{\text{periodic acid}}{2H10_4} \rightarrow \underset{\text{iodic acid}}{2H10_3} + \underset{\text{formaldehyde}}{2H{\cdot}CHO} + \underset{\text{formic acid}}{H{\cdot}COOH} + \underset{\text{water}}{H_2O}$$

The quantity of glycerol originally present in the sample is determined by titration with standard caustic soda of the formic acid formed under standard conditions. This test estimates as glycerol any compound which contains a groups $\begin{matrix} -CH & - & CH & - & CH- \\ | & & | & & | \\ OH & & OH & & OH \end{matrix}$ with three adjacent carbons each with a hydroxyl group attached. Such compounds include sugars and sugar alcohols (sorbitol, etc.) which are sometimes found in glycerines which have been contaminated with glycerine substitutes used in some food industries, or added in an attempt to defraud. On the other hand, TMG (trimethylene glycol, 1,3 dihydroxypropane, or propane 1,3 diol) and polyglycerols are not estimated as glycerol by this test. As considered later, TMG appears in some crude glycerines made from low-grade fats which have been stored badly, or, more particularly, from lyes which have been stored under conditions which permit destruction of glycerol by microorganisms. As well as indicating a destruction of glycerol, TMG in a crude glycerine can cause problems in the refining operations. Plyglycerols are formed by heating glycerol under certain conditions, particularly in the presence of alkaline, and other, catalysts. The reactions are of the type

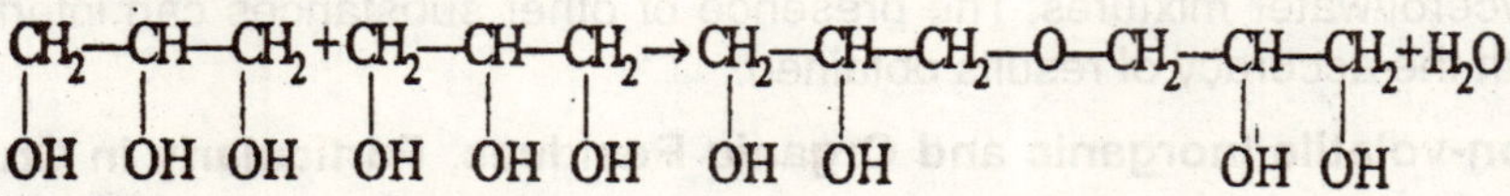

glycerol glycerol di-glycerol

Tri-glycerols, and higher members of the polyglycerol family, are formed by similar condensation reactions in which a molecule of water is eliminated between two hydroxyl groups to form an ether linkage. The reaction can occur between two primary alcohol,—CH_2OH, groups as shown, or a secondary alcohol group >CH–OH can be involved, so that many isomeric polyglycerols are possible.

Formation of polyglycerols, or, more strictly, avoidance of their formation, is important in glycerine distillation, and estimation of polyglycerols in still residues (foots) is often useful.

For many years before the development of the periodate method, the *acetin method* was standard for the estimation of glycerol. This involves acetylation of the glycerol with acetic anhydride and determination by hydrolysis with standard caustic soda, of the quantity of the ester tri-acetin formed. The acetin method includes as glycerol other hydroxyl compounds likely to be present, such as sugar, TMG and polyglycerols. Because of the elimination of hydroxyl groups when polyglycerols are formed, the acetin method does not return polyglycerols as the full amount of glycerols from which they were produced. Thus :

(i) Two molecules of glycerol contain 6 hydroxyl groups, but the diglycerol formed from them has only 4 hydroxyl groups.

(ii) Similarly tri-glycerol produced from three molecules of glycerol with 9 hydroxyl groups, contains only 5 hydroxyl groups.

The third important procedure for the estimation of glycerol is the *dichromate method.* This method, used particularly for soaps and lyes, involves removal of soapy, and other, impurities, followed by estimation of oxidisable matter calculated as glycerol. It includes all oxidisable compounds not removed in the preliminary purification of the sample. Because the condensation reactions in which polyglycerols are formed by elimination of water do not change the oxygen requirement for complete oxidation to carbon dioxide and water, the figure obtained for glycerol per cent includes any polyglycerols expressed in terms of the mass of glycerol from which they were formed.

For many purposes, the glycerol content of refined glycerines is estimated by determination of *specific gravity* at 15⁰C, or *relative density* measured at 20⁰C, and reference to tables giving the properties of pure glycerol/water mixtures. The presence of other substances can interfere with the accuracy of results obtained.

Non-volatile Inorganic and Organic Residues, Particularly in Crude Glycerines

The content of inorganic matter is determined as *percentage ash.* In the case of refined grades a little sulphuric acid is added during the determination to give *sulphated ash.*

For many years, important organic impurities in crude glycerines were estimated by determination of *total residue %,* the residue left after vapourisation of the glycerol under carefully controlled conditions in an oven at 160⁰C. The *organic residue (or)* was then total residue % – ash %.

More recently, organic residue has largely been replaced by *MONG %* (matter organic non-glycerol) which is defined as 100 – (ash + glycerol + water) %. Glycerol is determined by periodate and water by the Karl Fischer method. Determination of total residue is tedious and rather subject to error, so that MONG is more convenient. The figures found for OR and MONG are very similar for many crude glycerines, but there are differences which are significant under some circumstances :

(i) TMG is included in MONG, but not in OR, because it is more volatile than glycerol. Hence MONG should equal OR + TMG.

(ii) Any volatile alcohols, occasionally present in samples of glycerine including material from the alcoholysic of fats to form methyl, or ethyl, esters of the fatty acids, are included in MONG, but not OR.

(iii) Sugars, and other polyhydroxy compounds which increase the apparent glycerol content of a sample, artificially reduce MONG.

(iv) Polyglycerols and other relatively non-volatile organic compounds should be included in both MONG and OR, but substantial proportions of diglycerol, which is slowly volatile under total residue conditions, may make difficult the determination of the total residue end point (that is the stage at which the residue is deemed to have reached constant weight).

Nitrogen

Organic nitrogen which comes frm proteinaceous materials is sometimes found in quantities up to 0.5% as nitrogen in poor quality saponification crude glycerines made from low grade animal fats, although 0.025 – 0.15% is more usual. Crude glycerines with a high organic nitrogen content tend to give distillates with objectionable odours and colours. Many nitrogenous compounds have been found at low concentrations in such distillates, with 2-piperidone, a toxic substance, the most important. Washing the fats with sulphuric acid before they are split does not help much, but earth bleaching is often useful.

Arsenic

A limit for arsenic content is found in many glycerine specifications. At one time it was troublesome because of use in the factories which produced the crude glycerines of sulphuric acid contaminated with arsenic; but there is now seldom any problem.

Sodium Chlorate

Sodium chlorate is an unusual, and unexpected, constituent of crude glycerines, but it has sometimes been found in significant quantities which have caused explosions during distillation in some types of still. It arises from the use of caustic soda made in electrolytic cells which are incorrectly designed or operated. If crude glycerine containing sodium chlorate has to be processed, the chlorate can be reduced under strongly acidic conditions, for example with spent pickling acid derived from steel works which contains ferrous chloride and hydrochloric acid (see later for the possible use of such material in the purification of soap lyes).

Silver Tests for Reducing Substances in Refined Glycerines

Most specifications for refined glycerines include a test for reducing substances, such as aldehydes, which is based on the darkening which occurs with ammoniacal silver nitrate. In some cases comparison is made with the darkening produced by a standard quantity of dextrose (glucose). Different silver tests vary in sensitivity, so that conditions laid down in a particular specification must be followed precisely. Substances such as soluble phosphates derived from some activated carbons, can interfere with certain tests.

Fatty Acids and Esters in Refined Glycerines

The fatty acid and ester content of a refined glycerine is usually important; and most specifications include a test to measure the quantity of caustic soda reacted when the sample is boiled with an excess under standard conditions. For chemically pure grade this was known as soda absorption expressed in ml of N/10 NaOH absorbed in a standard test. Now it is commonly called saponification equivalent for all grades of refined glycerine and expressed as percentage Na_2O absorbed, or as milli-equivalents per 100 g. Fatty acids and esters in a distillate usually affect its odour and taste adversely.

Chlorides in Refined Glycerines

Most specifications include a test for sodium chloride based on reaction with silver nitrate. This may be expressed as maximum parts per million permitted, or in terms that the turbidity produced in the test is nil, or less than in a control. The sensitivity of this test makes important the almost complete exclusion of entrainment of still liquor when soap lye crude containing a high percentage of salt is being distilled. For specifications of glycerine (ref. BIS specification No. 12590-1988) and Glyceryl monostearate (ref. BIS specification No. 4236-1985).

Other Tests

Apart from tests for colour, odour, sugars, lead, and other heavy metals included in general specifications, some purchasers of glycerine impose tests specially relevant to the purpose for which they use the material.

Purification Of Soap Lyes And Sweet Waters

As already discussed soap lyes are now commonly neutralised with fatty matter before they leave the soapmaking department. They still contain some alkali, as well as soapy matter and other organic impurities, and a substantial percentage of salt (around 10%). If the older system of cooling and skimming, but not neutralisation, is used, the lyes contain a higher percentage of free alkali than in neutralised lyes. Sweet waters from high pressure splitters operated without catalyst only contain organic impurities of a fatty nature, plus some other compounds from the fats used. If the fats are split with the aid of a zinc oxide, or other alkaline, catalyst, the zinc, or other metal, leaves in the fatty acids, as a soap, and the sweet waters are little affected. Twitchell sweet waters contain some sulphuric acid, or sulphates, as well as organic impurities. The purification, or treatment, of the lyes, or sweet waters, is intended to remove organic compounds other than glycerol as completely as possible; and the success with which this is achieved is reflected in the MONG, or organic residue, of the crude glycerine produced.

The steps in the usual treatment of soap lyes are :

(i) *Acidification* to a pH of about 4.6 – 4.8, although this is often omitted if the lyes have been well neutralised with fatty acids. Acidification is preferably with hydrochloric, rather than sulphuric, acid to avoid introduction of sulphates into the system. It liberates fatty acids and those which are insoluble in water, although of elatively low molecular mass, separate on standing. They are removed from the settler, often periodically, and are sometimes returned to a low-grade soap, perhaps after filtration. These skimmed fatty acids are poor soapmaking material; they are low in molecular mass and contain hydroxy acids produced by oxidation, and they tend to give sodium salts which have little value and/or again dissolve in the next lyes.

(ii) *Purification* by addition of a soluble iron or aluminium salt, a stage normally called *first treatment.* The pH is kept at, or adjusted to, about 4.5–5.0 (often 4.6–4.8); and the mix is well agitated by compressed air blown in through perforations in a pipe near the base of the tank. This air also ensures that if iron is used it is oxidised to the ferric state and blowing should, if necessary, be continued until the mix is brown rather than greenish black. Oxidation is particularly necessary if sodium hydrosulphite is used in the soapmaking process. The precipitate may be ferric hydroxide, or aluminium hydroxide, on which fatty acids, proteinaceous matter, and other impurities are adsorbed; or basic salts of the low molecular mass fatty acids may be present, the precise chemistry is obscure. The two main precipitants are solutions of ferric chloride, $Fe\ Cl_3 6H_2O$, or of aluminium sulphate, sometimes called alum, $Al_2\ (SO_4)_3 18H_2O$. Ferrous chloride with excess acid, which is the residue left after hydrochloric acid has been used to pickle steel, state by bubbling in chlorine gas carefully through a porous diffuser. Excess acid can be reduced in concentration by allowing the spent pickling acid to stand in contact with scrap iron wire when additional iron goes into solution. It is preferable to use chlorides, rather than sulphates, in all additions to soap lyes, because otherwise sodium sulphate will build up in the recovered salt which is re-used in soapmaking, and because sulphates are liable to increase problems with scale in the evaporators. Aluminium chloride is, however, not a convenient material to handle; and when aluminium treatment is used the aluminium is usually added as a sulphate. Sodium aluminate can also be used as a source of aluminium, sometimes in conjunction with ferric chloride. Opinions differ as to the relative merits of iron and aluminium for the purification of soap lyes, but iron has the advantage that it can usually be added as chloride. The quantity of precipitant needed varies with the composition of the lyes, but about 0.1–0.2% of the hydrated ferric salt (added as a concentrated solution) is common, although more, up to about 0.4% may be required. The completion of the first treatment process is often checked by the filtration of a small sample and addition of a few drops of diluted precipitant to the clear filtrate. If the treatment process is complete, no precipitate should be produced, but a good end-point is not always obtained; the pH at which the test is carried out is important. The adequacy of the treatment is proved ultimately by the MONG of the crude glycerine produced. Lyes from soaps with a high proportion of good tallow are more easily treated than those from high lauric oil blends, or those from low-grade fats. A very high glycerol concentration in the liquor can also make effective treatment more difficult.

(iii) The first treatment mud is removed by filtration, normally with filter presses or leaf filters. It is often advantageous to allow the tank contents to settle, to filter first the lower layer, and to put the nearly clear upper layers through a clean press, or presses.

(iv) The filtrate is made slightly alkaline with caustic soda, in what is known as the *second treatment*. A pH of about 9 is common when the precipitant is iron, but a slightly lower alkalinity may be preferred with aluminium. Mixing and oxidation are again with air. A relatively small quantity of precipitate separates in the second treatment. It contains the excess iron or aluminium, silica, and a little organic matter.

(v) Finally, the treatment process is completed by a second filtration.

Variations in the details of the treatment process are possible, including estimation of the quantity of precipitant required by small scale tests. Single treatment processes have been devised in which, after precipitation of impurities with iron, or aluminium, as in the double treatment process, the mix is made slightly alkaline with sodium carbonate, or sodium bicarbonate, before being filtered once only.

Calcium chloride, followed by a second stage using sodium carbonate, has been used to treat soap lyes, but the purification is less good than with iron, or aluminium.

EVAPORATION OF PURIFIED LIQUORS TO CRUDE GLYCERINE

General

Many variations are possible in the design of plants for evaporation to crude glycerine. Points to be considered in the design of an evaporation plant to produce crude glycerine include :

(i) The capacity required in terms of water to be evaporated, crude glycerine produced, and, for soap lyes, salt to be separated.
(ii) Thermal efficiency and maximum consumption of steam.
(iii) Type of heating unit.
(iv) Arrangements for separation of salt, when relevant.
(v) Avoidance of undue losses of glycerol.
(vi) Vacuum equipment and other ancillaries.
(vii) Method of control.
(viii) Materials of construction.

Evaporation of Water, Separation of Salt and Production of Crude Glycerine

A simple procedure for the estimation of the relationships between the relevant quantities is illustrated by an example of a soap lye containing 4% glycerol, 11% salt and 85% water. Minor ingredients and losses are neglected.

	Lye	*Crude glycerine*	*Lye to produce 100 parts of crude glycerine contains*	*To be separated*
Glycerol	4	83	83	–
Salt	11	8	$\frac{11 \times 83}{4}$ x = 228	228-8 = 220
Water	85	9	$\frac{85 \times 83}{4}$ x = 1764	1764-9 = 1755
Total	100	100	2075	1975

Hence, to produce 1 part of 100% glycerol in crude :

(i) use $\frac{2075}{83} = 25.0$ parts lye

(ii) make $\frac{100}{83} = 1.2$ parts crude

(iii) evaporate $\frac{1755}{83} = 21.1$ parts water

(iv) separate $\frac{220}{83} = 2.7$ parts salt

(ii)–(iv) together: 25.0 parts

The results of similar calculations for lyes containing 4, 6, 10 and 15% glycerol respectively, plus 11% salt, evaporated to give a crude glycerine containing 83% glycerol, 8% salt and 9% water are sown in Table 6.1. The figures show how dramatically even a small increase in lye strength reduces the quantity of water to be evaporated, with consequent reduction in steam usage and evaporating capacity needed. It also reduces the quantity of salt to be recirculated. Similar calculations can be used to estimate quantities for the evaporation of treated lyes to semi-crude strength, or of sweet waters which do not separate salt.

Table 6.1. Quantities required and/or separated to produce 1 part of 100%glycerol in crude glycerine at 83% glycerol.

% glycerol in lye	*Parts lye used*	*Water evaporated*	*Salt separated*	*Crude glycerine produced*
4	25.0	21.1	2.7	1.2
6	16.65	13.7	1.75	1.2
10	10.0	7.8	1.0	1.2
15	6.65	4.8	0.65	1.2

Thermal Efficiency

In addition to steps to reduce the quantity of water to be evaporated, methods are available to minimise the usage of steam required to carry out the necessary evaporation. One kg of steam will evaporate approximately 1 kg of water fed at its boiling point, but less than 1 kg when the feed is at a lower temperature and sensible heat, which does not immediately produce vapour, has to be supplied before boiling commences. The boiling point of water, or any other liquid, falls as the pressure under which it is held is reduced. These simple facts provide the key to several ways in which the thermal efficiency of an evaporation system can be improved. Thermal efficiency is often and conveniently expressed in terms of kg of water evaporated per kg of steam supplied.

The main ways in which thermal efficiency can be improved are :

(i) *Multiple effect operation* in which the vapour from one evaporating vessel, or 'effect', becomes the heating steam in another effect operating under a lower pressure. In this way, the latent heat is used more than once.

(ii) *Vapour recompression* in which the vapour from a vessel is compressed, by a steam jet or by mechanical compressor, and returned as heating steam to the same evaporating unit. It will be appreciated that for the latent heat to be re-usable the pressue must be increased; and that a simple addition of superheat to the vapour will not do.

(iii) Selection of the optimum *method of feeding* the liquor to the evaporator; and/or the use of the heat exchangers. As discussed later, heat exchangers can be used internally between effects, or to recover heat from outgoing streams of vapour, condensate, or product.

(iv) Integration with other plants in the factory.

Before these procedures are considered, it is necessary to discuss boiling point elevation and temperature differences. Boiling point elevation is the difference between the boiling point of the solution in an effect and the boiling point of water under the pressure in the vapour space of the effect. It is due to two causes :

(i) *Boiling point elevation due to dissolved substances* in relation to fatty acid distillation, which increases as the concentration of dissolved substances increases. For semi-crude soap lye glycerine at 40–45% glycerol it is about 15°C; and for soap lye crude at 83% glycerol about 37°C.

(ii) *Boiling point elevation due to hydrostatic head.* When a liquid is heated at a distance below its surface, the pressure is that in the vapour space plus that equivalent to the head of liquid above the point at which the heat is supplied. 3 ft of glycerine of specific gravity 1.2 is equivalent to a hydrostatic pressure of 3 × 12 (1.2/13.4) = 3.2 inches of mercury, so that with a pressure of 2 inches Hg in the vapour space, the pressure at a depth of 3 feet is 5.2 inches Hg. The relative effect is clearly smaller when the pressue in the vapour space is higher. Boiling only occurs when the temperature reaches the boiling point under the prevailing pressure, but it is possible for the liquid to be heated to above its boiling point at the pressure in the vapour space and for it to flash when the liquid is circulated to a zone of lower pressure.

The apparent temperature difference, Δt_{ap}, is defined as the difference between the condensing temperature of the steam in the heater and the temperature at which water boils under the pressure in the vapour space. Consider, for example, a single effect evaporator in which the heating steam condenses at 5 psig, 109°C, and the vapour space has a pressure of 2 inches mercury at which water boils at 38°C. The apparent temperature difference is 109–38 = 71°C. If the liquid being boiled is crude glycerine with a boiling point elevation, bp_{elev} including any hydrostatic head effect, of 37°C, it will boil at 38 + 37 = 75°C; and the actual temperature difference Δt_{act}, is 109 – 75 = 34°C (or, alternatively, 71 – 37 = 34°C, the apparent temperature difference minus the boiling point elevation). This situation is depicted as case 1 in Fig. 6.1. If a double effect evaporator is used in which vapour from the first effect, which contains partially concentrated liquor with a boiling point elevation of 10°C boiling at 91°C, is used to boil crude glycerine under a pressure of 2 inches Hg in the second effect, the conditions are as shown as case 2. The various temperatures and pressures adjust themselves automatically to fulfil both heat transfer and heat balance requirements, so that the figures shown in Fig. 6.1 are approximate only and vary with conditions.

A positive Δt_{act} is essential in each effect in order to achieve heat flow and evaporation. With a natural circulation heater, particularly when the liquid is viscous, a Δt_{act} is required larger than the minimum which can be used with a forced (pump) circulation type of heater.

Case 3 in Fig. 6.1 shows approximate conditions for evaporation from lye to semi-crude glycerine in double effect using low pressure steam, a system which was once widely used.

Case 4 shows possible conditions for evaporation from lye to crude glycerine in triple effect using steam which condenses at 30 psig, 133°C.

Some general points related to these topics are :

(i) Boiling point elevation due to hydrostatic head varies with the design of the heaters and is assumed to be included in the figures for bp_{elev} used in Fig. 6.1. It does, however, reduce the effective temperature difference, even if the liquor is heated without boiling and only flashes when it arrives near to the liquor surface.

(ii) Boiling point elevation due to dissolved substances depends only on the composition of the liquor. It is high for crude glycerine; and this is a disadvantage of continuous operation in which the liquor in the effect from which the product leaves must be maintained at the product concentration. If an evaporator is operated semi-batch, that is the unit is fed with fresh liquor but the bulk of the product is not discharged unit its concentration reaches the desired level, the average boiling point elevation is lower and the average Δt_{act} higher, other things equal, than with continuous operation. At one time semi-batch operation to concentrate lye to semi-crude and, separately, semi-crude to crude glycerine was normal, but the usual advantages of continuous operation are now commonly considered to outweigh this disadvantage.

(iii) Forced circulation heaters, now often used in all effects, are particularly valuable for effects in which crude glycerine concentration is reached, as they permit operation with a low Δt_{act}, even when the liquid is quite viscous.

(iv) The need for an adequate Δt_{act} in each effect limits the number of effects which are physically with terminal conditions. In general, an increase in the number of leads to a reduction in steam consumption, but to an increase in capital cost. There is an economic optimum which may well use less than the maximum number of effects physically possible.

Double effect evaporators to concentrate lye to semi-crude were traditional for many years; and further concentration to crude glycerine was carried out in a separate single effect finisher, or in the second effect of the double effect unit operated either as a single effect using a connection directly to the steam supply, or as a double effect using water in the first effect. These plants used steam at only just above atmospheric pressure; and the supply commonly included exhaust from steam pumps and small steam engines. Increased emphasis on fuel economy led to the construction of at least one quadruple effect natural circulation evaporator to produce semi-crude glycerine from soap lyes. This was fed with steam at 90 psig and the pressure in the first effect heater rose to 30-50 psig depending upon conditions. Initially, this unit was operated semi-batch like its double effect predecessors, but it was found preferable to wok it continuously. Triple effect evaporators have been, and are, also used for soap lyes and sweet waters. They now commonly use forced circulation and take the concentration to crude glycerine strength. The concentration of glycerol in the lye, or sweet water, to be evaporated is an important factor in the design of the plant.

Vapour recompression evaporation with an electrically driven mechanical compressor is only likely to be economical when the compression ratio (that is, the ratio of the pressure of the heating steam to that of the vapour it produces by evaporation) is low, which means a low Δt_{app}. A low Δt_{act} can be achieved by the use of a forced circulation heater with a generous area of heating surface, but bp_{elev} is inevitably high if the unit is to produce

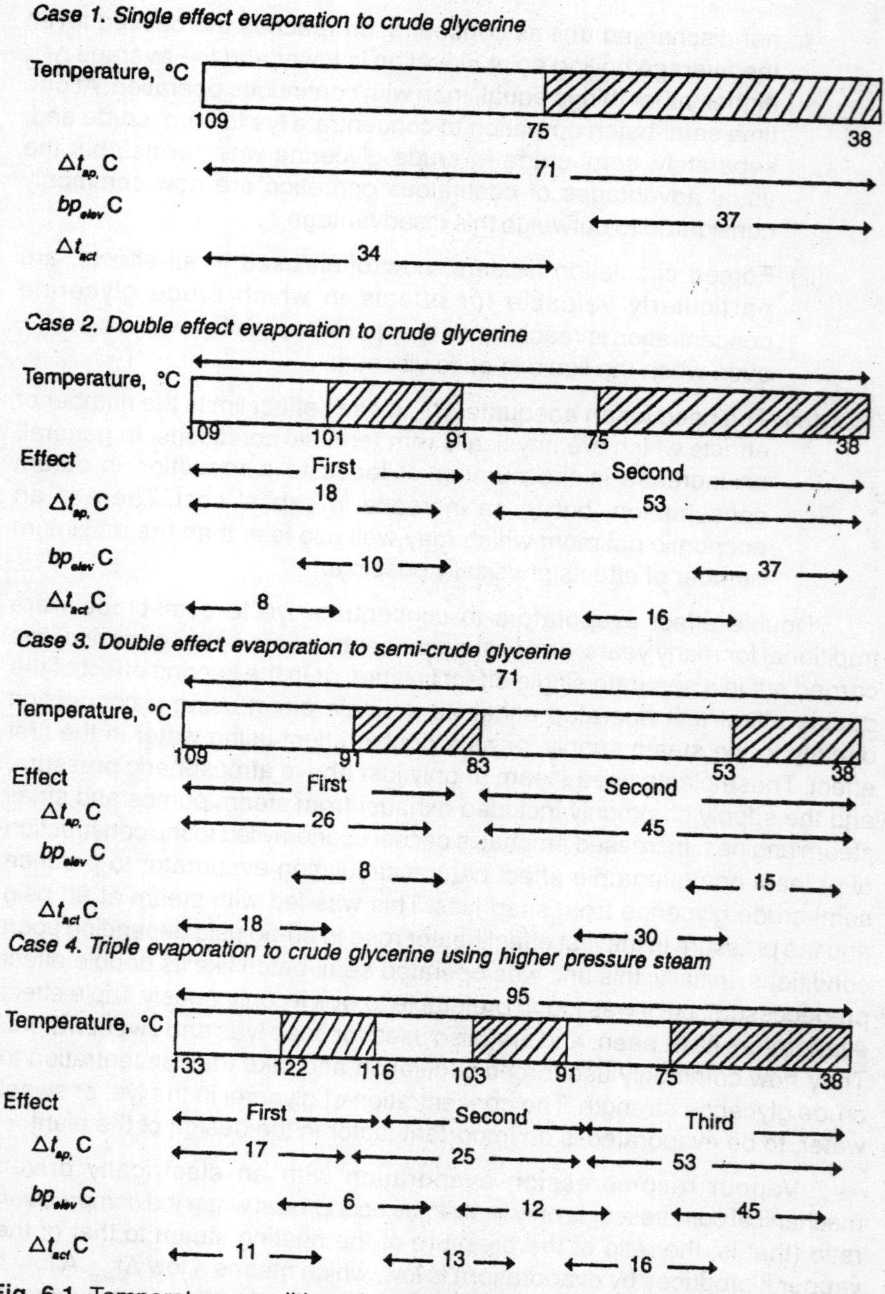

Fig. 6.1. Temperature conditions for single, double and triple effect evaporation to soap lye crude or semi-crude, glycerine.

crude glycerine; and mechanical recompression is not suitable for this duty. Jet recompression, combined with multiple effect operation, is valuable; and is now widely used steam at boiler pressure, rather than steam including low pressure exhaust, is to be the heating medium. Fig. 6.2 shows the main features of a triple effect system with jet recompression of part of the vapour leaving the first effect. Again, recompression is most effective when the pressure ratio is small, as it can be when the liquor concentration in the first effect is fairly low. When conditions permit satisfactory recompression, a useful improvement in thermal efficiency is achieved without increase in other costs and for only a very small additional capital cost for the jet.

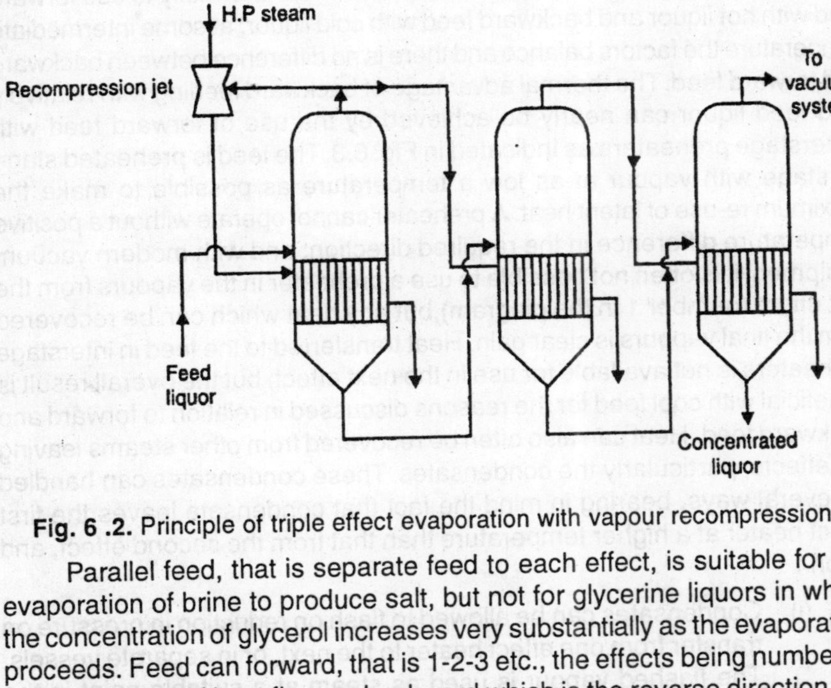

Fig. 6 .2. Principle of triple effect evaporation with vapour recompression.

Parallel feed, that is separate feed to each effect, is suitable for the evaporation of brine to produce salt, but not for glycerine liquors in which the concentration of glycerol increases very substantially as the evaporation proceeds. Feed can forward, that is 1-2-3 etc., the effects being numbered in the direction of heat flow; or backward which is the reverse direction, for example 3-2-1. The direction of feed often has an important influence upon steam consumption, depending upon the temperature of the feed liquor. If the feed is cold, it has to be heated to its boiling point under the pressure in the effect to which it goes. With forward feed, the temperature of the whole of the feed must be raised to the relatively high boiling point in the first effect by new steam and this sensible heat does not produce any vapour in that effect, although the heat in the party concentrated liquor does produce some vapour by flashing when it is transferred to the second and subsequent effects which operate under lower pressure than the first effect. With backward feed, a cold liquor is heated in stages as the unevaporated portion is transferred from effect to effect. Only the final portion which reaches the first effect is heated with new steam, and the sensible heating in the second and subequent effects is done by vapours from an earlier effect; that is by latent heat which has already been used one, or more, times in the evaporator. If the feed liquor is very hot, for example above the boiling point in the first effect, no sensible heat is required even with forward feed; and flash vapour is produced in each effect and forms part of the steam used in the next effect. With backward feed, the hot liquor flashes to the last effect and the latent heat is not used again, at least in the evaporator. The residual liquor then has to be re-heated to the temperature in its next effect, as for cold feed. These considerations show that it is beneficial thermally to use forward feed with hot liquor and backward feed with cold liquor; at some intermediate temperature the factors balance and there is no difference between backward and forward feed. The thermal advantage of backward feeding with relatively cold feed liquor can nearly be achieved by the use of forward feed with insterstage preheaters as indicated in Fig. 6.3. The feed is preheated stage by stage with vapour at as low a temperature as possible to make the maximum re-use of latent heat. A preheater cannot operate without a positive temperature difference in the required direction; and with modern vacuum equipment it is often not possible to use a preheater in the vapours from the last effect (number 1 in the diagram),but any heat which can be recovered from the final vapours is clear gain. Heat transferred to the feed in interstage preheaters is not available for use in the next effect, but the overall result is beneficial with cool feed for the reasons discussed in relation to forward and backward feed. Heat can also often be recovered from other steams leaving the effects, particularly the condensates. These condensates can handled in several ways, bearing in mind the fact that condensate leaves the first effect heater at a higher temperature than that from the second effect, and so on :

(i) Condensates can be allowed to flash on reduction in pressure on transfer from one effect heater to the next, or in separate vessels. The flashed vapour is used as steam at a suitable point in the system, and the residual hot, or warm, water remains available. This condensate can be re-used as process water in the soapmaking or fat-splitting process, as well as a source of heat.

(ii) Unflashed, or flashed, condensate can be used in a heat-exchanger.

Other factors to be considered in the selection of a system of feeling are :

(i) With forward feed the most concentrated liquor is evaporated at the lowest temperature, so that its viscosity is higher than that of the fully concentrated liquor using backward feed. This adversely heat transfer, particularly with natural circulation heaters.

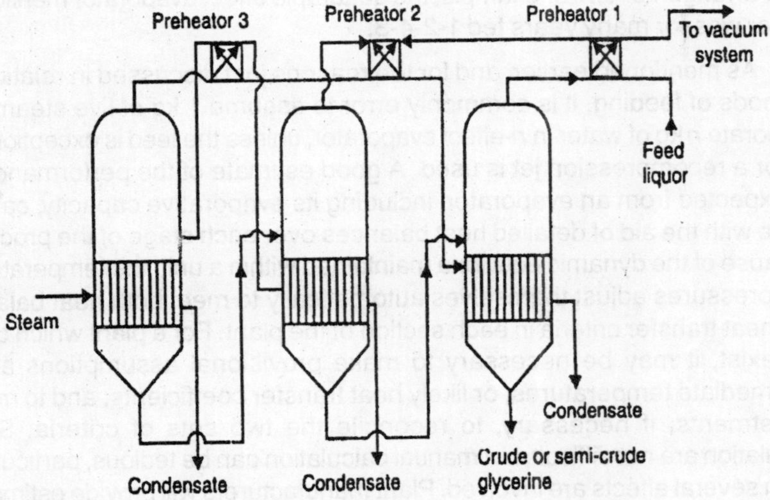

Fig. 6.3. Evaporation with forward feed and interstage preheaters.

(ii) More sensible heat leaves in the crude, or semi-crude, with backward than with forward feed; but some of this may be recoverable in heat exchangers.

(iii) Liquor can normally be transferred from effect to effect by pressure difference with forward feed, although a pump may be needed to introduce the feed liquor into the first effect. With backward feed it is normally possible to suck the feed liquor into the last effect, but pumps are needed for transfer from effect to effect, unless unusual levels are adopted which provide sufficient gravity head to more than offset the adverse pressure differences between the vapour spaces.

(iv) The salt crystals which separate during the evaporation of soap lyes are rather fine; and they tend to become finer with rise in the temperature at which they are separated and with increase in the glycerol content of the liquor. Fine crystals are more difficult to wash effectively than coaser ones. The same factors also tend to induce 'salting' of the heater tubes, a phenomenon discussed later. Salting can be a serious problem with natural circulation soap lye evaporators under some conditions and forward feed may then be advisable.

When the feed liquor is relatively cool it is usual to use forward feed with interstage preheaters. For special reasons, it is also possible to use other arrangements. For example, the quadruple effect evaporator mentioned earlier was for many years fed 1-2-4-3.

As mentioned earlier, and for the reasons just discussed in relation to methods of feeding, it is commonly error to assume 1 kg of live steam will evaporate *n* kg of water in *n*-effect evaporator, unless the feed is exceptionally hot or a recompression jet is used. A good estimate of the performance to be expected from an evaporator, including its evaporative capacity, can be made with the aid of detailed heat balances over each stage of the process. Because of the dynamic equilibria maintained within a unit, the temperatures and pressures adjust themselves automatically to meet both heat balance and heat transfer criteria in each section of the plant. For a plant which does not exist, it may be necessary to make provisional assumptions as to intermediate temperatures, or likely heat transfer coefficients; and to make adjustments, if necessary, to reconcile the two sets of criteria. Such calculation are not difficult, but manual calculation can be tedious, particularly when several effects are involved. Plant manufacturers will provide estimates in response to serious enquiries, doubtless by the use of computer programmes, but it is sometimes useful for an operator to estimate what is likely to result from changes such as the inclusion of additional heat exchanger, or a different feed arrangement. In making such estimates, it must be remembered that any change is likely to induce other changes to maintain the dynamic equilibria.

As a first approximation it is sometimes assumed that an *n*-effect evaporator costs *n* times as much as a single effect plant for the same duty, because the overall temperature difference is split between the effect with a consequent need for additional heating surface. This is also subject to considerable error. Estimates obtained some years ago from a well-known plant manufacture for single and double effect units for the same, rather small, duty showed that the cost of the double effect was substantially less than twice that for the single effect. At least in part this was because of the larger final entrainment separator, condenser, and vacuum equipment needed for the single effect unit in which the whole of the water evaporated passes to the condenser.

The discussion of thermal efficiency has so far considered the evaporator alone, but it is sometimes worthwhile to involve other plant. Steam from another unit which is not at high enough pressure to be used as first effect steam may be able to be introduced between effects.Similarly, vapour can sometimes be bled between effects for use elsewhere. Different plant units commonly do not synchronise at all times, so that it is usually necessary to provide an alternative steam supply, probably through a reducing valve. Surplus heat from a high pressure fat splitting plant can often be used in the evaporation of the sweet water.

Types of Heating Unit

Long tube climbing film heaters, in which much vapourisation takes place in the tubes, are used for sweet waters, but are not suitable for soap lyes, because the tubes would block with salt. Traditionally, short tube natural circulation evaporators were usual for soap lyes. These have a bundle of vertical tubes (say 1-2 m long) arranged in a steam chest to give what is called a calandria. Commonly calandrias built the main evaporator bodies, and provided with downcomers of various designs, such as a sector, a larger central hole, or a series of tubes larger than the boiling tubes, are used. The liquor circulates up the small tubes and returns through the downcomers. It is also possible to have natural circulation evaporators in which the liquor rises through the vertical tubes in an external heater and returns via the liquor reservoir in the main body. In order to obtain the maximum rate of heat transfer, and hence of evaporation, it is necessary to work with a static level of liquid below the top of the tubes, so that some vapourisation takes place in the tubes giving an increased rate of circulation due to the vapour lift effect. With soap lyes care must be taken to avoid too low a static level, as otherwise salt will deposit in the tubes in effects in which the liquor is saturated with salt. Salting of the tubes can sometimes occur when an evaporator is being operated in a way which would normally be satisfactory; this is presumably due to some small changes in the composition of the purified lye. It is also sometimes possible to operate natural circulation evaporators with a static level well above the upper tube plate of the calandria, particularly when finishing batchwise to crude strength. In this case, the liquid is heated in the tubes to above its boiling point at the pressure in the vapour space and flashed as it rises to a region of lower hydrostatic pressure. It is usually necessary to avoid operation at some intermediate levels at which 'priming', or boiling over, is liable to occur.

Evaporator effects in which salt separates usually need to be washed out at regular intervals with water, or with other liquor which is not saturated with salt. When a plant is operated semi-batch, rather than continuously, the charge of concentrated crude, or semi-crude, containing some salt, is discharged from the last effect; and it is common practice to start the next batch by refilling with unsaturated lye, or even water, to dissolve deposited salt. If the tubes become blocked with salt, it is necessary to soak with water and to boil as long as is needed to clear them. Mechanical methods are sometimes used, but care is necessary to avoid damage and this procedure is best avoided if possible. Various insoluble scales can build up slowly in the tubes of glycerine evaporator and these normally have to be removed mechanically. Scales can contain silica, but they are particularly common when lye, sweet water, or other liquor containing sulphate and calcium is introduced, for example, if the plant is washed out with hard water. Calcium carbonate scales are also encountered; can sometimes be removed by careful use of acid. The modern tendency is to use external calandries with forced circulation by pump. This system improves heat transfer, and so permits the use of less heating surface and/or a lower Δt_{act}. External heaters with forced circulation minimise the risk of salting and scaling; and an external heater can be arranged to permit machanical descaling more readily than an internal calandria. As mentioned earlier, forced circulation is useful for the final effect of an evaporator in which crude glycerine is produced.

Whatever type of heater is used, it is necessary for satisfactory heat transfer to remove effectively both condensate and non-condensible gases, mainly air. When the pressure in steam chest is above atmospheric, ordinary steam traps can be used for the condensate; and air can be discharged, with a little steam, through a slightly opened vent valve, or cock. For steam chests at below atmospheric pressure, the air must be vented through a small connection to a vapour space at a sufficiently low pressure; and a pumping trap, or used for the condensate. A convenient system for the condensate is shown in Fig. 6.4. The centrifugal pump runs continuously, but discharge of condensate is intermittent. The condensate is virtually at its boiling point at the pressure in the steam chest and can only be pumped when there is a sufficient head of liquid in the receiver to prevent vapourisation (cavitation) in the pump. The level in the receiver rises until the pump starts to discharge and then falls untill flow virtually ceases; the cycle being repeated indefinitely.

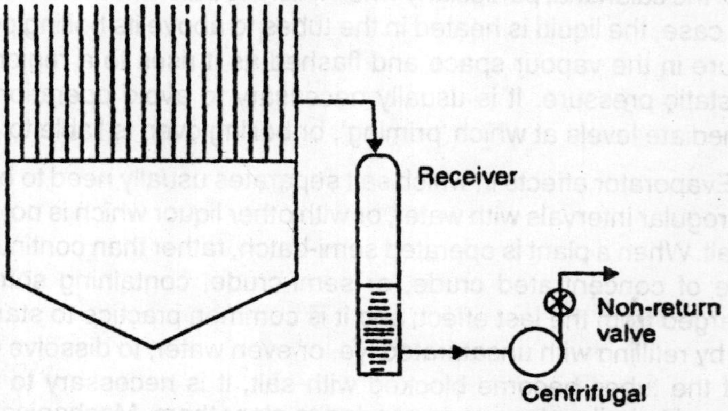

Fig. 6.4. Arrangement for discharge of condensate from a vessel at sub-atmospheric pressure.

Removal and Recovery of Salt in the Evaporation of Soap Lyes

All effects in which the lyes have become saturated, and solid separates, need a facility for the removal of the solid as soon as possible after it is formed and the crystals have grown to a reasonable size, otherwise the liquor may become unduly thick. Effects which do not normally produce salt may be fitted with simple vessels to collect sludge and any abnormal salt. Three systems are, or have been, used :

(i) Salt filters, or dry salt boxes.

(ii) Wet salt boxes.

(iii) Devices through which the effect content are circulated, a thickened slurry is discharged, and substantially clear liqour is returned to the effect.

Dry salt boxes are messy, labour intensive, and do not permit adequate removal of glycerol from the salt to meet the requirements of efficient modern soapmaking. In the larger, the more factories efficient, they were replaced many years ago, but they are still in use in some places. The other two systems remove the solid salt from the evaporator in the form of a slurry in a more, or less, concentrated glycerine liquor; and the separation process is completed in some form of centrifuge.

The operation of dry and wet salt boxes can be explained by reference to Fig. 6.5. In both types salt settles into the quite zone of the effect body below the calandria and down into the salt box. A sufficiently deep cone and settling zone is important; and, if the plant is to be operated semi-batch, sufficient liquor volume is necessary in the last effect to hold an adequate batch of crude, or semi-crude, glycerine. Consider now a dry salt box as shown in Fig. 6.5a. The salt settles onto the grid and filter gauze. When sufficient salt has collected, valve A is closed, valve B is opened, and the liquor is drawn back into the effect, helped by the pressure of the steam introduced through the valve at the top of the box. The bed of salt is washed with lye, and/or water, and the liquor is again displaced by steam. The steam valve and valve B are closed, the vent atmospheric opened, and the door on the box opened. The salt is shovelled out for return to the soapmaking department as solid salt, or as brine. The door of the box is closed, the box is evacuated through the balance valve C, and valve A opened to commence another cycle. It is particularly important to ensure that the box is fully evacuated before valve A is opened; otherwise expansion of the air from the box will cause the liquor in the effect to prime. It is also important to ensure that air cannot leak in through the valves; lubricated cocks have been found useful for these duties.

Wet salt boxes can be cylindrical drums, or vessels of any other convenient shape. They are operated in a manner similar to, but somewhat more simply than the dry boxes. When sufficient salt has accumulated, as judged by inspection through sight glasses, or in accordance with a time schedule, valve A is closed, valve B and vent are opened and the slurry is run out and/or blown out with steam after the vent has been reclosed. The box is evacuated via valve C before it is reconnected to the effect.

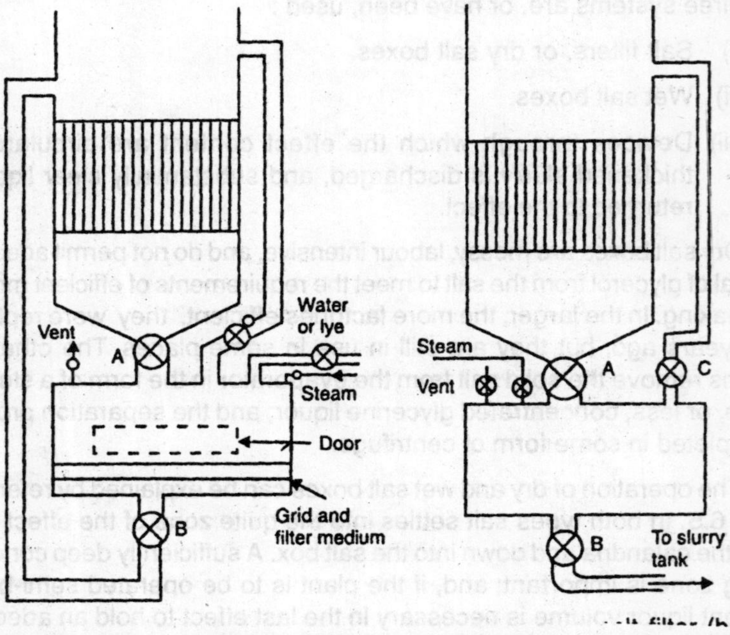

Fig. 6.5. The operation of salt boxes. (a) Dry salt box, or salt filter (b) Wet salt box.

Pairs of boxes, dry or wet, and used alternately, are common on effects in which larger quantities of salt are produced. If only one box is fitted, salt accumulates in the cone of the effect whilst the box is disconnected. Discharge by continuous pumping from the base of the effect is arranged as shown in Fig. 6.9 later for a evaporator which uses a baffled settling vessel. Thickened slurry is discharged from the base of the vessel and the rest of the liquor is returned to the effect and/or transferred to the next effect. Sufficient pressure is maintained in the circulation loop by the pump and the valves in the return and transfer lines to enable the discharge of thickened slurry to be controlled by a valve without another pump. Hydroclones (liquid cyclones) instead of the baffled vessels have been found very satisfactory separating devices for systems of this kind. Care must be taken not to interfere with the circulation through the heater tubes if a continuous pumping system is introduced into a natural circulation evaporator. An attempt to do this many years ago produced a well thickened slurry, but led to unacceptable salting of the calandria tubes. Return of the circulated liquor to the base of the effect, with sufficient volume below the calandria, may prevent this difficulty. The system works well forced circulation effects and is probably best modern practice.

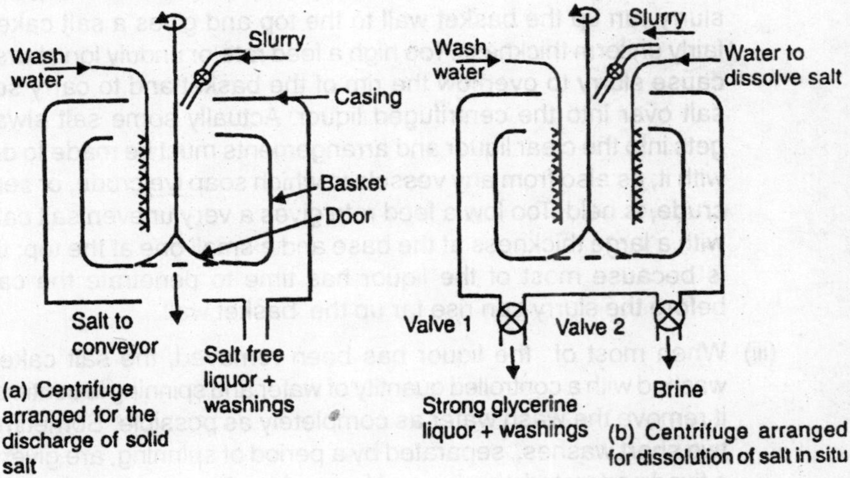

Fig. 6.6. Batch salt centrifuge, (a) arranged for the discharged of solid salt, (b) arranged for dissolution of salt in *situ*.

It is necessary to separate the solid salt in the slurry removed from the evaporator from the liquor, and to wash the salt as free from glycerol as is economically feasible. Some washing with lye may be possible, but mainly fresh water is used; and this water has to be evaporated, which sets a limit to the amount of washing which is worthwhile. Traditionally, basket centrifuges operated batchwise are used, and the salt is discharged as a crystalline powder. It is returned to the soapmaking department as such, or after solution in water, preferably condensate, to form a near saturated brine. Modern soapmaking plants use only brine; and systems have been developed in which the salt is dissolved in the centrifuge itself. Alternatively, the salt is dissolved in separate unit. When sulphate is introduced into the system, by use of aluminium sulphate or sulphuric acid, it is necessary to discard some recovered salt from time to time to prevent undue build up of sodium sulphate in the salt. The batch centrifuges used are normally of the suspended basket type; and some points regarding their use are discuused in relation to Fig. 6.6.

(i) Perforate basket machines are used; and the filter medium is a fine weave metal gauze backed by coarse gauze to facilitate drainage. A high speed to give a high centrifugal force is desirable to remove the liquors from the solid salt as completely as possible.

(ii) The slurry should be fed with confidence in intermittent bursts having a high rate of flow. A 4" pipe with a control cock operated with a long handle is convenient. This rate of feed makes the slurry run up the basket wall to the top and gives a salt cake of fairly uniform thickness. Too high a feed rate,or unduly long bursts, cause slurry to overflow the rim of the basket and to carry solid salt over into the centrifuged liquor. Actually some salt always gets into the clear liquor and arrangements must be made to deal with it; as also from any vessels in which soap lye crude, or semi-crude, is held. Too low a feed rate gives a very uneven salt cake, with a large thickness at the base and a small one at the top; this is because most of the liquor has time to penetrate the cake before the slurry can rise far up the basket wall.

(iii) When most of the liquor has been removed, the salt cake is washed with a controlled quantity of water and spinning is continued it remove the wash water as completely as possible. Sometimes two short washes, separated by a period of spinning, are given. If a fixed perforated pipe is used for wash water, care must be taken to ensure that it does not interfere with the discharge of the salt and a spray on a flexible hose is an alternative. Timers to help the operatives to adhere to a cycle laid down by the management are useful. in order to reduce the glycerol content of the salt to the required level with a minimum use of wash water, careful control is essential, particularly of the time during which the water is sprayed.

(iv) With the system shown in Fig.6.6(a),the machine is stopped, the door over the bottom outlet raised and held up on a hook, and the salt dug out to fall into a conveyor, or receptable, below. A narrow spade with the cutting edge cut at an angle is useful for this work. When lower speed, and less efficient, centrifuges were used, a rope placed roune the bottom of the basket before the slurry was fed provided a simple means to dislodge the salt cake. The end of the rope had a hook which held it to the upper rim of the basket; and this end was pulled to bring down the salt at the end of the cycle .However, well washed and dried salt in modern machines is normally too hard for this technique to be used.

(v) With the system shown in Fig.6.6(b),valve 1 is open and valve 2 closed during most of the cycle for the glycerine liquor and the washings to flow away. When the salt has been washed and dried, valve 1 is closed, valve 2 opened,and a controlled flow of water introduced to dissolve the salt. With proper adjustment of the conditions the salt can substantially all be dissolved to produce nearly saturated brine. Care is necessary to ensure that the casing is arranged to allow the two streams of liquid to drain with minimum contamination one with the other. Also that the valves close tightly, and that the operators control the valves and sprays with care. With proper precautions, this system can give very satisfactory results without the heavy manual labour required with system(a).

In large factories, the modern trend is to automatic centrifuges. Several types have been used, but some have not been very successful because either they could not handle fine glycerine salt satisfactorily, or because they need too much wash water to reduce the glycerol in salt to the required level. The best type is probably one in which the operation is very short cycle,automatic batch.The salt is discharged with a knife; and it is a useful refinement for the knife mechanism to be arranged so that the cut leaves a slightly different thickness of salt inconsecutive cycles in order to minimise the formation of a 'glaze' of very fine broken crystals which may impair drainage.

The glycerol left in salt varies considerably with the system employed,the quantity of wash water used, and the care with which the operation is carried out. With centrifuges 0.4 -0.6%glycerol on salt should be possible, but figures from 0.2 -0.1%are quoted. With dry salt boxes,1% is sometimes claimed, but 2-4% is probably more usual (corresponding figures calculated on saturated brine are about one quarter of those for salt).

Minimisation of Losses of Glycerol

During evaporation, liquor containing glycerol and salt can be lost by being carried out in liquid/solid form with the vapours and discharged in a condensate. The carry -over can be as droplets, foam, or, if a serious prime occurs, as bulk liquid. To minimise this loss:

(i) Adequate vapour space should be provided above the level of the boiling liquid.

(ii) Suitable separators, and external 'catchalls',usually cyclonic, should be included in the system. It is useful to provide sight-glasses in external separators, and/or the return lines, so that the plant operator can see immediately when any serious carry-over occurs and take remedial action,

(iii) The liquor levells in the effects should be controlled with care, automatically or manually.

(iv) The treatment of the lyes, or sweet water, should ensure that the liquors have no undue tendency to foam.

External catchalls are sometimes fitted only to the effect in which the concentration of glycerol is highest. Devices which measure roughly the electrical conductivity of the condensate from the evaporated vapours are very useful indicators of carry-over.That actually indicate the presence of salt, or other electrolyte, but this is relevant as salts and glycerol are carried over together.The main problem is to obtain a contonuous flow of condenser is used in the vacuum system; and the condensate is mixed with cooling water. It is not essential to obtain a representative sample of the vapours plus any entrained liquor; all that is necessary is to get a sample which will indicate when any abnormal amount of salt is present in the vapours, and this can often be achieved by the use of a small partial condenser in the vapour line. For example,a ring carrying cold water placed above a collecting tray, in vertical vapour main, as shown in Fig 6.9, can be used.There is a continuous flow of condensate through the box containing the electrodes which are connected to a suitable low A/c voltage and a measuring instrument or, better, recorder. An audible alarm can be included to draw immediate attention to any substantial increase in conductivity.

Losses of glycerol during evaporation can occur in other ways, for example, if a leak develops in a calandria. The effects are normally left containing water during shut-downs(to dissolve deposited salt) and ,if a leak is present, some salt solution can be drained from the steam chest of the calandria after the plant has stood for a period of time.

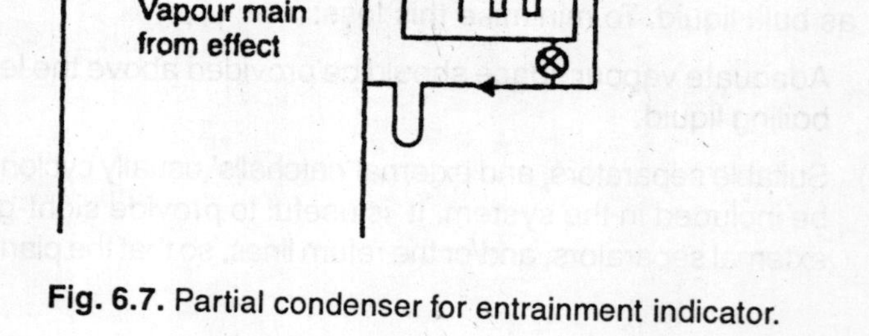

Fig. 6.7. Partial condenser for entrainment indicator.

Fig. 6.8 shows the flow of glycerol through a soap factory with glycerine recovery; and indicates the sources of loss. The diagram is drawn for a double-effect evaporator with direct contact condenser; and refers to closed coils in soap pans. Such coils are now obsolete, but they can be a serious source of loss of present. The diagram can readily be modified to suit other plant arrangements and similar ones prepared for the splitting route. It is useful to determine the recovery in each section of the factory, particularly if the overall loss is high,but this is usually not done easily;and, for routine purposes, those with limited resources may find it best to concentrate on checks on the controllable losses, and the important glycerol in re-cycled salt. Care is necessary to ensure that truly average samples of materials such as muds are tested. Misleading samples of treatment mud can be taken from near he point at which water is introduced into the filter presses.

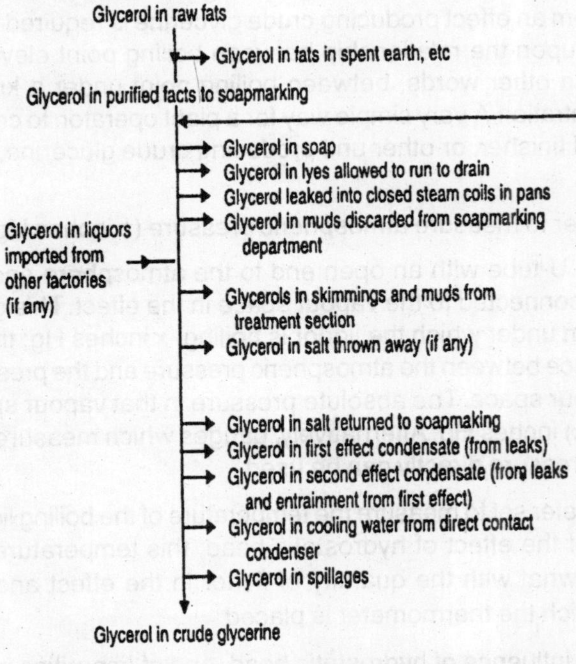

Fig. 6.8. Flow of glycerol through a soap and glycerine factory.

Vacuum Maintenance

Glycerine evaporators now normally operate at 2-4 inches Hg absolute pressure(28-26 inches Hg vacuum with 30 inches Hg barometric pressure); and a high-level direct contact condenser with barometric leg is commonly used. The non-condensible gas can be removed with a two-stage ejector system, with an intermediate condenser, or by a mechanical vacuum pump.

Because of the level of pressure needed in a glucerine evaporator,no booster jets are normally installed.The direct contact main condenser can be replaced by a surface condenser if the condensate from the last effect is required, for example,for use with other condensates in the splitting section of a fatty acid plant.

Evaporator Control

Traditionally glycerine evaporators were controlled manually,but standard instrumental control techniques are now used to make operation increasingly automatic. Possible difficulties due to dissolved and solid salt must be remembered with soap lye evaporators. Also,the influence of vapour on the apparent density of boiling liquid in, for example,a natural circulation evaporator.

A reliable indication of the concentration of glycerol in the material being discharged from an effect producing crude glycerine is required .This is frequently based upon the relationship between boiling point elevation and concentration; in other words, between boiling point under a known pressure and concentration.A very simple way for a plant operator to control a manually operated finisher, or other unit producing crude glucerine, is to provide:

(i) A barometer to measure atmospheric pressure (*b* inches Hg).

(ii) A mercury U-tube with an open end to the atmosphere and the other end connected to the vapour space in the effect. This gives the vacuum under which the liquor is boiling, *x* inches Hg; that is the difference between the atmospheric pressure and the pressure in the vapour space. The absolute pressure in that vapour space is thus (*b-x*) inches Hg. Alternatively, gauges which measure this absolute pressure directly can be used.

(iii) A thermometer set to measure the temperature of the boiling liquid. Because of the effect of hydrostatic head, this temperature will vary somewhat with the quantity of liquor in the effect and the point at which the thermometer is placed.

Because of the influence of hydrostatic head, and of impurities in the crude glycerine being produced, it is necessary to calibrate the system by the analysis of samples taken in relation to various sets of readings. Roughly, a boiling temperature of about 77°C with an absoluate pressure of 2 inches Hg indicates 83% glycerol in a soap lye crude glycerine. It has also been found that an extra 0.1 inch Hg pressure requires an extra 1°C in boiling liquor temperature. Hence, if 77°C is found to be correct for 2.0 inches Hg,

79°C will be about right for 2.2 inches Hg pressure, and 74°C for 1.7 inches Hg pressure.

Materials of construction for Glycerine Treatment and Evaporation Plants

Traditionally, mild steel, wrought iron, or cast iron tanks and pipes have been used for soap lye treatment plants, with cast iron filter presses clothed with cotton cloths. Particularly for the early stages of treatment carried out under acidic conditions, the presence of chlorides and blowing and blowing with air give highly corrosive conditions; and the life of tanks is short. The lining of such tanks with rubber, cement, or some acid resistant plastic coating, is highly desirable. Cast iron filter presses have a reasonably long life, although it is often useful to scarpe the grooves in the plates from time to time. Expensive polypropylene filter plates are now sometimes used; and it may be desirable to assess the economics of using polyester cloths.

For many years, cast-iron was used for the bodies of soap lye evaporators, with arsenical copper tubes in the caladrias and heat exchangers. Such evaporators lasted a very long time; examples are known where the cast-iron bodies were very difficult to break-up after a life of about forty years, although they had been re-tubed 3-4 times during this period. These evaporators used exhaust steam, plus make-up, at about 4 psig in the main, and less in the actual calandrias. The adverse effect of higher temperatures, resulting from the use of higher pressure steam, is shown dramatically by experience with the quadruple-effect evaporator mentioned earlier. The arsenical copper tubes in the first effect calandria lasted only 1-2 years; and the rate of corrosion fell with reduction in temperature from first to last effect. Experiments showed that monel metal was a particularly good material for tubes, but that the less expensive cupronickels (including the cheapest 90 : 10 type) were adequate for the duty. The cast-iron bodies also behaved less well than expected, but this may have been due, at least in part, to the quality of war time cast iron. Special cast irons, such as Ni-resist, have also been used for the bodies of soap lye evaporators. Copper has been used successfully for the bodies of sweet water evaporators.

These traditional materials are still recommended by some plant manufacturers, but others alternatives, include mild steel. Sacrificial anodes of aluminium have sometimes been found beneficial in reducing the corrosion of mild steel, or cast-iron, evaporators.

The baskets of centrifuges used for salt separation have to withstand high stresses as well as corrosive conditions. Mild steel was normally used, but, with modern, more efficient, machines, failures, particularly at welds, are known. High nickel alloys (or, perhaps certain stainless steels), with the necessary mechanical properties as well as corrosion resistance, should normally be selected. Design to avoid high stresses is very important, whatever metal is selected; and rivetted, rather than welded, side seams may be advantageous.

Complete Evaporation Plants

It will be appreciated that many combinations of plant elements are possible. Figs. 6.9 to 6.13 outline some examples. Fig. 6.9 shows a backward feed, double-effect, evaporator, for soap lyes, directly connected to a single effect finisher. Heating is in natural circulation calandrias; and extraction of salt slurry is by continuous pumping through separating vessels. Salt is recovered from the slurry in a batch centrifuge, or centrifuges.

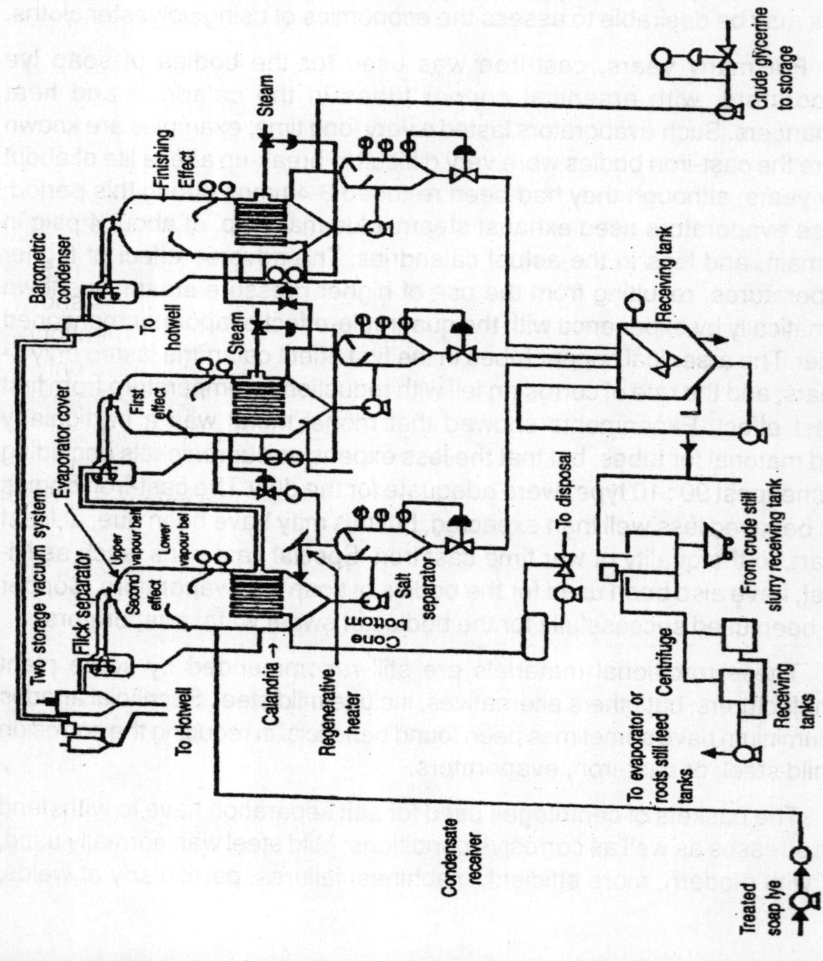

Fig. 6.9.Wurster and Sanger evaporator for soap lyes.

Fig. 6.10 represents a *Gianazza* evaporator for soap lyes. This unit is double-effect with forward feed; and uses jet recompression of part of the vapour from the first effect. External calandrias are used, with natural circulation for the first effect and forced for the second which produces crude glycerine. Salt slurry is extracted by pneumatically operated salt boxes, and from the crude glycerine in a static separator, for separation in a centrifuge. BO 1 is a direct-contact condenser with barometric leg and PV 01 a mechanical vacuum pump.

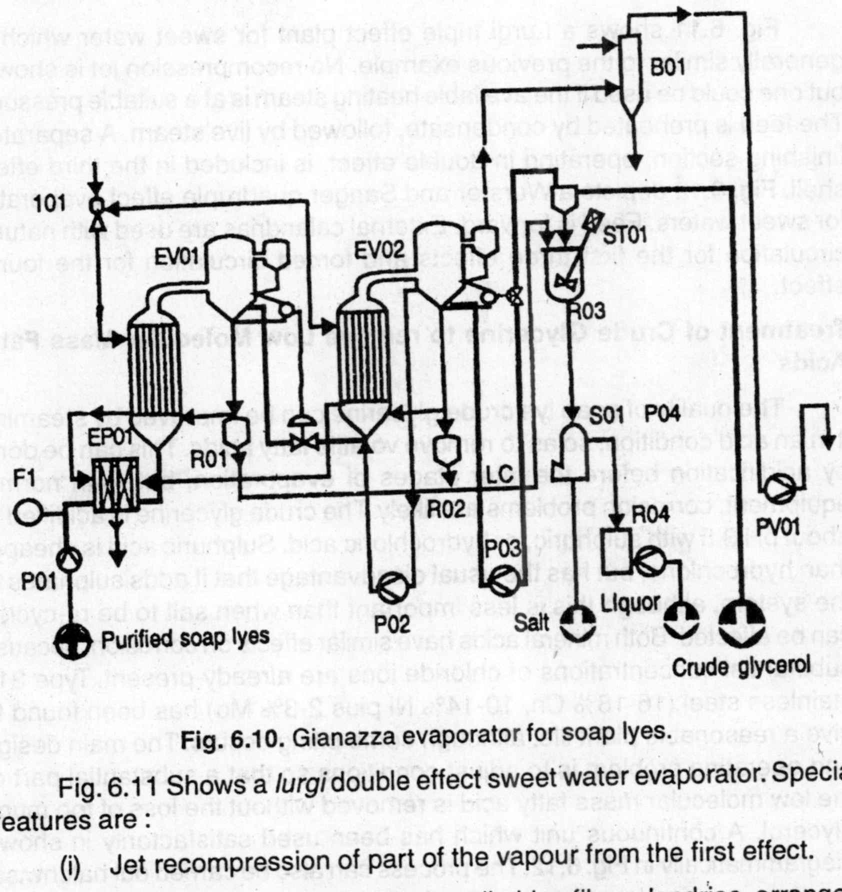

Fig. 6.10. Gianazza evaporator for soap lyes.

Fig. 6.11 Shows a *lurgi* double effect sweet water evaporator. Special features are :

(i) Jet recompression of part of the vapour from the first effect.

(ii) Multi-compartment, long tube, climbing film calandrias, arranged so that the liquid flow is once through each compartment in series, with the vapour discharge from each into a single space. The last part of the second effect is separated from the rest and is fed with steam directly from the recompression jet; that is the final concentration is in single effect. As an example, Lurgi quotes concentration from sweet water at about 10% glycerol to 25% in the first effect, to 70% in the second effect, and to 88% in the final stage.

(iii) A surface condenser is used for the final vapours to increase the quantity of condensate available for re-use.

(iv) The feed is preheated by the first effect condensates (including that from the final stage).

Fig. 6.11 shows a Lurgi triple effect plant for sweet water which is generally similar to the previous example. No recompression jet is shown, but one could be used if the available heating steam is at a suitable pressure. The feed is preheated by condensate, followed by live steam. A separated finishing section, operating in double effect, is included in the third effect shell. Fig. 6.12 depicts a Wurster and Sanger quadruple effect evaporator for sweet waters. Feed is forward. External calandrias are used with natural circulation for the first three effects and forced circulation for the fourth effect.

Treatment of Crude Glycerine to remove Low Molecular Mass Fatty Acids

The quality of soap lye crude glycerine can be improved by steaming it in an acid condition, so as to remove volatile fatty acids. This can be done by acidification before the later stages of evaporation, but, with normal equipment, corrosion problems are likely. The crude glycerine is acidified to about pH 3.5 with sulphuric, or hydrochloric acid. Sulphuric acid is cheaper than hydrochloric, but has the usual disadvantage that it adds sulphates to the system, although this is less important than when salt to be re-cycled can be affected. Both mineral acids have similar effects on corrosion, because substantial concentrations of chloride ions are already present. Type 316 stainless steel (16-18% Cn, 10-14% Ni plus 2-3% Mo) has been found to give a reasonable plant life, although some piting occurs. The main design and operating problem is to adjust conditions so that a substantial part of the low molecular mass fatty acid is removed without the loss of too much glycerol. A continuous unit which has been used satisfactorily in shown diagrammatically in Fig. 6.12. The process can also be carried out batchwise.

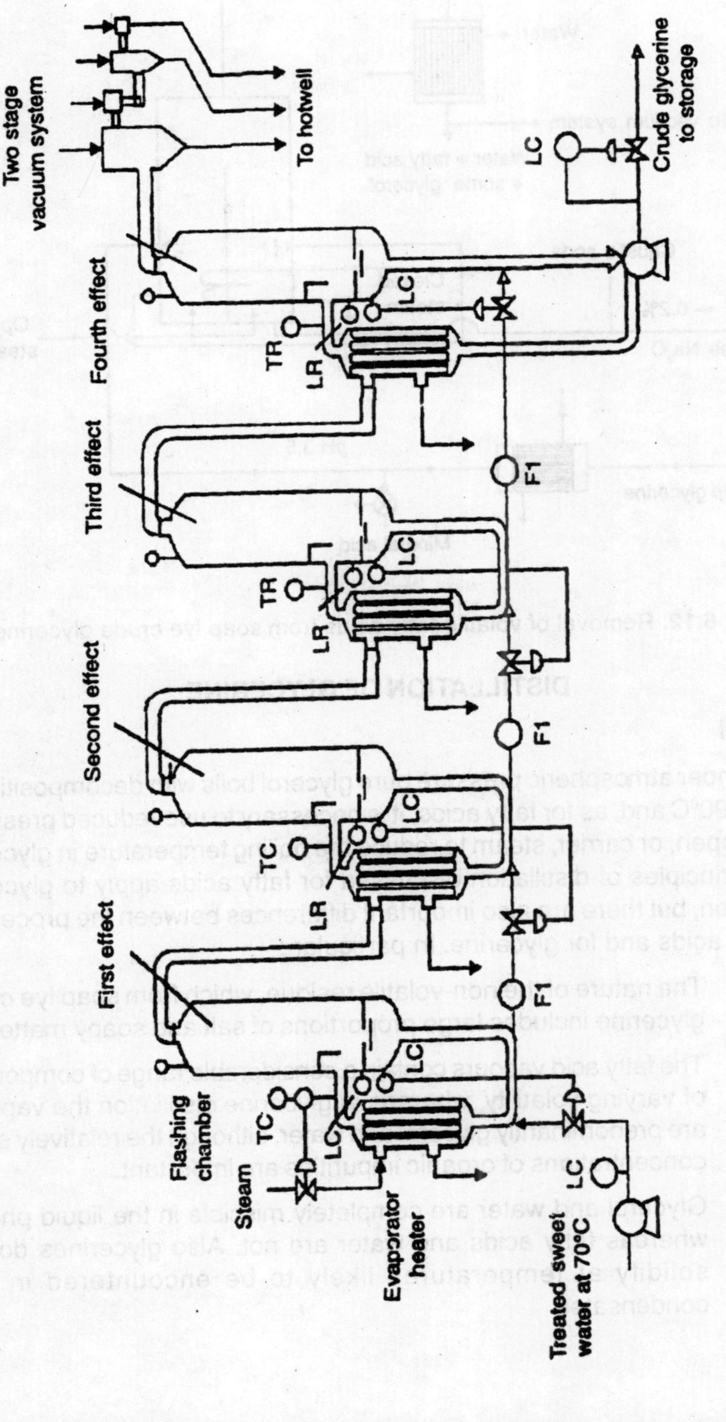

Fig. 6.11. Wurster and Sanger quadruple-effect sweet water evaporator.

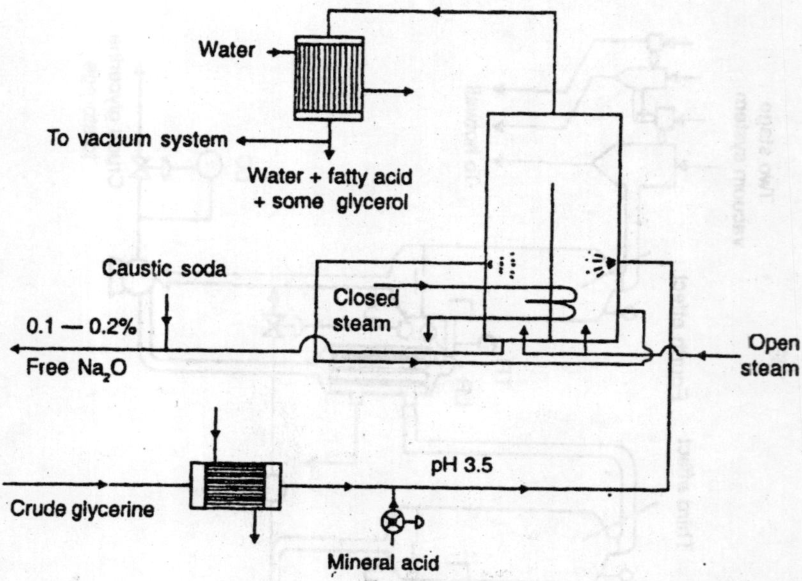

Fig. 6.12. Removal of volatile fatty acids from soap lye crude glycerine.

DISTILLATION OF GLYCERINE

General

Under atmospheric pressure pure glycerol boils with decomposition at about 290°C and, as for fatty acids, it is necessary to use reduced pressure, and/or open, or carrier, steam to reduce the boiling temperature in glycerine stills. Principles of distillation discussed for fatty acids apply to glycerine distillation, but there are also important differences between the processes for fatty acids and for glycerine. In particular :

(i) The nature of the non-volatile residue, which from soap lye crude glycerine includes large proportions of salt and soapy matter.

(ii) The fatty acid vapours contain a considerable range of compounds of varying volatility, whereas in glycerine distillation the vapours are predominantly glycerol and water, although the relatively small concentrations of organic impurities are important.

(iii) Glycerol and water are completely miscible in the liquid phase, whereas fatty acids and water are not. Also glycerines do not solidify at temperatures likely to be encountered in still condensates.

Chemical Aspects of Glycerine Distillation

Several important, but undesirable, reactions tend to occur in glycerine liquors held at still temperatures :

(i) Formation of volatile glyceryl esters by reaction between glycerol and the soaps of low molecular mass fatty acids.

$$C_3H_5(OH)_3 + R.COONa \rightarrow C_3H_5(OH)_2\text{—}O.CO.R + NaOH$$

glycerol soap mono-glyceride caustic soda

(ii) Formation of polyglycerols.

(iii) Formation of objectionable organic nitrogen compounds from proteinaceous residues in the crude glycerine.

(iv) Decomposition of glycerol to highly volatile compounds normally lost in the vacuum system.

Esters, fatty acids (if any), and the volatile nitrogenous bodies effect adversely the quality of distillates in which they are condensed. Polyglycerols are substantially non-volatile under distillation conditions; but they are undesirable because they represent a loss of glycerol, and because they modify the residue in ways which can be adverse. The condensation reactions by which polyglycerols are formed are not reversible and the ether links they contain are not broken under still conditions. Careful materials balances determined for glycerine distillations normally show a small unaccounted for loss, which may be associated with radical decomposition of glycerol to gaseous products.

Ester formation is a balanced reaction which is suppressed by the presence of caustic soda in the still vapouriser; and polyglycerol formation is catalysed by alkalis, with caustic soda more potent than the milder alkalis sodium carbonate and soaps. It is therefore, important to carry out the distillation with as little caustic soda in the still as will permit the production of distillates satisfactory as regards content of esters and faty acids (measured by the saponification equivalent, but also likely to affect taste and odour). Physical conditions of disstillation are very important. Increases in the time for which, and the temperature at which, glycerine is held in the still vapouriser both increase the formation of polyglycerols. There is an interaction between the two conditions, so that a very short time at a relatively high temperature may be less damaging than a longer time at a lower temperature. More severe physical conditions also increase the influence of alkaline catalysts, so that mild alkalis may not be very significant if the physical conditions are mild, but become important when they are more severe. It has also been shown that with a given crude glycerine the distillate is much lower in saponification when distillation is very rapid. Similar factors probably affect the formation of volatile nitrogenous bodies. The introduction of a small quantity of water into the still in, or with, the crude glycerine may also help to suppress polyglycerol formation, even though the water is rapidly vapourised. Under some conditions, the use of open steam may also help to reduce ester formation. When distillates needs to re-distilled, it is important to saponify any ester in them before the second distillation. This can be done by agitating the hot distillate with air after addition of caustic soda; and a suitable quantity of caustic soda is needed in the still during re-distillation to suppress re-formation of esters.

Formation of polyglycerols is commonly a major source of loss of yield in glycerine distillation; and it may be useful to estimate the polyglycerol in the still residues, which are often called foots. Elaborate separation procedures have been developed for special investigations, but the polyglycerol content is usually deduced from a periodate and an acetin, or dichromate, test on the foots, or, better, from all three tests. As explained the periodate test does not respond to polyglycerols and, unless sugar or other unusual substances are present, records only glycerol. The acetin test includes polyglycerols, so that the difference between glycerol estimated by acetin and glycerol estimated by periodate is a measure of the polyglycerol content of the sample. To convert this difference to the glycerol from which the polyglycerols were formed, it must be multiplied by a factor which depends on composition of polyglycerols. If di-glycerol is assumed, the factor is 6/4 = 1.5, and if tri-glycerol, it is 9/5 = 1.8. To obtain the general relationship, when *n* moles of glycerol condense, (*n*-1) ether links are formed with a loss of (*n*-1) × 5 2 hydroxyl groups. Hence, 3 *n* hydroxyl groups form a polyglycerol containing 3 *n*-2(*n*-1) hydroxyls. In practice, a factor around 1.8 is probably reasonable. Similarly, the difference between glycerol per cent by dichromate and glycerol per cent by periodate is a measure of the polyglycerols present, and in this case no factor is required. Some stills give a very poor distillation yield when found to be operating at 60-70 mm Hg absolute pressure in the still instead of the 10-14 mm Hg for which it was designed. This raises the boiling liquor temperature to 170-180°C, substantial quantities of caustic soda had to be used, and the yield is only about 75%. A sample of liquid residue run out of the still, not a true average sample of the foots, tested 7% glycerol by periodate and 37% by bichromate. It, therefore, contained 7% glycerol and 30% polyglycerol calculated as glycerol; and showed qualitatively that major conversion of glycerol to polycerol had occurred and was a major cause sof the very bad yield. In order to relate the polyglycerol found in foots to distillation loss due to this cause, it is necessary to test a true average sample of the residue and to find the quantity of this residue formed from a known quantity of crude glycerine by measurement, or by calculation from the salt contents of the two materials.

Vapourisation Principles

The Vapour pressure of pure glycerol is as shown in the table.

Temperature °C	120	130	140	145	150	155	160	165	170	175
Vapour pressure mm Hg	0.75	1.35	2.45	3.2	4.3	5.5	7.4	9.2	11.5	14.7
Temperature °C	180	190	200							
Vapour pressure mm Hg	18.5	29	45							

The more relevant part of this information is shown graphically in Fig. 6.13.

Glycerol and water are miscible in the liquid phase and no water remains still of distillation. That is $P_G + p_w = P_T$, where p_G is the vapour pressure of glycerol, p_W the vapour pressure of water, and p_T the total pressure in the still. The vapour pressure of glycerol in equilibrium with still liquor in lower than that of pure glycerol at the same temperature, because of boiling point elevation due to dissolved substances. This elevation varies with the composition of the still liquor, which, in turn, varies with the composition of the crude glycerine fed and the degree of concentration which has been achieved. In the case of soap lye, crude, from which salt leaves solution as the distillation proceeds, a figure based upon experience of roughly 10-15°C is assumed for the main part of the distillation. That is to say that the vapour pressure of glycerol in equilibrium with a still liquor at 155°C is taken to be about that for pure glycerol at 140-145°C, or about 2.5-3.2 mm Hg.

Substituting 92, the molecular mass of glycerol, and including the vapourisation efficiency E, the equation derived for steam distillation can be re-written, lb of open steam/lb glycerol distilled = $(P_T - Ep_G) \times 18)/(Ep_G \times 92)$. Table 6.2 gives estimated usages of open steam for a range of conditions with the provisional assumption that E = 1. These estimates, which show a wide variation with conditions, refer only to the major part of the distillation run; considerably more opensteam is used in the final stage when the residue is being worked down. Crude glycerines contain a small proportion of water; in some stills this is removed in a preliminery dehydrator, but in others it enters the main vapouriser, in which case it contributes to the open steam.

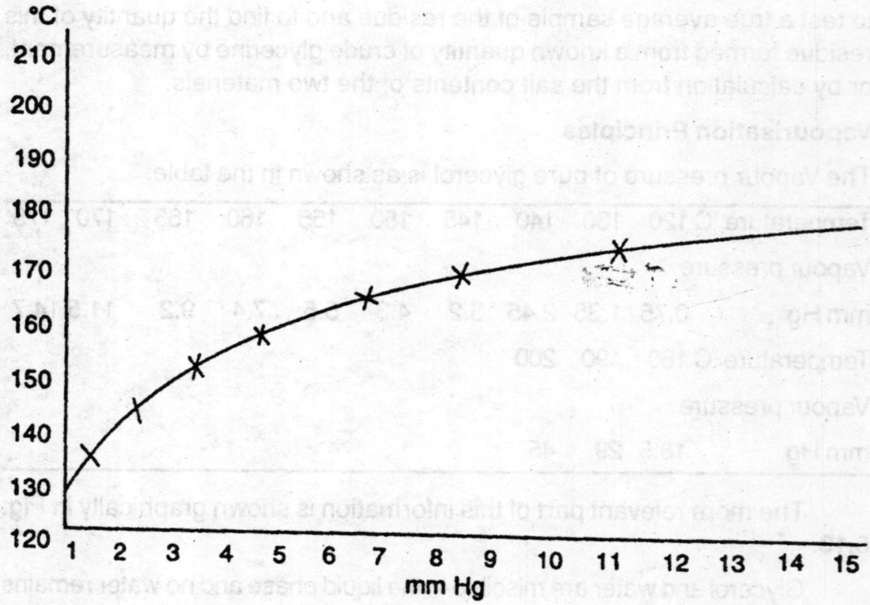

Fig. 6.13. Vapour pressure of pure glycerol

In a vapouriser which uses open steam as well as reduced pressure, the distillation conditions are established by automatic adjustment to meet three sets of requirements simultaneously :

(i) Heat transfer from the closed steam, or other heating medium.

(ii) Heat balance, which determines the rate of vapourisation of the glycerol plus that of any liquid water fed to the main still.

(iii) The partial pressure relationship just discussed.

If, for example, the rate of heat transfer is increased, the additional heat will vapourise more glycerol. With a fixed rate of open steam supply this reduces the open steam/glycerol vapourised ratio, which causes the boiling liquor temperature to increase to the level required by the new ratio. Similarly, if the flow of open steam is increased, and the vapour passages and steam condensing equipment are such that the total pressure P_T is not raised significantly, the increase in the open steam/glycerol vapourised ratio results in a fall in the boiling liquor temperature.

So far it has been assumed that E = 1, that is that the open steam becomes saturated with glycerol as it passes through the glycerine liquor in the vapouriser.

Table 6.2. Open steam usage for glycerine distillation under various conditions.

Approximate temperature of still liquor °C	150-155	160-165	170-175	180-185
Assumed equipment temperature of pure glycerol °C	140	150	160	170
Vapour pressure glycerol P_G mm Hg	2.45	4.3	7.4	11.5
Vapour pressure water,				
$p_W = p_T - p_G$				
If $p_T = 15$, $p_W = 15 - p_G$	12.55	10.7	7.6	3.5
$= 30, p_W = 30 - p_G$	27.55	25.7	22.6	18.5
$= 60,\ p_W = 60 - p_G$	57.55	55.7	52.6	48.5
$\frac{\text{Mass of water vapour}}{\text{Mass of glycerol vapourised}}$				
$\frac{(P_T - pG)}{pG \times 92} \times 18$				
If $P_T = 15$	1.00	10.49	0.20	0.06
$= 30$	2.20	1.17	0.60	0.31
$= 60$	4.60	2.53	1.39	0.83

The actual usage of open steam is much higher than that calculated with E = 1. It has been found that with allowance for boiling point elevation and excluding the work-down period, the calculations using E = 1 are in fair agreement with experience, for at least some stills. Analysis seems to provide some approximate support for this view as follows.

Assuming the soap lye crude used contained 83% glycerol and 7% water, and that the distillation came from crude glycerine containing $0.07/(0.83 \times 0.95) = 0.09$ lb of water.

For a Garrigue still, the findings are :

Heating steam in closed coils 175-200 psig (192-198°C)

Distillation temperature about 177°C.

Vapour leaving still 166-171°C.

Still pressure 40-50 mm Hg.

Open steam used during run 0.5 - 0.6 lb/lb glycerol.

Total open steam (including boil down and finishing of foots) 1-2 lb/lb glycerol.

From these figures it is assumed that the equivalent boiling temperature for pure glycerol was about 168°C, with a p_G of 11 mm Hg. With the mean operating pressure of 45 mm Hg, this gives (lb open steam)/(lb glycerol distilled) = $((45-11) \times 18)/(11 \times 92) = 0.60$. With allowance for the water in the crude glycerine fed, the ratio becomes 0.60-0.09 = 0.51.

For an Ittner still, the findings are :

Distillation temperature 166°C

Still pressure 10-15 mm Hg

Open steam used 0.25 lb/lb glycerol.

It is assumed that the equivalent boiling temperature for pure glycerol was about 155°C, with p_G = 5.5 mm Hg. With the mean operating pressure of about 13 mm Hg, the ratio = $((13-5.5) \times 18)/(5.5 \times 92) = 0.27$, which, with allowance for water in the crude, becomes 0.18.

Water in crude glycerine obviously becomes of increasing importance as the total usage of open steam falls.

Vapourisation Equipment

Soap lye crude glycerine contains some 10% of salt and soapy matter; and the disposal of this non-volatile material influences the choice of vapourisation equipment which can be used, and makes it usual with many types to operate semi-batch, rather than continuously. This problem is much reduced with saponification crudes, particularly those made from high pressure split sweet waters which contain little inorganic matter. For this reason, saponification crudes are often considered superior to soap lye crude, but, especially when produced from low grade fats, they are liable to contain nitrogenous and other impurities which can lead to problems with the quality of the distillates made from them.

As a batch of soap lye crude glycerine is distilled semi-batchwise, with additional crude fed to replace the glycerol vapourised, the concentrations in the residue of sodium chloride, other inorganic materials, and MONG increase; and the viscocity of the residue rises. The recovery of as much glycerol from this residue as is economically worthwhile is a major problem ; and several procedures are possible :

(i) Traditionally the main distillation was stopped whilst the residue was still liquid enough to flow out of the still. The residue was then diluted and purified as much as possible using treatments similar to those adopted for lyes or sweet waters. The purified liquor was re-evaporated to give 'foots crude', which was distilled separately to produce a low grade distillate. A variant was to return the still foots to the soap lyes before treatment. This was simple, but is not recommended because of the build-up of impurities in the system, despite some purification in the re-treatment.

(ii) Some plants removes residues from the main still in liquid form for the rest of the glycerol to be stripped in a separate foots still. This enables the main still to be operated more, or less, continuously, although it needs to be washed out from time to time. Recently the stills offered are of the type in which solid salt is separated in a centrifuge through which the liquor is passed on its way from the main still to the foots still. Apart from the cost of the additional equipment (offset by the additional capacity of the main still), the use of a foots still tends to increase the time during which the material is exposed to distillation temperatures. Separation of salt and other solids in a centrifuge helps the final stages of vapourisation, but exposure of hot liquor to air may entail some risk of oxidation of glycerol.

(iii) For many years it has often been found best to continue the main distillation until little more glycerol can be vapourised. With many still designs this involves a loss of glycerol in foots discarded to drain of at least about 2% of that fed. If a reasonably good quality soap lye crude glycerine has been distilled, and conditions are such that only a little polyglycerol is formed, the residue is so stiff that it cannot be run out of the still; and it has to be dissolved by being boiling with water. If the quality of the crude glycerine is poor, polyglycerol formation is high, or the final steaming has not been complete, some of the residue can be run out as liquid foots. When liquid foots are formed, investigation is desirable to ascertain the cause and, if possible, to arrange remedial action for future distillations.

In most stills the residue after as much glycerol as possible has been vapourised from a soap lye crude is a toffee-like material, but, as described later, it has been found recently that under some circumstances a dry, powdery, residue can be obtained from a once-through vapouriser.

When re-distillation of once distilled glycerine is used to produce chemically pure grade, a procedure which is no longer common, a liquid residue containing glycerol, polyglycerols, caustic soda, and soapy matter is left. From time to time, this needs to be transferred to a first distillation of crude glycerine.

Three major types of vapouriser are used in the distillation of crude glycerine :

(i) Pot stills, and variants, in which open and closed steam are used to provide natural circulation.

(ii) Stills with external heaters and forced circulation.

(iii) Scraped wall, once through, vapourisers.

Types 1 and 2 can be used for saponification as well as soap lye crudes, but type 3 cannot because the necessary dry, powdery, residue is not produced, unless a liquid residue can be discharged satisfactorily.

Natural circulation pot vapourisers are used in Van Ruymbeke stills, a type which was vary widely employed for many years; and in various other designs. In essence, they comprise pots fitted with closed heating coils (usually steam) and a perforated ring, or cross, near the bottom for the introduction of open steam. The Van Ruymbeke still operated at around 60 mm Hg; and hence required about 1-1.5 lb open steam/lb glycerol vapourised, with a boiling temperature around 170-175^{0}C. Steam in the closed coils at 175-200 psig (condensing at 192-198^{0}C) gives a reasonable temperature difference to induce heat flow and a good rate of distillation. One major installation with several Van Ruymbeke stills for the distillation of soap lye crude glycerine, plus two smaller stills for re-distillation to produce chemically pure grade, operated satisfactorily for many years with steam from Lancashire boilers at 150-160 psig (185-188^{0}C) which gave a rather small temperature difference. Special arrangements to make the best use of the available steam are shown diagrammatically in Fig. 6.14. Features are :

(i) A good flow of steam through the coils, with efficient removal of condensate and air, was induced by use of surplus steam which was recovered from the 90 psig collector.

(ii) Superheated steam was used in the crude still coils. This is contrary to the usual view that superheat in the steam used in heating coils reduces rather than increases heat transfer, but this use of superheat was found to increase distillation rate, presumably because it increased the temperature of the upper parts of the coils which were in contact with froth, as well as more compact liquor. Saturated steam was found advisable for re-distillation, when the boiling point elevation was lower.

Classical Van Ruymbeke stills included a 'superheater' for the open steam. This comprised a tube and shell heat exchanger in which the flow of open steam towards the perforated distributor in the still was exposed to heat from full pressure steam. The superheater was presumably intended to avoid the introduction of liquid water into the hot glycerine liquor where it might cause primes. It can, however, be shown by theoretical analysis, using the Fanno line technique, that expansion of steam through a control valve and pipe is very different from that through a nozzle, because of the 're-heating' effect of pipe wall friction as the linear velocity becomes very high; and that liquid water is unlikely to be formed. Later on it was found that these superheaters were unnecessary, and they were removed without any ill effect.

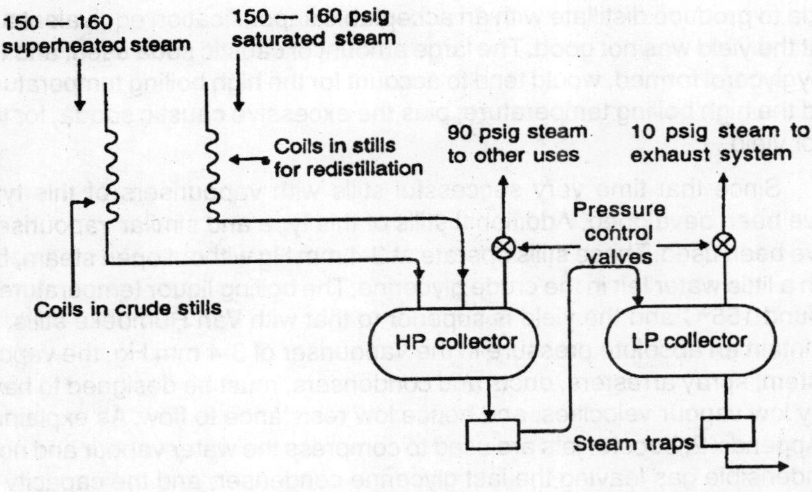

Fig. 6.14. Steam supply arrangements for a group of Van Ruymbeke stills.

In addition to its role as a carrier fluid, an important function of the open steam in pot-still vapourisers is to provide agitation, with proper circulation of the liquor over the closed coils without local overheating. Some plant manufacturers have introduced the open steam through jet-type vapour-lift devices to improve the circulation; for example up the centre of the pot and down over the annular heating coils. This is particularly useful when the still is designed to work at a relatively low absolute pressure and with a low open steam ratio.

It is important to ensure that flow passages through condensers and ducts are adequate to take the maximum requirement of open steam without undue pressure drop. Stills have been constructed in which this was not done, so that an adequate flow of open steam could not be used without a substantial increase in still pressure.

Several important modern stills use *external heaters and forced circulation* which permit operation at low pressure of about 2-4 mm Hg. Often no open steam is used during the main part of the distillation, but it is also possible to inject some open steam into the vessel to and from which the liquor is circulated; in which case a rather higher still pressure is usual. One early type was a Scott still for which the soap lye crude is dried before being fed into the still in which a pressure of about 2 mm Hg is maintained. This still is operated with a liquor temperature of 177^{0}C, which is surprisingly high for a pressure of 2 mm Hg, even with no water in the crude glycerine as fed to the vapouriser. Still of this type requires a large addition of caustic soda to produce distillate with an acceptable saponification equivalent and that the yield was not good. The large amount of caustic soda used, and the polyglycerol formed, would tend to account for the high boiling temperature; and the high boiling temperature, plus the excessive caustic sodda, for the poor yield.

Since that time very successful stills with vapourisers of this type have been developed. Additional stills of this type and similar vapourisers have been used. These stills operate at 3-4 mm Hg without open steam, but with a little water left in the crude glycerine. The boiling liquor temperature is around 155^{0}C and the yield is superior to that with Van Rumbeke stills. To maintain an absolute pressure in the Vapouriser of 3-4 mm Hg, the vapour system, spray arresters, ducts and condensers, must be designed to have very low vapour velocities, and hence low resistance to flow. As explained in Appendix 2, booster jets are used to compress the water vapour and non-condensible gas leaving the last glycerine condenser; and the capacity of the booster jet, or jets, is often the factor which limits the capacity of the still. This means that the water content of the crude glycerine should normally be kept low. The significance of the presence of a little water in the crude glycerine as fed to the vapouriser on polyglycerol and ester formation is not clear, but it may be important. To enable the distillation to be completed in the vapouriser, without a foots still, closed and open steam coils are fitted in the vessel, together with a damper in the circulation pipe, as shown in Fig. 6.15. During the main part of the distillation the butterfly damper is open and the liquor is circulated at a high rate by the centrifugal, or axial flow, pump through the external heater. It is returned to the vessel through a tangential inlet onto a ledge round which it swirls; vapour flashes off and the residual liquor runs back into the reservoir to be recirculated with the new feed. The closed and open steam coils in the still vessel are not used during the main part of the distillation. When sufficient crude has been fed, and the liquor worked down until its viscosity becomes too high for continued operation in this way, the damper is closed and the liquor in the circulating system is transferred by the small pump to the main reservoir. The residue is then worked to dryness using the closed and open steam coils, as for a pot still. During this final stage the pressure in the still and the liquor temperature are higher than for the main run.

A more recent development is the use of a *'once-through' scraped wall vapouriser* for the distillation of good quality soap lye crude glycerines. When conditions are right the glycerol is vapourised very rapidly and almost completely, without formation of polyglycerols, and a dry, powdery, residue is discharged from the base of the until. It the Gianazza still (Fig. 6.16) the residue is collected in a vessel from which it is said to be discharged once, or twice, a week. It is also possible to remove the residue continuously through an automatic air-lock system and screw conveyor. The vapouriser is heated with at, say, 250 psig (208°C); or with hot oil, or other high temperature heat transfer medium. A low pressure of a few mm Hg is maintained as for other stills not using open steam. Because of the very short residence time it seems probable that the working pressure may be less critical than with other type of vapouriser. Because of its almost instantaneous vapourisation, this type of unit has great advantages when it works well. The yield can be exceptionally high, because virtually no polyglycerol is formed, and vapourisation of glycerol is nearly complete. The formation of esters and other undesirable compounds is also substantially lower than with other vapourisers using the same crude glycerine. On the other hand, it can only work if a dry, powdery residue is formed; patches of toffee-like material can cause major problems. This requires the unit to be kept in good mechanical condition and capable of uniform heat transfer. It also requires a good soap lye crude glycerine with a sufficiently high ratio of salt to MONG; at least 3.5 is said to be a useful criterion. It has also been found that particularly good crude glycerines, which produce a very dusty residue at the base of the vapouriser, can cause some difficulties due to carry over of dust, because there is little organic matter to bind the particles of residue. The dry residue produced by this type of vapouriser may be more readily disposed of than the rather foul smelling and polluting liquors obtained when othertypes of vapouriser are washed out.

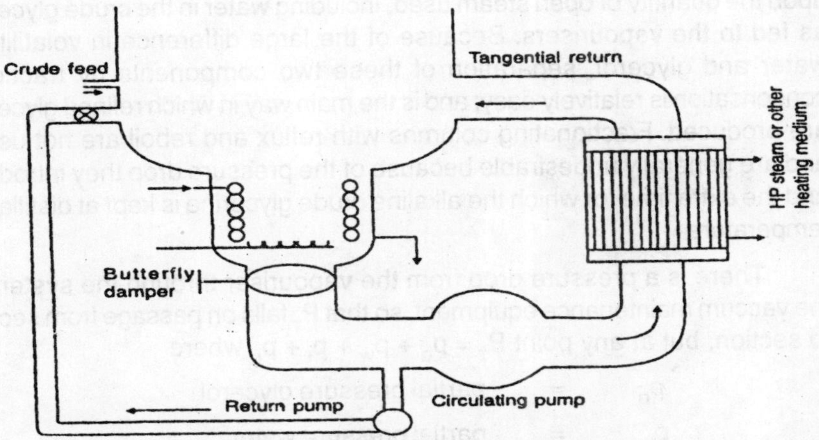

Fig. 6.15. Forced circulation vapouriser.

Spray Arresters

Traces of liquor, or solid residue, carried over in the vapours from the still can spoil a distillate, particularly the first (and best) when more than one fraction is collected. The strict limits for chlorides mentioned in the specification discussed earlier make this particularly critical with soap lye crudes.

The main problem is to remove without excessive flow resistance, especially in stills which operate at very low pressure. Thin beds of rings having a large cross-section, so as to minimise linear velocity and hence resistance, are now usual. Such beds are often situated in the upper part of the still vessel; and they should be provided with water sprays to enable them to be washed when the still is cleaned. Older stills, such as the Van Ruymbeke, which operated without jets, commonly used catch-all vessels.

Particularly when foots are worked down to dryness and considerable boiling out with water is needed to remove the residue, carry over is liable to occur during the wash out. Some stills include a large valve in the vapour line which can be closed to isolate the vapouriser from the condensing system during the washout. Such valve can be valuable; but care must be taken to avoid construction of vapour passages and the posssibility of in leakage of air.

Condensation, Condensers, Stripping Columns, Concentrators, and Deodorisers

Apart from any carry-over of droplets, the vapours leaving a glycerine still contain glycerol and water, plus small concentrations of esters, TMG, and other organic impurities. The proportion of water to glycerol depends upon the quantity of open steam used, including water in the crude glycerine as fed to the vapourisers. Because of the large difference in volatility of water and glycerol, separation of these two components by fractional condensation is relatively easy; and is the main way in which refined glycerine are produced. Fractionating columns with reflux and reboil are not usual; and are generally undesirable because of the pressure drop they introduce and the extra time for which the alkaline crude glycerine is kept at distillation temperature.

There is a pressure drop from the vapouriser through the system to the vaccum maintenance equipment, so that P_T falls on passage from section to section, but at any point $P_T = p_G + p_W + p_I + p_N$ where

p_G	=	partial pressure glycerol
p_W	=	partial pressure water
p_I	=	partial pressure organic impurities
and p_N	=	partial pressure non-condensible gas

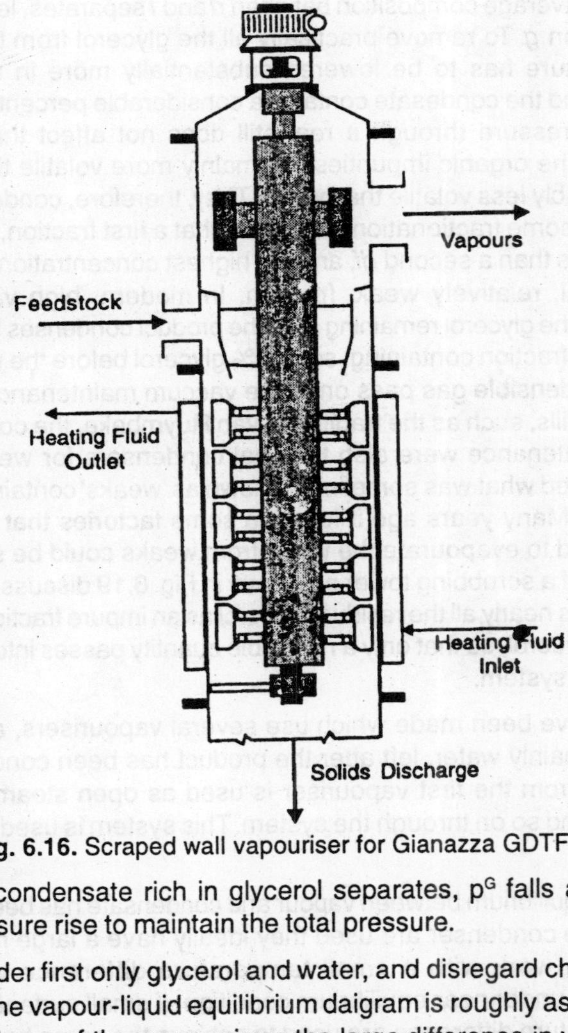

Fig. 6.16. Scraped wall vapouriser for Gianazza GDTF still.

As a condensate rich in glycerol separates, p^G falls and the other partial pressure rise to maintain the total pressure.

Consider first only glycerol and water, and disregard changes in total pressure. The vapour-liquid equilibrium daigram is roughly as shown in Fig. 6.17. The shape of the curve mirros the large difference in volatility of the components. If a superheated vapour containing 50% glycerol is cooled carefully, condensation will start at point a where the 50% vartical cuts the vapour line; and the drop of liquid which separates will, under equilibrium conditions, have composition *b* (that is it is nearly pure glycerol). As more heat is removed, further liquid will separate with compositions along the line *bd*; and the residual vapour composition, and temperature, will fall along the line *ac*. If the cooling in the first condenser stops at temperature t_2, the liquid condensed will have an average composition between *b* and *d*; and the remaining vapour composition *c*. Similarly, on further cooling to t_3, another fraction with average composition between *d* and *f* separates, leaving vapour of composition *g*. To remove practically all the glycerol from the vapour *g*, the temperature has to be lowered substantially more in a cold water condenser and the condesate contains a considerable percentage of water. The fall in pressure through a real still does not affect this qualitative discussion. The organic impurities are mainly more volatile than glycerol, but considerably less volatile than water. They, therefore, condense with the glycerol, but some fractionation occurs, so that a first fraction, *bd*, contains less impurities than a second *df*, and the highest concentration of impurities is in the final, relatively weak, fraction. In modern, high vaccum, stills practically all the glycerol remaining after the product condenses is condensed as an impure fraction containing, say, 60% glycerol before the water vapour and non-condensible gas pass on to the vaccum maintenance system. In some older stills, such as the traditional Van Ruymbeke, the condensers for vaccum maintenance were also the final condensers for weak glycerine which produced what was sometimes known as 'weaks' containing about 2-6% glycerol. Many years ago it found in some factories that much of the steam needed to evapourate the water from weaks could be saved by the introduction of a scrubbing tower as shown in Fig. 6.19 discussed later. This tower recovers nearly all the residual glycerol as an impure fraction containing about 60% glycerol, so that only a negligible quantity passes into the vaccum maintenance system.

Stills have been made which use several vapourisers, and in which the vapour, mainly water, left after the product has been condensed from the vapours from the first vapouriser is used as open steam in the next vapouriser; and so on through the system. This system is used in the Wood still.

So far equilibrium between vapour and condensate has been assumed. When surface condenser are used they ideally have a large heat transfer area; and so work with a small temperature difference which gives condensation under near equilibrium condition. If small surface area and a large temperature difference are used to achieve the same heat flow, local overcooling can occur with less fractionation. This point can be illustrated by the extreme, fortunately not real, case in which a pocket of vapour is condensed completely by itself; the condensate would then have the same composition as the vapour. It is possible to arrange contact between liquid and vapour after the initial condensation. Interchange of components then occurs in a move towards equilibrium. Hence counter-current condensers may be beneficial; and stripping, or washing, columns can be used to improve distillate quality. In such columns, distillate flows downwards in counter-current to rising vapours, usually directly from the still, which vapours are superior in quality to others left after some condensate has been separated. Stripping columns are sometimes used to correct for quality deficiencies due to condensation with a large temperature difference.

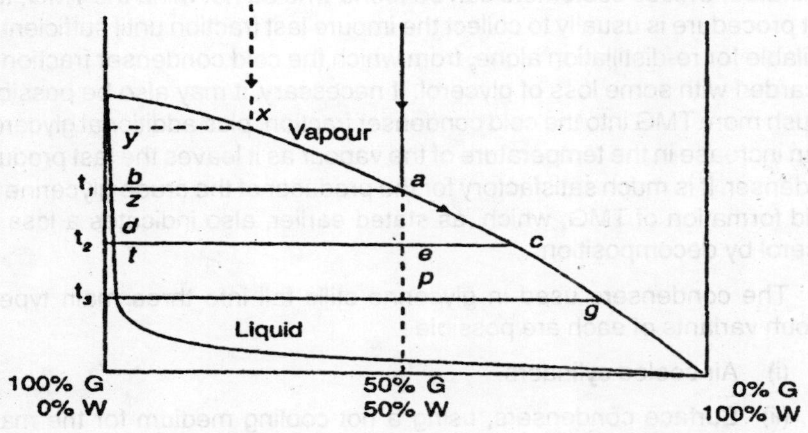

Fig. 6.17. Vapour/liquid equilibrium for glycerol and water.

Some stills, particularly small ones, have only one product condenser, but there are often advantages in havi g two. The best distillate, from the first condenser, is then available for the top quality product and the somewhat less good distillate from the second product condenser can be diverted to the less exacting grades. This may enable distillation to be carried out with less caustic soda in the vapouriser and so tend to a better yield. Fig. 6.17 shows that a little water condenses with the glycerol; and a comparison of routes *abdf* and *xyz* indicates that the amount is larger in stills using open steam than in modern high vaccum stills in which the vapours from the vapouriser little water. Concentration of the distillates is sometimes, but by no means always, needed to meet specification. This can be done in a separate evaporator, but stills in which concentration of distillate is needed may include vessels in which the distillate is subjected to heat from closed coils whilst under vaccum. Such vessels sometimes also use open steam, when they are known as deodorisers and are intended also to remove relatively volatile organic impurities which have condensed in the distillate. Older type stills, such as the Gairrigue which produce large quantities of weaks, sometimes include built-in concentrators which also produce open steam for use in the vapouriser.

TMG is more volatile than glycerol and concentrates in the later fractions. The final, impure fraction from the cold water condenser is normally returned for redistillation, after treatment with caustic soda and possibly concentration; and if the crude glycerine being used contains a relatively high concentration of TMG this compound may build-up in the system to the extent that the distillates cannot meet the high glycerol clauses in some specifications, such as the 99% in the Indian standards, even if all water is eliminated. Unless customers can be found who do not mind the TMG, the best procedure is usually to collect the impure last fraction until sufficient is available for re-distillation alone, from which the cold condenser fraction is discarded with some loss of glycerol. If necessary, it may also be possible to push more TMG into the cold condenser fraction, plus additional glycerol, by an increase in the temperature of the vapour as it leaves the last product condenser. It is much satisfactory for the producer of the crude glycerine to avoid formation of TMG, which, as stated earlier, also indicates a loss of glycerol by decomposition.

The condensers used in glycerine stills fall into three main types, althouh variants of each are possible :

(i) Air cooled cylinders.

(ii) Surface condensers, using a hot cooling medium for the main product condenser, or condensers.

(iii) Direct contact condensers.

Air cooled cylinders are now obsolete, but they were used in Van Ruymbeke and the even earlier direct-fired stills. The vapours from the vapouriser pass through a lagged catchall and then through a series of large unlagged cylinders. Some 8-12 cylinders are usual and they can be arranged in line, or in tiers, Heat is lost by natural convection and radiation from the surface of the cylinders. Distillation has to be continued for several hours after the commencement of a cycle to bring the system up to the temperatures necessary to produce satisfactory condensate. During this period the liquid condensed is returned to the still ; and this helps to remove impurities carried over into the cylinders during the washing out of the foots. When the return to still is closed, condensate collects in the cylinders, but, with some designs, 'drop-cylinders' are provided for removal of condensate during the run. The following temperatures for the sequence of cylinders in the condensing system of a Van Ruymbeke still are quoted as under :

Cylinder	1	2	3	4	5	6	7	8	9	10	11	12
Temperature °C	197	195	191	185	178	170	160	149	122	106	90	72

Distillation was said to commence at 199-203°C, using closed fed with steam at 225 psig (203°C). The distillation, and early condensing cylinder, temperatures seems rather high, but the figures illustrate :

(i) The favourable temperatures for near equilibrium condensation.

(ii) The way the condensing temperature falls slowly at first and then at an accelerating rate as the vapours are denuded of glycerol.

Objections to air condensers are the space required and the lack of possible control. However, with some designs, particularly the linear arrangement of cylinders, the condensates from the individual cylinders can be combined to suit the operator's requirements. For example, the best fraction might normally be taken from cylinders 1—5; but if a larger quantity of slightly lower quality is needed, a change might be made to cylinders 1—7.

Surface condensers using cooling media at relatively high temperatures and condensers of this type have been, and are, used in many more recent stills. The main features of one version of the Garrigue still are shown in Fig. 6.20, discussed later. The following temperatures for the vapours at various points in a Garrigue condensing system can be quoted as under :

Vapouriser→	Superheater→	First condenser→	Second condenser→	Coldwater condenser→	Vaccum system
166-171°C		149-154°C	121-124°C	60°C	29°C

Figures for the condensates from a modern still working at 3 mm Hg without open steam, other than from water in the crude glycerine, are :

Vapouriser →	First condenser →	Second condenser →	Cold water condenser →	Vaccum system
	↓ 130°C	↓ 75°C	↓ 15°C	

The actual temperatures needed at the various depend upon the distillation conditions and the quality requirements, but it will be evident that when two product condensers are used a cooling medium temperature above 100°C is normally required for the first condenser in order to achieve the appropriate cooling of the vapours with a modest temperature difference. In different designs this is obtained by :

(i) Condensers in which heat is removed by water boiling at a pressure, and temperature, controlled by conditions in an auxiliary steam condenser.

(ii) Circulation of hot water under pressure.

(iii) Circulation of a cooling liquid, such as glycerine at a suitable concentration, with a boiling point higher than that of water.

For the second product condenser, hot water is normally adequate. A cold water condenser separates most of the remaining glycerol as an impure fraction.

Direct contact towers containing a mesh, or other low pressure drop packing can be used as condensers by the circulation of suitably cooled glycerine condensate as shown diagrammatically in Fig. 6.18. Advantages of this system are :

(i) The condenser also functions as a stripping column in which the quality of the distillate is improved by counter-current contact with the best available vapours. A unit separate stripping section for the glycerine leaving the until can, if required, be installed below the condensing section round which condensate is circulated.

(ii) It is cheaper than a large surface condenser.

(iii) Control is simple; and considerable flexibility can be achieved.

The problem is to achieve adequate contact between liquid and vapour without excessive pressure drop. This may make the system more suitable for use with vapourisers which do not require very low absolute pressures of 2-4 mm Hg, such as those operating at 10-15 mm Hg with a little open steam, and those with once through, scraped wall vapourisers.

Points in the design of a direct contact condenser include:

(i) The quantity of heat to be removed from the circulated glycerine is controlled by the kg/hr of vapour to be condensed. The higher the flow of circulated glycerine, the smaller the decreaser in temperature required to achieve this heat removal. The extent to which the vapours need to be cooled is controlled by the vapour-liquid equilibrium discussed earlier. The temperature of the circulated liquid, which rises as it passes down the condenser, must be sufficiently below that of the vapour at all points in order to induce the required heat flow, but should be kept as near as possible to that required for equilibrium.

(ii) The diameter of the column must be selected so that the vapour velocity is sufficiently low to give an acceptable pressure drop with an adequate depth of packing; but also so that the liquid flow is enough to wet the packing properly without any risk of flooding.

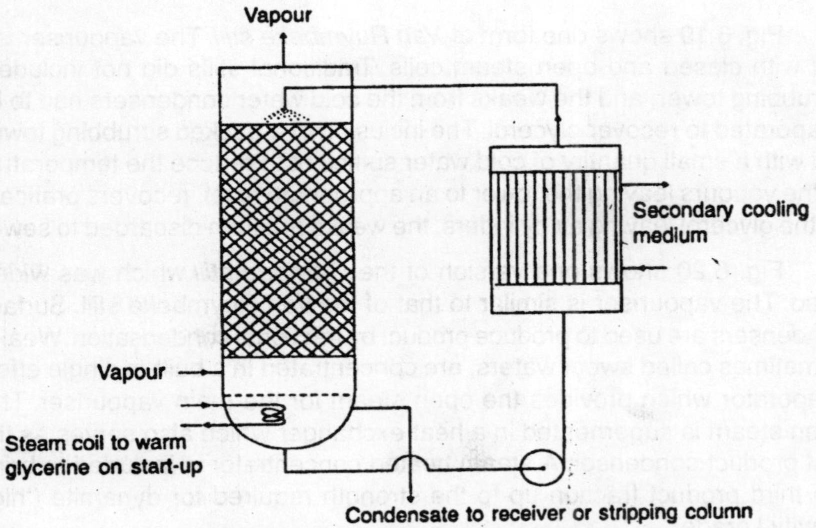

Fig. 6.18. Direct Contact Condenser

Materials of Construction for Glycerine Stills

The older stills, such as the Van Ruymbeke, were normally made of mild steel, with only a few parts, such as the perforated open steam distributor, and the valves, of more resistant metal, such as phosphor bronze. Some discolouration of distillate occurred. For the production of chemically pure grade by redistillation in mild steel equipment it is advisable whenever possible to use a separate still for the second distillation. Without the need to boil the foots from a distillation of crude glycerine with water, the condensing cylinders in the second still retain a film of concentrated glycerine which minimises contamination.

Most modern stills use stainless steel, or aluminum, for all parts in contact with the vapours and distillates. Some designers consider it worthwhile also to make the vapouriser of stainless steel.

Complete Stills

The various possible element considered in previous sections can be selected and combined in many ways to form complete glycerine stills; and many designs have been used and described. Some plant manufacturers have used widely differing designs at various times, so that mention of a plant manufacturer does not necessarily indicated the nature of a still. In this section, only two stills of particular historical importance, plus some designs from recent manufacturers are outlined.

Fig. 6.19 shows one form of *Van Ruymbeke still.* The vapouriser is a pot with closed and open steam coils. Traditional stills did not include a scrubbing tower; and the weaks from the cold water condensers had to be evaporated to recover glycerol. The inclusion of a packed scrubbing tower, fed with a small quantity of cold water sufficient to reduce the temperature of the vapours leaving the tower to an appropriate level, recovers pratically all the glycerol leaving air cylinders, the weaks are then discarded to sewer.

Fig. 6.20 shows one version of the *Garrigue still* which was widely used. The vapouriser is similar to that of the Van Ruymbeke still. Surface condensers are used to produce product by fractional condensation. Weaks, sometimes called sweet waters, are concentrated in a built-in single effect evaporator which provides the open steam for the main vapouriser. This open steam is superheated in a heat exchanger which also serves as the first product condenser. A steam heated concentrator is included to bring the third product fraction up to the strength required for dynamite ('high gravity') grade.

The *Gianazza* HPS still which is very similar to the *Frazer Scott,* glycerine is dehydrated before it is fed to the forced circulation vapouriser. Salt slurry, which separates as the crude glycerine losses water in the dehydrator, is returned to the crude glycerine department. Condensation is in surface condensers which use a circulated fluid cooled in auxiliary coolers. The *Gianazza GDTF 'Turbotherm'* still includes a scraped-wall, once-through, vapouriser, otherwise it is similar to the Gianazza type HPS.

In recent process developed by *Lurgi,* the *Lurgi* still preheated crude glycerine is vapourised in a vessel with one, or more, legs, each equipped with closed heating elements over which the liquor rises by the vapour lift principle induced by open steam injected at the base of the legs. With this steam also acting as carrier fluid, vapourisations is about 10 mm Hg total pressure. This vapouriser is similar in principle to that used in Lurgi fatty acid stills. In some large untis the multi-compartment vapouriser distils soap lye crude continuously, a liquid residue being withdrawn to be worked down in a separate foots still. Distillate from the foots still is redistilled. Other Lurgi stills of this type are operated on the semi-batch principle. The main condenser is of the direct contact type using glycerine cooled slightly in a heat exchanger in which it boils water. In addition to the stripping which occurs in the condenser, the product leaves through a separate stripping section of tower in which it contacts the vapours from the vapouriser. Practically all the glycerol left in the vapours leaving the main condenser is separated as a 90-94% glycerol fraction in a cold glycerine direct contact condenser. This fraction, which needs to be reprocessed, amounts to 6-10% of the total glycerol fed.

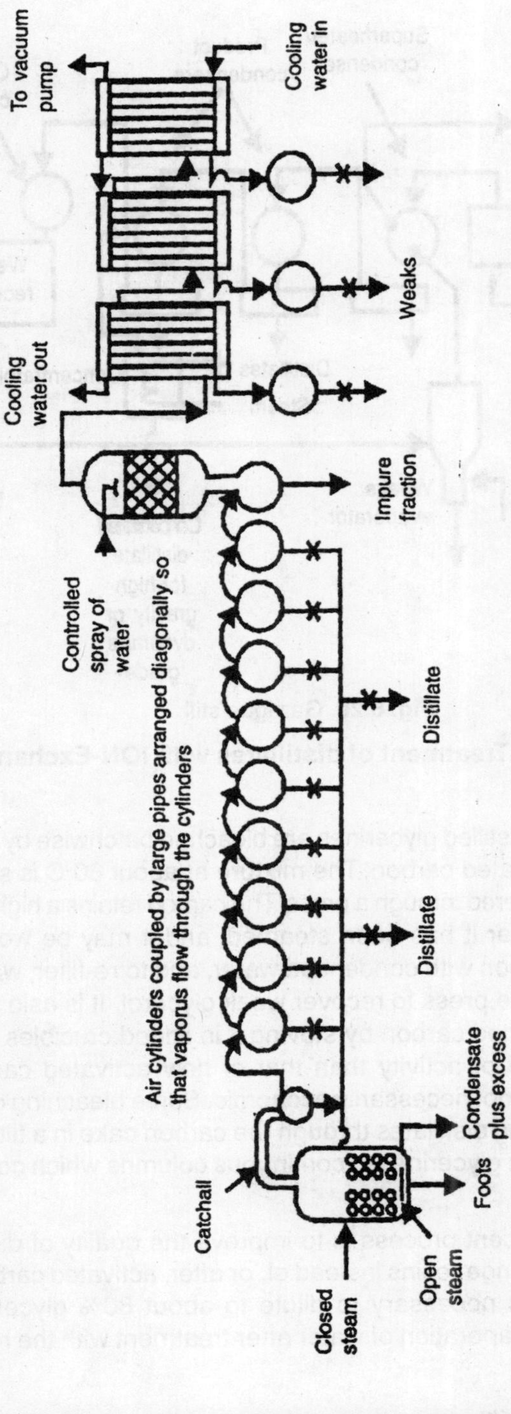

Fig. 6.19. Van Ruymbeke still

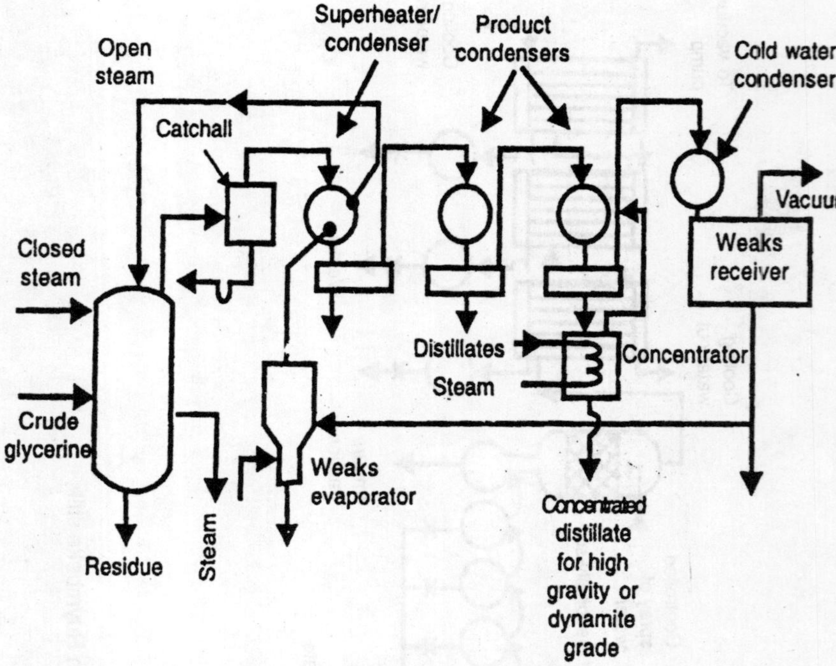

Fig. 6.20. Garrigue still.

Bleaching and the Treatment of distillates with ION-Exchange Resins to upgrade Quality

Traditionally, distilled glycerines are bleached batchwise by an addition of 0.2-2.0% of activated carbon. The mixture at about 80°C is stirred, held for 1-2 hours, and filtered through a press. The carbon retains a high proportion of glycerol even after it has been steamed; and it may be worthwhile to slurry the used carbon with condensed water, and to re-filter, wash, steam and/or air blow in the press to recover weak glycerol. It is aslo possible to re-activate the washed carbon by stoving it in lidded crucibles in an oven (although to a level of activity than that of new activated carbon). This recovery process is not necessarily economic. Some bleaching can also be achieved by pumping distillates through the carbon cake in a filter press. It is possible to bleach glycerines in continuous columns which contain beds of granular carbon.

A relatively recent process is to improve the quality of distillates by the use of ion-exchange resins instead of, or after, activated carbon. At one time it was through necessary to dilute to about 80% glycerol, and to reconcentrate by evaporation of water after treatment with the resins but it has since been found that useful purification can be achieved by the use of appropriate resins on undiluted distillates. Macrorecticular resins (which have large discrete pores capable of removing relatively large molecular mass compounds from the liquid) are normally best for this duty which demands the removal of organic, rather than ionic, impurities.

Deodourisation, using heat and open steam, under vaccum, is often necessary after a distillate has been passed through beds of resins to remove odours imparted by the resins.

Selection of the best combination of resins beds, possibly following an activated carbon treatment, requires experiments, and/or consultation with a resin manufacturer.

PRODUCTION OF REFINED GRADES OF GLYCERINE WITHOUT DISTILLATION

Ion Exclusion

The ion exclusion process for the partial purification of glycerine liquors is based on the fact that in a bed of granular resin (50-100 mesh) of a suitable type, such an 8% cross-linked medium porosity resin consisting of sulphonated styrene-divinyl benzene co-polymer fed with an impure glycerine solution, there are three phases; the resin, the liquor within the resin granules (called the resin liquor), and the surrounding liquor (called the interstitial liquor). Most low molecular mass substances of nonionic, or slightly ionic, nature (such as glycerol) diffuse freely out of the resin liquor and the interstitial liquor. Ionic substances, such as sodium chloride and sodium sulphate, are repelled by the ionic charges of the resin, and exist at a much lower concentration in the resin liquor than in the interstitial liquor. Thus when a mixture of ionic and non-ionic solutes is passed through a resin column and follwed by a water rinse, ionised solutes are excluded from the resin granules and leave the column first. The nonionic material is held back and appears in the rinse water. By the use of properly balanced flows of impure glycerine and of rinse water a partial purification can be achieved, as shown in Fig. 6.21. Purification can be completed by ion-exchange. It is said that Indian Pharmacopoeia grade can be produced from saponification crude glycerine without any distillation.

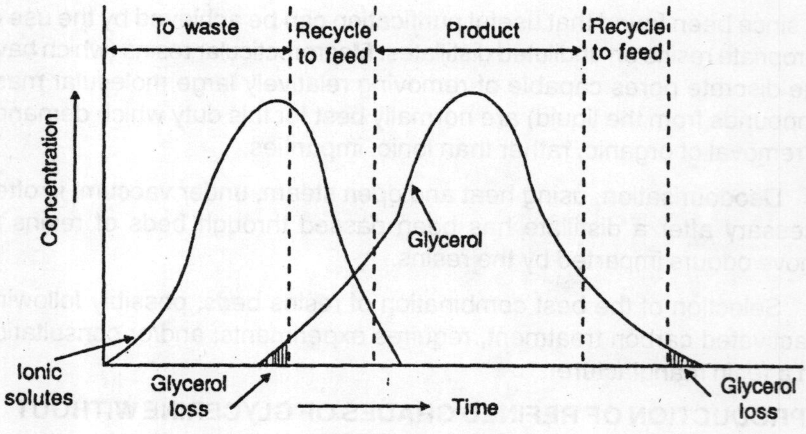

Fig. 6.21. Partial purification of glycerine liquors by ion-exclusion.

Ion Exchange

Glycerine liquors can be purified by the use of ion exchange resins in a process similar to that used for the de-mineralisation of water. The cations, Na^+, Ca^{2+} and $M_g{}^{2+}$ are exchanged for H^+ in a bed of cation resin (regenerated with hydrochloric or sulphuric acid); and the anions $C1^-$ and $SO_4{}^{2-}$ (or their acids) are removed by an anion resin (regenerated with caustic soda). Organic impurities are also removed. Because of the quantities of resins and of regenerating chemicals needed, the process is impracticable for soap lyes, but it was at one time considered at least marginally economical for soap lye crude glycerine diluted to 25-30% glycerol (much of the salt having been removed in the evaporation of purified lyes to crude glycerine). The weak base anion resins are most economical for the removal of the strong acids, hydrochloric and sulphuric, but they need to be 'backed' by a strong anion resin to remove weak organic acids.

Reverse Osmosis Using Semi-permeable Membranes

Experiments have shown that weak glycerol liquor can be concentrated some ten-fold by forcing water through a suitable cellulose acetate membrane under a pressure of 1500 psig (103 bar), with a recovery of 96% in the concentrate. This is an application of reverse osmosis in which preferential sorbtion of water by the membrane, as well as flow through capillary pores, is involved. This use of reverse osmosis might, perhaps, provide a basis for the recovery of glycerol from liqour which would otherwise be too weak to be processed.

7
Perfuming of Soaps and Detergents

Introduction

The terms 'fragrance' and 'perfume' are synonymous and are used interchangeably throughout the perfumery and cosmetics industries. This will also be so throughout this chapter. Fragrance (or perfume) is a blend of two or more materials characterised by having olfactive properties, and is incorporated into a preparation with the intention of imparting specific odours characteristics to that preparation. Very occasionally, the fragrance may consist of one raw material only.

The most important function of the perfume is usually to impart a pleasant and suitable odour to the product into which it is to be incorporated. It is the job of the creative and evaluation teams to define the terms 'pleasant' and 'suitable' for each particular brief that is received. The perfume may also be required to perform other roles in the product, which may take priority over, or be additional to the primary role of imparting odour.

Most soap products have a mild but detectable odour, which is derived from the raw materials in the formulation. Although this 'base' odour is usually inoffensive, it can detract from the overall aesthetic character of the product and should at least be 'masked'. This can be effectively achieved by the use of a suitable fragrance. Very pungent bases, such as permanent-wave lotions, are almost impossible to mask, even with the strongest of perfumes.

The role of the perfume in these products is therefore to produce as pleasant an odour as possible, and this can often be attained by harmonising the fragrance with the base odour.

Fragrances can be designed to give subliminal support to a particular product. For example, a fragrance may appear to make a shampoo wash the hair more cleanly, a perfumed night cream may seen more nutritional to the skin, or a perfumed body spray may appear to impart all-over freshness, all-day. In other words, the perfume may have the role of apparently enhancing product performance.

Some fragrance mate have antimicrobial activity, particularly against becteria. Both bac ostatic and becteriocidal properties are evident. Consequently, fragra ice blends often take on the antimicrobial activity of some of the individual components. Fragrances that have spicy and herbal notes usually exhibit some antibacterial activity owing to the presence of phenols such as eugenol (from clove oil), and thymol and carvacrol (from thyme oil). Consequently, the fragrance may also have the role of assisting the preservative system and even in extreme cases, of replacing the preservative system altogether. Similarly, the fragrance may assist a bacteriocide/bacteriostat in its effect on the skin's microflora (reducing body odour) or may be required to carry this attribute of the finished product on its own.

Types of Perfumes

The cost of soap is determined largely by the perfume. A perfect sample should be strong without being harsh and should retain its fragrance right up to the last thin wafer in use. The stability in the presence of alkali of the aromatic substances in any compound is of importance, as also any change in colour which they may effect in soap after manufacture. Successful soap perfuming therefore requires a knowledge of the durability of each individual raw material when in contact with the soap and any of its constituent impurities. One or 2 per cent of compounded perfume, spread through a large and non-volatile mass has to yield an odour suggestive of the finer alcoholic perfumes in which the solvent plays an important part in determining the delicacy of the finished odour. While alcohol develops the finer ingredients of a perfume, soap on the contrary the odour to such an extent as to often make it unrecognisable in the absence of correct blending. Raw materials listed in the odour classification under basic notes play an important part in solving this problem and the durability of a perfume in soap largely depends upon their correct selection. Natural oils and resins are often the key, and if price will allow they should be used liberally. Some makers rely upon very small range of raw materials, and in consequence their products lack variety. Many of the newer sythetics have proved of great value in soap perfumery, but in all cases, before adoption, experiment is necessary. For this purpose a miniature mill and plodder are used. To save expense, however, many chemists use an ordinary mincing machine, and after passing the perfumed ribbons through two or three, pound them into a mass in a mortar, and stand aside under ordinary commercial conditions for three months. At the end of this time the durability of any perfume compound can be well judged. To facilitate choice a list of substances with are discussed. The stability and keeping qualities their properties are indicated as follows—*very good, A; good, B; weak, C; poor, D.* These are all that are necessary for the standard lines of soap, but may be added to when creation of a new bouquet is desired:

Ajowan oil will replace thyme oil. It is stronger and imparts a pleasing freshness (*A*).

Almond oil, bitter, useful in acacia and fancy compounds, generally replaced by benzaldehyde, free from chlorine.(*C*).

Ambergris tincture, not often used excepting in very high-class soaps, generally replaced by labdanum (*B*).

Amyl cinnamic aldehyde, useful in jasmin soaps and very persistent.(*B*).

Amyl salicylate, very good in trefle compounds and quite strong and lasting in use.(*A*)

Aniseed oil, very powerful. Use traces only.(*B*)

Anisic aldehyde, excellent in May blossom and acacia compounds. About 10 per cent sufficient.(*A*).

Atlas cedarwood oil, excellent in acacia, mimosa, santal, and violet. Very strong and lasting. Resinoid also good in fern and chypre.(*A*).

Basil oil, indispensable for mignonette, but requires to be well blended(*B*).

Bay oil, sometimes used in place of clove oil.(*B*).

Banzaldehyde, cheap and useful in almond soaps, traces in fancy compounds yield pleasing results.(*C*).

Benzoin, used as a resinoid and also as a tincture made with industrial methylated spirit, inclined to darken soaps.(*B*).

Benzyl acetate, 5 or 10 per cent will give a refreshing and sweet odour to most soaps, useful in jasmin and orange blossom when blended with petitgrain oil.(*B*).

Benzyl alcohol, weak and faintly balsamic, useful as a diluent.(*C*).

Benzyl benzoate, a good solvent for musk xylene.(*A*).

Benzylidene acetone, useful in the sweet-pea type, blends well with bromstyrole for cheap bouquets. Owing to its irritating effect on the skin, should be used with care.(*B*).

Bergamot oil, very good, often replaced by lemon oil.(*A*).

Beta naphthol ethers, very powerful, but require to be well blended, otherwise coarse. Use in moderation.(*A*).

Bois de rose oil, indispensable in all flower compounds, much improves Bourbon geranium.(*A*).

Bornyl acetate, the base of all pine perfumes, useful in lavender compounds.(*A*).

Bromstyrole, very powerful and stable, good hyacinth base.(*A*).

Cananga oil, useful in violet and santalwood, not very strong and lacks body.(*D*).

Caraway oil, an indispensable constituent in brown windsor. Rather fleeting.(*B*).

Cassia oil, base for all brown windsors, good blender in bouquets, and should not be overlooked in some rose compounds. Causes darkening.(*A*).

Castoreum tincture, excellent and cheep substitute for made.(*A*).

Cedarwood oil, strong and persistent, good basis for violets.(*A*).

Cinnamic alcohol, weak but good hyacinth base.(*C*).

Cinnamic aldehyde, occasionally used to replace cassia oil.(*A*).

Cinnamon leaf oil, good substitute for clove oil, darkness in soap.(*C*).

Citral, sometimes used as a substitute for lemon oil.(*B*).

Citronella oils. Both Java and Ceylon very largely employed in all forms of cheap soap compounds, Ceylon frequently preferred and not always on account of its lower cost—very strong.(*A*).

Citronellol, useful in rose compounds.(*B*).

Citronellyl esters, useful as modifiers and blenders.(*C*).

Civet tincture, made with industrial spirit, often replaced by synthetic civets based on phenyacetic acid and skatole.(*A*).

Clove oil, much used for imparting a pleasant sweetness to compounds and indispensable in carnation, darkness rapidly.(*A*).

Copaiba resin (balsam), good fixative.(*A*).

Coumarin, very good in all compounds, not forgetting lavender. Gives a yellowish tinge in time.(*A*).

Para-cresol methyl ether, very strong and stable. Use only about 1 per cent.(*A*).

Diphenyl methane and oxide, very strong and stable, substitutes for geranium oil.(*A*).

Ethyl cinnamate, very powerful and balasamic.(*B*).

Eucalyptus oil, traces useful in fern compounds, much used in medicated soaps.(*A*).

Eugenol, good in carnation, but darkness less than clove.(*B*).

Fennel oil, very useful, requires moderation.(*C*).

Geraniol, stable in rose and other compounds.(*A*).

Geranium oils, both Algerian and Bourbon indispensable, latter rather coarse, equal parts of each give best results, used in rose and all bouquets.(*A*).

Geranyl acetate, excellent in rose and lavender.(*C*).

Ginger-grass oil, very good, but requires to be well blended.(*B*).

Guaiac–wood oil, an excellent base for all compounds.(*A*).

Heliotropin, only permissible in coloured soaps, odour good, and indispensable in heliotropes.(*A*).

Hydroxy–citronellel. Use the residues—quite stable and persistent.(*C*).

Ionone, unpurified 100 per cent or residues will yield good results, about 20 per cent sufficient in violets, less in bouquets.(*B*).

Iso–butyl esters, good modifiers and blenders, rather weak excepting the phenylacetate and salicylate.(*B*).

Iso–eugenol, excellent in carnation but darkens rapidly, colours the soaps containing it.(*B*).

Labdanum, very persistent in small quantities, will replace ambergris, good in lavender.(*A*).

Lavender oil, useless alone, must be strengthened and well blended, oakmoss excellent for purpose, also rose–mary, thyme, and borneol.(*B*).

Lavender oil, spike, powerful and very good in lavenders, ferns, etc.(*A*).

Lemon–grass oil, basis of all verbenas. Modify with bois de rose or palmarosa—turns the soap yellowish.(*C*).

Lemon oil, inclined to darken slightly. Ten per cent will make a marked difference to many compounds, indispensable soaps, but must be well fixed to retard oxidation of terpenes.(*C*).

Linalol. Better use bois de rose oil.(*A*).

Linalyl acetate, good, but better to use bergamot oil.(*B*).

Methyl acetophenone, must be used in small quantities and requires well blending, useful in acacias and mimosas.(*A*).

Methyl anthranilate, very cheap and strong, but inclind to darken.(*A*).

Methyl benzoate, very strong and stable.(*A*).

Methyl cinnamate, better than ethyl ester, small quantities give an amber note.(*A*).

Methyl heptine carbonate, traces sometimes used in violets, sharp at first but softens after a few days.(*C*).

Methyl salicylate, used in chypre and fern soaps.(*B*).

Mirbane oil. Dont't use it.(*B*).

Musk ambrette, about 2 per cent is excellent, more gives a sickly sweetness. Residues are good and cheaper.(*A*).

Musk tincture, seldom, employed.(*B*).

Musk xylene, very useful, but make sure it is all dissolved, otherwise the soap will be spotty—turns yellowish in time.(*A*).

Nutmeg oil, used occasionally in lavender compounds.(*D*).

Oakmoss, excellent in lavender and fern, much used in fancy bouquets, very persistent. The green resin is good enough for all purpose.(*A*).

Orange oil, excellent sweetener but must be well fixed, inclined to darken.(*C*).

Orris oil concrete, much used in violets, but often replaced with the olec–resin or extracted from the spent rhizomes. Industrial tinctures of this material useful.(*B*).

Palmarosa oil, good and stable, useful in rose and similar compounds.(*A*).

Patchouli oil, very good stable, more than 10 per cent becomes unpleasant, much less generally enough, useless in rancid bases.(*A*).

Pepper oil, traces employed in fancy bouquets and carnation compouns.(*B*).

Peppermint oil, traces are useful for developing other odours.(*A*).

Peru balsam, imparts warmth, darkness in time.(*A*).

Petitgrain oil, good in many compounds, but turns yellowish in time, often used for predominating note in glycerine and cucumber and Cologne soaps. Very durable.(*B*).

Phenylacetic aldehyde, not very valuable in soap, better use bromstyrole.(*D*).

Phenylethyl alcohol, useful in all flower compounds.(*A*).

Phenylethyl esters, good blenders, rather weak.(*B*).

Rhodinol, excellent in rose and other compounds, usually too expensive. Use Bourbon Geranium.(*A*).

Rosemary oil, good and stable, imparts freshness, useful in many compounds, especially lavender.(*A*).

Safrole, much used in cheap soaps.(*A*).

Sandalwood oil, excellent blender in violets and roses, requires to be developed in santal soaps.(*A*).

Sassafras oil, indispensable in chypre.(*A*).

Spearmint, powerful at first but evanescent.(*C*).

Storax, the best all–round resinous fixative.(*A*).

Terpineol, often the only perfume in cheap soaps, excels rather as a basis on which to build fanciful odours. Use 10 per cent or thereabouts very stable and strong.(*A*).

Terpinyl esters, fair blenders, but not so stable.(*B*).

Thyme oil, excellent for imparting freshness to all kinds of soap compounds, antiseptic value good.(*A*).

Tolu balsam, good fixative, but inclined to darken.(*B*).

Vanillin, traces useful in fancy bouquets, turns the soap yellowish.(*B*).

Vetiveri oil, small quantities are most persistent, good in violets.(*A*).

FLower oils are only used in the highest priced soaps. They yield ecellent results. A cheaper jasmin is made at Grasse by distilling the flowers with cedarwood oil. This product is of considerable value. Mimosa absolute should not be overlooked since it is fairly cheap.

Matching a Perfume

Matching a perfume of known composition requires experiment and is often necessary when a toilet soap is included in any series of cosmetic products. As will be readily understood it would be impossible, from a pecuniary point of view, to use a first-class compound in soaps. From another point of view it would be equally unsatisfactory, since some of the ingredients might undergo decomposition, cause discolouration, or generally upset the finished odour to such an extent as to make it unrecognisable. A formula therefore requires very careful examination and analysis. Those ingredients which are known to be stable and not too dear are allowed to remain although the quantities may have to be adjusted. The others are eliminated but replaced with raw material having similar odours. Other substances may have to be added to diffuse the perfume. The most important point is to choose the right combination of basic notes and add just sufficient to regulate the volatility of perfume. There are, of course, many essential oils having distinctive odours which at the same time act in this way as for instance, vetivert and santal in violets; patchouli and guaiac–wood in roses. These are often more stable than synthetics but, nevertheless, gum-resin in liberal quantity are imperative constituents. The soap perfumer's stand-by is styrax, but this is by no means the only one of value; almost all the resinous substances are excellent and many useful variations can be made with them. It should be noted that it is useless to judge the odour of a soap compound by the usual methods. The perfume must be incorporated in the soap by milling and the finished tablet left on one side for three months. The experiments leading up to this stage may be carried out with a mincing machine.

In order to indicate the lines upon which matching may be conducted an example of violet will be examined. A good quality compound for general use in perfumery will be approximately as follows :

Formula 1

500	Ionone alpha (1)	500
80	Orris oil, concrete (2)	80
50	Heliotropin (3)	50
150	Bergamot oil (4)	150
30	Ylang–ylang oil, Manila (5)	30
40	Sandalwood (6)	40
30	Violet leaf absolute (7)	30
25	Cassie absolute (8)	25
50	Jasmin absolute (9)	50
1	Aldehyde C_{12} (10)	1
25	Rose otto, Bulgarian (11)	25
20	Benzoin R. (12).	20
1001		1001

This formula would be adjusted as follows :

Replace 1 with ionone 100 per cent for soaps and reduce the quantity: Replace 2 with orris oleo–resin and reduce, only when costs compel: Retain 3 and 4 : Replace 5 with cananga oil and increase: Increase 6: Replace 7 with methyl heptine carbonate and reduce: Omit 8: Replace 9 with benzyl acetate or inexpensive jasmin compound: Omit 10: Replace 11 with Algerian geranium oil and increase: Retain 12: To strengthen and diffuse add cedarwood, clove, and vetivert oils, terpineol and musk xylene or residues.

The formula for the violet soap compound having a similar odour to the above would therefore read (Formula 1a)

Formula 1(a)

Ingredient	Parts
Ionone, 100 per cent for soaps	200
Orris oleo–resin	80
Heliotropin	50
Bergamot oil	150
Cananga oil	50
Sandalwood oil	60
Methyl heptine carbonate	1
Benzyl acetate	50
Algerian geranium oil	40
Benzoin R.	20
Cedarwood oil	130
Clove oil	20
Vetivert oil	30
Musk residuces	50
Terpineol	70
	1000

In making violet soaps some manufactures add palm millings which emit a violet–like odour. Others add powered orris–roots, but the use of the oleo resin dispenses with the necessity.

Formulation of Perfumes in Soap Compounnds

Two examples of each of principle toilet soap perfumes will now be given. The first and better quality one being based where possible largely upon essential oils, and the second and cheaper more particularly upon synthetics. They are all workable and are capable of endless modification to suit individual tastes. By applying the principles outlined above it will be quite easy to further cheapen the compounds as desired. With a view to assisting the experimenter in the choice of raw materials for odours of spacific type, the more important components are enumerated in accordance with the classification of odours (Formula 2)

Formula 2

Acacia soap (Based on essential oils)

Rosewood	100
Methyl acetophenone	20
Petitgrain para	200
Terpineol	50
Bergamot	50
Methyl cinnamate	20
Cananga	40
Anisic aldehyde	200
Methyl anthranilate	50
Clove	20
Geranium, African	50
Methyl naphthyl ketone	50
Santal	50
Tolu balsam	30
Vetivert	40
Musk xylene	30
	1000

Formula 3

Acacia soap (Based upon synthetics)

Rosewood	50
Petitgrain para	100
Bromstyrole	20
Tempineol	100
Geraniol, Java	100
Cedarwood	100
Methyl cinnamate	20
Cananga	40
Anisic aldehyde	200
Ionone	50

Methyl anthranilate	50
Clove	20
Methyl naphthyl ketone	50
Styrax resin	70
Musk xylene	30
	1000

Formula 4

Almond soap

Benzaldehyde	400
Rosewood	150
Clove	100
Geranium, African	50
Orris resin	70
Peru balsam	100
Santal	100
Musk xylene	30
	1000

Formula 5

Amber soap

Rosewood	150
Phenyl ethyl alcohol	50
Bergamot	150
Amyl salicylate	100
Geranium, Bourbon	40
Castoreum absolute	10
Coumarin	100
Labdanum resin	200
Musk xylene	30
Oakmoss	20
Phenyl acetic acid	50
Resin (styrax)	100
	1000

Formula 6

Cedarwood

Santal	150
Bromstyrole	10
Cananga	100
Terpineol	100
Methyl ionone	150
Cedarwood	250
Geranium, Bourbon	100
Vetivert	30
Orris resin	60
Heliotropin	50
	1000

Formula 7

Carnation soap

Amyl salicylate	100
Geranieol, Java	100
Eugenol	450
Geranium, African	50
Cassia	30
Orris resin	50
Iso-Eugenol	70
Musk xylene	30
Pepper	20
Peru balsam	100
	1000

Formula 8

Chypre soap

Bergamot	400
Methyl ionone	100
Geranium, African	100
Civet absolute	5
Orris resin	50
Castoreum absolute	5

Coumarin	50
Musk xylene	30
Pakmoss	50
Patchouli	30
Santal	80
Peru balsam	100
	1000

Formula 9

Cologne soap

Petitgrain para	200
Lavender	50
Bergamot	200
Lemon	150
Lemongrass	50
Methyl anthranilate	40
Rosemary	60
Geranium, African	100
Citral	100
Methyl naphthal ketone	50
	1000

Formula 10

Heliotrope soap

Benzaldehyde	10
Benzyl acetate	40
Bromstyrole	10
Phenyl ethyl alcohol	90
Geraniol, Java	100
Sweet orange	50
Heliotropin	300
Anisic aldehyde	50
Ionone	50
Benzoin resin	100
Musk xylene	50
Peru balsam	100
Vanillin	50
	1000

Formula 11

Herb

Thyme, red	100
Rosemary	100
Lavender, spike	200
Fennel	50
Spearmint	50
Geranium, bourbon	300
Cassia	50
Clove	100
Camomile	50
	1000

Formula 12

Herb compound	500
Citronella, Java	100
Terpineol	300
Rosewood	100
	1000

Formula 13

Bergamot	200
Rosewood	200
Geranium, Algerian	100
Miel compound	100
Amyl cinnamic aldehyde	50
Civet absolute	10
Peru balsam	60
Musk xylene	30
Phenylethyl alcohol	150
Terpineol	100
	1000

Formula 14

Honey

Citronella	450
Lemon	200
Cinnamon leaf	100
Bay	50
Iso-butyl phenylacetate	20
Phenylethyl alcohol	100
Phenylacetic acid	30
Musk residuces	50
	1000

Formula 15

Hyacinth soap

Benzyl acetate	200
Rosewood	200
Brometyrole	50
Phenyl ethyl alcohol	100
Methyl cinnamate	30
Cananga	50
Ionone	50
Clove	70
Geranium	50
Galbanum resin	50
Amyl cinnamic aldehyde	50
Styrax resin	100
	1000

Formula 16

Jasmin soap

Benzyl acetate	200
Rosewood	100
Petitgrain para	80
Phenyl ethyl alcohol	100
Bergamot	100
Amyl salicylate	70

Sweet orange	25
Cananga	100
Clove	50
Civet absolute	3
Orris resin	50
Undecalactone	2
Amyl cinnamic aldehyde	40
Liquidambar resin	50
Musk xylene	30
	1000

Formula 17

Jasmin *(Another formula)*

Benzyl acetate	200
Rosewood	200
Terpineol	100
Petitgrain para	150
Amyl salicylate	50
Cananga	50
Ionone	50
Methyl anyhranilate	50
Clove	20
Amyl cinnamic aldehyde	50
Musk xylene	30
Resin (styrax)	50
	1000

Formula 18

Lavender soap

Bergamot	70
Geraniol, Java	50
White thyme	20
Spike lavender	100
Lavender	130
Rosemary	100
Clove	10
Orris resin	30

Benzoin resin	70
Coumarin	50
Musk xylene	30
Oakmoss	30
Patchouli	10
Santal	30
	1000

Formula 19

Lily soap

Benzyl acetate	50
Rosewood	200
Terpineol	200
Citronellol	200
Bergamot	100
Cananga	50
Heliotropin	50
Ionone	30
Hydroxy citronellal	100
Cyclamen aldehyde	10
Amyl cinnamic aldehyde	20
Coumarin	10
Styrax resin	80
	1000

Formula 20

Musk

Musk ambrette	20
Musk ketone	30
Vetivert	40
Santal	100
Methyl ionone	200
Liquidambar resin	70
Bergamot	100
Geranium, Bourbon	200
Musk extract, 3 per cent	100
Civet absolute	5

Castoreum absolute	5
Terpineol	100
Cassia oil	30
	1000

Formula 21

Palm and olive oils

Palm compound	500
Terpineol	200
Lavender, spike	300
	1000

Formula 22

Frose soap

Citronellol	200
Phenyl ethyl alcohol	200
Geraniol palmarosa	200
Verbena	20
Ionone	50
Clove	10
Geranium, African	150
Orris resin	50
Musk xylene	30
Santal	50
Trichlor phenyl methyl carbinyl acetate	30
Vetivert	10
	1000

Formula 23

Santal soap

Rosewood	100
Geraniol, Java	100
Clove	30
Geranium, African	50
Orris resin	50
Coumarin	70

Musk zylene	30
Patchouli	20
Peru balsam	100
Santal	400
Vetivert	50
	1000

Formula 24

Violet soap

Rosewood	100
Bergamot	150
Methyl heptine carbonate	10
Cananga	40
Methyl Ionone	300
Mimosa absolute	20
Anisic aldehyde	30
Ionone	200
Orris resin	50
Iso-eugenol	10
Musk xylene	30
Styrax resin	30
Vetivert	30
	1000

Antiseptic and Medicated Soaps

Antiseptic and medicated soaps are made up with all kinds of medicaments, such as iodoform, thymol, phenol, betanaphthol, sulphur, etc. Many of the essential oils used in perfuming the soaps are highly antiseptic.

Perfuming Boxes

When packing wrapped soap it is advisable to spray the boxes with perfume–an example of which is given :

Formula 25

Violet soap

Bergamot oil	30
Geranium oil, Algerian	40
Rose, synthetic	30
Jasmin, synthetic	10
Tuberose, synthetic	20
Oakmoss	5
Benzyl cinnamate	20
Coumarin	20
Musk ambrette	10
Tincture of civet, 3 per cent	100
Tincture of benzoin, 10 per cent	715
	1000

8
Testing of Soaps and Detergents

Introduction

For a practical and realistic evaluation of quality of soap and detergents, performance test constitute the ideal yardstick. Thus the need of the testing is to prove performance that is material has to pass through various specification in a process. Phsico-chemical analysis alone is not adequate. This chapter highlights current practices followed during testing from time to time improve their precision and accuracy.

Test Methods

Few methods for measurement of physico-chemical properties of surface active agents have been various industries. Since there are upwards of thousand available surface active agents whose claims of activity widely overlap, for chioce of the best agent for a given purpose it is necessary that all their properties be recognised and selection made accordingly. Certainly if an agent is not stable to hard water is resembles soap, and must possess other properties sufficiently different from soap to make it competitive. Screening tests can save much effort and can increase the general knowledge of utility when properly used. The tests described have been used successfully for years and cover the general properties of synthetics which make them industrially useful.

An over simplified statement of the detergent process indicates that it is the removal of soil (matter out of place) from a surface in some medium, generally through the application of mechanical force, and most frequently in the presence of a substance which may lower the adherence of the soil to the surface, then maintain the soil in suspension so that it can be rinsed or flashed away. When it is considered that the medium in which the cleansing can take place may be aqueous, nonaqueous, or mixed, that the force applied may be of almost any kind, and that the surface and soils to be separated are legion, then the real complexity of the detergency picture becomes apparent. Since some surface may be satisfactorily cleaned in one or more media using a wide variety of cleaning agents on any of them, a choice must be made which will prove economically satisfactory. When all these factors are recognised it may not appear so unusual that no accord has been reached as to recognised testing methods.

The most effective methods, and the most reasonable one, is to perform the laboratory screening tests, meanwhile building up a fund of data to be coorelated with practice, progressing as soon as feasible to a semi-or full-scale trial under practical conditions of operation. Regardless of verbal expression to the contrary, this is the procedure most generally followed.

Statistical Presentation of Data

Knowledge of the reliability of result obtained in any test is necessary. Frequently this is accomplished simply by comparison with standard samples. Certainly the use of samples of known characteristics for comparison purposes is highly desirable but this method lacks precision. In the presentation of data the ASTM Manual on Quality Control of Materials is a useful reference.

In the operation of a test method it should be realised that the error of the average obtained is inversely proportional to the square root of the number of observations made. This simply means that in order to improve upon the information obtained, the method must either be improved to reduce variables which are recognised in lack of control, or the number of replicate samples must be increased. However this can be carried to extremes when it is recalled that the average of four observations reduces the error of the average only to half that of the single observation. Likewise that the average of 16 samples or observations has 1/4 the error of the single observation. It quickly becomes apparent that for minimisation of effort that the test method itself should be more rigidly controlled if this is possible.

The minimum data which should be presented in recording experimental results is the mean ($\overline{x}$), the standard deviation (σ), the number of observations (n) and sometimes the range. From these data it is a relatively simple matter to compare results and certainly offers much over no statistical data of any kind, as means for ascertaining the reliability of the experimental work.

Having developed the experimental data, the next question that will arise is whether samples which have been tested actually differ. It is suggested that a rough approximation of the differences between two mean values can be obtained by applying the twice standard error criterion to the data. In other words, if the difference between two mean values is equal to, or greater than twice the larger standard error, the chances are roughly 95 out of 100 that the two samples are different. This is a useful and reliable method when more than six replicate samples have been used in the observation of the mean value. However, for less than this number of replications the approximation becomes even more rough. The significance level between the difference of two mean values can be ascertained more accurately by several methods (Ref. Table I in the ASTM Manual) which present the factors for calculating 90, 95, and 99% confidence limits for averages which includes the number of observations from 4 up to 25 and greater. These values were computed from Fisher's table of "*t*". Application of this method will indicate for these several levels of confidence whether the differences between observed mean values are real.

Still a further method is use of Student's *t* for the comparison of two means. The calculations used are given below :

$$t = \frac{\overline{X} - \overline{X}'}{\sigma}\sqrt{\frac{n_1 \times n_2}{n_1 + n_2}}$$

where

$$\sigma^2 = \frac{\left[\Sigma(X'^2) - \frac{(\Sigma(X'))^2}{n_2} + \Sigma(X^2) - \frac{(\Sigma(X))^2}{n_1}\right]}{n_1 + n_2 - 2}$$

Although these calculations may look rather formidable they actually are relatively simple and straight forward. Having calculated σ^2 it is possible to enter student's table of *t* for the number of degrees of freedom observed, to determine the significance of the difference between two means.

In analytical work it is generally assumed that the reproducibility of data should lie within the 99.25% range. In other words, the chances of being in error should be extremely small. However, in tests such as those described here, where control of many factors is very difficult, the significance level may be considerably broader. Whether this is a 95 or 90% level of significance depends upon the number of samples used, the reproducibility of the method, and the judgment of the operator. Obviously the significance level should be as high as possible, without, as previously suggested, increasing the number of observations too extrensively.

Radioactive Tracer Technic

As a new medium, this tachnic offers possibilities for the investigation of the quantitative characteristics of a system not readily susceptible to other methods. It also makes possible the estimation of extremely minute amounts of materials. Other uses for the radioactive tracer technic lie in the calibration of other methods of examination and in some instances can be used in certain industrial applications for estmation of quality or quantity.

There are two general classifications in the detergent industry to which this method has been applied. One is in estimating the surface active characteristics of agents and the other has been applied to metal cleaning processes. In the former investigation agents were synthesized containing a radioactive isotope and the orientation of these at solution–air interfaces measured. The adsorption or relative solubility of ordinarily insoluble salts of surface active agents was measured using a radioactive calcium salt as the insolubilising agent. In the metal cleaning application tagged hydrophobic materials such as stearic acid were used in the soiling medium and the ease of removal from metal surface was measured.

Health hazards in the use of radioactive materials must always be considered and it was this that ruled against the use of graphitised carbon 14 as a constituent of a graphite soil for fabric.

In general the radioactive tracer technique would appear to be a most useful tool where the sensitivity of a method is to be determined or for which the usual methods of investigation fail. It currently appears that for the detergent industry, the radioactive tracer technic will find its greatest use in research rather than in regular control operations.

Water Hardness

The water hardness values chosen were for both soft and hard areas in order that detergent might be evaluated for use under the extremes of operating conditions ordinarily encountered. The water itself is comprised of Ca and Mg salts in the ratio of 60 to 40. There are those who object correctly that many synthetic detergent are more affected by the Ca in the water than by the Mg ions, hence that the ratio of Ca in the water should be incraesed. Others will criticise the range of water hardnesses chosen. The obvious answer to both criticisms is that a really effective agent will be only mildly affected by either type of water hardness, and that at any rate a full investigation of the characterisitics of a material will include concentration-water hardness curves for a range up to 1,000 ppm. The present method has successfully served the purpose of screening potential detergents :

2000 ppm. water

Ratio of Ca: Mg of 60:40 is 29.6 g. $MgSo_4 \cdot 7H_2O$, 26.4 g. $CaCl_2.2H_2O$

Dissolve separately in distilled water and make up to 15 litres. Dilution to hardness desired :

$$\frac{\text{No. of m l. wanted} \times \text{hardness}}{2000} = \text{(A) m l. of 2000 pp m. water to use}$$

Make (A) up to volume wanted with distilled water.

Screening Tests

With so many available agents it is desirable to use screening tests to minimise the effort involved in running laborious detergency evaluation, since there are frequently other factors involved which may aid in controlling their application. Frequently the conditions which either precede or follow a deterging or cleansing operation, or the chemicals with which they may come into contact may control the type of agent which may be used .

It frequently is necessary that the agent to be used in a plant must not only be an effective detergent, but must perform several other additional functions. For example, it may be necessary that the detergent be an excellent wetting agent, must have high effectiveness for promoting emulsion formation, or if not completely rinsed from the fabric may beneficially aid in rewetting that fabric satisfactorily.

The tests which follow are designed to differentiate between the characteristics of surface active agents so that suitable selection may be made. These tests can frequently be initiated prior to wash testing to save much time and effort. The discussion which accompanies each test will further suggest some of the applications for these or other similar materials and reasons for choice.

Acid Stability

A surface-active agent chemically unaffected by acid has many potential uses. Soap is not useful under these conditions since it is decomposed, forming inactive, and many times obnoxious, oily or waxy fatty acids. In the textile industry, the acid-stable agents are used among other purposes for acid-dyeing operations and in carbonising baths. The metal trades utilise them in pickling and electroplating baths, and they may even be used in the acidisation of oil wells.

Chemical stability may very markedly among the available agents. Esters may be stable to slight acid concentrations for some time, but increase in acid concentration, temperature, or time of exposure may induce decomposition. Sulphonic acid types of agents generally are quite stable to acids, but sulphonic acid separation may be mistaken for decomposition.

One possible method for evaluating these agents is to add a known excess of acid to given solution of the agent, boil under reflux, then back titrate, thus quantitatively measuring any change. This method, while quantitatively, does not provide acid concentrations of the degree many times encountered in industry. Consequently the qualitative method later described has given adequate results.

The other agents may therefore be used in acid media of considerable strength, but a further elimination would be required by evaluation under conditions approaching actual use as closely as possible. Combinations of tests such as acid stability, surface-tension measurements in acid media, and stability to metallic ions under acid conditions may prove adequate means for comparison of several otherwise almost identical materials.

Acid stability test method

Apparatus : 250 ml wide-mouth extraction flasks, Allihn condensers, four-bulb, Porous plate fragments.

Procedure : Transfer 100 ml of a solution containing 1.0 g. of agent to a 250 ml. wide-mouth extraction flask and add a piece of porous plate to prevent bumping. Attach condenser.

Bring to the boil and record appearance.

Add 0.1 per cent (1 ml. of 10 per cent) sulphuric acid and boil 15 min. Record appearance. Lack of stability is exhibited by turbidity, separation of an oil, and loss of lathering power.

If no change occurs or the change is minor, add acid to provide 1 per cent acidity (0.5 ml of concentrated sulphuric acid) through the condenser. Boil for 15 min. and again record appearance.

If no change occurs, or the change is minor, add acid provide 3 per cent acidity (1.0 ml. of concentrated sulphuric) and boil a further 15 min. period.

If the product is still stable add sufficient acid for 10 per cent concentration (6.5 ml. concentrated sulphuric). Again boil 15 min. If no change occurs record this fact and discontinue test. At this acid concentration there may be a separation of oil which may perhaps be sulphuric acid insoluble at the conditions prevailing. Dilute with an equal volume of water and agitate vigorously to determine whether foaming power has been destroyed. If separated sulphonic acid has resulted this test indicates its stability but relative insolubility.

Record as "stable," "partially decomposed," or "decomposed" at the acid concentrations indicated.

Alkali Stability and Solubility in Caustic Soda Solutions

Although soap is chemically stable to alkali, it may be salted out and loses its effectiveness whenevre high caustic alkali concentration is reached.

Consequently, there is a definite place for an alkali-soluble surface-active agent. Perhaps the outstanding use for an agent of this type is in mercerisation, but surface-active agents are also used in manufacture of viscose yarn. There are many other processes where lower alkalinity values are used in which fully soluble, active agents may be effective. It is obvious, however, that such agent must not be subject to decomposition, so that a suitable test may serve to screen out those agents most likely to successful application under the foregoing conditions of usage.

A second test of a more quantitative nature is used to determine the approximate solubility of the wetting agent in sodium hydroxide solutions, while saponification determiations may be made if the materials are of saponifiable nature and such quantitative data may prove necessary.

Few materials are fully soluble in 25 per cent caustic soda solutions, but in many cases such an agent is most desirable, so that an adequate screening tests amy materially simplify practical testing.

The low surface tension of the more dilute solutions of surface-active agent in dilute alkali are to be expected, but what actually is desired is surface tension lowering even in concentrated alkali, as shown by Areskap 100. However, lowered effectiveness of even this compound may be expected at caustic soda concentrations in excess of 21.6 per cent, or Areskap concentrations greater than 0.8 per cent at 21.6 per cent NaOH solution.

Test method—alkali stability

Apparatus : 250 ml. wide-mouth extraction flasks. Allihn condensers, four-bulb, Porous plate fragments.

Procedure : Dissolve 1.0 g. of sample in 74 ml. of water. Add 25.0 g. of sodium hydroxide (c.p.) and a small piece of porous plate and swirl to dissolve the sodium hydroxide. Record appearance of system after sodium hydroxide is dissolved.

Boil under reflux for 15 min. and again record appearance which most generally will be a salting-but effect.

Cool the contents of the flask. Decant the solution through a fluted filter.

Transfer the insoluble agent from the paper to a beaker containing 25ml. of distilled water. Add 3 drops of methyl orange indicator solution, stir and titrate with dilute acid to a faintly acid end point.

Stir thoroughly, heat to boil, permit to cool to room temperature, and note separation of oil. If oil separates under these condition, and material has proven unstable to dilute acid, record the material as being "unstable." If the insoluble material completely dissolve in acidified solution and shows no separation, consider the product as "stable."

Test method—solubility

Apparatus : 1 - litre Erlenmeyer falsk, Dispensing burette.

Reagents : Solution sodium hydroxide, c.p., 30 g. per 100 g. of solution.

Procedure : Dissolve 1.0 g. agent in 9.0 g. distilled water, add 90 g. of 30 per cent sodium hydroxide solution and transfer to a 1-litre Erlenmeyer flask. Rinse the beaker in which the solution was preared into the flask with small increments of distilled water. Continue the addition of distilled water either until the solution becomes clear and free from undissolved particles, or when 900 ml. of water have been added.

The surface tension of resultant solution is measured at 25 ±1 C.

Calculations :

$$\text{Percentage Agent} = \frac{1.0}{\text{wt. water (g.)} + 100\text{ g.}} \times 100$$

$$\text{Percentage NaOH} = \frac{27.0}{\text{wt. water (g.)} + 100\text{ g.}} \times 100$$

Stability toward Metallic Ions

Water solubility of the metallic salts of surface–active agents will greatly influence their application. First, these agents must be stable to the calcium and magnesium ions of hard water, since one of the factors unfavourable to soap is its ready formation of insoluble, sticky lime and magnesia soaps. In textile processing many operations require the use of acids, as for example, in dyeing, and metal from equipment may be dissolved, so that in this case the agent must not only be a good wetting agent but must be chemically stable both to acid metallic salts incidentally formed. In carbonising wool a wetting agent may find considerable usage, but must stable acid or to a combination of acid and aluminium salts. For scouring pulled wool, a detergent is required which is stable to lime salts. Other agents may be useful in metal salt solutions as in electroplating, pickling or soldering fluxes. Although the foregoing is but a partial list of uses where metallic salts are encountered, it should be evident that knowledge of solubility of the metallic salts of the surface-active agent should be available.

There are two general methods for obtaining these solubility data: One is to prepare the salts by metathesis or other process and determine their solubility; the other is to add the metallic ion in question to a solution of the agent and determine the point at which a given maximum degree of turbidity is obtained, where lathering ceases, or both. There are advantages to both methods. The preparation of the pure compound permits accurate measurement of values, but experience with metallic soaps. for example, has shown that the solubility characterisitics entirely different after drying than they are in solution or dispersion, prior to drying. Furthermore, attempted preparation of a salt will present an entirely different problem from one in which the ion represents a small portion of the system. Casual contamination in many cases will different results from an attempt to measure the solubility of the salt in water, since the pH value of the solution will have profound effect upon degree of solubility.

The specific metallic ions are chosen for this test for the following reasons:

(a) Calcium and magnesium because they are responsible for water hardness.

(b) Copper and nickel because of possible contamination from processing equipment.

(c) Aluminium and iron salts because they readily form insoluble salts and any agent stable to them should prove useful for many purpose.

(d) Barium was chosen because sulphates and even sulphonates are precipitated or become turbid in its presence.

(e) Heavy metal salts because they are represented by lead contamination.

(f) Zinc salts since they are somewhat amphoteric in nature and are present in certain processing baths.

(g) Other salts or varying concentrations at varying pH values may advantageously be evaluated, but their applications are more specific.

Test method

Samples : 1.0 per cent solution in distilled water.

Metallic Salt Solution: 1.0 per cent solution (dry weight basis) of the following c.p. salts are used :

Salt	Weight for 1 per cent (dry basis) g. per 100 ml.
$CaC1^2 2H_2O$	1.327
$MgSO_4.7H_2O$	2.048
$CuSO_4.5H_2O$	1.564
$A1_2(SO_4)_3.18H_2O$	1.948
$BaC1_2.2H_2O$	1.173
$Fe_2(SO_4)_3.xH_2O$	—
$Pb(NO_3)_2$	1.000
$ZnSO_4.7H_2O$	1.781
$Ni(NO_3)_2.6H_2O$	1.591

Dissolve the required amount of salt in water, cool if necessary, and make up to volume.

Equipment : 50 ml. Erlenmeyer flasks, Mohr measuring pipettes.

Procedure : Transfer 10 ml. volumes of 1 per cent surface-active agent solution to each of Erlenmeyer flasks.

Add solution of metallic salt dropwise from a Mohr measuring pipette to the solution of surface-active agent until the solution becomes turbid or precipitation is noted. Record the volume of metallic salt solution used, and heat the flask containing the mixture to the boil. If the solution becomes clear, add additional metallic salt: (*a*) Until 10 ml. of metallic salt solution has been added. (*b*) Terminate the test when the addition of metallic salt causes no further precipitation or when lather no longer is formed.

The total volume metallic salt solution used to attain the end point is recorded.

Calculation : Metallic ion stability = volume metallic ion solution × 10.

Surface and Interfacial Tension Values and Spreading Coefficient

Potential detergent and wetting action may be ascertained by measurement of surface and interfacial tension. In general, the greater the ability to reduce surface tension and to lower the interfcial tension between oil and water, for example, the more useful the composition may be for producing desired effects under actual conditions of usage. These measurements have a practical application since dilution effect and quality may thus be indicated. The activity of certain baths, as for example electroplating baths, in which a surface-active "anti–pitting" agent has been used, may be controlled by use of these methods.

Surface-tension measurements generally refer to the liquid-air interface, while interfacial tensions refer to interfaces such as liquid-liquid or solid-liquid. Since these interfaces are so interrelated, it is difficult to discuss them separately, but an attempt will be made to do so as a means for simplification.

Surface tension

(a) Capillary height or pressure.

(b) Drop weight.

(c) Maximum bubble pressure.

(d) Capillary waves.

(e) Vibrating jet.

(f) Drop height.

(g) Drop-shape.

(h) Maximum pressure in drops.

(i) Method of Sentis (capillary tube hanging drop and measurement of meniseus height in tube above drop).

(j) Ring method.

Interfacial tension

Wetting of liquid by a liquid, or solid by a liquid may be estimated by several methods. The solid-liquid interface may be measured by several techniques which require estimation of the angle of contact :

(a) Pressure of displacement.

(b) Horizontal plate.

(c) Vertical bar.

(d) Deposited film.

Liquid-liquid interfaces may be determined by several methods :

(a) Stalagmometer.

(b) Drop weight (Millard)

(c) Ring

(d) Ripple.

The facility with which a solution may wet another surface, whether solid or liquid, may have considerable influence upon subsequent operations. Cleaning or dying a fibre, wetting a metal surface or foliage, and formation of emulsions all are dependent upon optimum interfacial tension properties.

The lower the surface and interfacial tensions of a system, the better the chance of forming an emulsion or wetting a given surface. Cupples has applied these data to foliage wetting by utilising the measurement of surface tension against air and against mineral oil. The spreading coefficient (SC) of a system may be calculated as follows :

SC = surface tension oil — (surface tension solution + interfacial tension) (1)

The more positive the value obtained, the greater the spreading value of a system. Consequently, the possible utility of the wetting agent for insecticidal sprays may be predicated as as emulsifier for mineral or other oil, or as a means for wetting oiled soiled surfaces.

In general, the du Nouy instrument may most satisfactorily be used for liquid-liquid systems. One instrument may furthermore be used for the determination of both surface and interfacial tensions. For control purposes, the dial reading after calibration may be adequate, but if highest accuracy is desired, ring corrections have been developed.

Surface Active Agents

Since surface activity is increased by this addition, the term "builder" for added sodium sulphate is warranted, and this effect may be attributed at least in part to orientation of the surface-active agent at the interfaces involved.

The generally high surface activity of these agents upon dilution indicates their potential utility for the wide variety of uses open to surface-active agents. Those materials with most highly positive spreading coefficients are potentially useful as insectidical spreading agents and are most likely to be good emulsifying agents.

Test Method

Apparatus : Either the precision (surface tension) or interfacial tensiometers may be used.

Calibration :

(a) Level the tensiometer.

(b) Adjust the torsion wire until it is taut.

(c) Adjust vernier of scale to zero.

(d) Adjust platinum ring.

(e) Place piece of paper on ring and adjust until index level of arm is opposite reference line of mirror (thus compensating for weight of paper).

(f) Place weights totalling 600 mg. on paper platform.

(g) Turn adjusting head (controlling dial reading) until the index level of the arm is opposite the reference line of mirror. Record dial reading to 0.10 division.

(h) Calculate scale reading as follows : Weight added to ring (*m*) = 0.600 g. Mean circumference of ring (*L*) = 4.00 cm. Acceleration of gravity (*G*) = 980.3 cm. per sq. sec. (at Chicago) :

$$Y = \frac{MG}{2L} = \frac{0.600 \times 980.3}{2 \times 4.00} = 73.52 \text{ dynes per cm.}$$

For the interfacial tensiometer substitute the pertinent values in the above equation.

(i) If the recorded value is greater than the calculated value of *h,* shorten the torsion arm, or lengthen it if the recorded value is less.

(j) Repeat the calibration procedure, readjusting to the zero position after each change of torsion arm length until the dial reading corresponds to the calculated value.

(k) Adjust the dial reading to zero, remove the weights and the paper platform and readjust so that the torsion arm indicator is in alignment with the reference line of the mirror.

Precautions :

(a) The wire of the ring should lie in one plane, be horizontal, and round.

(b) The vessel holding the liquid should be large enough so that curvature of the free surface shall have no effect upon the shape of the liquid column raised by the ring.

(c) The liquid surface should be free from motion.

(d) The ring should be only very slowly raised.

(e) There should be no evaporation or coating of the surface.

Procedure : Prepare 1.0 per cent solutions of the agents in distilled water. Retain a portion of dilution. Determine surface tension by averaging four measurement. The reading is taken at the point where the film breaks, while evary effort is made to maintain the torsion arm indicator exactly opposite the reference line of the mirror. The interfacial tension measurement is made by immersing the ring in the aqueous layer, then carefully flowing a sufficient depth of layer of paraffin oil (Nujol) over the aqueous surface that the inverted V of the ring shall at all times during the measurement be immersed in the oil. The measurement is carefully made, since extremely low interfacial tensions are hard to discern, and in some instances no more than one measurement may be made because of preferential wetting of the ring by the oil. The results are averaged and recorded.

The ring is cleaned between determination by immersion in turn in carbon tetrachloride and dilute hydrochloric acid solution followed by flaming.

Similar readings are obtained for 0.25 per cent solutions of the agents, and 0.0625 per cent solutions.

Corrections for surface tension measurements may be made by reference to calibration curves or to the data developed by Harkins and Jordan (4) or Zuidema and Waters (7) for interfacial measurements.

Lime Soap Dispersion

The synthetic surface–active agents will themselves form calcium and magnesium salts of varying degrees of solubility, and highly effective compounds will exhibit exceptional tolerance for these ions. A possible use for these agents is in combination with soda soap as a dispersant for subsequently formed insoluble soaps. This lime soap dispersing action has been put to use in the war effort since both the Army and Navy use certain synthetics in combination with soap in their all-purpose or sea–water detergents. A further possibility is that these synthetics may be used to cleanse lime soap—containing garments, since these soaps may readily be removed either by solubilising them or removing them by peptisation or emulsification. In such cases high washing temperatures will have important effect upon degree of removal by the synthetic. Two possible conditions may thus be encountered : (1) presence of large amounts of insoluble soap; (2) presence of relatively light films of insoluble soap. Laboratory test conditions should be chosen which will duplicate the most severe conditions which will be encountered, so that relatively large amounts of soap should be present in the test medium.

Nonlathering agents may also be useful for lime soap dispersion (phosphates) but in cases where soap is actually regenerated, by exchange of ions to form a soluble calcium or magnesium complex, a lessr amount of lime soap should be used or formed in situ, and the solution should be titrated with the regenerating agent to permanent lather.

Test Method

Reagents : 2.3 per cent sodium oleate (dry weight). Either pure sodium oleate or oleate flake soap.

0.34 per cent $CaC1_2$ solution.

0.2 N HC1.

Methyl orange–xylene cyanole indicator solution (Eastman No. 2216).
10 per cent volume solution of auxiliary agent under investigation.

Procedure :

(a) *Add* 1–ml. increments of auxiliary or dispersing agent up to 8 ml. to separate 20 ml. volumes of 2.3 per cent soap soiution in 125 ml. flasks. The solutions are then shaken and to them are added 25 ml. of 0.34 per cent calcium chloride. Heat for 15 min. on a water bath, then suction filter through a prepared No. 4 Whatman paper on a Gooch crucible. The flask and crucible are then washed with three 10 ml. portions of distilled water. If complete filtration is impossible with 8 ml. of auxiliary agent, this fact is recorded without further examination.

(b) The filtered solutions are titrated with 0.2 N HCI to the xylol–cyanole end point which is gray in colour. A blank for each agent comprising 20 ml. of soap solution, 25 ml. of calcium chloride solution, and the volume of auxiliary agent required, are titrated without filtration. When the filtered test sample has a titration value practically equal to that of the blank, the volume of auxiliary agent required to produce complete dispersion is recorded.

(c) The results are expressed as centigrams of auxiliary agent required to disperse 45.5 mg. of calcium oleate formed. One millilitre of auxiliary agent is equal to a dispersion number of 10.

Calculation : Dispersion number = ml. auxiliary agent × 10

Practical Wetting Tests

Since the usual surface and interfacial tension measurements limit the systems under investigation to liquid-air, liquid-liquid, or liquid-solid, more practical systems may prove useful in evaluation. In these systems capillarity may be a sufficient criterrion of suitability, and the height to which the solution rises in a strip of fabric or paper may provide adequate comparisons. In these cases the interfaces involved may be liquid-solid-air-oil, but other materials may further complicate the picture.

Generally Draves-Clarkson skein test and the canvas disk method are used. The canvas disk test can readily be used under conditions not suited to the use of skeins.

Regardless of what test surface is used, standardisation of the test is necessary. With skein preparation wetting times will vary for a given weight of skein with humidity, spool, tension on the skein winder, and age of yarn or variation from lot to lot. The canvas used may age to give progressively slower wetting times as the finishing agents become progressively more water repellent. In fact, whenever *any fibre, yarn* or fabric is used, steps should be taken to standardise against a stable wetting agent under a given set of conditions, and this standardisation made periodically, to save embarrassment. The Draves–Clarkson and canvas disk tests have in their favour simplicity of operation, minimum of equipment, and adequate reproducibility. Both methods are subject to variation in the standard fabric or yarn used in the determination, either as a result of aging or actual variation in the character of the manufactured article. They furthermore have been most widely used, and evalution data on either basis are available from the literature. Either method provides data which, under careful control, can be used for the evalution of comparative wetting efficiency, but their values are not directly comparable.

***Test method :* Draves–Clarkson test**

Equipment : 500 ml. graduate.

Hook or sinker, 1.50 g. in weight (of No. 12B. and S.gage copper: with ¼-in. hood opening

Anchor, 20 g. in weight.

Skeins : A 5.0 g. skein of two–ply (70/2 combed peeler yarn) is prepared such that an 18–in. loop can be formed. The yarn may best be standardised against a standard sample of wetting agent, adjusting the weight of skein to yield a specific wetting time.

Wetting Test :

(a) Prepare 500 ml. of 1.0 per cent test solution.

(b) Transfer 250 ml. of 1.0 per cent solution to a 600 ml. beaker, add 250 ml. distilled water and adjust the temperature to 25 ±1 C.

(c) Transfer the temperature-adjusted 0.50 per cent solution to a 500 ml. graduate.

(d) Attach the hool or sinker to the 18-in loop, hold the skein in the middle and cut the end opposite the hook.

(e) Transfer the hook, anchor, and skein to the graduate of solution and dip the hook into the solution until the surface is just touched, then drop the skein and start the stopwatch simultaneously.

(f) The sinking time is attained when the skein sinks, and the hook just reaches the level of the anchor, at which time the stopwatch again is snapped.

(g) Repeat steps d, e, and f until five replicate skeins have been tested,using the same solution throughout.

(h) In a manner similar to step c, prepare an 0.25, 0.125, 0.0625 or further dilution until a wetting time in one dilution of + 180 sec. is attained for two replicate skeins. The test is then terminated.

(i) The mean values for each dilution shall then be reported.

Note : This test is applicable to acid, alkaline, or saline conditions.

Canvas disk test method

Equipment : Vernon duck.

Steel die, 1 in. in diameter.

Carbon filter tube of 75 mm. stem and 38 mm. inside top diameter.

600 ml. Griffin beaker with spout.

Disk : The disks may best be cut using a 1-in. steel die. Cut the disks on a smooth, hardwood surface. The disks for use must be flat and free from rough edges and raveling. Cut the disks from the fabric area bounded by 1 in. within either side of the selvedge.

Wetting Test :

(a) Transfer 500 ml. of test solution at 25 ± 1 C. to a 600 ml. beaker.

(b) Drop the flat canvas disk into the funnel and quickly invert and immerse in the test solution.

(c) Start the timer as soon as the disk enters the solution. The individual test is considered as terminated when the disk first being to sink.

(d) Four replicate tests shall be made for each dilution tested.

(e) The average results shall be reported as seconds wetting time for each of the concentration tested, which shall be 0.5, 0.25, 0.125, 0.0625 or further dilution until the disks give wetting times greater than 180 sec., at which point the test shall be terminated.

Note : This test is applicable to acid, alkaline, or saline conditions.

The test equipment should be so aligned that a disk held horizontally by the filter tube should be 1 in. below the surface of the liquid.

Rewetting Test

If frequently is desirable to know whether the agent in question is suitable for rewetting purposes since this may be an important factor in its choice for subsequent processing.

Briefly, this test consists of applying the solution of rewetting agent by means of dipping in a bath and running through squeeze rolls (a pair of regular hand wringer rolls will prove satisfactory). Good impregnation is obtained by running two ends (i.e. opposite end of tape fed through wringer first) at a sufficiently high roll pressure to give a 100% weight pick-up. The test strips are then either air or oven force-dried and allowed to condition over night. The next morning the rewetting times are run in much the same manner as wetting times. Though pretested, the tape has been found to vary from lot to lot, and drying conditions have been found to alter the rewetting times considerably so that it is necessary to run a standard agent for comparison with the experimental sample.

Test Method

Equipment : Stopwatch, 500 ml. graduate, Hook, 1.00 g., Anchor, 40 g., Distance hook to anchor, 20 mm., Tape, length 9 in., width 1¼ in, Laboratory padder or wringer rolls.

Impregnation : A 21 in. length of tape (sufficient to allow for shrinkage and trimming) is required for duplicate determinations at each concentration of surface active agent.

An initial bath concentration of 0.0625% is suggested, through this may be adjusted to double or half this concentration, depending upon effectiveness in speed of wetting.

The bath temperature is adjusted to 70°C.

The tape is run through the padder or wringer twice, reversing ends at 200 pounds pressure (20 lb. pressure/inch face). Adjustment of add-on or solution pick-up is made for 100% weight increase of tape.

The tape is oven-dried 10 minutes at 105 C. or dried overnight and conditioned overnight in either case at 70 °F. and 65% R.H.

Rewetting time :

(a) The 500 ml. graduate is filled with water at the required temperature. (A fresh portion of water is used for each test to avoid contamination by surfactant).

(b) The hook is inserted through the tape about ¼ in. from one end on the centre line.

(c) The tape is held by the free end so that the anchor and bottom hook are just submerged in the liquid in the graduate.

(d) The tape is dropped and the stopwatch is started when the anchor strikes the bottom of the graduate.

(e) When the hook and tape start to sink at a constant rate the sinking time (rewetting time) is reached and the watch is stopped.

Lather Values

The relative lathering action of surface-active agents is obviously important with detergents and wetting agents used largely for their foaming action. Soap, as the time-recognised detergent, foams profusely in soft water or even in hard water if a sufficient amount is present to overcome both water hardness and the insoluble soap formed. As a consequence, foam is now considered a requisite to detergent action. Many detergent adjuncts, which are detergents in their own right, produce no foam. These adjuvants are the alkaline salts such as the carbonates, silicates, borates, and phosphates. The fact that these materials did not foam disproved the theory that foam was useful as a measure of detergency, but the volume of foam formed is still a very valuable property of surface-active materials. Ability to foam at extreme dilution or under adverse conditions may be an important factor in application. Wetting agents have been used in the wash water of conditioning systems to remove foreign substances, but excessive foam would be a liability rather than an asset.

Many methods for measuring foaming characteristics of compositions have been devised. From the consideration of equipment involved they may be calssified as follows :

(a) Bubble cylinder.

(b) Manual manipulation of closed container.

(c) Capillary under constant pressure.

(d) Solution drop, open cylinder.

(e) Mechanical agitation in closed vessel.

(f) Single bubble.

The subject of foams is a complicated one, but for many purpose a measurement of foam height will suffice as a means for preliminary comparison. The method often used in the absence of other equipment is to shake a volume of solution in a stoppered graduate in a standard manner,and measure the foam formed. The method provides only a rough estimate, since a variation of ± 15 per cent is about the best that may be expected under carefully controlled conditions.

The most satisfactory method for the evalution of foaming agents is that developed by Ross and Miles. This test is easy to make, the equipment made according to ASTM specifications is commercially available and relatively inexpensive, outside variables are reduced to a minimum, and reproducibility is good. Fig. 8.1 and 8.2 give the necessary specifications which must be checked against the equipment as supplied. Careful evalution will require tests over a range of concentrations and temperatures.

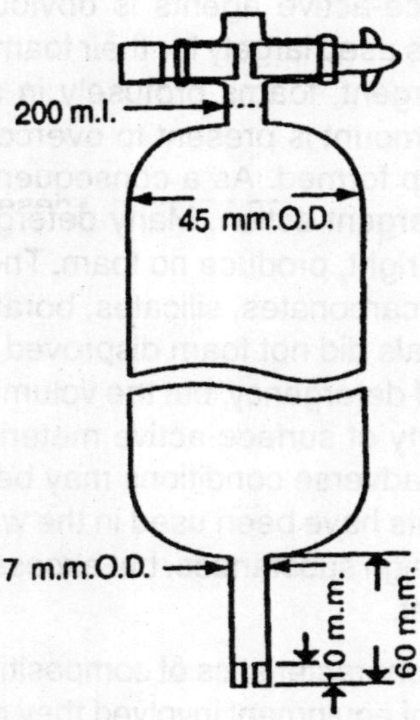

Fig. 8.1. Ross-Miles lather test foam pipette.

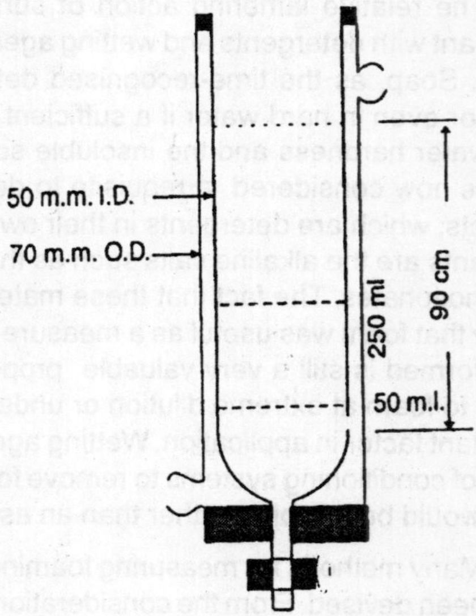

Fig. 8.2. Ross-Miles lather test foam receiver.

The anionic synthetic detergent will form salts of varying degrees of solubility and these will foam to greater or lesser extent. Consequently, hard water (calcium or magnesium ions) will have more or less effect upon the lather of the sodium salts. In some cases, the calcium and magnesium ions may depress foam formation, in others foam may be increased, while in still others no change will be observed.

Test method : Ross-Miles pour foam test

Apparatus : Level cylinder so that drops fall vertically into centre of liquid at bottom of cylinder.

Solution Preparation :

(a) Dissolve sample in distilled water at double the concentration desired by bringing to the boil then cooling to 25°C.

(b) Make back to weight with distilled water for loss by evaporation.

(c) Dilute to correct concentration by using water at 25°C. of double the hardness or strength finally required.

Procedure :

(a) Start circulation pump on column to maintain temperature at 25 ± 0.2°C.

(b) Rinse cylinder walls with distilled water, drain 10 min. and close stopcock.

(c) Age solution for 10 min. in constant temperature both 25 ± 0.2°C.

(d) Wet down walls of cylinder with 50 ml. of test solution by washing walls in circular motion with 50 ml. pipette of solution.

(e) Immediately transfer 200 ml. of test solution to tipped pipette. Insert in holder in position vertical to base and open stopcock.

(f) Record later height in centimeters, at once, and in 5 min.

(g) Drain cylinder, rinse with distilled water, and permit to drain for 10 min.

(h) Repeat steps of through g for next sample making one determination for each sample.

Solubility—Organic Solvents

In spite of the presence of polar groups, many compounds are soluble in nonpolar solvents. Their possible applications under these conditions are in paints, dry cleaning solvents, insecticides, printing inks, and as self-emulsifying agents.

Since the surface active generally is added to produce some given effect, it is not necessary that solubility be determined under conditions of greatest accuracy : Small amounts of agent are generally sufficient or must be maintained. It is therefore felt that the accuracy of the method used is entirely adequate.

Only the pure materials are evaluated for this purpose, since even traces of inorganic salts or of water will reduce actual or apparent solubility.

Other solvents may be used in this test when further information is desired, although chlorinated hydrocarbons, a polar solvent, and a hydrocarbon are represented.

Test Method

Sample Weight : 0.50 g.

Equipment : 16-oz glass stoppered bottles dispensing burettes.

Temperature : 25 ± 3^0C.

Solvents : Transfer 0.50 g. of sample to the glass-stoppered bottle. Add 1.0 ml. of solvent, shake thoroughly, and determine whether solution has taken place. Continue adding increments of solvent, either until solution is effected, or until 450 ml. of solvent has been added.

Calculation :

$$\text{Percentage solubility} = \frac{0.50}{\text{vol. solvent} \times \text{sp. gr.}} \, 100$$

Cotton Washing

Through the process of forming fibre into yarn and into fabric, and prior to conversion into garments, rigorous cleaning chedules are followed which require considerable amounts of detergent. When of sufficiently high tensile strength characteristics, those fibres and fabrics which can withstand the cleaning process most satisfactorily will be chosen for the hardest wear. Cotton still retains its historic leadership even though the synthetic fibres are gaining much favour. Indeed several of the synthetic fibres are simply cellulose which has been treated to provide fibres differing from the original cotton in luster, evenness of character, and offering opportunities for styling that cotton does not provide. Cotton as well as many of the fabrics made from these fibres can washed repeatedly, wear well, and retain their dimensional stability. These are the fibres which are washed most often and their cleansing represents the large outlet for cleansing agents.

The controversy as to whether an applied soil simulate a "real" soil or be a synthetic one continues. Practically speaking, the soil and its method of application and the laboratory machine used in washing are minor factors so long as they remain constant, provided that the data so obtained can be correlated with practice. Advancement from the laboratory to the practical scale for proof of utility is a "must" and should proceed as soon as laboratory data are convincing.

Water Hardness

In general, most detergents becomes less effective when water hardness increases. Certain of anionic type synthetics are improved in detergency in the presence of moderate amounts of calcium and magnesium salts but excesses render surface active agent totally ineffective or at least reduce effectiveness in cleansing action. Calcium is the ion which causes most difficulty. Nonionics are generally only slightly affected by water hardness.

Exactly what ratio of calcium to magnesium to use and what shall be the water hardness for detergent testing are factors which must be decided. Many investigators have used a ratio of calcium to magnesium of 60 to 40 while others have increased the ratio or have excluded magnesium entirely. Regardless of the ratio used it is desirable that the detergency test be made over a range of water hardnesses, and if this is done, and the range is sufficiently extended, the effect of having used only calcium as the hardening ion will have been equivalated.

A standardised water hardness is desirable and one which can be made in a stock solution for dilution purposes should be used. For general screening purposes hardness levels of 50 and 300 ppm. have been used successfully. First and most important, they demonstrate the comparative effectiveness of a detergent when subjected to hard water usage; and second they represent levels of practical signficance. A 50 ppm. level probably represents the maximum (with exceptions) for the large population areas, while the 300 ppm. hardness is one frequently approached in hard water areas.

Because of test discrepancy, suspected inaccuracy in preparation of standard water, or necessity for analysis of unknown water, it is valuable to have several test methods available. Both of the following have been used successfully : Langelier methods or the Versenate method. The former is a variation of the soap titration method, and the latter a colorimetric titration procedure. The APHA soap titration method is still useful, but in inexperienced hands can prove misleading and takes longer to perform than either of the foregoing methods.

Machines

When a decision has been reached as to the manner in which mechanical action shall be applied in the washing operation, the machine should then be designed so that all of the other factors involved in the washing operation can be controlled. It should be obvious that mechanical action is applied in the washing operation and depending upon the fibre and fabric, and the state of manufacture, the application of mechanical "elbow grease" may be varied.

A very short review of some of the operations washing (scouring or cleansing) may indicate why some of the types of washing have been developed. In the manufacture of textile fibres there are many points where cleansing must be performed before subsequent processing can be properly controlled. In the cotton mill raw cotton is mechanically cleaned of burrs and extraneous matter and formed into yarn which is then woven into a fabric. Before this fabric can be further processed it must be kiered, which is simply removal of the cotton wax and lignin-like materials inherent to the cotton; then it is bleached and further processed. Following the dyeing operation it generally is necessary to "soap off" or scour for final finishing. Washing of fabrics in the home may take many forms. It may be simple hand washing or it may be accomplished with any one of several different types of washing machines, either manually or automatically operated. Here the detergent is selected with a view to providing the greatest soil removal for the amount of mechanical energy applied to the fabric in scrubbing and removing the closely adherent soil.

Many laboratory machines have been designed which provide control of operating conditions for the evaluation of detergents, most of them varying in the method of applying force to the cleaning operation. Generally the evaluation of a washing machine, as contrasted with detergent testing, will be accomplished on a full scale basis.

Standard Cotton Soil Fabric Preparation

The requirements for a standard soiled fabric are :

The fabric should be uniform.

The soiling operation should provide the same initial amount of soil, and the same removal value for any given detergent under identical conditions of cleansing.

The soil removal values should be reproducible, preferably of analytical accuracy.

The effect of aging should be minimised.

The method for determination of soil removal or retention should be reproducible, preferably quickly accomplished, and closely coorelated with actual practice.

The process of preparing a standardised soil fabric may be subdivided as follows : fabric, desizing of fabric, soil, soiling machine, wash test machine , wash test method, storage, evaluation of washed swatches, soiled fabric testing, statistical data.

Fabric choice

Indian Head fabric is a plain weave sheeting, has a thread count of 48 × 54, is available in several widths, and has a weight of 5 ounces to the square yard. To minimise the desizing problem, purchase is made on specification requiring from the manufacturer a scoured, bleached, dried, but unmercerized or otherwise finished grade. This meant that chemical change or deposition of chemicals liable to change the surface reactivity of the fabric were eliminated since a mercerized or chemically treated surface is much more reactive than one not so treated.

Desizing

For purposes of uniformity all sizing should be removed. Variation in fabric characteristics resulting from small scale operation led to desizing in a 25 × 25 in. pony wash wheel.

Soil

A test solid generally will comprise a binding agent and a material which permits quantitative estimation of removal and which in itself may be a natural soil. Since soot is a common soiling agent and certainly lends itself to reflectance measurement against a while fabric, it is not unusual that carbon in some form should be used. Carbon will vary widely in composition depending upon method of manufacture. Some may be very finely divided, others coarse, and the particle size distribution may vary widely. Some carbons may be predominantly oil-dispersible and others water-dispersible, but apparently satisfactory result have been obtained using either type.

Oildag concentrate has been used satisfactory for at least 12 years and is comprised of colloidal graphite and apparently an oil-soluble dispersing agent, dispersed in mineral oil. This forms relatively stable dispersions in nonaqueous solvents. So long as the code number which appears on the Oildag package is specified, satisfatcory reproducibility by the manufacturer has been noted. The binding agent for the graphite may be chosen from a wide variety of agents, but preferred is a vegetable oil such as Wesson oil, though Mazola oil can be substituted for it. Others have used lard, tallow, or other natural oils. Yet others have used mineral oils because they are not readily susceptible to atmospheric oxidation. Wesson oil was chosen because when it was properly aged or cured on the fabric, it made the graphite much more difficult to remove than did mineral oil, giving a satisfactory spread in soil removal. The difficulty in the use of an oxidizable oil however is that the degree of oxidation must controlled and the storage conditions maintained at an optimum to prevent further oxidation.

The medium to be used for dispersion of the carbon and oil is obviously important. In some systems graphite or carbon is deposited upon the fabric in water, loose carbon removed, and the soiled fabric used as such or the dried fabric impregnated additionally with an oil. Water is a safe and inexpensive medium for soil application, but the fabric must be treated to remove wrinkles and loose carbon. Choice of a chlorinated solvent may be preferable to a naphtha solvent wherever fire hazard is involved, though the latter is less expensive and relatively nontoxic.

A technical grade of carbon tetrachloride has been used and while there is no evidence that inhibitors added to the carbon tetrachloride may affect oxidation, this is a possibility which has been explored.

The soiling solution (or suspensive) used has the following composition :

5.0 grams Wesson oil

10.0 grams Oildag concentrate (Acheson Colloids Corp.)

12.0 litres carbon tetrachloride (Dowelene, Dow Chemical Co.)

The amounts of Wesson oil and oildag are weighed to the accuracy indicated, and the carbon tetrachloride measured from a two-litre graduate. Care is taken to disperse the Wesson oil and Oildag thoroughly during dilution.

Soiling machine

The soiling operation is important, and insure reproducibility of application it is general practice to use a machine of some sort. Generally a chlorinated solvent or hydrocarbon is used as a means for uniformly applying them to the fabric. The machine was developed from an initially hand operated heated tube to the presence equipment. Since moisture as dew deposited on the fabric (as a result of solvent volatilisation) has such a marked effect upon soil characteristics, the machine was designed to minimise the effect of condensed moisture by raising the dewpoint.

Soil storage

The ideal soiled test fabric should be completely stable toward ageing or storage. The soil described continues to age over a considerable period of time, but to minimise this effect it was found that ordinary mechanical refrigeration during storage of the soiled cloth in a dry atmosphere will prevent change in soil removal characteristics over a period of a month. All of the usual methods for inhibiting oxidation such as vaccum, absence of light, inert atmosphere, desiccator, etc. (and other than the use of an inhibitor) were evaluated in arriving at the most desirable storage conditions noted above.

Evaluation of washed swatches

Since the soil is designed to permit a spread of results from original soil to original white (which seldom if even is attained), and since this is what the eye sees, regardless of actual weight percentage soil distribution, a photometric method for soil removal evaluation is indicated. Other investigators prefer the measurement of soil removed from the fabric and held in suspension in the solution. This latter method utilises the photometer, reading transmittance against a curve for removal, but possible turbidity of detergent in solution interferes, and somewhat narrows the utility of this method.

Standardisation of Solid Fabric Testing

Since every load of samples includes at least one standard detergent product, for many years it was considered sufficient simply to use the soiled fabric as it was cured or artificially aged and without preliminary evaluation. Apparently this is the general method followed by a large proportion of the investigators detergency data.

In an attempt to improve reproducibility each roll soiled fabric is tested immediately after preparation and without further treatment. There are variations from roll to roll as evidenced through the use of the standard detergent sample. Having ascertained the degree of soil removal immediately after soiling, and knowing the degree of retentivity of soil desired, the freshly produced fabric is then baked in a circulatory oven in festooned form for periods of time which experience indicates will provide adequate resistance to removal. After baking, the soiled fabric is again tested under standard conditions to be certain that specified control has been attained.

Cotton Wash Test Methods

The wash test method chosen will depend to a considerable extent upon the soiled test fabric and the washing machine available. Depending upon the mechanical energy expended in the washing operation, a soiled fabric may be of single or multiple wash characteristics.

Frequently, a soiled fabric designed for one type of operation will be found useful for others, and the influence of the washing will be minimised.

Having decided that the fabric may prove satisfactory with the available washing machine, a decision will be made as to single or multiple washing operation shall be followed. Home laundering may encompass prewash and wash operation; a single or multiple rinse procedures. Power launderies follow a multiple suds, multiple rinse procedure. Which procedure is chosen will be arbitrary, since the laboratory machine used frequently cannot be compared exactly with a full scale washer.

Next the duration of the wash period must be decided. It should be long enough that stabilised conditions of soil removal can be attained, but not so long that unnatural redeposition of soil can occur. For laboratory work where many samples must be screened under a variety of concentrations and water hardnesses, the washing period (within reason) the greater will be the work output.

Whether the rinse shall be by machine or by hand, and whether the test pieces shall be wrung out by hand or by using wringer rolls will depend upon the degree of stability of soil removal. Certainly, if the rinse removes considerably further amounts of soil, this should be done under controlled conditions and not haphazardly, and the rinse will be by machine. However, if the soil removed in the rinse is negligible, a simple hand-rinsing is indicated to save time and effort. The same argument is applicable to hand vs. roll wringing of swatches, but in either case the rinse water should be as well removed as possible to prevent possible migration of soil or retained discoloration.

Drying of the washed swatches is important. Migration frequently may occur when the test pieces are laid out flat on a line and permitted to dry overnight. Forced hot air drying in either vertical or horizontal position is therefore indicated.

Deter-Meter Test Method

Dynamics. General testing, 120 cycles/minute. 50 min. amplitude. No. 2 impact surface spacing. 5 minute wash time.

Concentrations. At three chosen levels.

Temperature. 120, 140 160°F.

Replicate Tests. Three, using fresh swatches in each. Where a relatively large number of concentrations or temperatures are involved two swatches at each point are suggested.

Sensitiveness of Test Method. Ability is claimed to distinguish between concentrations which differ as little as 0.01% with a single swatch at each concentration.

Conventional Washer Method

The water capacity of machine with an 8-pound load (or other recommended load) is determined for calculation of detergent requirement. The load is weighed into the machine and should consist of normally soiled, fast-coloured or garments.

Test Cloth Preparation. Each load contains, in addition to the soiled garments, five 5 × 6 inch swatches of soiled fabric marked for identification.

Changing the Washer.

(a) The machine is filled to the predetermined level with water at 120°F.

(b) The detergent is added with the agitator in motion to permit rapid solution.

(c) The 8-pound weighed load is added.

(d) The load is washed for 10 minutes.

(e) The garments are then wrung into a stationary tub of 9 gallons of water of the same hardness as the wash, at 100 ± 5⁰F.

(f) A hand rinse is administered in the water of step (e) by thoroughly moving the garments up and down in the water.

(g) The rinsed garment are wrung into the machine filled with 17 gallons of fresh water of the hardness in use at 100 ± 5⁰F.

(h) A machine rinse is made for minutes.

(i) The garments are wrung from the rinse.

Drying the Washed Swatches. The soil swatches are removed and pressed dry at a low iron temperature in a flat work ironer.

Practical Wash Tests

For complete assurance that any developed detergent composition is satisfactory for the purpose designed, it is necessary that the product at least be pilot-plant tested. Satisfactory screening on a full scale with home washer and on a pilot scale with a pony washer for commercial laundering has been the rule.

Home laundering

It after completion of small scale bench testing of the detergent an apparently satisfactory product has been developed, it is then reasonable that the sample be evaluated under conditions which at least approximate those for large scale use. For the home washing machine this means that a load of fabric of about a maximum of 9 lbs. dry weight (depending upon machine capacity) will be required. Obviouly a mechanical set-up for the supply of water of the proper temperature and hardness is necessary. Quite satisfactory results have been obtained with several types of home washing machines.

Sea Water Detergency Tests

A sea water detergent should be soluble in this medium, and should exert reasonable soil removal characteristics. Any detergent which can be operated successfully in this medium can probably be used in the hardest of waters. This led to a combination of tallow soap, as a binder, and alkyl benzene sulphonate as the active detergent ingredient.

Detergency methods

These methods can be made to exactly duplicate fresh water tests with the possible exception that a final fresh(distilled) water rinse may be used. In laboratory as well as power laundry trials this rinse will remove some of the stiffness from the fabric without markedly increasing soil removal : for garments it is feasible aboard ship and improves the wearer's personal comfort.

A *synthetic sea water* used and successfully applied to evaluation either in laboratory machines or the 25-pound capacity pony wash wheel follows:

1.60	g.	$CaCl_2.2H_2O$
11.00	g.	$MgCl_2.6H_2O$
4.00	g.	Na_2SO_4 anhydrous
25.00	g.	NaCl

Dissolve in 500-700 ml. of distilled water then make up to 1 litre.

Concentration. For laboratory evaluation it may be desirable to cover a range of sample concentrations such as 0.10, 0.20, and 0.40%. For power laundry work the several materials used successfully have been used at near normal power laundry concentrations of near 0.1%.

Redeposition

Soap is relatively effective in preventing redeposition of soil once it has been removed from the fabric, but this property not a "built-in" attribute to most synthetic detergents. It is understood that the synthetic detergents are less colloidal in character than soaps, and consequently lack certain properties of which this is one. Certain soaps may likewise be lacking in these redeposition-preventing characteristics, but these are not the soaps generally used in commercial work.

Even though the individual factor or factors involved in preventing redeposition have not been isolated, it is possible to measure the effectiveness of detergent compositions in preventing this occurrence. It has long been recognised that some detergent type materials may remove soil from a fabric and then redeposit it in such a form that the washed fabric is darker than the original before immersion in the test solution. It is this redeposition of soil particles under conditions of high soil, adverse temperature conditions, low solution volume and low detergent concentration that promotes graying of fabrics.

It has been recognised that synthetic detergents were deficient in preventing redeposition of soil and developed sodium carboxymethyl cellelose to remedy this shortcoming. This is one of the very few materials for use with synthetic detergents which redeposition of loosened soil. So extensive now is the use of CMC that almost without exception, there are no synthetics detergents on the market which do not contain this compound in greater or lesser proportion.

General methods

The evaluation of redeposition in washing compositions, and of agents potentially useful for this purpose, can be accomplished by two general methods. In one case a sample of soiled fabric for the wash test is accompanied by a swatch of white fabric, and the net detergency or the soil redeposition measured photometrically after a proper washing period. The second and preferred method is to add a known amount of soiling agent to the detergent solution, add a swatch of white fabric, then determine the reflectance of the swatch after washing. The second method permits better control of amount of soil used than the first and is generally under better statistical control.

Redeposition test procedure

Launder-Ometer. In duplicate swatches per sample.

Time of Wash. 20 minutes.

Temperature. 140 ± 2_0F.

Water. 300 ppm. hardness unless otherwise noted.

Fabric. Indian Head Permanent Finish as received. Cut into swatches 6 × 5 inches and mark for identification.

Standard Value. This is obtained by making 6 or 8 readings on the Hunter Reflectometer on swatches taken at random from those to be used in test. This standard value is repeated for each separate test.

Solution Preparation. Make 200 ml. of 0.2% concentration as following : Weigh 0.4 g. of sample and dissolve in 100 ml. of water of desired hardness. After sample is dissolved, add 2 ml. of 10% Aquadag suspension and 98 ml. of water of same water hardness. If excessive heating is required to dissolve sample, enough water should be added to maintain total volume at 200 ml.

Preheating. The solutions are preheated on a hot plate to 60°C. They are then transferred to jars in the preheating tray on Launder-Ometer, each jar to contain 100 ml. of solution and 10 rubber balls.

Washing. After all solutions have been transferred to the preheating tray, the test swatches are transferred to them. The jars are at once tightly capped, tested for leaks and placed in the Launder-Ometer.

Blotting. At the end of the 20-minutes wash period, the jars are removed from the Launder-Ometer and the contents poured into a stainer. Each duplicate set of swatches is removed before another set is poured into the strainer. The swatches *without being squeezed,* are placed between filter papers (or paper towels). The papers are then placed between glass plates and a 5 or 6 lb, weight applied for one minute.

Rinsing. While the wash is running, the rinse is prepared. Water of the same hardness is heated on the hot plate to 60°C and 100 ml. is transferred to each jar. 10 rubber balls are included in the rinse. After all swatches have been blotted they are placed in the jars for rinsing. The jars are tightly capped and tested for leaks as before, and then placed in the Launder-Ometer and run for 5 minutes. At the end of the rinse period the swatches are removed, as before and blotted.

Drying. The swatches are then either air or preferably oven dried, and the reflectance measured on the Hunter Reflectometer.

Record of Values. Standardise the Hunter instrument and record the reflectance values for swatch and average them.

Redeposition Index

$$\frac{\text{Reflectance after treatment}}{\text{Reflectance of whites watches}} \quad 100 = \text{Redeposition index}$$

Standard Sample. A standard comparison sample of known quality is desirable, and should be included with each wash load.

Wool Washing

Detergents and their evaluation, or the evaluation of cleansing methods are important throughout the processing of wool, from the scouring of raw wool, back washing, wash-off after dyeing or fulling to the cleasing of soiled garments after the wool has been fabricated and worm. This may be simplified to: raw wool scouring, in-process scouring, and finished fabric cleansing.

Raw Wool Scouring

The first requirement in the treatment of raw wool is mechanical removal of the dirt and extraneous matter by a simple opening and beating or picking operation. Following this, the raw wool is generally carried through what is known as a train of scouring bowls which vary in number. Since wool is sensitive to mechanical action in the scouring operation, the agitation involved in the wool scouring train is mild and accomplished by rakes which simply pull the mass of raw wool through each of the bowls between a nip, sometimes rinsed between bowls, passing into the next bowl in the train. In general these bowls consist of a steep bowl where the greatest portion of the dirt is removed and where some of the fatty acids are saponified (by soda ash, a desirable sodium bicarbonated content being built up). The second bowl consists of a detergent-builder mixture, either soap and soda ash (or modified soda) or synthetic detergent and soda ash. The next bowl may either be a final rinse bowl in simpler operations, or is a second soap-detergent bath of lower concentration, followed by one or two water rinses. Temperatures of scour and rinse are carefully controlled and seldom exceed 130^{0}F.

Laboratory evaluation of raw wool scouring is difficult unless a satisfactory sample of raw wool of the type expected to be used in the plant is available. To satisfy this requirement a quantitative method for the evaluation of wool-scouring detergents has been developed by using small skeins of wool-in-the-grease (in this case carpet yarn), the use of a laboratory bowl (beaker) scouring train and determination of the point at which the bath became exhausted or lost its effectiveness in the removal of the grease (as determined by solvent extraction of the skeins and determination of residual grease content). The method is reasonably reproducible from laboratory to laboratory and has the decided advantage that it closely approximates plant scouring conditions using wool which might actually be encountered. This method has been used successfully in the evaluation of surface active agents for this purpose, and detergents tested in the laboratory by this method have been taken directly to the mill and have met successful acceptance.

Continuous scouring of raw grease wool

This specification covers a method for the laboratory evaluation of continuous wool scouring. It is adaptable to the comparison of detergents, builders, and other chemical factors in the scouring operation; and also to the study of mechanical and other control variable, such as temperature, the number of bowls, immersion time, etc.

A standard apparatus and set of operating conditions are specified for purposes of calibration. Beyond that, conditions are specified for varied in accordance with the desires of the operator to study any particular system which may exist in this own plant.

The criterion for scouring effectiveness is the extent of grease removal. Extraction is done by agitating the scoured and dried wool specimens in a piston and cylinder system while immersed in carbon tetachloride. An aliquot sample of the carbon tetrachloride is then evaporated in a tared aluminium cup on an infrared dryer to determine the grease residue.

In-Process Scouring

The Detergency Comparator for the evaluation of detergents on wollen and worsted materials is used.

The Detergency Comparator is constructed of stainless steel and has a thermostatically controlled, electrically-heated outer water bath, and the solution may be circulated by means of an electric pump to further insure close temperature control. Stepped pulleys are used for speed selection and it has Hyear-covered nip rolls (3 inch diameter), driven take-off rolls, baffles to prevent suds from cross-contaminating the detergent solutions under test and subs boxes with piping arrangements to permit the expressed liquor to be returned to the main washing tank either by cascading or by-passing through the pipe drains or to be drained off into the waste line. The adjustable pot eyes help to prevent the formation of hard creases in the knitted tubing samples. The rinsing process is controlled using a reservoir fitted with calipered openings and a valve for close control.

The Detergency Comparator is said to be the only device that will compare detergents under the conditions of high concentration and low bath ratio similar to those obtained in good plant practice.

1. **Soiled Suspension.** The composition recommended follow : commercial grease oil 50% (by wt.); refined mineral oil 50% (by wt.).

   To one gallon of the oil blend was added ½ pound of Bear Brand Lamp Black (Monsanto). This was mixed thoroughly before use.

2. **Soiled Fabric Preparation.** The mixture of oil and lamp black was applied to worsted top sliver during the first drawing operation so as to deposit 5.0 to 5.5% oil on the stock. The worsted stock was then drawn and spun to 2/40's count and 1.75 inch wide knitted tubing was prepared (2 yards long weighing 40 grams).

3. **AATCC Detergency Comparator Test Method.** This method of test is applicable to the evaluation of detergents on woolen and worsted material. It provides an ideal method for classification without conducting costly, time-consuming plant runs.

Finished Fabric Scouring

In comparison with cotton, much less effort has been spent on the standardisation of a test method for wool. The soil or soils vary, but in general are similar to those used for cotton. The fabric chosen should be scoured, in the grey, neutral, and as free from adsorbed soap or synthetic detergent as possible. The laboratory washing machines can be the same as those used for cotton, the wash temperature being adjusted to a level to prevent excessive felting.

Wash test method

Soiled Fabric Preparation. The fabric is Botany Worsted Mills, Style 404, prescoured.

The proportions for the soiling ingredients are :

Edible tallow	2.0 g.
Nujol	6.0 g.
Grinders	0.125 g.
Lamp black	

These ingredients are mixed in the Waring Blender then passed through a homogeniser. To 8.125 g. of the homogenised mixture add 4 litres carbon tetrachloride and mix thoroughly.

Using the soiling machine a 7 inch width of fabric 22 feet long, is passed six times through the soiling bath and machine until a reflectance of 28.32% is obtained. This soil is baked one hour at 90^{0}C.

WASHING PROCEDURES FOR OTHER FIBRES

The increasing number of new fibres and mixtures of them with cotton or wool may change some of the practical washing procedures mainly as to temperatures used, but laboratory wash test procedures described in Section 12.3 and 12.4 are applicable.

Dry Cleaning

Dry cleaning establishments are as numerous as power laundries and indeed both are frequently maintained.

The effect of the moisture regain and the relative humidity of the air in the cleaning operation, and of added moisture in certain instances has marked effect upon both soil removal and soil redeposition. It has been found that when the relative humidity is lower than 40% that 1.5-3.0% water, added on the weight of the fabric, will reduce soil redeposition. It has been investigated that of a variety of detergents tested, certain ones were more susceptible to the addition of moisture or to relative humidity conditions than others. Thus it was found that both Stoddard solvent and tri-chloroethylene were beneficiated in preventing redeposition, when the garments were preconditioned, or when water was added to the cleaning solution.

Evaluation can consist either of redeposition or soil removal, or both. In any event, the effect of preconditioning the fabric or of adding water to the cleaning medium must be considered.

Shampoos

Since the materials which may be used in the production of shampoos are legion, it might be expected that fairly well defined methods would exist for their evaluation. The reverse is true, howevere, since the cleansing of the scale is a rather difficult process to control. Generally the evaluation of shampoos has been performed either through experienced operators in beauty parlors or by the panel technique.

One of the important factors in a shampoo is the abundance and stability of the lather formed, and this phase of the evaluation can be performed in the laboratory and separately from the actual cleansing operation. A recent innovation for detergency evaluation has been the use of a variation of the raw would scouring technique.

Detergency method

Fabric. Wool yarn "in-the-grease" is used for this test. A small skein about 4 inches from end to end when stretched is prepared from a 20 foot length of yarn and will weigh between 4.5 and 5 grams.

Detergent Solution. A sample of detergent weighing 0.50 g. (100% basis) is dissolved in 200 ml. of water (hardness selected). The solution is adjusted to 38°C.

Procedure

(1) Accurately weight the skein of wool yarn.

(2) Transfer to a 500 ml. Erlenmeyer flask containing the temperature-adjusted detergent solution and stopper.

(3) Slowly invert flask back and forth 50 times per minute for 4 minutes.

(4) Remove skein and either hand or wringer-squeeze to remove excess solution.

(5) Drain and rinse flask, add 100 ml. of water of hardness in use at 38°C and add the squeezed skein of yarn.

(6) Rinse by shaking for 2 minutes in same manner as before.

(7) Remove wool, squeeze as before and repeat rinse as above for 1 minute.

(8) Remove wool, squeeze to remove water and dry in an oven at 45°C.

(9) During drying of scouring yarn accurately weigh two 400 ml. extraction flasks and a second skein of wool yarn.

(10) Place washed sample and unwashed control in separate extraction thimbles and reflux each with 200 ml. of petroleum ether to remove residual grease.

(11) Remove solvent in hood over a steam bath and dry to constant weight. (this generally will take one hour).

Calculation for the *Control* :

$$\frac{\text{(wt. flask + contents)} - \text{wt. empty flask}}{\text{wt. of wool sample}} \times 100$$

= % grease content

For the *scoured wool* sample :

$$\frac{\text{grease content of control - grease content scoured sample}}{\text{grease content of control}} \times 100$$

= % grease content

Lather - Shampoo

This method is a tentative standard for the American Society for Testing Materials, D-1173, Method of Test for Foaming Properties of Surface-Active Agents.

Use of soiling agents in combination with the foaming agents under test is not convenient with the Ross-Miles test equipment because it is so difficult to clean. Consequently other methods for estimation of foam volume and stability in the presence of soils must be devised. Moderately successful results have been obtained using a simple stirrer agitation method in a graduated, temperature controlled vessel, to which may be added successive increments of a chosen soil such as lanolin, mineral or vegetable oil.

Hard Surface Cleaning

Hard surfaces as contrasted with soft, or textile surface, exhibit several differences which strongly affect detergency operations. In general, hard surfaces have a comparatively restricted surface area, though still of considerable dimensions when closely examined.

Metal Cleaning

A metal surface offers a number of conveniences in the estimation of soil removal. Though it may seem perfectly flat, when observed microscopically may contain a tremendous number of pores or hills. Many of the metals are chemically reactive and either oxidize rapidly, presenting an adsorptive surface, or can react preferentially to provide chemisorbed surface as with adsorbed corrosion inhibitors, etc. Another factor which may have influenced the extensive investigation in this field is the tremendous tonnages of metal processed.

Performance tests

The main performance test is effectiveness of soil removal under actual (orsimulated) conditions of use. However, there are many individual factors which can be measured and when properly used can be made excellent supplements to detergency testing. The more generally investigated performance tests are :

pH and titration values
Colloidal properties
Water softening
Conductivity
Solvent action
Surface and interfacial tension measurements
Emulsification
Rinsability
Stability under conditions of usage

A very short review will indicate the variety of metal cleaning processes:

Wiping (by hand or machine)
Brushing (by hand or machine)
Sand blasting
Tumbling
Hydraulic spraying
Steam gun spraying
Dipping in still tank
Machine washing
Electrolytic cleaning (anodie or cathodie)
Continuous acid or alkaline dip
Vapour degreasing
Solvent degreasing.

To this may be added :

Emulsion degreasing : (1) Organic solvent containing oil soluble emulsifying agent. (2) Organic solvent containing oil-soluble emulsifying agent mixed with kerosence and solvent to form emulsion.

Diphase cleaning

The main general types of cleaning, however, may be reduced to the following:

- Soak tank cleaning
- Mechanical tank or spray cleaning
- Eletrolytic cleaning (anodie, cathodie, alternate current)
- Solvent or vapour degreasing
- Emulsion degreasing
- Diphase cleaning.

Surfaces

Cleaning of metals represents the entire gamut of pure metals and alloys. All must be cleaned to a greater or lesser extent for either processing or for use as a finished product. The chemical reactivity of the surface to form either oxide coating or reactions with components of corrosion inhibiting compositions or cleaning compounds, may greatly influence the effectiveness of the compositions used and of the finished product. Lard oil which has a stronger bond of attachment for metal than mineral oil, is readily removed by the addition of surface active agents in contrast with mineral oil which is not. Presence or absence of oxide film is an important factor in the ease with which oil be may be removed, since this probably depends upon the bond between the oil and the metal surface. The effect of freshly pickled surfaces in increasing the attraction of the oil for the metal is an important one and is most marked mineral oils. In contrast, fatty oils containing considerable amounts of free fatty acid are more strongly adsorbed by the oxide films. Condition of the metal as it is to be worked in the plant will be the controlling factor in metal cleaning operations.

Soils

The variety of soils encountered in the cleaning of metals is numerous. Generally, however, they are comprised of fatty or mineral oils, debris from previous processing, corrosion inhibitors, drawing compounds and the like. These oils act as entraining for solids which may be oxides or simply debris picked up in the processing operation.

Machine for removal

Probably the simplest device which is used in the metal cleaning industry is the so-called soak tank method of cleaning. This may be manually or mechanically operated and in either event is strongly dependent upon the temperature of the bath and the degree of agitation (with steam, air or pump) to provide the desired amount of mechanical action.

Laboratory machines for duplicating the results obtained in plant machines are simple and are frequently quite representative of what can be done in the plant, particularly when samples of the actual soiled surface can be cleaned with the material expected to be used. Generally the simple soak bath is used in laboratory evaluation but spraying operations may be set up with spray nozzles and pump which simulate plant application. A device which agitates the article to be cleaned in the soak bath been suggested. Whichever piece of machinery is used for laboratory evaluation is not as important as control of the surface prior to , and subsequent to, the cleaning operation and full recognition of the desired state of cleanliness is important for maximum economy.

Sample

The size and shape of the panel to be soiled and cleaned can vary at will. Disks one inch in diameter to panels 6 × 6 inches or more have been used. The shape of the panel can likewise vary, some being perforated at two points on one edge so that when held at an angle they drain from a corner, while still another was like a flat spearhead so that drainage can be made to take place from the tip.

Estimation of soil removal

In general, either a metal surface is clean or it is not, and any degree between these two extremes may be considered unsatisfactory. In effect, this is a "go," "no go" type procedure. However, for the estimation of the effectiveness of cleaning agents in the laboratory it is desirable that satisfactory quantitative methods be available. Historically the water-break method is the one which has provide most satisfactory. It can be made in the plant as well as in the laboratory, and is indicative of general cleanliness. In either case, maximum advantage is obtained by an acid dip prior to evaluation of the degree of soil removal. An obvious method of attack is to submit the cleaned sample to *solvent extraction* and to weigh the oil or soil which is removed. In cases where almost complete cleanliness has been obtained, sensitivity of this test is obviously dependent upon technic and a sufficiently sensitive weighing device. The *radioactive trace technic* has been used in the evaluation of metal cleaning compositions and likewise for the evaluation of the several methods available to determine the cleanliness of cleaned metal surfaces. The *copper dip method* has been used for the estimation of the cleanliness of surfaces which are to be electroplated. The adherence and the brightness of the copper coating which results from dipping the cleaned ferrous metal in an acid copper sulphate solution is indicative of the quality of electroplate to be expected. The *fluorescent dye method* depends upon the inclusion of an ultraviolet sensitive fluorescing material combined with the oil used as a soiling agent. This has certain advantages for pretorial evaluation of data but is not entirely satisfactory as a quantitative method for estimation.

Dishwashing

The cleansing of dishes has been investigated with one or more objectives which are: deposition of hard water film, soil removal, bacteriological cleanliness, and washing machine design and efficiency.

Frequently several of these factors can be combined and a clear over-all conception of the effectiveness of the detergent solution or of the machine design can be obtained. Mahlmann and his co-workers in a number of different publications. It has been found that for bacteriological cleanliness a temperature of not less than 170°F. in the wash and rinse will generally provide the desired bactericidal action. Consequently the temperature of wash and of the abundance of the supply of wash water to a mechanical washing machine is most important.

Prior to the introduction of polyphosphates there was considerable difficulty in the deposition of an insoluble hard water film upon glassware which was most unsightly and could potentially harbor bacteria and the soil particles. It has been found that the inclusion of polyphosphates in the washing composition is most beneficial in reducing hard water precipitate and deposition. The essentials of a test for dish washing evaluation are comprised of the following :

Soil

In evaluation the removal of these soils it generally is necessary that a tracer compound of one sort or another be added with the expectation that it will be removed in the same ratio as soil itself and thus can be used as a device to measure the soil retained on the surface. Agents which have been used for this purpose are lamp black, India Ink, a combination of printing ink and lineseed oil, a test organism suspension, and also ferric chloride.

The most recent thinking on this general subject is that the method for deposition of the soil is important to the extent that the viscosity of the soil medium should be adjusted and the soil applied in some given and reproducible manner.

Measurement of soil retention (or removal)

A number of different photometers, colorimeters and glossimeters are available on the market and it seems hardly necessary that special design of equipment now be developed. Obviously if the desire is to ascertain bacteriological cleanliness, a properly standardised plating technique will be used and several of these have been described.

Machines for washing

Most of the small scale laboratory devices for evaluation of washing efficiency have been based on the use of microscope slides and either an agitating rocking or rotating device in which these slides are held while immersed and moved by mechanical action in the bath to provide soil removal.

Miscellaneous Tests

There are several tests which may prove useful in the further evaluation of compounds to be market tested. Most synthetic detergents are deficient in the ability to suspend soil once it is removed from a fabric surface. The redeposition method will indicate the comparative ability of a composition to prevent this graying, effect. A compound almost universally used for this purpose is carboxymethylcellulose, and it might be thought that its isolation from the detergent composition and its analysis would prove the most effective method for estimation. Such is not the case even though methods of analysis exist, and the redeposition characteristics will be fully as revealing as an analytical procedure. Furthermore, though there are a few other compounds which posses this same power to prevent redeposition, analysis means little when measure of comparative effectiveness is desired.

Another useful addition to the detergent field, and used both in soaps and synthetic detergents, is the fluorescent dye. These are also called brightening or "bleaching" agents. The best criterion of effectiveness again is a direct comparison, under use conditions of either competitive detergents or competitive dyes. While not actually increasing detergency or soil removal, the effect is as if increased cleanliness had occurred and is especially evident in actual practice over a sequence of washings.

Determination of pH can be very helpful, but properly executed, can be most misleading. This determination should be a routine operation.

A product, before introduction to the market, should be as free from possibility of harm to equipment as possible. Corrosion of metal, glass or vitreous enamel surfaces can cause many complaints and even result in rejection of a product. The methods chosen cover aluminium and vitreous enamel surfaces.

Brightening Agents

These compounds are colourless to the eye but are excited by ultraviolet light, fluorescing blue. They have been termed "bleaching" agents because they are so effective in converting daylight ultraviolet to visual, making white fabric appear bleached or brightened in comparison with one not so treated. Brightening is a better term since colours are also increased in intensity as well.

The most generally used dyes are chosen for their substantivity to cellulosic fabrics, though some less generally used are available which exhaust onto wool rather than cellulose. Depending upon chemical structure, these dyes will fluoresce as a reddish blue or preferably as a brilliant, almost true blue colour.

Choice of brightening agents will depend upon the hue of the dye, the degree of substantivity or exhaustion from the bath, stability toward excess untraviolet illumination, stability toward bleaching compositions, buildup of colour and cost. A reddish blue fluorescence may not have the intensity of a dye giving a deep blue. Unless the dye is evenly adsorbed in a short time, and essentially quantitatively, it may fail under adverse conditions of operation or in the small amounts used. Some dyes will "sunburn" when exposed continuously to ultraviolet, producing an undesirable visual colour. Other dyes may be oxidised to undesirable visual "off" colours by the common bleaching agents. Early experience with these agents in repeated washing resulted in "off" shades of pink built up by adsorption on the fabric. The evidence of the effectiveness of well selected brightening agents is so clear that a detergent manufacturer can hardly afford not to use them, especially as they are used in such minor percentages.

The evaluation of these dyes can be complicated or relatively simple, depending upon the size of the detergent operation, and upon the accuracy and sensitivity of the method chosen. Certainly a dye manufacturer can afford a complicated evaluation method if it will either control his operation or permit development of better, more effective agents. The detergent manufacturer is interested in producing maximum effectiveness at minimum cost of dye and of process control and the method which follow has proved quite adequate.

Evaluation

Machine. Launder-Ometer, or Terg-O-Tometer, set at 345^0 rotation and 117 half-cycles per minute.

Fabric. Desized Indian Head or white terry cloth towelling, 8 × 9 inch size.

Temperature. 120^{0}F.

Detergent concentration. 0.25%

Volume of solution. 1000 ml. Terg-O-Tometer. 200 ml. Launder-Ometer.

Time of wash. 10 minutes.

Time of Rinse. 5 minutes.

Procedure

(1) Wash for 10 minutes.

(2) Remove swatches, run through hand wringer.

(3) Rinse for 5 minutes.

(4) Remove swatches, run through hand wringer.

(5) Oven dry.

Number of washes. Selection of fabric swatch size will make it possible to remove a portion after every wash or alternatively after the fifth and tenth was periods.

These same tests can be performed in varying water hardness with various fabrics, and in the presence of commercial bleaching agents in the amounts recommended by the bleach manufacturer. If temperature of wash water or rinse is important, tests can be made to cover a range to indicate effectiveness of the agent.

pH Determination

The pH values of soaps, alkalies, and detergents are valuable indications useful in application. It should be recalled that soaps, as "neutral" salts of fatty acids, have pH values much higher than organic sulphates or sulphonates, Should soap pH values fall in a lower than those for the normal salts, difficulty in the way reduced detergency or actual deposition of insoluble fatty acids may be expected. The surface active sulphate or sulphonates may be finished off at pH values over a considerable range, but they generally closely approach pH 7 as the normal salts.

"Building" of soaps or synthetic detergents with alkaline salts frequently is accomplished to conform to some predetermined pH level dependent upon the sensitivity of the product or equipment with which they are to be used. Most built soap or synthetics to come into contact with the hands are maintained at levels below pH 10.5 since otherwise they may cause excessive skin irrizitation. This buffering ability to maintain a given level is most readily ascertained using a combination of pH and titration methods.

Colorimetric methods for pH determination can be most useful, but for precise estimation the electrometric method is to be preferred. Simplified apparatus is available for electrometric, largely with the glass electrode which may be operated from line current or from batteries and may be secured for versatility of measurement in different media.

The first item to recall in making pH measurements is that distilled water unless freshly boiled may absorb much carbon dioxide from the air and will then have been a quite acid value. Freshly boiled distilled water is indicated for the measurement of pH values for detergent solutions since the synthetic detergents are frequently poorly buffered. The fact is that very many of the neutral or sodium sulphate-built detergents will simply asssume the pH of the water used in the test. Attempts to obtain check pH values between laboratories may frequently fail unless this precaution of using freshly boiled distilled water is observed.

The second item of importance is to standardise the pH meter with appropriate standard buffer solutions using the proper glass electrode for the pH range and temperature used.

The American Society for Testing Materials Specification E-70 is a tentative method for Determination of the pH of aqueous Solutions of Soaps and Detergents with the glass electrode and gives specific data for the proper use of this equipment.

Proposed method of test for pH of aqueous solutions of soaps and detergents

Scope. This method covers procedures for the preparation of aqeuous solutions of soaps and detergents and for the determination of their pH.

Sampling. The material shall be sampled in accordance with the Standard Methods of Sampling and Chemical Analysis of Soaps and Soap Products, or the Standard Methods of Sampling and Chemical Analysis of Alkaline Detergents, whichever is applicable.

Reagent, Distilled Water. Distilled water shall be boiled thoroughly, or purged with CO_2-free air, to remove CO_2 and shall be protected with soda-lime or soda-asbestos (Ascarite) while cooling and in storage. The pH of this water shall be between 6.2 and 7.2 at 25°C. the residue on evaporation,when heated at 105°C for 1 hr., shall not be more than 0.5 mg. per litre.

Preparation of solutions. Weigh 1 ± 0.001 g. of the detergent and transfer to a 1-liter volumetric flask. Partially fill the flask with distilled water and agitate until the sample is completely dissolved. Adjust the temperature of the solution and the distilled water 25 ± 0.5°C. and fill to the calibration mark with distilled water. Stopper the flask, mix thoroughly, and allow the solution to stand at a temperature of 25°C. for 2 hours prior to measuring the pH.

Determination of pH. Measure the pH of the solution as directed in the Tentative Methods for Determination of the pH of Aqueous Solutions with the Glass Electrode (A.S.T.M. Designation: E-70). Use the "low sodium-error" glass electrodes for solutions having pH values higher than 9. Use type I or type II meters.

Corrosion

Detergent compositions are designed for many purposes, but one thing they should *not* do, is to cause corrosion or protective coatings. Dishwashing compositions should not remove decorative decals or overglazes, nor should they cause corrosion of silverware or of the machines in which they may be used. Washing machine detergents should not cause corrosion of metal parts of the machine, nor remove vitreous enamel or damage organic finishes. The machine designer and the metallurgist can do much to eliminate complaint, but because detergent compositions contain alkaline builder salts and are generally very effective electrolytes, they must be suitably inhibited to minimise attack.

Aluminium is a metal commonly found in machines and is rather easily attacked by either acid or alkaline media, but can be protected through the use of silicates in alkaline compositions. Chrome or nickel plating, when available and well deposited, prove quite satisfactory but when skimped are quickly removed. Substitute platings frequently are less resistant and may even cause electrolytic corrosion with repid removal and complaint. This latter difficulty can be alleviated by sound metallurgy, but in any event, the less corrosion caused by the detergent, the better the washer.

polyphosphates have been shown to remove vitreous enamel under conditions of high temperature and high concentration but even this corrosion can be controlled. In this same category would be removal of ceramic overglaze from chinaware. Complaints from organic finishes originate from wear, brittleness, crazing or impact, with exposure of base metal to electrolytes; however under normal conditions they are unaffected by detergents.

Corrosion and corrosion inhibition studies can be carried out using the following two methods as applied to metal or to ceramic surfaces.

9

Manufacturing Process and Formulations of Various Soaps

Various types of soaps are being used now these days i.e. powder form, cake form, bar form and liquid form. All these soaps are used in India continuously but in this modern age liquids soaps preferred to use everywhere. Liquid soap are most popular for normal use of soap in public wash rooms. These are used widely in public buildings, schools, hotels, hospitals and institutions. Besides providing better rinsing than cake or powdered soaps, liquid soap is more and more economical. It is manufactured in large batches and sold bulk and it does not need to pass through crutcher, dryer, milling machine and grinder etc. With it various other soaps manufacturing process and formulation are given in brief:

(A) **Washing Soaps**

1. Washing Soap with Soap Stone (by Cold Process)

Ingredients	*Parts by weights*
Coconut oil	50
Mahua oil	150
Til oil	40
Castor oil	20
Soapstone powder	40
Soda caustic lye (36°B')	130

Process

Heat the oil in an iron pan till these are bearable hot. Now add the soap stone powder and mix well. When the soap stone powder have completely mixed and formed a homogeneous mass add the soda caustic lye. Stir it well. When the soap becomes homogeneous, put it into the frame. When the soap has set, cut it into cakes or bars of desired size and weight.

2. Washing Soap with Soda Silicate (by Cold Process)

Ingredients	*Parts by weight*
Rice oil	10
Mahua oil	10
Coconut oil	1
Linseed oil	10
Castor oil	1
Soda silicate	10
Soda caustic lye (36°Be')	16

Process

Put the oils in an iron pan. Mahua and rice oil is generally in semi-solid form in winter therefore, these should be melted alongwith the other oils. The purpose is not to boil but only to make them fluid so that a uniform oil mixture may be obtained. When the oils have mixed up well, remove the fire.

Pour the soda silicate in an another pan. Add the soda caustic lye to it and agitate it with wooden lathe. Heating a little will make the process go easier. If soapstone powder is also to be used as adultrant, it should first be mixed in the mixture of oils with constant stirring. There should not be any lump left in the oil mixture.

When the oil mixture becomes fluid, the soda silicate-lye mixture is added in a thin stream with constant gentle stirring in one direction only. The mixture at once begins to thicken and when it reaches to such a stage of thickness that the stirrer leaves a mark in the mixture, it is transferred into the frame, which is well greased before hand.

In the cold process, saponification is completed in the frame. At this stage the temperature of the mixture is about 180°F. It takes about 24 hours to complete the saponification but if the soap is heavily adultrated it may be completed in 3 or 4 hours only.

The frame must be covered with wooden planks and gunny bags to prevent the loss of heat due to radiation and the soap formed is allowed to cool slowly.

3. Washing Soap

Ingredients	*lbs.*
Coconut oil	20
Castor oil	12
Tallow	12
Caustic soda lye (37°Be')	22
Water	4
	Grains
Metanil yellow	15

Process

Melt the oils and tallow in an iron pan till these are bearable hot. Now add the soda caustic lye. Let the heating be continued slowly at low temperature. When the mixture begins to foam and threatens to go out, put out the fire altogether. Now pour into it 4 lbs. of water (in which metanil yellow colour has already been dissolved) and stir it well. When the mass becomes homogeneous, add perfume at this stage, if desired and pour it immediately into the frame. Cut into cakes or bars of required weight and size.

4. Sunlight Type Washing Soap

Ingredients	*Grains*
Coconut oil	300
Palm oil	400
Castor oil	100
Rosin	50
Soda caustic lye (36°Be')	400
Yellow soap colour	1
Sunlight type perfume	15

Process

Take all the oils in an iron pan. To this add rosin and melt on gentle heat. Dissolve the yellow soap colour in caustic lye, then add this coloured lye to the mixture of the oil and rosin. It should be stirred constantly and heated, but in no case should the temperature be allowed to cross 90°C. When the mass becomes homogeneous and starts thickening, remove the pan from fire and stir it well for a few minutes. Then pour it into the greased frames and allow to cool slowly. When the soap is ready, take it out from the moulds and cut it into cakes or bars of the required size and weight.

5. Sunlight Type Washing Soap (Other Formula)

Ingredients	*lbs.*
Castor oil	12
Coconut oil	20
Tallow	12
Caustic soda lye (37°Be[1])	22
Water	4
	Grains
Metanil yellow	*15*

Process

Heat the oils and tallow together till these are bearable hot. Now add the lye. Let the temperature be slowed down by removing some fire from below. When the soap begins to effervesce and threatens to overflow, put out the fire altogether. Let it stand for a few minutes. Now dissolve colour into 4 lbs. of water and add it to the above mixture and stir well. When the soap becomes homogeneous, mix the perfume, if desired, and pour it immediately into the frame. Cut up into cakes or bars of the required weight and pack them for sale in the market.

6. Washing Soap made *of* Groundnut Oil Residue

Ingredients	*Parts by weights*
Groundnut oil residue	100
Mahua oil	100
Rice oil	150
Coconut oil	100
Rosin	20
Soapstone powder	50
Soda caustic lye (36°Be[1])	220
Soda silicate	100

Process

Mix the soda caustic lye and soda silicate together in an iron pan and heat. The soda silicate should be completely dissolved in caustic lye.

In an another pan melt the rosin and oil together. When the rosin has completely melted and mixed well with the oils, add the soapstone powder and mix it well again. To this then add the mixture of caustic lye and soda silicate prepared already as explained in the first paragraph. It should be kept stirred constantly till a homogeneous mixture results. When it cools and starts thickening,, pour into frames and cut into bars or cakes of the required size and weight.

7. Washing Soap (from Linseed Oil)

Ingredients	*Parts by weights*
Linseed oil	100
Coconut oil	50
Mahua oil	200
Soda silicate lye (36°Be')	125
Soda silicate	150

Process

Same as above.

8. Washing Soap (made of Cottonseed Oil)

Ingredients	*Parts by weights*
Cottonseed oil	130
Mahua oil	100
Coconut oil	30
Soda caustic lye (36°Be')	10
Soda silicate	100

Process

Same as mentioned above:

Note- If soapstone powder or soda silicate is to be added to reduce the cost, its proportion should not increase more than 25 per cent of the total weight of mixture of oils.

Nerol Soap

(1)	*Ingredients*	*Parts by wt.*
	Castor oil	20
	Rice bran oil	15
	Caustic soda (40°Be')	25
	Soda ash	5
	Sod. silicate	5
	Multani earth	15
	Soap stone powder	20
	Perfumes	0.5

(2)	*ingredients*	*Parts by wt.*
	Rice bran oil	15
	Acid oil	18
	Rosin	2
	Residual earth (from vegetable oil refining industry)	15
	Soapstone	10
	Caustic soda lye (36°Be[1])	20
	Sodium silicate	7
	Soda ash	3

(3)	*Ingredients*	*Parts by wt.*
	Oil of cheap quality	25
	Castor oil	10
	Caustic soda lye (36°Be[1])	30
	Rosin	2
	Soap stone	10
	Sodium silicate	5
	Residual bleaching earth (of oil refining plant)	15
	Multani earth	7
	Perfumes	0.5

Process of Manufacturing

First prepare lye solution by mixing caustic soda and water and stir well to mix completely and heated to achieve the specific quality.

Then take the oil in a Epoxy Coated M.S. pan and heat it. Then mix the other oils and heat it. Now add caustic lye solution and stir it with heating.

Then add other ingredients and continue stirring with heating till viscose mass is achieved. The product is now moulded in aluminium moulds. After 1-2 day the soap will hard and it will be wrapped in wax paper with appropriate brand name perfume. They arc fully kneaded on a three roll soap mill for transfer to a plodding machine, where it is extruded out in the form of soap bar. These bars are cut, and at the same time, shaped in a soap-stamping machine.

9. Other Selected Formulas of Washing Soaps

(i)

Ingredients	*Parts by wt.*
Acid oils	1
Cottonseed oil	4
Rice oil	2
Rosin	1.5
Soda silicate	4
Scapstone powder	2
Soda caustic lye (36^0 Be[1])	4.5

Process

Same as given above.

(ii)

Ingredients	*Parts by wt.*
Mahua oil	20
Rosin	2.5
Soda caustic lye (36°Be[1])	22.5
Soapstone powder	15
Acid oil	20
Castor oil	2.5
Soda silicate	24.5

(B) Nerol Washing Soap

(1)

Ingredients	*Parts by wt.*
Castor oil	20
Rice bran oil	15
Caustic soda (40°Be[1])	25
Soda ash	5
Sod. silicate	5
Multani earth	15
Soap stone powder	20
Perfumes	0.5

Ingredients	*Parts by wt.*
Rice bran oil	15
Acid oil	18
Rosin	2
Residual earth (from vegetable	

Contd...

oil refining industry)	15
Soapstone	10
Caustic soda lye (36°Be[1])	20
Sodium silicate	7
Soda ash	3

Ingredients	*Parts by wt.*
Oil of cheap quality	25
Castor oil	10
Caustic soda lye (36°Be[1])	30
Rosin	2
Soap stone	10
Sodium silicate	5
Residual bleaching earth (of oil refining plant)	15
Multani earth	7
Perfumes	0.5

Process of Manufacturing

First prepare lye solution by mixing caustic soda and water and stir well to mix completely and heated to achieve the specific quality.

Then take the oil in a Epoxy Coated M.S. pan and heat it. Then mix the other oils and heat it. Now add caustic lye solution and stir it with heating.

Then add other ingredients and continue stirring with heating till viscose mass is achieved. The product is now moulded in aluminium moulds. After 1-2 day the soap will hard and it will be wrapped in wax paper with appropriate brand name perfume. They are fully kneaded on a three roll soap mill for transfer to a plodding machine, where it is extruded out in the form of soap bar. These bars are cut, and at the same time, shaped in a soap-stamping machine.

(C) Toilet Soaps

For manufacturing toilet soaps, a suitable mixture of fats and oils, is put in a soap boiling pan. The contents are heated and continually agitated with the addition of caustic soda lye in small amounts. Thus the fats and oils are saponified producing a mixture of soap and glycerine.

When saponification is complete, a suitable amount of salt water is added to it. As soap does not dissolve in salt water it floats on the surface of water as a separate layer, while soap spent-lye, which contains glycerine, sinks in salt water. The lower layer, namely, the soap-spent lye solution, is drawn out from the lower part of the soap boiling pan or tank, and collected in a soap spent-lye tank.

In order to ensure further saponification, caustic soda solution is again added to soap for heating, after which it is left alone for ten to twenty hours.

At the above stage, the content in the soap boiling pan is divided into three layers, the upper layer which is soap, the middle layer consists of metallic soap and protein, and the bottom layer is of soap spent lye.

The soap layer is pulled out and stored in an another tank equipped with a steam jacket. Now it is cooled and turned into suitable chips. These chips are dried by hot air. When these have lost moisture to the extent of 12 to l6 percent, the chips leave the dryer for storage.

After having been weighed, dry soap chips are mixed in a mixing machine with a suitable amount of colouring material and perfume. They are fully kneaded on a three roll soap mill for transfer to a plodding machine, where it is extruded out in the form of soap bar. These bars are cut, and at the same time, shaped in a soap-stamping machine.

Toilet Soap Composition

	Ingredients	*BY wt. %*
a.	Coconut oil	20-40
b.	Tallow	30-50
c.	Rosin	10-20
d.	Castor oil	10-15
c.	Sugar	5-7
f.	Glycerine	5-8
j.	Perfume	2-3

Selected Formulas for Toilet Soaps

A full-boiled soap, consisting of 20 per cent of coconut oil and 80 per cent of fancy tallow, properly milled and pressed, gives satisfactory performance. A 200 lbs. milling batch should contain

Ingredients	*lbs.*
Soap chips (containing about 12 per cent moisture)	200
Perfume (as desired)	l to 2
Titanium dioxide (for whiteness)	0.5

There are many ingredients which may be added in the milling, as paraffin, petroleum, bees wax and dibromo and tribromosalicylanilide (as in cuticura soap) and tri-methyl thuramdisulphide (as in lifebuoy).

Notes- (1) About one to two per cent perfume is sufficient for toilet soaps.

(2) The coaltar dyes may be used to colour the soap. About 1 to 2 parts of colour is sufficient for 1000 parts of soap. The following colours are suggested for colouring the soaps:-

For Green Tint - Soap green or ultramarine green or chlorophyll.

For Violet Tint - Acid violet 6 B ; or add a very small quantity of rhyodamine in acid violet 6 B-for dull violet colour ; and for light violet tint, add a mixture of a little ultramarine blue with acid violet B.

For Brown Tint - Caramel.

For Red Tint - Eocine ; fuchsine of rhodamine dye may be used.

(D) Carbolic Soaps

1.

Ingredients	*grams*
Soda caustic lye (10°Be[1])	600
Coconut oil	900
Soda lye (20°Be')	375
	C. C.
Water	500
Common salt	375
Alcohol	50
Soap colour (red or brown)	as desired

Process

Prepare coconut oil soap according to the following method :-

600 grams of soda lye (10°Be[1]) is boiled in a porcelain vessel and 900 grams of coconut oil is gradually added while heating the mixture continuously. When the mixture becomes homogeneous 375 grams of soda lye (of 20°Be[1] is added. The mass now becomes thicker. The mixture is tested from time to time. When the test portion of it solidifies on cooling the heat is stopped immediately. Then about 500 ccs of water is added the whole mass is heated to boiling and 375 grants of common salt is added when the soap separates out and floats on the surface. The mixture is then cooled, the water drained out, the mass mixed twice with a twenty percent salt solution and finally with cold water. The water is allowed to drain out from the sieve, and the mass pressed to remove the excess of water.

The soap so obtained in the form of paste, is brought to a suitable consistency by heating it at moderate temperature in a drying oven. Now 50 grams of alcohol is added gradually to the coconut oil soap already prepared. Add the colour dissolved in water. The mixture is then made homogeneous by agitating it thoroughly with wooden laddle. It is then cut and pressed into tablets and embossed with the trade mark and dried at a temperature 30 to 50°C.

2. Lifeboy Type Soap

Ingredients	*grams*
Coconut oil	800
Groudnut oil	960
Castor oil	160
Caustic soda lye (36°Be')	1 kg.
Red soap colour (water soluble)	2
Water (to dissolve colour)	100
Carbolic acid	20

Process

Pour the oils in a soap boiling pan and heat upto 90°C.

Dissolve the colour in 100grams of water,and strain through a cheese cloth. Add this filtered colour solution to the soda caustic lye and shake well. Then add this coloured lye with the oil mixture at 90°C temperature. Stirring should be continued. Now add the carbolic acid. When the mass becomes thick and homogeneous, pour it into frames to cool and solidify and then cut into cakes of required size.

3. Transparent Soap (Pears Type)

Ingredients	*grams*
Refined tallow	240
Refined coconut oil	200
Refined castor oil	200
Soda caustic lye (36°Be')	350
Crystalline sugar	180
Distilled water	180
Glycerine	20
Crystal soda	40
Dark brown soap colour	1
Pear's type soap perfume	4 c. c.

Process

Melt tallow and oils in a soap boiling pan. When the tallow has completely mixed with the oils, add soda caustic lye with constant stirring. When the mass becomes homogeneous leave it undisturbed for about 24 hours. Now heat it again with continuous stirring. When the mass becomes viscous and smooth (like honey), add the sugar solution and the mixture of caustic soda solution and oils and agitate it again vigorously until it becomes homogeneous. Now remove the soap pan from fire and add perfume. When the perfume is mixed, run it into the soap frames, and cool till they solidify. Then cut into the cakes of desired size.

Transparent Soap (Another Formula)

Ingredients	*grams*
Stearic acid	100
Refined coconut oil	220
Refined castor oil	80
Soda caustic lye (37°Be)	200
Industrial spirit	240
Crystalline sugar	80
Glycerine	80
Colour (as desired)	to suit
Perfume (as desired)	to suit

Process

Add the stearic acid with refined coconut oil and castor oil and melt. Then add the soda caustic lye. Now leave this mass for two or three days. After that add the spirit and dissolve the soap mass in spirit.

When the soap has dissolved in the spirit, heat it in a steam jacketed kettle from 130 to 160°F temperature, until the mass becomes clear and transparent. Now pour this mass into a 'still' fitted with a 'condenser'. Evaporate the spirit and separate the soap mass.

Now the glycerine and sugar solution is added with the soap mass obtained as above. Heating and stirring is continued till the mass becomes uniform and viscous like honey. Then add colour and perfume as desired and run it into frame. Cool till it solidifies.

(E) Shaving Soaps

	Ingredients	*grams*
1.	Tallow	200
	Coconut oil	24
	Soda caustic lye (38°Be')	100
	Caustic potash lye (38°Be')	16
	Perfume	*10 ml.*

Process

Mix soda caustic and caustic potash lye together. Melt tallow and coconut oil together and heat upto 90°C. Now remove the pan from fire and add the mixture of caustic soda and potash lye gradually with continuous stirring till the mass becomes thick and uniform. Then pour it into frames to cool and solidify. When the soap is ready cut into the shape of cakes and emboss it with the trade mark with soap-stamping die.

	Ingredients	*grams*
2.	Tallow	400
	Coconut oil	48
	Caustic potash lye (38°Be')	24
	Soda caustic lye (38°Be')	100
	Gum tragacanth	4
	Perfume (as desired)	sufficient

Process

Melt tallow and coconut oil together in a big pan. Mix soda caustic and caustic lye together and add this lye to the melted coconut oil and tallow mixture, with constant stirring. When the mass becomes uniform add the gum tragacanth (in powdered-form) and mix well. Then remove it from fire and add the desired perfume in sufficient quantity so that the product gives the aroma of the perfume.

This soap is slight softer than of toilet soap, it produces lather easily highly and nonirritant. Following raw materials require for the desired properties.

		Ingredients	%
3.	a.	Coconut oil	10
	b.	Palm oil	10
	c.	Tallow	10
	d.	Stearic acid	35
	e.	Highly hardened fats	10
	f.	Caustic potash	8
	g.	Glycerine	5
	h.	Gum arabic	7
	i.	Boric acid	4
	j.	Perfume	2

(F) Special Soaps

1. Borax Soap (for Pimples)

Ingredients	*lbs.*
Coconut oil	16
Tallow	4
Soda caustic lye (38°Be')	I
Borax	1.5 *pints*
Boiling water	2

Process

Melt tallow and mix it with coconut oil. Then add soda caustic lye with continuous and uniform stirring in one direction. When the mass becomes homogeneous, add the borax solution in water. Then add perfume, if desired.

Note- To perfume the above soap, anyone of the following compounds may be used :-

Ingredients	*oz.*
Bergamot oil	1.5
Lavender oil	1.5
Citronella oil	1.3

2. Borax Soft Soap

	lbs.
Tallow	100
Soda caustic lye (15°Be')	60
Caustic potash lye (10°Be)	60
Borax solution (10°Be')	15

Process

Melt tallow and soda caustic lye with constant stirring. Heating should be continued till it forms a clear liquid. When the mixture is homogeneous the potash lye and borax solutions are added. It should be a semi-solid translucent paste.

3. Soft Soap (Other Formula)

Ingredients	*lbs.*
Linseed oil	250
Cottonseed oil	250
Rosin	50
Caustic potash lye (20°Be')	145
Pearl ash	25

Process

Take half the quantity of the oils and saponify with half the volume of potash lye. Pass steam through it and stirrwell. When the mass fobs add more lye and boil Do not heat the oils to boiling. When the oil and lye have completely mixed, add rest of the oil and lye of 22°Be' and boil. Add hot water to keep the mass thin. Whe the soap is clear and transparent, it is ready to be framed. Now crutch the silicate of soda in the ratio of 7 lbs. to 9 gallons of soap. Next prepare mixture of starch and caustic soda lye 24°Be. Heat to about 159°-169°F and add farina in small quantities at a time, taking care that the previous lot added should have dissolved before the addition of next lot. The farina is added until a mass of the required consistency of soft soap is obtained.

4. Rug Cleaning Soaps

The combination of a soap and a chlorinated or hydrocarbon solvent produces an excellent rug cleaner. An emulsion of solvent, soap, and water removes grease, tar, and paint more readily than does soap and water. The amine soaps, being soluble in these solvents, form a clear, homogeneous and suitable emulsion of solvents soap, and water which can be stored indefinitely without separation. The colours in the rugs or carpets will not fade, rather will be distinct and brightened after cleaning with such an emulsion.

A standard formula of rug cleaning soap is given below :-

Ingredients	*Parts by weight*
Oleic acid	28
Ethylene dichloride	13
Isopropanol (99 per cent)	14
Butyl cellosolve	5
Triethanolamine	16
Water	125

Process

Mix the oleic acid, ethylene chloride, isopropanol, and butyl cellosolve ; and add the triethanolamine. Stir until thoroughly mixed. Then add water. If the mixture is misty, add sufficient isopropanol to clear it.

Note- An emulsion made of equal volumes of the above soap and water is recommended for cleaning rugs and carpets.

Caution- Adequate ventilation should be provided, and special care should betaken, to avoid inhaling the vapours and repeated contact with the skin whenever chlorinated solvents are used.

5. Dry-Cleaning Soap (Liquid)

Ingredients	*Parts by weight*
Oleic acid	197
Naphtha	25
Butyl cellosolve	27
Triethanolamine	21
Potassium hydroxide (100 per cent)	8.3
Water	13.5

Process

Mix oleic acid, butyl cellosolve, and naphtha, and heat to 140°F. In a separate container, dissolve the potassium hydroxide in the water and add the triethanolamine. This solution is then added to the oleic acid solution prepared above. Stirring should be continued for about 30 minutes to react all of the potassium hydroxide. The solution should be clear.

Caution - Do not use near *an* open flame.

Note-Mixed isopropanolamines may be used to replace triethanolamine in the above formula, to produce greater oil solubility.

6. Soap used in the Bleaching of Jute

Ingredients	*Pts. by wt.*
Fish oil	1
Linseed oil	2
Caustic potash lye (20°Be')	6

Process

Take half the quantities of oil together and saponify these with half of its volume of potash lye of l0°Be'. Pass steam and stir well. When the mass fobs, add more lye and boil. Take care that the oils do not boil. When the oils and lye have formed a uniform and homogeneous mass add rest of the oils and lye of 20^0 Be' and boil. To make the mass of required consistency add hot water and stir. When the soap is clear and transparent, it is ready to be framed. Then it is cut into bar or cakes of the required size and weight.

7. Built Soaps for Cottons and Linens

This is a soap suitable for high-temperature laundering of all types of cottons and linens, but not silk and woollens. The soap is prepared by full-boiled process, with tallow and caustic soda. The crutching formula is as follows :-

Ingredient.	*lbs.*
Kettle soap	800
N-brand silicate	250
(37^0 Be') caustic soda	10
Soda ash	140
Perfume	q.s.
Total	1,200

Process

All the constituents are mixed in a pan, heated and stirred to form a homogeneous mixture.

It is possible that a little hot water will be necessary to plasticize the mixture in the crutcher. The soap is then run on the dryer, so regulated as to yield a chip of about 16-17 per cent moisture. Alternatively, the mixture may be run into frames, and cooled to solidfication. Then it may be slabbed, barred, racked off to dry. Now it is ready to be chipped on the chipping wheel. This method is for plants which do not have a chip dryer. The chips may be dried on trays to proper moisture and then ground in the mill.

8. Sandle Soap

The specification covers one type of sandle soap, that is used to clean and to a certain extent, preserve and extend the useful life of such items as shoes, handbags, leather coats, upholstery, gloves, belts, sports equipment, etc.

The soap shall be a non-flowing smooth paste, over a temperature range of 5°C to 38°C with no separation of vehicle. It is in the form suitable for ready use with a brush or cloth without crumbling.

This may be either a half-boiled or a whole-boiled soap.

The fats used may consist of 25 percent nigre palm oil and 75 percent house grease.

A crutcher batch, made from whole-boiled soap, will consist of :

Ingredients	*lbs.*
Kettle soap	400
Sodium silicate	5
Hot water	717
Beeswax	36
Neatsfoot oil	36
Silicone	6
Total	1,200

Process

Pour the soap into the crutcher, add hot water and silicate. Stir until a nice smooth slurry is formed and then add the other ingredients. The beeswax may be melted with the neatsfoot oil and both added together, followed by the silicone. When the batch has been stirred to a smooth homogeneous mass, it may be run into cans to cool. The cans should be covered when the soap is cold, to avoid deposit of moisture on the lids.

(G) Vaseline Soap

Vaseline soap is most important and vigorously used now in the homes. It is one of the best toilet soap uses for various types of skin. Formulation of this soap is:

Ingredients	*lbs.*
Coconut oil	200
Vaseline (petrolium jelly)	25
Caustic soda lye (40°Be')	95
Water	50
Total	370

Process

Heat the coconut oil in the steam heated pans, add vaseline into it. In another vessel dilute half the quantity of 40°Be caustic soda lye with 35 parts of water and add it to the above mixture when the temperature rises to about 100°C with stirring boil the mixture. When whole of the alkali has been absorbed by the oil, add the rest of the caustic soda lye and continue boiling. Add water from time to time if necessary. When the saponification has taken place completely, the mass is run down to frames, cooled and cut into cakes of the required size and weight. Colour, and perfume added in requisite proportions as desired.

(H) Liquid Soap

Liquid soap is used to dry cleaning the clothes in home. This reduces expenditure of washing in laundary:-

Ingredients	*kgs.*
Coconut oil	130
Caustic potash lye (28°Be')	125
Sugar	72
Borax	2
Water	267
Total	596

Process

The oil run into a jacketed kettle and heated to about 120°F. The potash lye is then added to the oil and sulphonation takes place. The mass expand rapidly and may overflow unless a kettle of about four to five times the capacity of the total charge of soap is used. When the saponification has completed, the sugar, borax and glycerine are added. Then water is added and the mixture stirred well until the soap has thoroughly dissolved. Heating may be necessary to dissolve the soap. The soap is then allowed to cool and removed as it floats separately on the surface. If' colour and perfume are to be added, these are added at this stage with uniform stirring.

(I) Girt Soaps

1.

Ingredients	*lbs.*
Laundry soap flakes	10
Soda ash	2.5
Pumice	32.5
Perfume	0.1
Water	54.9
Total	100

Process

Dissolve the soap flakes in hot water at 150°F and strain through a screen to remove undissolved particles. Add soda ash and stir till a smooth gel is obtained without froth. At about 135°F add pumice and perfume, and stir until uniform mixture results. Run soap into cans or jars, at a temperature that will allow the soap to gel before the pumice sinks to the bottom. The temperature can be best determined experimentally. In summer, it may be necessary to use fans to cool the soap in the containers, to speed up the congealing.

If the soap seems to be too hard or brittle, reduce the amount of soda ash. It will thin the gel.

2. Hand Soap Paste with Mineral Abrasive

Ingredients	*lbs.*
Powdered laundry soap	20
Soda ash	4.5
Pumice	75.5
Perfume	0.1
Total	100

Process

Blend all in a ribbon-type mixer. When the entire mix is uniform, it can be packed.

3. Powdered Hand Soap with Vegetable Abrasive and Lanolin

	Ingredients	*lbs.*
(a)	Powdered laundry soap	32
	Soda ash	7
	Corn cob meal	52

	Ingredients	*lbs.*
(b)	Lanolin	3
	Kerosene (deodorized) or	6
	Chlorothene NU (DOW)	6

Process

Mix all the ingredients of 'b' and get the solution. Place ingredients of 'a' into a ribbon type mixer and while the batch is mixing, pour the solution from 'b' slowly over the entire length of the mixer. When the batch is uniform, it may be spread out on a concrete floor near a window, to facilitate evaporation of the solvent. The mass can be turned over with a shoe several times. Perfumes may be added, if desired.

Notes-The specification states that it shall be uniform, free-flowing,non stratifying mixture of clean corn meal, corn cob meal, or a combination there of thoroughly saponified soap, and lanolin, in powdered form. The mixture shall contain no rosin, sugar, pine oil, nor mineral abrasives such as lava, pumice,sand or quartz. Corn meal used shall be degerminated.

If the mixture does not yield sufficient suds in accordance with test methods as in specification, powdered toilet soap should be used in preference to laundry soap.

If the corn meal is used, the free fatty acid-content shall be 2.5 percent at the maximum.

(J) Depilatory Soaps

(1)	*Ingredients*	*grams*
	Coconut oil	600
	Groundnut oil	300
	Starch	*200*
	Soda caustic lye (36°B&)	450
	Barium sulphide	600
	Citronella oil (for perfume)	*20* ml.

Process

Take coconut and groundnut oils together in a pan. If the coconut oil is in solid form, melt it. When both the oils have mixed with each other, add starch and stir well till the mass becomes uniform. Now add the barium sulphide and mix well. Remove the pan from fire and add perfume. Stir well. Then pour this mass into soap frames. When the soap is ready, cut it into the cakes of desired size and emboss these with your trade mark, with the help of soap stamping die.

(2)	*Ingredients*	*parts by weight*
	Coconut oil	180
	Castor oil	100
	Glycerine	30
	Starch	*20*
	Soda caustic lye (30°Be[1])	160
	Sodium sulphohydrate	80
	Citronella oil (for perfume)	10 ml.

Process

Mix oils and glycerine together and add caustic soda lye. Stir well till the mass becomes homogeneous. Then add starch and sodium sulphohydrate and mix thoroughly. Then add citronella oil. Pour this mass into soap frames. When the soap has cooled and solidified, take it out from the frames and cut into the cakes of the desired weight and size.

(K) Metallic Soaps in protective coating industry

This soap have large application in industrial and pharmaceutical and industrial application. Metallic soap are the combination of following metals and fatty acids.

Ingredients

Fatty acids	Abictic
Stearic acid	Naphthonic acid
Oleic acid	Palmitic acid
Linoleic acid	Phathalic acid

Metals

Ingredients

Calcium	Lead
Cobalt	Magnesium
Aluminium	Manganese
Copper	Zinc etc.
Cerium	

Various uses of metallic soaps in protective coating industry:-

1. Suspended agents in heavily pigmented paints to prevent excessive settling and hard caking of pigments.
2. Drier or catalysts to accelerate the drying of oil, natural and synthetic, varnishes and enamel films.
3. Anti-fouling agents as ingredients of ship-bottom paints.
4. Flatting agents ; ingredients in various finishes to decrease the degree of gloss.

The protective coating industry uses a large number of metallic soaps.The linoleates, resinates, and naphthalates are used as driers. The naphthalate, oleate palmitate and stearate, of aluminium are used as thickening and suspending agents for paints. The stearates of aluminium, calcium and zinc are used for flatting purpose in varnishes and liquors.

Method of Precipitation

Resinates, palmitates and stearates of calcium, lead, aluminium, magnesium and *zinc* are prepared by this method. These are powdered metallic soap. The fatty acid saponified with requisite quantity of caustic soda, to get a water soluble soap. Then the soap of desired salts is, added to this soluble soap. The chemical reaction taking place is as follows :-

(i) $C_{17}H_{35}COOH + NaOH \rightarrow C_{17}H_{35}COONa + H_2O$

Stearic Acid Caustic Soda Sod. Stearate

(ii) $2C_{12}H_{35}COONa + CaCl_3 \rightarrow (C_{17}H_{35}COO)_2Ca + 2NaCl$

Calcium stearate Metallic soap

The resulting metallic soap which precipitates is subsequently filtered, washed, dried and ground. In case of calcium stearate the moisture content is kept at 2.5%. A disintegrator such as a hammer mill is used to obtain a fine, fluffy powder of the product fusion method for manufacture of metallic soap.

Oils or fatty acid is heated with oxides, hydroxides, carbonates, or other easily dissociates salts of metals, to get metallic soaps. Temperature by maintained during the reaction at about 100°C with the result that the products have a much lighter colour when glycerine are used, the temperature may go as high as 200°C. For manufacturing, the fatty acids are heated in a steam jacketed kettle with constant agitation while the oxides or carbonates of the desired metal is sifted into them slowly. The chemical reaction taking place is as follows :-

$$2C_{17}H_{33}COOH+PbO\text{-}Pb(C_{17}H_{33}COO)+H_{2}0$$

Oleic acid litharge lead oleate

As the temperature in the reaction is high, the water formed in the reaction is constantly driven off as steam. The lead oleate thus obtained is fused, paste masses of varying consistency. Aluminium oleate is hard tough mass, while nickel oleate is liquid at room temperature.

(L) Liquid Dental Soap

This soap is widely used for the cleaning of teeths. Its process is simple, Saponify the oil with caustic potash and dissolve in equal parts ofalcohol then pour the water and glycerine with good agitation and warm water and glycerine before adding. Then keep it for cooling for some time and then add the rest of the alcohol and perfume and agitate it. Let settle it for 8-15 days in small vessels and then filter it. Composition of its components.

Ingredients	kgs.
Alcohol	280
Glycerine	230
Olive oil	70
Caustic potash(38^{0}Be'')	35
Water	350

(M) Medicated Soap

Neem Soap

Formulations

Ingredients	*kg.*
Neem oil	I
Coconut oil	5
Caustic soda (70° Be')	I
Water	2
Blue colour	q.s.
Yellow colour	q.s.

Caustic soda dissolved in water and make a solution of it. Add this solution in the other vessel of oil slowly with continuous agitation. When the whole mixture has acquired the consistency of thick paste the colours are intimately incorporated into it after being finely ground and the creamy substance is allowed to settle for 2 days.

10

Miscellaneous Formulae

Peroxide Gel Dentifrice

Component	*Composition (W/W)%*
Carbopol 940	1.50
Polyethylene glycol 400	30.00
Glycerine 99.6%	25.00
Butylated hydroxy anisole	0.50
Hydrogen peroxide (35% solution)	10.00
Sodium saccharin	0.50
Mixed flavour oils	1.00
Calcium pyrophosphate	29.00
Sodium lauroyl sarcosinate	1.50
Tetrasodium pyrophosphate	1.00

High Lather Cream Rinse Shampoo

Component	*Composition(W/W)%*
Sodium lauroyl sarcosinate, 30%	20.0
Coco betaine, 35%	10.0
Lauramide DEA	5.0
Cetrimonium chloride, 30%	0.8
Steralkonium chloride, 25%	0.1
Disodium EDTA	0.2
Water, perfume,preservative	q.s.
Adjust pH to 6.7	

Antidandruff Shampoo

Component	*Composition (W/W)%*
Sodium lauroyl sarcosinate, 30%	4.0
Colloidal sulfur	4.0
Sodium chloride	6.0
Sodium coconut alkyl glyceryl sulfonate	30.0
N-cocoyl sarcosine	0.7
FD&C blue dye no.1	0.4
Perfume	0.5
Succuinic Acid	1.0
Disodium cupric ethylenediaminet-etraacetate	0.5
Distilled water	q.s.

Antidandruff Shampoo for Oily Hair

Component	*Composition(W/W)%*
Sodium lauroyl sarcosinate, 30%	10.0
TEA dedecyl sulfate, 40%	25.0
Zinc pyrithione, 48%	4.2
Magnesium aluminum silicate	1.0
Hydroxypropylmethyl cellulose, E4,000	1.25
Water, perfume, colour	q.s.

Disperse magnesium aluminium silicate and HPMC, E4,000 in water and allow to stand overnight. Add the rest of the ingredients.

Crystal Clear, Acid Balanced Shampoo

Component	*Composition(W/W)%*
Part 1:	
Sodium lauroyl sarcosinate, 30%	30.0
Lauryl dimethyl amine oxide, 30%	5.0
Polyquaternium 7 (Merquat 550)	1.0
Part 2:	
Polyol alkoxy ester (Crothix)	0.7
Disodium EDTA	0.3
Water	64.0

Disperse Crothix in hot water and add with strong agitation to Part 1. A clear solution forms. While still hot, adjust pH to 5.7 by adding citric acid solution with strong agitation

Sarcosinate Shampoo

Component	*Composition (W/W)%*
Triethanolamine lauryl ether sulfate (3 moles ethylene oxide)	4.0
Triethanolamine cocoyl sarcosinate	10.0
Monoethanolamide of coconut fatty acids	3.0
Diethanolamide of coconut fatty acids	3.0
EDTA, partialthiethanolamine salt	0.65
Ethanol	7.0
Methyl cellulose (4000 cps)	0.75
Perfume	0.75
Water	q.s.
pH adjusted to 6.7	

Clear Facial Cleanising Gel

Component	*Composition (W/W)%*
Sodium cocoyl glutamate	40.0
Sodium lauroyl sarcosinate	10.0
Cocamide DEA	10.0
Glycerol	5.0
Water, perfume, preservative	q.s.

Mix ingredients, heat to 50°C until clear, cool.

Mild Shower Gel

Component	*Composition(W/W)%*
Cocoamphoglycinate	23.0
Sodium lauryl sarcosinate, 30%	20.0
Sodium dodecyl sulfate, 30%	20.0
Hydroxypropyl methylcellulose (E4M)	0.3
Water, perfume, preservative,	q.s.

Mix ingredients, Heat to 50°C and adjust pH to 7.0 with lactic acid, cool.

Liquid Bath Foam

Component	*Composition(W/W)%*
Na alpha-olefin sulfonate, 40%	10.0
Ammonium lauryl sulfate, 30%	30.0
Cocoyl sarcosine	3.0
Ammonium chloride	3.0
Water, preservative, etc	q.s.

Mix surfactants, dissolve ammonium chloride in warm water, and add. Adjust pH to 4.8.

Liquid Toilet Soap

Component	*Composition(W/W)%*
Sodium (C14-16) olefin sulfonate, 40%	20.0
Sodium lauroyl sarcosinate. 30%	10.0
Cocamide MEA	3.0
Ammonium chloride	2.0
Disodium EDTA	0.2
Water, perfume, colour, opacifier, preservative	q.s.

Add first two ingredients to water, heating to 80°C. add cocamide MEA and heat with stirring until clear. Add remaining ingredients and adjust pH to 5.5 with citric acid.

Cationic Skin Cleanser

Component	*Composition (W/W)%*
Sodium lauroyl sarcosinate, 30%	50.0
Oleoyl sarcosine	1.0
Lauramide DEA	5.0
Tetrasodium EDTA	0.4
Cetrimonium chloride, 29%	3.4
Water	q.s.

Surgical Scrub Liquid

Component	*Composition(W/W)%*
Sodium C14-16 olefinsulfonate, 40%	20.0
Sodium lauroylsarcosinate, 30%	10.0
Cocamide MEA	3.0
Choroxylenol	1.0
Ammonium chloride	2.0
Disodium EDTA	0.2
Water	q.s.
Adjust to pH 5.5	

Facial Cleanser for Oily Skin

Component	*Composition(W/W)%*
TEA lauroyl sarcosinate, 40%	20.0
Hydroxypropylmethyl cellulose, E4000	2.0
Salicylic acid	1.0
Methyl paraben	0.2
EDTA	0.2
Water	q.s.

Disperse thickener in hot water before adding other ingredients.

Acne Lather Scrub Gel with 10% Benzoyl Peroxide

Component	*Composition (W/W)%*
Sodium lauroyl sarcosinate, 30%	30.0
Oleth-10	15.0
Benzoyl peroxide, 70%	14.3
Magnesium aluminum silicate (Veegum - R.T Vanderbilt Co.)	1.0
Disodium EDTA	02.
Water	q.s.

Disperse Veegum in hot water with high shear mixing and allow to stand overnight. Mill benzoyl peroxide with Veegum suspension. Mix remaining ingredients, heat to 50°C and mill to uniform texture. Fill warm into containers. A stiffer gel may be obtained by increasing the oleth-10 to 20.0%.

Emollient Gel

Component	*Composition*
Coal tar extract	50 mg
N-lauroyl sarcosine	30 mg
Glyceryl capric/caprylic ester	800 mg
Propylene glycol	20 mg
Glyceryl tris 12-hydroxy	
stearate	100 mg

Sunscreen Lotion

Component	*Composition*
A:	
Veegum	1.5
Water	78.5
Triethanolamine	4.0
B:	
Myvacet 9-40	4.0
Cetyl alcohol	0.5
Stearic acid	1.5
Cocoyl sarcosine	5.0
C:	
P-aminobenzoic acid	5.0

I. Rehydrate Veegum in water. Add Tea and heat to 65°C.

II. Heat B to 70°C, then add to 1 with agitation.

III. Add paba with agitation until 35°C is reached.

Note: Because of the possible formation of suspected cancer causing compounds. p-Aminobenzoic Acid (PABA) should be replaced with some other UV blocker, such as Benzophenone-4 or Octyl Methoxycinnamate.

Aerosol Shave Cream

Component	*Composition(W/W)%*
A:	
Veegum	1.5
Water	76.0
Sorbitol (70% solution)	3.0
Triethanolamine	6.0
B:	
Stearic acid	6.5
Cocoyl sarcosine	7.0
Preservative	q.s.
Perfume	q.s.

I. Add the VEEGUM to water slowly, agi-tating continually until smooth. Add sorbitol and triethanolamine. Heat to 70°C

II. Heat B to 75°C.

III. Add 11 to I and mix until cool.

Aerosol Depilatory Spray

Component	*Composition(W/W) %*
Sodium N-lauroyl sarcosinate	1.5
Sodium metasilicate penthydrate	1.0
Thioglycolic acid (80% solution)	7.5
Sodium hydroxide	5.36
Urea	10.0
Perfume	0.45
Water	q.s.

Deodorant Stick

Component	*Composition(W/W)%*
A:	
Veegum	2.0
Water	q.s.
B:	
Zinic stearate	5.0
C:	
Cocoyl sarcosine	2.0
D:	
Pyrax B	90.5
Vancide 89RE	0.5

Add the Veegum to about 30 parts water, agitating continually until smooth. Add the zinc stearate with agitation. Add the cocoyl sarcosinate to the paste. Premix D, add to A, B and C and work into a smooth paste (add more water if necessary to get a paste). Pack into stick mold and allow to dry. (Final pH should be about 5.0.)

Analgesic Cream

Component	*Composition(W/W) %*
A:	
Hectabrite DP	1.75
Klucel J	1.75
Water	40.75
Ethanol	36.75
B:	
Eucalyptus oil	0.20
Menthol	0.40
Peppermint oil	0.40
Triethanolamine	3.00
Methyl salicylate	5.00
Cocoyl sarcosine	10.00
Preservative	q.s.

Phase A: Dry blend Hectabrite DP and Klucel J and add to the water and ethanol slowly, agitating continually until smooth.

Phase B: Combine, stiring to dissolve crystals, and add to

Phase A: with slow mixing. Mix until unifrom

Surfactant Base Shower Gel Formulation

Ingredient	*Chemical Name*	*A-1785*	*B-1352*
PHASE A			
Empicol ESB3/ A&W	SLES (30%)	30.0	30.0
Oramix N S 10 / Seppic	Decyl Glucoside (50%)	5.0	5.0
Amonyl 380 BA / Seppic	Cocamidoporpylbetaine (30%)	10.0	10.0
Brij 30 / ICI	Laureth-4	2.0	2.0
Sepigel 305 / Seppic	-----	2.0	2.0
Water		Up to 100	
PHASE B			
DC 1785/DowCorning	Silicone Emulsion	8.3	0.0
DC 1352 DowCorning	Silicone Emulsion	0.0	3.0
PHASE C			
NaCl		0.5	0.5

Soap Base Shower Gel Formulation

Ingredient	*Chemical Name*	*Ratio (%)*
Natrosol 250HR/Aqualon	Hydoxyethylcellulose	0.65
Edenor C 18 98/100/Henkel	Stearic Acid	2.00
Edenor C 14 98/100/Henkel	Myristic Acid	9.00
Edenor C 12 98/100/Henkel	Lauric Acid	14.00
K0H 85% flake	—	7.06
Propylene Glycol	—	2.00
Glycerin	—	2,00
Ethylene Glycol Monostearate	—	2.00
EDTA-4Na	—	0.10
Citric Acid	—	0.20
Germall II	—	0.20
Perfume	—	1.50
DC1497 Emulsion	Silicone Emulsion	2.50
Water	—	Up to 100

Procedure

- Dissolve HEC into 40% weight of water
- Add 0.1% KOH, mix until uniform
- Heat to 70°C, add PG and Glycerin - A
- Heat all acid to 70°C and agitation until uniform - B
- Add B into A, mixed and maintain 70°C
- Add residue KOH (50% solution) slowly, mixed and maintain 80c, mixed 10 min more after finished neutralization
- Add EGMS when 60c, get well dissolution and start cooling system Add DC 1497 emulsion when 50c
- Add residue ingredient like citric acid, EDTA-4Na, Germall 11 and perfume when 40c or below

Mixed Base Shower gel Formulation

Ingredient	*Chemical Name*	*Ratio (%)*
PHASE A		
Aculyn 33/ISP	Acrylates Copolymer	1.4
Aculyn 22/ISP	Acrylates/Steareth-20 Methacrylate Copolymer	1.4
Water	—	10.0
TEA	—	0.8
PHASE B		
Liquid Soap SFP/Goodway	Potassium Soap (30%)	38.9
Mirataine BET C-30/Rhodia	Cocamidoporpylbetaine (35%)	3.4
Texapon N70/Henkel	Sodium Laureth Sulfate (18%)	32.2
Plantacare 1200/Henkel	Lauryl Polyglucosides (50%)	1.0

Mixed Base Shower Gel Formulation

Ingredient	*Chemical Name*	*Ratio (%)*
PHASE C		
Cetyl Alcofhol/Merk	—	1.0
EGMS	—	1.4
EGDS	—	0.5
PHASE D		
Liquid Germall Plus/ISP	—	0.5
DC 1352/DC 1497 Emulsion/Dow Corning		3.3
Perfume	—	0.6
Water		Up to 100

Procedure :

1. Mixed part A and B separately and agitate together until uniform
2. Heat to 70°C, add ingredient of group C, cool the whole system
3. Add part D by mild mixing
4. Adjust pH value to 8.3-8.7 with citric acid or TEA, add salt to adjust viscosity

Soap Base Shower Gel Formulation

Formulation	*A*	*B*	*D*	*E*
D.I Water	41 14	43.64	46.14	46.44
Natrosol 250HR	*0.65*	*0.65*	*0.65*	*0.65*
C 18 Fatty Acid (99%)	*2*	*2*	*2*	*2*
C 14 Fatty Acid (99%)	*14*	*14*	*14*	*14*
C 12 Fatty Acid (99%)	*9*	*9*	*9*	*9*
K0H (85-%)	7.49	7.49	7.49	7.49
Propylene Glycol	2	2	2	0
Glycerine	2	2	2	6
EGMS	2	2	2	2
FDTA-4Na	0.1	0.1	0,1	0.1
Citric acid	0.2	0.2	0.2	0.2
Germall II	0.2	0.2	0.2	0.2
PCA-Na	0	0	0	0.3
Perfume	1.5	1.5	1.5	1.5
DC 2-1497	0	2.5	5	3

Suractant Base Shower Gel Formulation

Ingredient	*Chemical Name*	*Ratio (%)*
PHASE A		
Empicol LS 30P/A&W	SLS(30%)	25.0
Empilan Fd/A&W	Coconut diethanolamide	3.0
Empigen BS-AU/A&W	Cocamidoporpylbetaine (30%)	5.0
Extrapone Seaweed/Dragoco	Plant Extract	3.0
Carbopol 2020 (4%)/BF.	Acrylic copolymer (4%)	15.0
Water		44.0
PHASE B		
Suttocide A/ISP	Sodium Hydroxy Methyl Glycinate	0.8
PHASE C		
DC 1227 emulsion/Dow Corning	Silicone Emulsion	4.0
Perfume		0.2
Color		q.s.

Daily Protection Facial Lotion (SPF 25)

K 18/1-22026/E

Ingredients	*INCI Name*	*% (w/w)*
PART A:		
Crodafos MCA	Cetyl Phosphate	1,50
Cutina MD	Glyceryl Stearate	2,00
Lanette 16	Cetyl Alcohol	1,00
Cetiol SN	Cetearyl Isonanoate	4,00
Myritol 318	Caprylic/Capric Triglyceride	5,00
Witconol TN	C12/15 Alkylbenzoate	5,00
Prisorine 3505	Isostearic Acid	1,00
Copherol 1250	Tocopheryl Acetate	0,50
Solbrol P	Propyl Paraben	0,10
NEO HELIOPAN BB	BENZOPHENONE 3	1,50
NEO HELIOPAN 303	OCTOCRYLENE	5,00
PART B:		
Demineralized Water	Water	QS

Contd......

NEO HELIOPAN HYDRO	PHENYLBENZIMIDAZOLE SULFONIC ACID	2.00
NaOH Solution	Sodium Hydroxide Solution	QS
Glycerin 99%	Glycerin	3.00
Solbrol M	Methyl Paraben	0.20
Carbopol ETD 2050	Carbomer	0.20
PHENOXYETHANOL	Phenoxyethanol	0.70
PART C:		
ALPHA BISABOL NAT H&R	Bisabolol	0.10
PERFUME OIL	FRAGRANCE (PARFUM)	0,30

Dental Cream

Component	*Composition (W/W)%*
Calcium Carbonate	12.1
Dicalcium phosphate dihydrate	36.2
Sodium N-lauryl sarcosinate	2.0
Glycerine	30.6
Water	15.3
Irish moss	1.0

Mouthwash

Component	*Composition (W/W)%*
Sodium N-lauroyl sarcosinate	0.2
Ethyl alcohol	10.0
Flavor	0.15
Saccharin (Soluble)	0.012
Distilled water	q.s.

Dental Cream

Component	*Composition (W/W)%*
Sodium lauroyl sarcosinate	4.1
Stannous fluoride	0.2
Sec. calcium phosphate dihydrate	86.0
Magnesium silicate	7.0
Flavoring materials	2.5
Saccharin (Soluble)	0.2

Mouth Rinse

Component	*Composition (W/W)%*
Diisobutyl cresoxyethoxlethyl-dimenthylbenzyl ammonium chloride	0.03
Sodium N-lauroyl sarcosinate	0.20
Polyoxyethylene tridrcyl alcohol (EO12)	0.25
Ethanol	15.0
Adjuvants (colours, flavour, fragance)	0.20
Water (distilled)	84.32

Commercial Baby Shampoo

PEG-80 Sorbitan Laurate	
Cocamidopropyl Betaine	
Sodium Trideceth Sulfate	
Lauroamphoglycinate	
PEG-150 Distearate	
Sodium Laureth-13 Carboxylate	
Performance :	
Lather Drainage Time	
(2% Solids)	15 Seconds
ET-50 (10% Solids)	8 Hours

Formula 1

Component	*(W/W)%*
Hampshire Sodium LED3A	3.2
Sodium Myristoyl Sarcosinate (Hamposyl ® M-30)	3.2
Sodium Lauryl Ether Sulfate	3.2
Polyquaternium 7	0.4
Water	100
Performance:	
Lather Drainage Time	
(2%Solids)	101 Seconds
Et-50 (10% Solids) :	15 Hours

Formula 2

Component	*(W/W)%*
Hampshire Tris LED3A	5.0
Cocamphodiacetate	5.0
Water	90.0
	100.0
Performance:	
Lather Drainage Time (2% Solids)	103 Seconds
ET-50 (10% Solids) :	5.3 Hours

Formula 3

Component	*(W/W)%*
Hampshire Sodium LED3A	5.0
Alkylppolyglycoside 1200	5.0
Water	90.0
Performance :	
Lather Drainage Time (2% Solid)	50 Seconds
ET-50 (10% Solids) :	19 Hours

Formula 4

Component	*(W/W)%*
Hampshire Sodium LED3A	3.3
Sodium Lauryl Ether Sulfate	3.3
Sodium Cocamidopropyl Betaine	3.4
Water	90
	100.0
Performance :	
Lather Drainage Time (2% Solids)	57 Seconds
ET-50 (10% Solids) :	24 Hours

Formula 5

Component	*(W/W)%*
Hampshire Sodium LED3A	3.3
Sodium Lauryl Ether Sulfate	3.3
Sodium Cocamidopropyl Betaine	3.4
Water	90
Ca/Mg Hardness to 3,000 ppm	—
	100
Performance :	
Lather Drainge Time (2% Solids)	49 Seconds
ET-50 (10%Solids) :	24 Hours

Instant Polish

Ingredients:	*% Wt.*
Phase A	
Exxsol D40 (ExxonMobil)	25.0
DC 200 Fluid, 350 cSt (Dow Corning)	1.4
DC 200 Fluid, 1,000 cSt (Dow Corning)	1.0
DC 5200 Formulation Aid (Dow Corning)	2.0
Phase B	
Water	57.6
Sillikolloid P.87 (Hoffmann Minerals)	8.5
Wax emulsion (35% activeblend of soft/hard waxes)	2.5
50% sodium citrate in water	2.0

Procedure: Blend phase A ingredients in the main vessel under low shear. In an auxiliary vessel, load phase B ingredients in the order listed. Mix with low shear. Add phase B to phase A very slowly under high shear until the emulsion begins to form. The remainder of phase B can then be added at a faster rate. When addition is complete, mix with high shear.

Comments: The blend of fluids in this formulation yields high gloss in an easy-to-use product form.

Amide-free Liquid Dishwash

Ingredients:	*%Wt.*
Dodecylbenzene sulfonic acid	21.5
Caustic soda	5.4
Sodium laureth sulfate (60%)	4.0
Mackam 35UL (McIntyre Group) (cocamidopropyl betaine)	5.5
Sodium xylene sulfonate (40%)	8.0
Water, dye, fragrance	q.s. to 100

Procedure: Add caustic soda to water and adjust pH to 7.0-8.0 with dodecylbenzene sulfonic acid. Add remaining components and adjust pH to 6.5-7.0 with citric acid. If necessary, lower viscosity with sodium xylene sulfonate, or raise viscosity with sodium chloride.

Comments: Solids, %: 30 +/- 1.0 pH: 6.5-7.0 viscosity (cps, 25°C): 260-350.

Aloe Vera SPF 10 Sun Protection Gel

Ingredients:	*%Wt.*
CoVera (RTD HallStar) (aloe barbadensis leaf juice)	14.77
Triethanolamine	2.18
Phenylbenzimidazole sulfonic acid	4.00
Allantoin	0.10
RTD Glycerin 99.5% (RTD HallStar) (glycerin)	5.00
CoSept M (RTD HallStar) (methylparaben)	0.20
Imidazolidinyl urea	0.15
Water (deionized)	1.00
Carbopol 940 (carbomer)	1.50
Water (deionized)	(to 100) 58.10
Triethanolamine	3.00
Water (deionized)	10.00

Procedure : Add CoVera to Vessel one and with good mixing, add triethanolamine (2.18% of formula) and then phenylbenzimidazole sulfonic acid. When homogeneous, add allantoin, RTD Glycerin 99.5% and CoSept M in order and heat batch to 70°C. Maintain until homogeneous (but at least 15 minutes) and then start cooling. Dissolve imidazolidinyl urea in water (1 % of formula) and when batch is at 45°C, add it to the batch. In vessel two, disperse Carbopol 940 in deionized water (58.10% of formula) and mix until uniform. In vessel three, dissolve triethanolamine (3% of formula) in deionized water (10% of formula). Add vessel three to vessel two with strong mixing but without aeration. When homogeneous, add the batch in vessel one to vessel two and mix to homogeneity. Continue cooling and mixing until the completed batch is at desired filling temperature. Perform quality assurance checks.

Comments: pH: 6.0. Viscosity: 24 cps.

Gentle Baby Shampoo

Ingredients:	*%Wt.*
Deionized water	q.s. to 100
Tego Betaine L-7 (cocamidopropyl betaine)	18.5
Neosorb 70/20 (sorbitol)	16.9
Plantaren 1200 UP (lauryl glucoside)	15.9
Plantaren 818 UP (coco glucoside)	12.5
Amisoft LS-11 (sodium lauroyl glutamate)	5.0
Antil 141 (propylene glycol(and) PEG-55 propyleneglycol oleate)	2.2
D-panthenol USP (D-panthenol)	1.0
Sensomer CI-50 (Ondeo Nalco) (hydroxypropyltrimonium chloride)	0.5
Crotein HKP Powder (keratin amino acid)	0.4
Fragrance	0.1
Preservative	q.s.

Procedure: Add water first and heat to approximately 40°C. Add the remaining ingredients to the water in the order listed. Mix until uniform at a low speed (under 100 rpm). Cool to room temperature.

Comments: Makes a clear, colorless shampoo formulation.

Vitamin Skin Lotion

Ingredients:	*%Wt.*
Deionized water	79.1
Carbomer 941	0.2
Glycerine	5.0
Paragon G-2	0.5
Fancorsil Lim-1	0.5
Mackstat DM	0.5
Triethanolamine	0.2
Hydrobrite 1000 (Crompton)	10.0
Crodafos CES	2.0
Shea butter	1.0
Uvinul MC-80	0.2
Vitamin E acetate	0.3
Fragrance No. 225404	0.5

Procedure: Premix deionized water and Carbomer 941 cold with high agitation. Heat to 70ºC and add glycerine, Paragon G-2, Fancorsil Lim-1 and Mackstat DM in order. Add triethanolamine and maintain heat at 70°C. Premix Hydrobrite 1000, Crodafos CES, shea butter and Uvinul MC-80 in oil kettle; heat to 70°C. Add oil phase to water phase at 70°C. Mix for 30 minutes; cool to 50°C. Add vitamin E acetate and fragrance. Mix and package at room temperature.

Kids Foaming Conditioning Shampoo

Ingredients:	*%Wt.*
Deionized water	72.27
Celquat L-200(National Starch)(polyquatemium-4)	1.00
Amaze (National Starch)(corn starch modified)	1.00
Tego Betaine L-7 30%(Goldschmidt)(cocamidopropyl betaine)	13.33
Mackanate EL 40%(McIntyre Group)(disodium laureth sulfosuccinate)	5.00
Tween 20 (Uniqema) (polysorbate 20)	1.00
Glydant (Lonza) (DMDM hydantoin)	0.40
Isobutane	6.00

Procedure: In a mixing vessel, add deionized water and Celquat L-200. Mix until dispersed, and add Amaze. Once dispersed, add remaining inuredients one at a time until homogeneous. Filter and fill aerosol containers. Charge with propellants.

Comments: Valve type: Seaquist VX-81 Stem: 018 Length: 0.343" Gasket: Buna-P 0.045" THK Code: 150 Spring: SS Cup: High profile OS OD, epoxy top, laminate bottom, dimpled, Taperseal; Code: 1625 Actuator: Mousse spout short neck, short spt (S4LS OFF)

Gel Sanitizing Vertical Surface Cleaner

Ingredients:	*%Wt.*
Deionized water	40.0
50% NaOH	5 0
DeMox CSG-30 (DeForest)	15.0
Sodium hypochlorite 10%	40.0

Procedure: Add first three ingredients and mix well until thick and fully dissolved. Add the chlorine bleach last, mixing well as it is added. A visco-elastic gel is formed.

11

Scouring Bar

The scouring Bar commonly employed for the cleaning of household utensiles is known as utensils scouring bar. It is available in the market in various trade names such as 'Vim' bar and any others. These trade names are from reputed and big concern whereas there are number of manufacturers of this product in india, so many entrepreneurs manufacture it on a small and tiny scale as well.

Process of Manufacture of Scouring Bar/Dish Washing Bar

The manufacturing process of scouring bar can be divided in the following step.

Formulation	%
Alkyl Benzene Sulphate (65-85% Active)	20
Sodium Lauryl Sulphate	15
Tallow Coco Soap (80% : 20% Ratio)	35
Calcium Stearate	6-0
Titanium Dioxide	1-5
Tri-Sodium Polyphosphate	16.2
Perfume	0.3
Water	6.0
Total	100.00

The manufacturing process of detergent bar can be divided into the following main head :

1. Ingredient Dosing.
2. Slurry Preparation.
3. Cooling and refining.
4. Extrusion.
5. Conditioning.
6. Stamping.
7. Packing and forwarding.

PLANT ECONOMICS

Rated Plant Capacity = 2.00 MT/Day

Land & Building (Land 700 sq.mts.) = Rs. 12,75,000.00

Plant & Machinery

1. Amalgamator
2. Milling Machine
3. Bar Cutting machine
4. Stamping Machine
5. Neutraliser
6. Mixer or Blender
7. Mini Boiler
8. Trays/Pan
9. Packing Machine (Semi Automatic)
10. Weighing Machine
11. Misc. Laboratory equipments, Storage vessels, tools etc.

FIXED CAPITAL

1. Land & Building	Rs.	12,75,000.00
2. Plant & Machinery	Rs.	5,50,000.00
3. Other Fixed Assets	Rs.	1,35,000.00
Total	Rs.	19,60,000.00

Raw Materials

1. Tri Sodium phosphate
2. Sodium Carbonate
3. Sodium meta silicate, Pentahydrate

4. Sodium Tri poly phosphate
5. Linear Alkyl Benzene sulphonate
6. Talcum Powder
7. Misc packaging materials, colour, etc.

TOTAL WORKING CAPITAL/MONTH

1. Raw Material	Rs.	14,65,000.00
2. Salary & Wages	Rs.	1,03,740.00
3. Utilities & Overheads	Rs.	71,250.00
Total	Rs.	16,39,990.00

TOTAL CAPITAL INVESTMENT

Total Fixed Capital	Rs.	19,60,000.00
Total Working Capital for 3 Months	Rs.	49,19,970.00
Total	Rs.	68,79,970.00

TURN OVER/ANNUM

Receipt By sale of Scouring Bar/ Dish washing Bar 600 MT	Rs. 2,28,00,000.00

PROFIT SALES RATIO = 9.02 %

RATE OF RETURN = 29.91 %

BREAK EVEN POINT (B.E.P) = 48.04 %

12
Detergent Cake & Powder

Detergents are defined as complete washing or cleaning products which contain among their ingredients an organic surface-active compound (Surfactant) that passes soil-removal properties. Frequently the term detergent is used synonymously with surfactant but common industry practice treats the surfactant as one component of a done here. Additionally this discussion treats primarily, only the so called synthetic detergents, excluding those products in which soap is the sole or predominant surfactant.

Soaps, the alkali salts of long chain fatty acids, differ significantly in certain important performance properties from the synthetic surfactants.

Detergent Cake Formula and its Manufacture

Formulation

Ingredients	
Alkyl Benzene Sulphate (65-85%) ACTIVE)	20
Sodium Lauryl Sulphate	15
Tallow Coco Soap (80% : 20% RATIO)	35
Calcium Stearate	6-0
Titanium Dioxide	1-5
Tri-Sodium Polyphosphate	16.2
Perfume	0.3
Water	6.0
Total	100.00

The manufacturing process of detergent bar can be divided into the following main head :

1. Ingredients Dosing.
2. Slurry Preparation.

3. Cooling and refining.
4. Extrusion.
5. Conditioning.
6. Stamping.
7. Packing and forwarding.

PLANT ECONOMICS

Rated Plant Capacity	=	500.00 KG/Day
Land & Building	=	Rs. 1,21,000.00
(Land 500 sq.ft.)		

Plant & Machinery

1. Analgamator Milling Machine
2. Cake cutting Machine
3. Stamping Machine
4. Empty Drums for Mixing and storage
5. Neutralizer (Extra kettle of stainless steel)
6. Mixer or Blender (Semi automatic
7. Trays/pan made of stainless steel
8. Pulverising machine (Grinding machine)
9. Weighing Machine
10. Weighing Balance for packing
11. Miscellaneous items, like Blowers Trolleys and Bag Sewing Machine etc
12. Bhatti (Chulla)
13. Laboratory equipments

FIXED CAPITAL

1. Land & Building	Rs.	1,21,000.00
2. Plant & Machinery	Rs.	1,81,000.02
3. Other Fixed Assets	Rs.	5,000.00
Total	Rs.	3,07,000.02

Raw Materials

1. Acid Slurry (LABS)
2. Sodium Tripolyphosphate
3. Carboxy Methyl cellulose
4. Optical Whitening Agent
5. Foam Booster
6. Sodium Silicate
7. Sodium Sulphate
8. Acid Slurry
9. Soda Ash
10. Sodium Silicate
11. Marble chips powder
12. Packaging Material
13. Detergent Cake packaging

TOTAL WORKING CAPITAL/MONTH

1. Raw Material	Rs.	1,00,150.00
2. Salary & Wages	Rs.	10,000.00
3. Utilities & Overhesds	Rs.	5,500.00
Total	Rs.	1,15,650.00

TOTAL CAPITAL INVESTMENT

Total Fixed Capital	Rs.	3,07,000.02
Total Working Capital for 3 Months	Rs.	3,46,950.00
Total	Rs.	6,53,950.02

TURN OVER/ANNUM

1. By sales of 30000 Kgs (30 MT) (300000 Pcs of 100 grms. each) of detergent cake
2. By sales of 120000 Kgs. (120 MT) of detergent powder

Total Rs. 21,00,000.00

PROFIT SALES RATIO = 24.70 %

RATE OF RETURN = 79.33 %

BREAK EVEN POINT (B.E.P) = 34.05 %

13
Toilet & Herbal Soap

Formulation for Toilet Soaps

By Cold Process

Fats should be used purely of high quality. Weigh fats and lye accurately and in case lye is more. The soap will become strong and harmful to skin, and if lye is low, the fats will not be saponified properly.

White Toilet Soap

Coconut Oil	44 Parts
Tallow	60 Parts
Castor Oil	4 Parts
Caustic Soda lye 40° Be	55 Parts

Process

Melt oil and fat in one vessel then filter to remove any impurity. Now add caustic soda lye in the oil slowly and stir continuously when the oil is fully saponified, add perfume and dye and pour into molds.

Process Descriptions

Following is the manufacturing process of toilet soap based on the hot process.

1. Manufacturing Section

a. Saponification

Fats or oils the raw materials used for making soaps are heated, as they are agitated with the addition of caustic soda solution. The fats and oils are decomposed, there-by producing mixture of soap and glycerine.

b. Salting Out

When saponification is over a suitable amount of salt water is added. As soap does not dissolve in salt water, it floats in water in the form of a layer, while soap lye which contains glycerine, sinks in slat water, there by also forming a layer.

The lower layer, namely the soap spent lye solution, in drawn out from the lower part of the soap boiling tank to be passed into a soap spent lye tank. In order to insure further saponification, caustic soda solution is again added to soap for heating, after which it is left alone for 10-20 hours.

Through the above process, the content in the soap boiling pan is divided into three layers the upper layer which is soap, the middle layer which consists of metallic soap and protein, and the bottom layer which is soap spent lye. The soap layer is pulled out and stored in an intermediary tank equipped with a steam jacket.

c. Cooling

Soap is cooled by means of a cooling roller, and it is simultaneously turned into the form of a thin ribbons, which are out to suitable lengths.

Driving

Soaps chips available to the above manner are placed in a dryer. There is a wire not like conveyor installed in the dryer. Soap chips are dried by hot air, while it is being carried on the conveyor. Having lost moisture to the extent of 12-16 percent, the chips leave the dryer for storage.

2. Finishing Section

a. Mixing

After having been weighed, dry soap chips are mixed in a mixing machine with suitable amounts of colouring material and perfume. They are fully kneaded on a three roll soap will for transfer to a plodding.

b. Plodding

Soap is extruded out of a plodding machine in the form of soap bar.

c. Stamping

As they come out of the plodding machine, soap base are cut and, at the same time shaped in a stamping machine. Soap which may be produced on the above occasion are sent back into the plodding machine.

Process of Herbal Soap Making

Due to the complexity of the full boiling process, it is generally not used in small and village scale soapmaking. However, the semi-boiling and the cold process normally used by the small-scale soapmakers are not suitable for use with non-edible oils due to fact that majority of these oils have deep colour and bad odour. Instead, a combination of the full-boiling and semi-boiling process is used.

In the combined process, the deep coloured and bad smelling non-edible oils to be purified are first saponified, and then grained to remove the colour and odour. The grained soap obtained is used in soapmaking together with other pale coloured oils, using the semi-boiled process.

A typical formulation and process involving the use of neem, castor and physic nut oils is described as follows:

Raw Materials

Neem Oil	60 Kg.
Physic nut oil	35 Kg.
Castor Oil	5 Kg.
Caustic Soda	14 Kg.
Sodium Carbonate	25 Kg.
Common Salt	8 Kg.

PLANT ECONOMICS

Rated Plant capacity = 500.00 Kgs./Day

Land & Building = Rs. 42,50,000.00

(Land 1000 sq.mt.)

Plant & Machinery

1. Boiling Kettle
2. Mixing & Kneading Machine
3. Chilling rolls
4. Dryer
5. Plodder Machine
6. Cutting machine
7. Semi-auomatic stamping press
8. Miscellaneous like pipe fitting, conveying system etc.
9. Complete Plant for Manufacturing of Herbal Toilet Soap with Cosmetics Products

FIXED CAPITAL

1. Land & Building	Rs.	42,50,000.00
2. Plant & Machinery	Rs.	7,52,500.00
3. Other Fixed Assets	Rs.	27,500.00
Total	Rs.	50,30,000.00

Raw Materials

1. Neem Oil Castor Oil, Soap Noodles, Common Salt etc. for Herbal Soap
2. Coconut oil
3. Castor oil,
4. Caustic Soda lye
5. Carbolic acid (Phenot)
6. Color,
7. Palm Rosa oil and other perfume

TOTAL WORKING CAPITAL/MONTH

1. Raw Material	Rs.	5,71,225.00
2. Salary & Wages	Rs.	51,750.00
3. Utilities & Overheads	Rs.	73,850.00
Total	Rs.	6,96,825.00

TOTAL CAPITAL INVESTMENT

Total Fixed Capital	Rs.	50,30,000.00
Total Working Capital for 1 Months	Rs.	6,96,825.00
Total	Rs.	57,26,825.00

TURN OVER/ANNUM

By sale of 1,50,000 Kg. of Toilet Soap and Herbal Soap	Rs.	1,09,50,000.00

PROFIT SALES RATIO = 14.86 %

RATE OF RETURN = 28.42 %

BREAK EVEN POINT (B.E.P) = 49.00 %

14

Laundry Soap

Laundry soaps are among household soaps which comprise various types of soaps available in difficult forms. Household chipped or flaked soaps used for laundry purpose are generally a little lower in moisture content than the corresponding bar soaps. a representative composition is moisture 10-20%; soap 50-60; tetrasodium pyropheesphate-15%; sodium metasilicate -7%; and soda ash 8 per cent.

Formulation		*(In Kgs.)*
1.	Mahua Oil	4
2.	Rice Bran Oil	4
3.	Water	7.5
4.	Starch	4
5.	Common Salt	1
6.	Soda Ash	0.5
7.	Caustic Soda lye 35°Be	5

		(In Kgs.)
1.	Coconut Oil	25
2.	Mahua Oil	20
3.	Rosin	10
4.	Soap Stone (Talc)	27
5.	Water	50
6.	Silica of Soda	10
7.	Soda Ash	5
8.	Caustic Soda lye 25°Be	57

MANUFACTURING PROCESS OF LAUNDRY SOAP FROM SOAP FLAKES

The process employed for this purpose is called full boiled process. The various charges involved in this process are :

1. The first brine charge
2. The second brine charge
3. The finish
4. Crutching and filling
5. Cooling frame
6. Slabbing & cutting
7. Drying and packing

PLANT ECONOMICS

Rated Plant Capacity = 1.00 M.T/Day

Land & Building = Rs. 7,30,000.00

(Land 500 Sq.mts.)

Plant & Machinery

1. Reaction Vessels (S.S.Vessels)
2. Moulds.
3. Oil Fired open hearths or gas
4. Automatic Soap Cake Cutting Machine
5. Soap Stamping Machine.
6. Miscellaneous viz. Weighing Scale, Testing Equipment, Fire Fighting Equipment etc.

FIXED CAPITAL

1. Land & Building	Rs.	7,30,000.00
2. Plant & Machinery	Rs.	3,79,000.00
3. Other Fixed Assets	Rs.	4,95,000.0
Total	Rs.	16,04,000.00

Raw Materials

1. Soap flakes
2. Caustic Soda solution for making 20 degree Be' lye
5. Salt,
6. Packaging Material.
7. Miscellaneous, Additives, Chemicals.

TOTAL WORKING CAPITAL/MONTH

1. Raw Material		Rs.	2,37,500.00
2. Salary & Wages		Rs.	1,06,400.00
3. Utilities & Overheads		Rs.	1,78,700.00
	Total	Rs.	5,22,600.00

TOTAL CAPITAL INVESTMENT

Total Fixed Capital		Rs.	16,04,000.00
Total Working Capital for 3 Months		Rs.	5,67,800.00
	Total	Rs.	31,71,800.00

TURN OVER/ANNUM

By Sale of Laundry Soap, 300 M.T.	Rs.	75,00,000.00

PROFIT SALES RATIO = 9.13 %

RATE OF RETURN = 21.58 %

BREAK EVEN POINT (B.E.P) = 73.65 %

15

Liquid Soap

Liquid Hand Soap Formulation			%
1.	Distilled Palm Kernel Fatty Acids	-	15.00
2.	Tallow Fatty Acids	-	5.00
3.	Crodolene LA 1010	-	2.50
4.	Potassium Hydroxide	-	5.60
5.	Empicol LQ27	-	10.00
6.	Formalin	-	0.20
7.	Water (Deionized)	-	61.70
8.	Perfume	-	9.5

Blend all components except water, formaline and KOH by heating to 80°C heat water and KOH to similar temperature, then add to the molten oil phase. Stir until clear solution forms, then add formalin.

PLANT ECONOMICS

Rated Plant Capacity = 200.00 Kgs/Day

Land & Building = Rs. 5,27,500.00
(Land 350 Sq.mts.)

Plant & Machinery

1. Reaction Kettle
2. Storage Tank
3. Filter Press with Accessories
4. Baby Boiler
5. Pump set
6. Automatic weighing filling and sealing machine

FIXED CAPITAL

1.	Land & Building	Rs.	5,27,500.00
2.	Plant & Machinery	Rs.	2,95,000.00
3.	Other Fixed Assets	Rs.	75,000.00
	Total	Rs.	8,97,500.00

Raw Materials

1. Coconut oil
2. Caustic Potash
3. Sequestering Agent, perfume colour
4. Packaging material

TOTAL WORKING CAPITAL/MONTH

1.	Raw Material	Rs.	1,30,395.00
2.	Salary & Wages	Rs.	36,360.00
3.	Utilities & Overheads	Rs.	20,800.00
	Total	Rs.	1,87,555.00

TOTAL CAPITAL INVESTMENT

Total Fixed Capital	Rs.	8,97,500.00
Total Working Capital for 2 Months	Rs.	3,75,110.00
Total	Rs.	12,72,610.00

TURN OVER/ANNUM

By sale of 60000 kgs of liquid soap Rs. 33,00,000.00

PROFIT SALES RATIO = 23.88 %

RATE OF RETURN = 61.91 %

BREAK EVEN POINT (B.E.P) = 40.48 %

16

Nerol Laundry Soap

Manufacturing Process of Best Quality Nerol Soap

Formula No. 1

(For Best Nerol Soap of Neem oil)

(i)	Sediments of groundnut	:	40 kg.
(ii)	Caustic Soda Lye 36^{0}Be	:	160 kg
(iii)	Rice Oil	:	60 kg
(iv)	Neem Oil	:	2 Quintals
(v)	Salt	:	50 kg
(vi)	Water	:	8 Cansster**s**

The procedure for the manufacture is very clear in the flow sheet . It is described as below:-

It is manufactured by undergoing followed steps of operations in sequence order:-

1. Mixing of Sediments of Groundnut with the Rice Oil & Neem Oil.
2. Addition of Water.

3 A. Preparation of Caustic Soda lye

3. Addition of Caustic Soda lye
4. Addition of Salt
5. Cooking of Soap Compound
6. Test for Proper Cooking
7. Settling and Moulding
8. Cake Cutting & Stamping
9. Packing, Casing, Marketing & Stamped

PLANT ECONOMICS

Rated Plant Capacity	=	1.00 M.T/Day
Land & Building (Land 500 Sq.mts.)	=	Rs. 13,30,000.00

Plant & Machinery

1. Cauldron for Mixing, Cooking at various stages.
2. Moulds.
3. Coal Fired open hearths.
4. Automatic Soap Cake Cutting Machine
5. Soap Stamping Machine.
6. Miscellaneous viz. Weighing Scale, Testing Equipment, Fire Fighting Equipment etc.

FIXED CAPITAL

1. Land & Building	Rs.	13,30,000.00
2. Plant & Machinery	Rs.	2,41,000.00
3. Other Fixed Assets	Rs.	82,000.00
Total	Rs.	16,53,000.00

Raw Materials

1. Sedimeats of Ground nut (or Ground Nut cake),
2. Caustic Soda Flakes (for making 36 degree Be lye or 45 % Solution),
3. Rice Bran,
4. Neem Oil,
5. Salt,
6. Packaging Material.
7. Miscellaneous.

TOTAL WORKING CAPITAL/MONTH

1. Raw Material	Rs.	2,85,665.00
2. Salary & Wages	Rs.	1,56,000.00
3. Utilities & Overheads	Rs.	1,65,300.00
Total	Rs.	6,06,965.00

TOTAL CAPITAL INVESTMENT

Total Fixed Capital	Rs.	16,53,000.00
Total Working Capital for 3 Months	Rs.	18,20,895.00
Total	Rs.	34,73,895.00

TURN OVER/ANNUM

By Sale of Nerol Laundry Soap,

300 M.T. Rs. 90,00,000.00

PROFIT SALES RATIO = 12.53 %

RATE OF RETURN = 34.25 %

BREAK EVEN POINT (B.E.P) = 65.41 %

17

Liquid Shoe Polish Puff

The puff and support used in puffed liquid shoe polish, are made of expanded plastic more of flexible and less flexible respectively. The puff, made of flexible expanded plastic, are made of flexible polyurathane foams. This foams are produced by the exothermic reaction of polyisocyante and a polyol in the prescene of a catalyst, to control the speed of reaction plus a surfactant to stabilize the rising foam and provide uniform cell size, and a foaming or blowing agent-either carbondioxide or an inert blowing agent such as fluorocarbon. In some flexible foam formulation based on the use of Co_2 the action can be boosted with another gas such as methylene chloride, to provide added softners. The density can also be veried from less than 1 to 41b/cuft. It is produced in the form of 1" thick sheets.

The support is also expanded plastic but it is less flexible and differ in formulation with the puff. The support is made of expanded polyethylene of density around 2 lb/ft^3. This expanded polyethylene is made by mixing a foaming agent with hot, molten polymer under pressure, then releasing the pressure and cooling. Control of cooling time and, in certain cases, application of ionizing radiation, permit the monituring the cell structure of the foam. It is used mostly as a padding material.

PROCESS OF MANUFACTURE

The process involved in the production of puff liquid shoe polishes has the following steps.

1. Setting the support sheet from and puff sheet with adhesive.
2. Cutting the set support and puff in required dimension.
3. Formulating the liquid shoe polished to be absorbed.

The equal dimension in length and breath of expanded polyethylene and polyurathane foam are pasted each other by rubber based adhesive.

After pasting the support sheet and puff sheet, these are cut according to the specified dimension by hydratilic double action press. In this way all the puff with support are cut into sizes.

Now, the polished to be filled in the poses of puff is prepared.

PLANT ECONOMICS

Rated Plant Capacity	=	500.00 Nos./Day	
Land & Building (Land 100 sq. mt.)	=	Rs.	2,00,000.00

Plant & Machinery

1. Melting tank,
2. Mixing tank, complete with all accessories
3. Weighing scale
4. Perforated tray
5. Hand operated, hydraulic press
6. Thermoforming press (hand operated)
7. Misc.

FIXED CAPITAL

1. Land & Building	Rs.	2,00,000.00
2. Plant & Machinery	Rs.	66,000.00
3. Other Fixed Assets	Rs.	8,500.00
Total	Rs.	2,74,500.00

Raw Materials

1. Expanded polyethene sheet
2. Polyurethane foam sheet
3. P.V.C. Sheet
4. Beeswax
5. Montan (Refined) Wax
6. Carnauba Wax
7. Turpentine oil
8. White spirit
9. Adhesive

TOTAL WORKING CAPITAL/MONTH

1.	Raw Materials	Rs.	37,688.00
2.	Salary & Wages	Rs.	32,625.00
3.	Utilities & Overheads	Rs.	16,800.00
	Total	Rs.	87,113.00

TOTAL CAPITAL INVESTMENT

Total Fixed Capital	Rs.	2,74,500.00
Total Working Capital for 3 Months	Rs.	2,61,339.00
Total	Rs.	5,35,839.00

TURN OVER/ANNUM

By Sale of 1,50,000 Nos. of Puffed Liquid Shoe Polish	Rs.	22,50,000.00

PROFIT SALES RATIO = 47.19 %

RATE OF RETURN = 198.1

BREAK EVEN POINT (B.E.P) = 26.36 %

18

Soap Stone Powder from Raw Soap Stone

PROCESS OF MANUFACTURE

Purification of Talc

It is seldom that soap stone can be used without some kind of treatment which shall enable it to mix easily with water and to be easily worked process of purification generally followed is as follows:-

(i) Weathering

The Natural agencies of wind, rain & frost may well be made use of in this connection supplemented if necessary by washing grinding & pugging. The object of exposing the soap stone to the action of the weather especially in the winter month is to bring about its disintegration. The chief agents concerned with the weathering of soap stone are water & frost. The water get absorbed into the porous of the soap stone and the expansion of water on cooling in some cases of low temp. even freezing leads to the formation of fine soap stone.

Hence the soap stone should therefore be kept sufficiently moist by watering and should be spread out in such a way that has large surface as posssible should be readily and completely exposed to frost. In the absence of water supply under sufficient pressure hose pipe is used for watering the soap stone. Many soap stones disintegrate easily but some besides the physical action of water requires the chemical action of air mover may require even more time (usually 8 hours).

The water can be made to ester the soap stone by means of external pressure applied by machinery but still the soap stone acted upon by weather is easily worked upon. Pressurised water can be supplied with the help of nozzle.

Weather of soap stone is an important step inorder to have high quality end product especially in case of non-uniformed soap stone, which may arise even due to the additives in order to improve the qualities and in that case if milled immediately without weathering will not get ground uniting ultimately to obtain good quality will prove to be difficult.

Excessive weathering should be avoided or the soap stone particles may get washed of in rain or by wind leaving a non-plastic residue behind.

It is therefore important if the soap stone worker requires his material to be acted on by frost he should estimate in the early autumn what will be his daily requirement of soap stone during the entire year and to arrange for spreading it out to weather.

Care must be taken to avoid the formation of crust of dry soap stone on the surface of the material and in case it appears it, should be removed and should be sent to recrushing consequently converting it into paste.

In addition its physical disintegeration action on soap stone, the weather oxidises some of the impurities in the soap stone and if oxidised products are soluble then may be washed away in the drainage water and some of the insoluble impurities are rendered more conspicuous and very easily picked out. Some organic compounds present in soap stone are decompose which helps in increasing the plasticity of the soap stone of raw soap stone. It is a valuable means of breaking down some hand materials which are not appreciably effected by ordinary weathering.

(ii) Removal of Foreign Materials

The foreign materials which cannot be handpicked are screened according to presence of impurities.

(iii) Cleaning

For the purpose of cleaning the soap stone cleaner is used. The material in the cleaner is fine.

The soap stone and the acceptable fine particles pass through but the unacceptable particles viz. fine stones and other fibrous materials are rejected. In case of selection of cleaner proper consideration should be given to the power consumption as it plays important role in its economy.

(iv) Crushing

Talc when mixed is available in form of big lumps. These lumps are crushed in a Jaw crusher and are reduced to the smaller sizes as desired.

(v) Crushing and Grinding

The Talc once passed through the hammer mill is again put into the hopper and the hammer mill started. Material is finely ground. It is passed through coarse screens once again. Then finally the material is passed through a micropulveriser and then again screened through B.S. standard 200 mesh screen. This set sieve designation pertains to an equivalent through and is comparable to seive designation of which pertains to an aperture of 15 microns.

Packaging

After pulverising and sieving through fine sieves the Talc which is now ready for use in different products is packed in jute bags.

PLANT ECONOMICS

Rated Plant Capacity	=	50.00 Ton/Day
Land & Building	=	Rs. 1,35,95,000.00
(Land 14000 sq.mts.)		

Plant & Machinery

1. Jaw Crusher
2. Rotary Dryer
3. Roller Mill (fine Roller)
4. Micro Pulveriser
5. Coarse screening set
6. Fine screens complete with screening machine
7. Electrical hoist for lifting drums etc.
8. Other accessories
9. Soap stone cleaner
10. Starter
11. Weighing Bridge
12. Electric Motor for Roller Mill
13. Magnetic separator
14. Electric Motor for Pulverizer
15. DG set
16. Electric Motor for Whizzer
17. System Fan
18. Electric Motor for Jaw Crusher

19. Laboratory Equipments
20. Plant Equipment accessories
21. Other miscellaneous equipment

FIXED CAPITAL

1. Land & Building	Rs.	1,35,95,000.00
2. Plant & Machinery	Rs.	1,28,90,000.00
3. Other Fixed Assets	Rs.	2,86,500.00
Total	Rs.	2,67,71,500.00

Raw Materials

1. Soap stone (mineral ore)
2. Misc. chemicals

TOTAL WORKING CAPITAL/MONTH

1. Raw Materials	Rs.	31,00,000.00
2. Salary & Wages	Rs.	1,19,500.00
3. Utilities & Overheads	Rs.	6,20,000.00
Total	Rs.	38,39,500.00

TOTAL CAPITAL INVESTMENT

Total Fixed Capital	Rs.	2,67,71,500.00
Total Working Capital for 3 Months	Rs.	1,15,18,500.00
Total	Rs.	3,82,90,000.00

TURN OVER/ANNUM

By sale of 15000 tonnes of Talc powdered for various purpose. Rs. 6,00,00,000.00

PROFIT SALES RATIO = 16.25 %

RATE OF RETURN = 17.94 %

BREAK EVEN POINT (B.E.P) = 60.70 %

19

Complete Plant Suppliers

Eurrestra Industries Ltd.
Plot No. 56,
Thane - Belapur Road,
Thane - 400605
Tel : 7602712/13, 7601124, 7690065
Fax : 7691177, 7602709
E-Mail : eurestra@bom3.vsnl.net.in

Ballestra S.P.A
Via P. Portaluppi,
17-20138 Milano
Italy
Tel : + 39 02 50831
Fax : + 39 02 5801 8449
E-Mail : mail@ballestra.com
www.ballestra.com

Japro Group of Co.
206, Neelam, Seaface Road,
Worli, Mumbai - 400 018
Tel : 91-22-4932114/8202/9434
Fax : 91-22-4950440
E-Mail : jan@japrogroup.com

Patil Machines Pvt. Ltd.
36D, kandivali Ind. Estate,
Kandivali (West),
Mumbai - 400 067
Tel : 8683501/8683991
Fax : 91-22-8686175
E-Mail : pmplbom@vsnl.com

Munshi and Co. Pvt. Ltd.
Dargah Road,
Bhandup Sonapur, Bhandup (W), Mumbai - 78
Ph : 5614700/5621808/5643196/5692682
Fax : 5612240
E-Mail : munshico@bom8.vsnl.net.in
Website:www.munshico.com

Milindia Ltd.
W-31, Sector - XI,
Noida - 201 301 (U.P)
Tel : 91-95120-4536772/4536773
Fax : 91-95120-4553342
E-Mail : milmàzz@vsnl.com
Website : milindia.com

Hi-Tech Engineers
4507, Phase-4,
GIDC, Vatva,
Ahmedabad - 382445
Tel : 079-5840350
Telefax : 91-79-5840350, 5840897

Micro Machines
Plot No. 2, Dharmajivan Ind. Estate,
Gokuldham Main Road,
Rajkot - 360004
Ph : 91-281-368564
Fax : 91-281-366010
E-Mail : micro_machines@yahoo.com

Zanjrukiya Engg. Cons.
C-1/37, Aji Ind. Estate,
Rajkot - 360 003 (India)
Ph : 387758, 362768, 388181
Fax : 0281-387758
www.zanjrukiya.com
E-mail : zanjrukiya@yahoo.com

SUPPLIERS OF SOAP WRAPPING MACHINES/PACKING MACHINES

Orum Engg. Pvt. Ltd.
42/43, Kiran Ind. Estate,
M.G. Road,
Goregaon (W)
Mumbai - 400 062
Tel : 8774573
E-Mail : orum@vsnl.net

Precise Packing Machines
Ashirwad Ind. Estate,
Building No. 4,
Gala No. 5, Ram Mandir Road, Goregaon (W),
Mumbai - 400 104
Telefax : 022-8687919

20

Suppliers of Fragrances, Flavours, Perfumes for Soaps

FFC Aromas Pvt. Ltd.
Plot No. A-42, St. 2,
MIDC, Andheri (E)
Mumbai - 400093
Tel : 022-8385996, 8213481
Fax : 91-22-8364491
E-Mail :
sales@ffcaromas.com
www.ffcaromas.com

Khattri Fragrances and Flavours Ltd.
Lucknow -Kanpur Road,
P.O. Sohramau,
Unnao - 209 859 (U.P)
Ph : 05143-45271, 45272
Fax : 05143-45276

Lalji Aromatics Pvt. Ltd.
253/44, Nadan Mahal Road,
Lucknow - 226004
Ph : 266650/265165/265171
Fax : 91-522-265165

Sachee Aromatics Ltd.
Y-4, Okhla Ind. Area,
Phase - 2
New Delhi - 110 020
Tel : 26310404, 26310405
Fax : 91-11-26310304
E-mail :
manojaro@del3.vsnl.net.in
www.sachee.com

Sonarome Chemicals Pvt. Ltd.
Peenya Ind. Area, II Stage,
Bangalore - 560 058
Tel : 080-8360595/8360804
Fax : 080-8363791
E-Mail :
sonarome@sonarome.com
www.sonarome.com

Maschmeijer Aromatics (India) Ltd.
P.B. No. 3, G.S.T. Road,
Chromepet
Chennai - 600 044 (T.N)
Ph : 2368788, 2368789
Fax : 044-2366828, 4981188
E-Mail :
maschmeijer@pobox.com

SUPPLIERS OF COLOURS FOR SOAPS

Neelikon Food Dyes and Chemicals Ltd.
D-8, D-17, Everest,
Pandit M.M. Malavia Marg,
Tardeo Circle
Mumbai - 400 034
Tel : 91-22-4980572, 4986159
Fax : 91-22-4964945
E-Mail :
neelikon@bom3.vsnl.net.in

21

Suppliers of Soaps Manufacturing Chemicals

New India Detergents Ltd.
Detergent Intermediates Divn.
Flat No. 205, 206, 4855-56/ 24, Ansari Rd.
New Delhi -110002
Tel : + 91 (0) 11 3251694
Fax : + 91 (0) 11 3256694
E-mail: newindia@nde.vsnl.net.in

Sarachem Surfactants Pvt. Ltd.
DSIDC Shed, Phase-I,61
New Okhla Indl. Cmplx.
New Delhi -110020
Tel : + 91 (0) 11 6810171

Apar Chem Products
203, "Kailash" I, 2nd Flr.
Nr. Jain Temple
B/h Navrangpura Post
Ahmedabad,
Gujarat - 380009
Tel : + 91 (0) 79 6560448
Fax : + 91 (0) 79 6561094
E-mail : vishal707@hotmail.com

Gujarat Alkalies & Chemicals Ltd.
P.O. Petrochemicals
Vadodara, Gujarat-391346
Tel : + 91 (0) 265 372681
Fax : + 91 (0) 265 372130
E-mail: nksachar@gujaratalkalies.com

Saurabh Products Pvt. Ltd.
46, Mithila Soc.
Nr. Shreyas Crossing
Ambawadi
Ahmedabad,
Gujarat - 380015
Tel : + 91 (0) 79 6604116

Shreeji Chem
Plot No. 2210, Nr. Post Office
GIDC Est. Ankleshwar,
Gujarat-393002
Tel : + 91 (0) 2646 52476

Siddharth Chlorochem Pvt. Ltd.
L-5, 3/82 , Shastri Ngr.
Ankur Rd., Naranpura
Ahmedabad
Gujarat - 380013
Tel : + 91 (0) 79 7435874
Fax : + 91 (0) 79 7433702
E-mail: scpladz@sanchar net.in

Starco Arochem Pvt. Ltd.
708, Parekh Tower
Nr. Diwan Ballubhai School
Kankaria
Ahmedabad
Gujarat - 380022
Tel : + 91 (0) 79 5463458
Fax : + 91 (0) 79 5469119
E-mail : rpg@starcoindia.com

Whitex Chemicals
104, Yogi Smruti, 2
Nutan Bharat Soc., Alkapuri
Vadodara, Gujarat-390007
Tel : + 91 (0) 265 340314
Fax : + 91 (0) 265 354047
E-mail: sdci@satyam.net.in

National Industries Co.
P.O. Box 2302
74, Magadi Rd.
Bangalore
Karnataka-560023
Tel : + 91 (0) 80 3351183

Shanti Chemical Works
709/2, Indl. Area
P.O. Udyambag
Belgaum
Karnataka - 590008
Tel : + 91 (0) 831 440416
Fax : + 91 (0) 831 441390
E-mail: dhananjaypatel@indiatimes.com

The Travancore-Cochin Chemicals Ltd.
P.O. Box 4004
Udyogamandal P.O.
Ernakulam
Kerala - 683501
Tel : + 91 (0) 484 551011
Fax : + 91 (0) 484 532420
E-mail: tccudl@kelnet07.xlweb.com

TMV Aromatics
No. 66-C, Major Indl. Est.
Kalamassery Devp. Plot P.O.
Kalamassery
Kerala-683109
Tel : + 91 (0) 48455 361330

Fairdeal Chemicals Ltd.
1/2, Murai Mohalla
Indore
Madhya Pradesh-452001
Tel : + 91 (0) 731 463122

Ava Chemicals Pvt. Ltd.
1/20 B, Narayan Plaza
26-A, Chandivli Rd.
Mumbai
Maharashtra-400072
Tel : + 91 (0) 22 8523955
Fax : + 91 (0) 22 8525790
E-mail: ava@bom2.vsnl.net.in

Lalit Nitro-Chem Pvt. Ltd.
Plot No.14, F-II Block,
MIDC, Pimpri Area
Pune, Maharashtra-411018
Tel : + 91 (0) 20 7485272
Fax : + 91 (0) 20 7477693
E-mail: shubham@pn2.vsnl.net.in

A&M Group
P.O. Box 5653, Dadar
Mumbai
Maharashtra-400014
Tel : + 91 (0) 22 4142634
Fax : + 91 (0) 22 4144260

Fancy Industrial Corp.
405, Veena Chmbrs.
Clive Rd., Dana Bunder
Mumbai
Maharashtra-400009
Tel : + 91 (0) 22 3738244
Fax : + 91 (0) 22 3738304
E-mail: fancy@vsnl.com

Galaxy Surfactants Ltd.
C-49/2, TTC Indl. Area
Pawne, Navi Mumbai,
Maharashtra - 400701
Tel : + 91 (0) 22 7616666
Fax : + 91 (0) 22 7615883
E-mail: galaxy@giasbm01.vsnl.net.in

Hindustan Lever Ltd.
Chemicals Divn.
ICT Link Rd., Chakala
Andheri (E), Mumbai,
Maharashtra - 400099
Tel : + 91 (0) 22 8329471
Fax : + 91 (0) 22 8225708

Kripa Chemicals Ltd.
'Kripa House', 6
Bhusari Cly, Paud Rd.
Pune, Maharashtra-411038
Tel : + 91 (0) 20 5283245
Fax : + 91 (0) 20 5280290

LN Chemical Industries
150, Adarsh Indl. Est.
Sahar Rd., Chakala
Andheri (E), Mumbai,
Maharashtra - 400099
Tel : + 91 (0) 22 8225719
Fax : + 91 (0) 22 8366434
E-mail : inchem@vsnl.com

Modhera Chemicals Pvt. Ltd.
101-A, Sanjay Bldg. No. 2
Mittal Indl. Est.
Andheri Kurla Rd.
Andheri (E), Mumbai,
Maharashtra - 400059
Tel : + 91 (0) 22 8500179
Fax : + 91 (0) 22 8503534
E-mail: modhera@vsnl.com

Subhash Chemical Industries
Shed W-2, S-Block
MIDC, Bhosari
Pune, Maharashtra-411026
Tel : + 91 (0) 20 7120632
Fax : + 91 (0) 20 7122554
E-mail: subhaschem@vsnl.com

Devarsons Industries Ltd.
443, GIDC Indl. Est.
Nr. Water Tank, Odhav
Ahmedabad
Gujarat - 382415
Tel : + 91 (0) 79 2871092
E-mail: devarson.coldyes@gnahd.global.net.in

Dinesh Chemicals
Nr. CMC India
Associated Indl. Est.
Odhav Rd.
Ahmedabad
Gujarat - 382415
Tel : + 91 (0) 79 2872324
Fax : + 91 (0) 79 2872325
E-mail: associat@wilnetonline.net

Paramount Minerals & Chemicals Ltd.
33, Old Hanuman Lane
1st Cross Lane, 2nd Flr.
Kalbadevi Rd.
Mumbai
Maharashtra-400013
Tel : + 91 (0) 22 2039301
Fax : + 91 (0) 22 2054108
E-mail: info@pmclindia.com

Privi Organics Pvt. Ltd.
205, Princess St.
Mumbai
Maharashtra - 400002
Tel : + 91 (0) 22 2062626
Fax : + 91 (0) 22 2080282
E-mail: privi@bom3.vsnl.net.in

Shree Diamond Silicate Company Pvt. Ltd.
D-29/16, MIDC
TTC Indl. Area
Navi Mumbai
Maharashtra - 400705
Tel : + 91 (0) 22 7632688
Fax : + 91 (0) 22 7632688
E-mail: diamondsilicate@rediffmail.com

Vinamax Organics Pvt. Ltd.
205, Vyapar Bhawan, 49
P D'Mello Rd.,
Carnac Bunder
Mumbai
Maharashtra - 400009
Tel : + 91 (0) 22 3758568
Fax : + 91 (0) 22 3782306
E-mail: sainathpower@xescts.net.in

Caliron Chemicals Pvt. Ltd.
5, Nirankari St., Miller Ganj
Ludhiana, Punjab -141003
Tel : + 91 (0) 161 534753
Fax : + 91 (0) 161 533203

Astha Technocrats
F-36, Chambal Indl. Area
Kota, Rajasthan-324003
Tel : + 91 (0) 744 420274
Fax : + 91 (0) 744 450276

Guljag Industries Ltd.
Nahata Bhawan
Chopasni Rd.
Jodhpur, Rajasthan-342003
Tel : + 91 (0) 291 435581
Fax : + 91 (0) 291 435670
E-mail: guljag@jp1.dot.net.in

Apex Polymers
159,
Govindappa Naicken St.
Chennai
Tamil Nadu-600001
Tel : + 91 (0) 44 569841
Fax : + 91 (0) 44 659841
E-mail: labdhi@md3.vsnl.net.in

Asian Peroxides Ltd.
69, Leelavathi Bldg.
Armenian St.
Chennai
Tamil Nadu - 600001
Tel : + 91 (0) 44 5226559
Fax : + 91 (0) 44 5229600
E-mail: cps@giasmd01.vsnl.net.in

Gee Gee Khay Chemical Industry
A-16, PIPDIC Indl. Est.
Mettupalayam
Tamil Nadu - 641309
Tel : + 91 (0) 4254 275397
Fax : + 91(0) 4254 371650

Kiran Pondy Chems Ltd.
81, New Avadi Rd., Kilpauk
Chennai
Tamil Nadu-600010
Tel : + 91 (0) 44 6441232
Fax : + 91 (0) 44 6446303
E-mail: kiranindia@kiranindia.com

Kiran Silicates Pvt. Ltd.
81, New Avadi Rd., Kilpauk
Chennai
Tamil Nadu-600010
Tel : + 91 (0) 44 6441232
Fax : + 91 (0) 44 6446303

Malpro Silica Pvt. Ltd.
400, Bhavani Main Rd.
Ashokapuram
Erode, Tamil Nadu -638004
Tel : + 91 (0) 424 293474
Fax : + 91 (0) 424 293894
E-mail: malpro@vsnl.com

Sri Kiran Chemicals
81, New Avadi Rd.
Kilpauk, Chennai
Tamil Nadu-600010
Tel : + 91 (0) 44 6445848
Fax : + 91 (0) 44 6446303
E-mail: raahull@md2.vsnl.net.in

Varuni Chemicals Pvt. Ltd.
72, Medavakkam Tank Rd.
Kellys, Chennai
Tamil Nadu - 600010
Tel : + 91 (0) 44 6417096
Fax : + 91 (0) 44 6426202

Gujarat Heavy Chemicals Ltd.
B-38, Institutional Area
Sect. 1
Noida
Uttar Pradesh - 201301
Tel : + 91 (0) 120 4536572
Fax : + 91 (0) 120 4535209
E-mail : nsr@ghclindia.com

Shabroc India
15/72-D, Civil Lines
Kanpur
Uttar Pradesh - 208001
Tel : + 91 (0) 512 311765
Fax : + 91 (0) 512 311765
E-mail: sunil16july@rediffmail.com

Vidisha Chemicals Pvt. Ltd.
3/12, Vishnupuri
Kanpur
Uttar Pradesh-208002
Tel : + 91 (0) 512 553431
Fax : + 91 (0) 512 553431
E-mail: vidishatraders@rediffmail.com

Durgapur Chemicals Ltd.
6, Little Russel St.
Kolkata
West Bengal - 700001
Tel : + 91 (0) 33 2471556
Fax : + 91 (0) 33 2400340

Gem Chemicals Industries
Suite F, 4th Flr., 25
R N Mukherjee Rd.
Kolkata
West Bengal - 700001
Tel : + 91 (0) 33 2483650

Kolmak Chemicals Ltd.
21-A
Shakespeare Sarani
Kolkata
West Bengal - 700017
Tel : + 91 (0) 33 2477512
Fax : + 91 (0) 33 2406476
E-mail: tioxide@cal2.vsnl.net.in

Kumar Chemical Industries
78, Bentinck St.
Kolkata
West Bengal - 700001
Tel : + 91 (0) 33 2362368
Fax : + 91 (0) 33 2363278
E-mail: kci@cal3.vsnl.net.in

Precision Balance (I)
6, Wood St.
Kolkata
West Bengal - 700016
Tel : + 91 (0) 33 2403476
Fax : + 91 (0) 33 2402427

Process Chemicals Co.
Powertool Bhavan, 3rd Flr.,
2, BBD Bag (E)
Kolkata
West Bengal - 700001
Tel : + 91 (0) 33 2481340
Fax : + 91 (0) 33 2430571
E-mail: pcccal@cal2.vsnl.net.in

Sai Sulphonates Pvt. Ltd.
2nd Flr., 21, Princep St.
Kolkata
West Bengal - 700072
Tel : + 91 (0) 33 2363055
Fax : + 91 (0) 33 2219145
E-mail : sai@cal.vsnl.net.in

Bihar Caustic & Chemicals Ltd.
A J.V. Of Aditya Birla Group & Bihar SIDC
Ghanshyamkunj
Garhwa Rd., P.O. Rehla
Palamau
Jharkhand - 822124
Tel : + 91 (0) 6584 87221
Fax : + 91 (0) 6584 87205

Chemtech Acids & Chemicals Pvt. Ltd.
Flat No. 119
Sanali Heavens Apts.
Nagarjuna Ngr.
Hyderabad
Andhra Pradesh - 500073
Tel : + 91 (0) 40 3748372
Fax : + 91 (0) 40 3748374
E-mail: chemtechltd@yahoo.com

Kalpana Chemicals Ltd.
Indl. Developed Area
Rd. No. 5, Nacharam
Hyderabad
Andhra Pradesh - 500076
Tel : + 91 (0) 40 7175802
Fax : + 91 (0) 40 7171946
E-mail: kalpand@hd2.dot.net.in

Kurre Polymers Pvt. Ltd.
1-3-46, St. No. 5
Habsiguda
Hyderabad
Andhra Pradesh - 500007
Tel : + 91 (0) 40 7171166
Fax : + 91 (0) 40 7171166

TGV Group
6-2-1012, TGV Towers
Khairthabad
Hyderabad
Andhra Pradesh - 500004
Tel : + 91 (0) 40 3313841

22

Present Manufacturers

Shivalik Soap & Detergents Works Pvt. Ltd.
D-103, Indl. Area-VII
Chandigarh (UT) -160054
Tel : + 91 (0) 172 672079

Vindarvind Hygine Products Pvt. Ltd.
98, Indl. Area-II
Ramdarbar
Chandigarh (UT) -160002
Tel : + 91 (0) 172 548449
E-mail: varkemi@123india.com

Bakemans Industries Ltd.
A-4/B1
Mohan Co-Op. Indl. Est.
New Delhi - 110044
Tel : + 91 (0) 11 6943479
Fax : + 91 (0) 11 6941044

Biba Chem Pvt. Ltd.
138-A/2, Munirka
New Delhi - 110067
Tel : + 91 (0) 11 6168053

Charkha Detergents & Soap Enterprises Pvt. Ltd.
A-3, Wazirpur Indl. Area
Delhi -110052
Tel : + 91 (0) 11 7212043
Fax : + 91 (0) 11 7214976

Gora Mal Hari Ram Ltd.
Indl. Area, 39, Najafgarh Rd.
New Delhi -110015
Tel : + 91 (0) 11 5450555
Fax : + 91 (0) 11 5433555
E-mail: goramal@del2.vsnl.net.in

Metropol India Pvt. Ltd.
262, Phase-III
Okhla Indl. Est.
New Delhi - 110020
Tel : + 91 (0) 11 6911372
Fax : + 91 (0) 11 6842429

Nahar Industrial Enterprises Ltd.
1107, Ashok Est. Bldg.
24, Barakhamba Rd.
New Delhi - 110001
Tel : + 91 (0) 11 3311069
Fax : + 91 (0) 11 3311009

Quartz Home Care (I) Pvt. Ltd.
A-2, 1st Flr., Ring Rd.
Rajouri Garden
New Delhi - 110027
Tel : + 91 (0) 11 5109038
Fax : + 91 (0) 11 5416563
E-mail: qhcindia@ndb.vsnl.net.in

Siel Ltd.
15, Shivaji Marg
New Delhi - 110015
Tel : + 91 (0) 11 5100190
Fax : + 91 (0) 11 5432600

Mohanlal Vensiram
Plot No. C2/319
GIDC Est.
Jamnagar, Gujarat-361004
Tel : + 91 (0) 288 77954

Nirma Ltd.
Nirma House
Nr. Income Tax Circle
Ashram Rd.
Ahmedabad
Gujarat - 380009
Tel : + 91 (0) 79 7546565
Fax : + 91 (0) 79 7546601
E-mail: nirma_ho@sify.com

Vinay Solvent Extraction Industries Pvt. Ltd.
C/O. Vijay Proteins Ltd.
Outside Majevadi Gate
Junagadh, Gujarat-362001
Tel : + 91 (0) 285 661797
Fax : + 91 (0) 285 660944
E-mail: piyush_domadia@hotmail.com

BNG Products
Chandigarh Rd.
Uklanamandi
Haryana-125113
Tel : + 91 (0) 1693 33184
Fax : + 91 (0) 1693 33439
E-mail: mumtajtea@yahoo.co.in

Jagdamba Soap Factory
Approach Rd.
Uklana Mandi
Hissar, Haryana - 125113
Tel : + 91 (0) 1693 34184
Fax : + 91 (0) 1693 33184
E-mail: alfasoapin@yahoo.co.in

Peshawar Soap & Chemicals Ltd.
Vill. & P.O. Khandsa
Gurgaon, Haryana-122001
Tel : + 91 (0) 124 6372866
Fax : + 91 (0) 124 6372963
E-mail: pesco@nda.vsnl.net.in

Annapoorna Chemical & Fertilisers Pvt. Ltd.
#43, Kengeri Town
Mysore Rd.
Bangalore
Karnataka - 560060
Tel : + 91 (0) 80 8483041

Binani Chemicals
D-18, Flat # 107BDA
MIG Flats, Domlur Stage
Bangalore
Karnataka-560071
Tel : + 91 (0) 80 5511457

Kamal Cottage Industries No. 9
3rd Cross
Nehru Rd., N G Halli
Mysore Rd.
Bangalore
Karnataka - 560026
Tel : + 91 (0) 80 6675787
E-mail: kamalcottagessoaps@usa.net

Srivatsa Industries
45/12
Gubbana Indl. Est., 6 Block
Raj Ngr.
Bangalore
Karnataka - 560010
Tel : + 91 (0) 80 3306023

Ashique Exports Pvt. Ltd.
1/432, Poothikkad
Poomala P.O.
Sulthan Bathery
Kerala - 673592
Tel : + 91 (0) 4968 621151
Fax : + 91 (0) 4968 621161
E-mail: global@thaigroupcos.com

Pankaj Chemicals
18/21, Palluruthy Rd.
Kochi, Kerala - 682005
Tel : + 91 (0) 484 232501
Fax : + 91 (0) 484 231239
E-mail: pankaj@md3.vsnl.net.in

Acme Soap Works
308, Veer Savarkar Marg
Dadar (W), Mumbai,
Maharashtra - 400028
Tel : + 91 (0) 22 4452706
Fax : + 91 (0) 22 4440282
E-mail : aacash@vsnl.com

Aero Pharma Ltd.
W-34 B, T T C Indl. Area
Rabale
Navi Mumbai
Maharashtra - 400701
Tel : + 91 (0) 22 7690020
Fax : + 91 (0) 22 7692637

Dyesfast
5/2, Sfurti Soc.
28, Mumbai-Pune Rd.
Wakdewadi
Pune, Maharashtra-411003
Tel : + 91 (0) 20 7120078
Fax : + 91 (0) 20 5816699
E-mail: naishadh@giaspn01.vsnl.net.in

Fem Care Pharma Ltd.
Plot No. 34, Fem House
Kherwadi
Ram Mandir Rd.
Bandra (E), Mumbai
Maharashtra - 400051
Tel : + 91 (0) 22 6437230
Fax : + 91 (0) 22 6402093
E-mail: femcare@com.5.vsnl.net

Godrej Soaps Ltd.
Pirojshahnagar
Eastern Express Highway
Vikhroli (E), Mumbai
Maharashtra - 400079
Tel : + 91 (0) 22 5188010
Fax : + 91 (0) 22 5188074

Harish International
318, C H St.
Marine Lines
Mumbai
Maharashtra - 400002
Tel : + 91 (0) 22 2011496
Fax : + 91 (0) 22 2054838
E-mail: harishintl@vsnl.com

Hindustan Lever Ltd.
HL House, 165/166
Backbay Reclm
Mumbai
Maharashtra - 400020
Tel : + 91 (0) 22 2827405
E-mail: moulindu.banerjee@unilever.com

Ivory Soap Works Pvt. Ltd.
H-44, MIDC, Ambad
Nasik, Maharashtra-422010
Tel : + 91 (0) 253 381654
Fax : + 91 (0) 253 803426
E-mail: ivory@bom6.vsnl.net.in

Jay Kay Dye Chemical Corp.
27/201, Motilal Ngr. No. 3
Goregaon (W), Mumbai
Maharashtra - 400090
Tel : + 91 (0) 22 8729509
Fax : + 91 (0) 22 8211749

Muller & Phipps (I) Ltd.
Queen's Mansion
A K Naik Marg, Fort
Mumbai
Maharashtra - 400001
Tel : + 91 (0) 22 2072544
Fax : + 91 (0) 22 2071097
E-mail: muller.phipps@gms.vsnl.net.in

Nand Kishore Khanna & Sons
102, Arun Chmbrs.
Tardeo Rd.
Mumbai
Maharashtra - 400034
Tel : + 91 (0) 22 4960818
Fax : + 91 (0) 22 8368916
E-mail: homacol@bom3.vsnl.net.in

Procter & Gamble India Ltd.
Tiecicon House
Dr E Moses Rd., Mahalaxmi
Mumbai
Maharashtra - 400011
Tel : + 91 (0) 22 4980679
Fax : + 91 (0) 22 4953399

Reeshab Teelak Chemicals Pvt. Ltd.
20/21, Amrit Niwas, 165
Lohar Chawl
Mumbai
Maharashtra - 400002
Tel : + 91 (0) 22 2013509
Fax : + 91 (0) 22 2085282
E-mail : reshab@vsnl.com

Swastik Surfactants Ltd.
Industry Manor, 442
Marathe Marg, Prabhadevi
Mumbai
Maharashtra - 400025
Tel : + 91 (0) 22 4224419
Fax : + 91 (0) 22 4224033
E-mail: shikakai@bom5.vsnl.net.in

Tirupati Industries (India) Ltd.
123-125, 1st Flr.,
Daya Mandir
Mumbadevi Rd.
Mumbai
Maharashtra - 400003
Tel : + 91 (0) 22 3428859
Fax : + 91 (0) 22 3428859

VVF Ltd.
Opp. Sion Fort Garden
109, Sion (E), Mumbai,
Maharashtra - 400022
Tel : + 91 (0) 22 4073221
Fax : + 91 (0) 22 4091554

Chamba Detergents Pvt. Ltd.
Shop No. 1, Chamba Tower
Ludhiana, Punjab -141008
Tel : + 91 (0) 161 726097

Manak Chemicals
Cinema Rd.
Adjoining Raikhy Theatre
Talab Mandir Rd.
Ludhiana, Punjab-141008
Tel : + 91 (0) 161 721964
Fax : + 91 (0) 161 721770
E-mail : manakchem@satyam.net.in

Shree Gopal Udyog
578, Indl. Area-B
Ludhiana, Punjab -141003
Tel : + 91 (0) 161 531327

Cholayil Pharmaceuticals
15th Main Rd., J-Blk.
Anna Ngr. (W)
Chennai
Tamil Nadu-600040
Tel : + 91 (0) 44 6280801
Fax : + 91 (0) 44 6214974
E-mail: mfc.mds@gnmds.globalnet.ems.vsnl.net.in

The Calcutta Chemical Company Ltd.
69-74
Ambattur Indl. Est.
Chennai
Tamil Nadu-600058
Tel : + 91 (0) 44 6258224
Fax : + 91 (0) 44 6258299
E-mail: cccamb@giasmd01.vsnl.net.in

Ahuja Enterprises
C-149, Site No. 1, Indl. Area
Bulandshahr Rd.
Ghaziabad
Uttar Pradesh - 201009
Tel : + 91 (0) 120 4702214
Fax : + 91 (0) 120 4731849

Amar Gram Udyog Sewa Sansthan
Khasra No. 67, GT Rd.
Chapraula
Gautambudh Nagar
Uttar Pradesh-201306
Tel : + 91 (0) 118 4674671

Berlia Udyog
E-47, Indl. Area
Bulandshahar Rd.
Ghaziabad
Uttar Pradesh - 201001
Tel : + 91 (0) 120 4700998

Chaudhary Soap & Chemicals
C-127, Indl. Area
Bulandshahr Rd.
Ghaziabad
Uttar Pradesh - 201009
Tel : + 91 (0) 120 4701930

Mital Chemical Industries
E-47, Foundry Ngr.
Agr Uttar Pradesh-282007
Tel : + 91 (0) 562 345273
Fax : + 91 (0) 562 580926
E-mail: vinod@agr.dot.net.in

Northern Aromatics Pvt. Ltd.
C-10, Chander Ngr.
Ghaziabad
Uttar Pradesh - 201011
Tel : + 91 (0) 120 770536

Pee Cee Cosma Sope Ltd.
19/9, Khatena Rd.
Loha Mandi
Agra Uttar Pradesh-282002
Tel : + 91 (0) 562 310277
Fax : + 91 (0) 562 310171
E-mail: pcsoap@vsnl.com

Perfect Cosmetics India
E-5, Sarojini Ngr. Indl. Area
Kanpur Rd.
Lucknow
Uttar Pradesh - 226012
Tel : + 91 (0) 522 436721

Vijay Soap Industries
1, New Arya Ngr. Indl. Area
Meerut Rd.
Ghaziabad
Uttar Pradesh - 201001
Tel : + 91 (0) 120 4735371
Fax: + 91 (0) 120 4792570

Vivek Soap Industries (Regd.)
21-E
New Arya Ngr. Indl. Area
Ghaziabad
Uttar Pradesh - 201003
Tel : + 91 (0) 120 4712108

Bengal Chemicals & Pharmaceuticals Ltd.
6, Ganesh Chandra Avenue
Kolkata
West Bengal - 700013
Tel : + 91 (0) 33 2259502
Fax : + 91 (0) 33 2257697
E-mail: bengchem@cal.vsnl.net.in

India Alkalies Ltd.
5, Garstin Place
Kolkata
West Bengal-700001
Tel : + 91 (0) 33 2103439

Swaika Vanaspati Ltd.
18B, Brabourne Rd.
Kolkata
West Bengal - 700001
Tel : + 91 (0) 33 2351827
Fax : + 91 (0) 33 2350413

The Scientific & Chemical Products Pvt. Ltd.
226, Bagmari Rd.
Kolkata
West Bengal - 700054
Tel : + 91 (0) 33 5515121

Utkal Soap Products Ltd.
Tobaco House, 1 & 2
Old Court-House Corner
Kolkata
West Bengal - 700001
Tel : + 91 (0) 33 2207445
Fax : + 91 (0) 33 2420628
E-mail : uspl@cal2.vsnl.net.in

Jocil Ltd.
P.O. Box 216, Arundelpet
Guntur
Andhra Pradesh-522002
Tel : + 91 (0) 863 290190
Fax : + 91 (0) 863 290090
E-mail: jocil@jocil.xeevga.xeemail.ems.vsnl.net.in

Sree Rayalaseema Alkalies & Allied Chemicals Ltd.
KJ Cmplx., Bhagyanagar
Kurnool
Andhra Pradesh - 518004
Tel : + 91 (0) 8518 21933
Fax : + 91 (0) 8518 26973
E-mail: jaleel2010@rediffmail.com

Vijeta Crane Chemicals & Cosmetics
2nd Lane
Ramanama Kshetram
Guntur
Andhra Pradesh - 522004
Tel : + 91 (0) 863 223311
Fax : + 91 (0) 863 356712

117. MANUFACTURE OF TIN CONTAINERS
118. MANUFACTURE OF STORAGE TANKS, PRESSURE VESSELS, HEAT EXCHANGERS
119. MARK II HAND PUMPS
120. MARUTI WORKSHOP CUM - SERVICE STATION
121. MECHANICAL JACKS
122. METAL CUTTING DIE DESIGN
123. METAL CUTTING OF AND GRINDING WHEELS (ABRASIVE CUTTING WHEELS)
124. METAL HOOKS & CLIPS
125. METAL SEPARATION (COPPER , TIN, LEAD) FROM SPENT WASH ACID
126. METALLIC RING JOINTS
127. METALLIC GASKET (SPIRAL WOUND)
128. MICROVEE & ABSOLUTE FILTER
129. MICROWAVE OVEN
130. MILD STEEL INGOTS
131. MINI STEEL PLANT
132. MODERN VEHICLE WORKSHOP
133. MOPED
134. M.S.HINGES
135. M.S.INGOT AND HR. STEEL STRUCTURALS
136. M.S.INGOT BY INDUCTION FURNACES
137. M.S.PIPES
138. M.S. WELDING ELECTRODE
139. MUFFLERS & SILENCERS FOR THREE WHEELERS
140. NAIL CUTTER WITH FILER & MANICURE
141. NICHROME WIRE
142. NICKEL LINED SCREENS
143. NON-FERROUS ALLOY ROLLING
144. NON-FERROUS FORGING
145. NON-FERROUS FOUNDRY
146. NON PRESSURE
147. INCANDESCENT LAMP
148. NUMBER COMBINATION LOCKS FOR LUGGAGES
149. NUTS & BOLTS
150. PAPER COATED ALUMINIUM AND COPPER WIRE
151. PETROMAX CONTAINER
152. PHOTO ETCHING OF STAINLESS STEEL PLATES
153. PIPE GALVANIZING PLANT
154. PISTON RING-AUTOMOBILE
155. PLANT PROTECTION EQUIPMENTS
156. PLATINUM LABORATORY APPARATUS
157. PRESSURE COOKER & ALUMINIUM UTENSILS
158. PRESSURE COOKER (ALUMINIUM)
159. PRESSURE DIE CASTING
160. PRINTED ALUMINIUM COLLAPSIBLE TUBES
161. PRINTED TIN CONTAINERS
162. PRINTING PRESS (CYLINDER MACHINE)
163. PUMPS FOR CHEMICAL INDUSTRY (SPECIAL)
164. RAILWAY SLEEPERS (M.S.)
165. RAZOR TWIN BLADE
166. R.C.C SPUN PIPES
167. RECONDITIONING OF M.S. DRUMS/BARRELS
168. RE-ROLLING COPPER AND BRASS SHEET AND RODS
169. RE-ROLLING MILLS
170. RESIN COATED SAND
171. RESIN CORED SOFT SOLDER WIRES
172. ROLLING MILL (BY INDUCTION FURNACE) & MANUFACTURE OF BARS, ANGLES, SQUARES, TUBES AND OTHERS
173. ROLLER BEARING & FORGING
174. ROLLING OF STAINLESS STEEL PATTA
175. RUBBER INSULATED PLIERS (HAND TOOLS)
176. RUBBING COMPOUND FOR AUTOMOBILES
177. SCIENTIFIC LABORATORY EQUIPMENTS
178. SCOOTER ASSEMBLING
179. SECONDARY LEAD EXTRACTION BY SCRAP BATTERY PLATES,PIPES & SHEET
180. SEAMLESS M.S. TUBES & PIPES
181. SELF TAPPING STEEL SCREW
182. SEWING NEEDLES
183. S.G. IRON & ALLOY STEEL
184. SHEET METAL PRODUCTS, (FERROUS/NON-FERROUS)
185. SHIP/MARINE CONTAINER
186. SHOCK ABSORBERS
187. SHOE EYELETS
188. SHOT AND GRITS BY AUTOMIZATION PROCESS
189. SHOVELS
190. SILICO MANGANESE ALLOYS
191. SILENCERS (MUFFLERS) EXHAUST & TAIL PIPE FOR ALL TYPES OF VEHICLES
192. SINTERED BEARING
193. SINTERED BUSHES
194. SINTERED METAL PRODUCTS
195. SOFT AND HARD FERRITES
196. SPANNERS
197. SPARK PLUGS
198. STEEL PLANT (ELECTRIC ARC FURNACE BASED- EAF)
199. SPHERIODAL GRAPHITE CAST IRON
200. SPRAY DRYER
201. STAINLESS STEEL HINGES
202. STAINLESS STEEL SHEET ROLLING TO PRODUCE STAINLESS STEEL UTENSILS
203. STAINLESS STEEL UTENSILS
204. STAPLE PINS,PAPER PIN , GEM CLIPS ETC.
205. STEEL CASTINGS
206. STEEL CHAIN
207. STEEL FOUNDRY
208. STEEL FURNITURES AND ELECTRICAL APPLIANCES
209. STEEL PLANT (MINI)
210. STEEL RODS AND COILS FROM SCRAPS
211. STEEL ROLLING MILL
212. STEEL STRIPS (COLD ROLLED) SILICON WITH GRAIN RIENTED FOR ELECTRIC USE
213. STEEL TRANSMISSION LINE TOWERS & ROLLING MILL TO PRODUCE STEEL SECTION
214. STEEL FURNITURES AND ELECTRICAL APPLIANCES
215. STEEL WIRE DRAWING AND GALVANIZING
216. STEEL WOOL
217. SUBMERGED ARC WELDED PIPES
218. SUBMERSIBLE PUMP MANUFACTURING
219. SUPER ENAMELLED COPPER WIRE
220. THREE WHEELERS
221. TIE-ROD ENDS
222. TIN CONTAINERS
223. TOOLROOM AND SHEET METAL PRODUCTS
224. TRACTOR TRAILERS
225. TRANSMISSION POWER FITTING
226. TUBULAR POLES
227. SUPER ENAMELLED COPPER WIRES
228. TUBULAR POLES FOR ELECTRICAL TRANSMISSION (BY FABRICATION PROCESS)
229. TUBULAR POLES OF M.S. & HIGH TENSILE STEEL
230. VACUUM CLEANERS
231. VACUUM FLASK (STAINLESS STEEL)
232. VALVES FOR REFRIGERATION AND AIR-CONDITION
233. VEHICLE WELDING & PAINTING
234. VENETION BLIND
235. WASHING MACHINES (AUTOMATIC & COMPUTERISED)
236. WATER CONTROLLER (AUTOMATIC)
237. WATCH STRAPS/CHAINS/ BRACELETS/BELT BRASS & STAINLESS STEEL
238. WATER COOLERS
239. WELDED WIRE MESH
240. WELDING ELECTRODES
241. WICK STOVES
242. WIND MILL WINDOW FRAME (FERROUS & NON-FERROUS)
243. WRIST WATCH

359. DI ETHYL OXALATE
360. DI METHYL ORTHOPHTHALATE
361. DI-METHYL PHTHALATE
362. DICLOFENAC GEL
363. DIOCTYL PHTHALATE (DOP)
364. DI PHENYL GLYCERINE
365. DI PHENYL OXIDE
366. DINITRO-CHLORO BENZENE
367. DISTILLED WATER
368. DODECYL BENZENE SULPHONATE
369. DUSTLESS CHALK
370. EDTA & ITS SALTS
371. ELECTROLESS NICKEL PLATING ON PLASTICS
372. ENDOSULFAN
373. EPOXY RESIN BASED COMPOUND
374. ETHYL ACETATE
375. EHTYL ETHER
376. ETHYL ALCOHOL (POTABLE LIQUOR)
377. ETHYL HEXANOL
378. EXTRACTION OF ESSENTIAL OILS BY SUGAR CRITICAL FLUID (CARBON DIOXIDE) METHOD FROM FLOWERS, HERBAL & SPICES
379. FERRIC ALUM
380. FERRO CHROME LIGNO SULPHONATE
381. FERRO MANGANESE
382. FERRO SILICONE
383. FERRO VANADIUM FROM VANADIUM SLUDGE
384. FERROUS SILICATE
385. FERROUS SULPHATE
386. FERTILIZER FROM ANIMAL BLOOD & LEATHER WASTE
387. FLUORESCENT TUBE LIGHT POWDER
388. FOAMED PVC COMPOUNDING & ITS PRODUCTS
389. FORMALDEHYDE
390. FRACTIONAL DISTILLATION OF D.M.O (DEMENTHOLIZED OIL)
391. FRACTIONAL DISTILLATION OF ESSENTIAL OIL & MEDICINAL PLANT EXTRACT
392. FRICTION DUST (LIQUID & POWDER) FROM CNSL
393. FRUIT FLAVOURS
394. FURFURAL FROM RICE HUSK
395. GARLIC ACID
396. GASKET SHELLAC COMPOUND
397. GEAR OIL
398. GIBBERELLIC ACID
399. GLASS PUTTY
400. GLYCERINE
401. GOSSYPOL (POLY PHENOL) FROM COTTON SEED OIL
402. GUAR GUM POWDER
403. HAIR FIXER (HAIR GEL TYPE)
404. H - ACID
405. HENNA PASTE MAKING
406. HEPTAL DEHYDE
407. HIGH CARBON FERRO CHROME
408. HYDRATED CALCIUM SILICATE BRICK
409. HYDRATED LIME FROM SEA SHELL
410. HYDROCHLORIC ACID
411. HYDRO FLUORIC ACID
412. HYDROGEN PEROXIDE (BY AUTO-OXIDATION PROCESS)
413. ICE PACKS (SOLUTIONS TYPE, WHITE GEL TYPE, VIOLET SEMI SOLID POLYMER TYPE)
414. IMPROVING DROP POINT PARAFFIN WAX FROM 45-50°C TO 75-80°C
415. INDUSTRIAL ALCOHOL
416. INTEGERATED COMPLEX OF EASTER & ALLIED PRODUCTS (D.O.P, D.B.P, ETHYL ACETATE WIRE ENAMEL & CABLE JELLY)
417. IMFL (WHISKY) & COUNTRY LIQUOR
418. IRON OXIDE FOR MAKING FERITTE
419. IRON SULPHIDE
420. JUTE BATCHING OIL
421. KESH KALA TEL (HAIR DYE LOTION) (VASMOL 33, BLACK NITE TYPE)
422. L-LYSINE MONOHYDROCHLORIDE
423. LACTIC ACID FROM WHITE SUGAR BY FERMENTATION PROCESS
424. LDPE GRANULES FROM VIRGIN (LDPE RESIN)
425. LEAD EXTRACTION FROM BATTERY SCRAP
426. LEAD OXIDE (A) LEAD MONOXIDE (B) LEAD TETRA OXIDE (C) GREYLEAD OXIDE
427. LIQUID GLUCOSE & ITS BY PRODUCTS
428. LIQUID OXYGEN BOTTLING PLANT
429. LIQUID SHOE POLISH
430. LIQUID FLOOR POLISH
431. LUBE OIL VISCOSITY IMPROVED FOR P.P.G/P.E.G.
432. LUBRICANTS ASHLESS 100% COMBUSTION
433. MAGNESIUM CARBONATE AND MAGNESIUM BICARMONATE
434. MAGNESIUM HYDROXIDE POWDER
435. MAGNESIUM SILICATE
436. MAGNESIUM SULPHATE
437. MALACHITE GREEN
438. MALEIC ANHYDRIDE
439. MANGANESE SULPHATE
440. MANUFACTURING OF CARBON MONO-OXIDE WATER GAS
441. MENTHOL BOLD CRYSTALS FROM FLAKES
442. MENTHOL CRYSTAL & MENTHA OIL
443. MERCURIC OXIDE
444. METAL PRE-TREATMENT CHEMICALS
445. METHANE GAS BY SODIUM ACETATE & SODA LIME
446. METHYL ACETYL RICINOLATE
447. METOL
448. METOL FROM HYDROQUINONE & METHYLAMINE
449. MICANITE
450. MICRO NUTRIENT MIXTURE
451. MINERAL WATER
452. MINERAL WATER AND PET BOTTILNG PLANT
453. MINERAL WATER IN BOTTLES, GLASS AND POUCHES
454. MINI CEMENT PLANT (BY ROTARY KILN PROCESS)
455. MIXED FERTILIZER
456. MOSQUITO & FLIES REPELLENT AGARBATTI (INCENSE STICKS)
457. MONO CHLORO ACETIC ACID
458. MONOCROTOPHOS (TECHNICAL)
459. MOSQUITO COIL
460. MOSQUITO COIL & MAT
461. MOSQUITO MAT
462. MOTHER TINCTURE & BIO CHEMIC MEDICINES
463. NAPHTHALENE & PHENYL (INTEGRATED UNIT)
464. NATURAL MINERAL WATER BY REVERSE OSMOSIS PROCESS
465. NICKEL PLATING BRIGHTNER (PRIMARY OR CARRIER BRIGHTNER & SECONDARY BRIGHTNER)
466. NICKEL SULPHATE
467. NICOTINE FROM TOBACCO WASTE
468. NICOTINE SULPHATE FROM TOBACCO WASTE
469. NITRO BENZENE
470. NITRO CELLULOSE SANDING SEALER/LACQUER
471. NITRO MUSK
472. NITROGEN & OXYGEN GAS PLANT
473. NON-IONIC SURFACTANT (WETTING AGENT)
474. NO-CARB PASTE
475. OCTANOL
476. ORTHO NITRO PHENOL
477. OXALIC ACID FROM MOLASSES
478. OXALIC ACID FROMRICE HUSK
479. OXALIC ACID FROM TREE BARK
470. OXALIC ACID FROM WASTE VEGETABLES
471. OXYGEN GAS PLANT
472. OXYGEN GAS PLANT (AIR SEPERATION METHOD)
473. PARA-AMINO BENZOIC ACID
474. PARA-AMINO PHENOL
475. PARA TOLUENE SULPHONIC ACID
476. PECTIN FROM RAW PAPAYA
477. PERFUME (LEMON & OTHERS)

CRUDE NAPHTHA
570. TRIMETHYL AMMONIUM CHLORIDE
571. TRIPHENYL PHOSPHITE (T.P.P)
572. ULTRAMARINE BLUE (LIQUID)
573. UREA FORMALDEHYDE & MELAMINE FORMALDEHYDE POWDER
574. UNDECYLINIC ACID
575. VINYL ACETATE MONOMER
576. VITAMIN C
577. VITAMIN E
578. WASTE WATER TREATMENT PLANT FOR INDUSTRIAL SECTOR IN INDIA (ONLY MARKER SURVEY)
579. WIRE DRAWING LUBRICANT
580. WIRE ENAMEL
581. XANTHATES
582. YELLOW DEXTRIN
583. ZINC CHLORIDE
584. ZINC OXIDE
585. ZINC PHOSPHATING BY COLD PROCESS
586. ZINC SILICATE
587. ZINC STEARATE
588. ZINC SULPHATE
589. ZINC SULPHATE MONOHYDRATE
590. ACID BLACK
591. AURAMINE'O'
592. AZO DYES STUFF
593. DYE & DYE INTERMEDIATE
594. DYE INTERMEDIATES
595. MALACHITE GREEN
596. METHYLENE BLUE
597. PHTHALOCYANINE BLUE
598. PHTHALOCYANINE BLUE & GREEN
599. REACTIVE DYES
600. SULPHUR BLACK DYE
601. VAT DYES
602. WATER CHILLING PLANT
603. WADDING OIL (100%) FOR WADDING OF COTTON HOSIERY CLOTH IN THE DYEING PROCESS
604. WHITE OIL
605. WAX FLOOR POLISH

ELECTRICAL, ELECTONICS, COMPUTERS AND INFOTECH/IT PROJECTS

606. AIR CONDITIONING
607. ALUMINIUM ALLOY CONDUCTOR
608. ALUMINIUM CABLE
609. ALUMINIUM ELECTROYTIC CAPACITORS
610. AUDIO CASSETTE ASSEMBLING & RECORDING
611. AUDIO CASSETTES DUPLICATING RECORDING
612. AUDIO CASSETTES & AUDIO STUDIO
613. AUDIO CASSETTES PLANE & RECORDED
614. AUDIO MAGNETIC HEADS
615. AUDIO MAGNETIC TAPE
616. AUDIO/VIDEO CASSETTES
617. AUTO BULB/LAMPS
618. AUTOMATIC VOLTAGE STABILIZER
619. BATTERY PLATES
620. BACK OFFICE (Rs. 5000/-)
621. B/W TV & COMPUTER MONITOR PICTURE TUBE
622. BREAD BOARDS
623. CALL CENTRE
624. CAMERA (35 MM)
625. CAPACITORS
626. CARBON ELECTRODE USED FOR BATTERY CELL
627. CARBON POTETIOMETERS
628. CEILING FAN
629. CERAMIC INSULATOR
630. CHILDREN INFOTECH TRAINING INSTITUTE (Rs. 5000/-)
631. CHOKE AND PATTI
632. CHOKE AND STARTER
633. CHOKE USED FOR FLUORESCENT LAMPS
634. COLOUR TELEVISION
635. COLOUR AND BLACK & WHITE TELEVISION
636. COMPACT DISC
637. COMPACT DISC PLAYER (AUDIO/VIDEO)
638. COMPUTER EDUCATION INSTITUTE
639. COMPUTER ASSEMBLY
640. COMPUTER HARDWARE
641. COMPUTER KEYBOARD
642. COMPUTER PERIPHERALS
643. COMPUTER PRINTERS
644. COMPUTER RIBBON
645. COMPUTER RIBBON REINKING OR REFILLING
646. COMPUTER STATIONERY
647. COMPUTER STATIONERY &

IMPORTED HARDWARE PARTS
648. COMPUTER TERMINALS
649. COMPUTERISED WASHING MACHINE (AUTOMATIC)
650. COMPUTER SOFTWARE
651. CONDENSER FOR MOTOR USING MPP FILM
652. CONTENT DEVELOPMENT CENTRE (EOU) (Rs. 5000/-)
653. CONTROL PANEL BOARD
654. COOLING COIL FOR AIR CONDITIONERS
655. COPPER STRIP COIL FROM SCRAP
656. CORDLESS TELEPHONES
657. CYBER CAFE
658. CYBERKIOSK (Rs. 5000/-)
659. DATA PROCESSING CENTRE (Rs. 5000/-)
660. D.C. MICRO MOTORS
661. D.G.SETS
662. DISH ANTENNA AND CABLE T.V. NETWORK EQUIPMENT
663. DISTRIBUTION TRANSFORMERS & REPAIRS
664. DOMESTIC ELECTRICAL APPLIANCES- ROOM COOLER, WASHING MACHINE, WATER HEATER, ELECTRIC ROOM HEATER
665. E-SCHOOL
666. E-COMMERCE/BUSINESS
667. ELECTRIC ENERGY METER
668. ELECTRIC FANS
669. ELECTRIC HORN FOR AUTOMOBILE
670. ELECTRIC LAMP/GLS (INCANDESCENT LAMP)
671. ELECTRIC MIXER
672. ELECTRIC MOTORS UP TO 10 HP. REWINDING OF ALL TYPES OF MOTORS WATER PUMPS
673. ELECTRIC MOTOR WINDING (FOR FAN, MIXIES, ETC.)
674. ELECTRIC STEAM IRON
675. ELECTRICAL APPLIANCES
676. ELECTRICAL FIXTURES
677. ELECTRICAL STAMPING
678. ELECTROLYTIC CAPACITORS
679. ELECTROMAGNETIC RELAY
680. ELECTRONIC BALAST/CHOK
681. ELECTRICAL CHOKE
682. ELECTRONIC DIGITAL WATCHES
683. ELECTRONIC DIGITAL WEIGHING MACHINE
684. ELECTRONIC FIRE ALARM
685. ELECTRONIC GAS STOVE LIGHTERS
686. ELECTRONIC PRESSURE INDICATORS, ELECTRICALS, ELECTRONIC LIQUID LEVEL INDICATORS, ELECTRONIC TEMPERATURE INDICATOR, DIGITAL TACHOMETER
687. ELECTRONIC TELEPHONE INSTRUMENTS
688. ELECTRONIC TOYS
689. ELECTRONIC WATCHES & CLOCKS
690. FAX MACHINES
691. F.H.P MOTORS
692. FLOPPY DISKETTES
693. FLUORESCENT LAMP STARTER
694. FLUORESCENT TUBULAR

Above all the Detailed Project Reports are available at *"ENGINEERS INDIA RESEARCH INSTITUTE"*. 4449, Nai Sarak (D), Main Road Delhi - 110 006

● Ph : 91-11- 23918117, 2391 6431, 23840361, 31082370 ●Fax : 91-11- 2391 6431

●E-Mail : eirisidi@bol.net.in

LAMPS WITH INTRODUCTION TO MERCURY VAPOUR LAMP
695. FRANCHISEE COMPUTER EDUCATION CENTRE (Rs. 5000)
696. GAS DETECTOR (L.P.G)
697. GENERATOR SET & PUMP SETS
698. GENERATOR (BATTERY OPERATED)
699. GIS SERVICE CENTRE (GEOGRAPHICAL INFORMATION SYSTEMS)
700. HARDWARE FITTING FOR TRANSMISSION LINE OVERHEAD LINE MATERIAL
701. HEADERS FOR TRANSISTOR ICS SEMI CONDUCTOR
702. H.T & L.T INSULATORS
703. H.T & M.V INDUSTRIAL CUBICAL SWITCH BOARD
704. INFORMATION MOVING DISPLAY (L.E.D TYPE)
705. INSURANCE CLAIM PROCESSING CENTRE (EOU) (Rs. 5000/-)
706. INTEGRATED CIRCUITS
707. INTERNET BASED STOCK TRADING (Rs. 5000/-)
708. INTERNET SERVICE PROVIDER (I.S.P.)
709. JELLY FILLED TELEPHONE CABLES
710. LAP TOP COMPUTERS
711. LEAD ACID BATTERIES
712. LEAD ACID BATTERY PLATES AND ASSEMBLING OF BATTERY
713. LEGAL TRANSCRIPTION & SECRETARIAL SERVICES CENTER (EOU)(Rs. 5000/-)
714. LIGHT EMITTING DIODES (L.E.D)
715. LINEAR ICS TRAINER KIT
716. LOUD SPEAKER
717. L.T TRANSFORMER REPAIRING
718. MEDICAL TRANSCRIPTION CENTRE
719. METAL FILM RESISTORS
720. METALLISED POLYPROPYLENE, POLYESTER FILM CAPACITOR
721. MICA BASE ELECTRONIC COMPONENTS
722. MICA PAPER WASTE PAPER FROM MICA WASTE
723. MICRO PROCESSORS TRAINER KITS BASED ON MICRO PROCESSORS
724. MINI COMPUTER (PERSONAL COMPUTER)
725. MINIATURE CIRCUIT BREAKER (M.C.B)
726. MINIATURE WATCH BATTERIES (BUTTON CELL)
727. MIXER/GRINDER (MIXI)
728. MONO CHROME COMPUTER MONITOR
729. MOTOR START ELECTROLYTIC CAPACITOR
730. MULTI LAYER P.C.B
731. MULTIPLE RELAY FOR LOW VOLTAGE
732. NEON INDICATOR
733. NEON SIGN MANUFACTURE
734. OPTICAL FIBRE CABLES
735. ON LINE SHOPPING MALL (Rs. 5000/-)
736. OPTO MECHANICAL & ELECTRICAL EQUIPMENTS
737. PHOTO COLOUR LAB
738. PICTURE TUBE (B/W)
739. PLAIN PAPER COPIER
740. PLASTIC FILM CAPACITORS
741. POLYESTER CAPACITORS
742. PORTABLE GENERATOR SET
743. PORTAL
744. PORTABLE TELEVISION(TV)
745. POWER CAPACITORS
746. POWER INVERTERS
747. POWER PLANT
748. POWER TRANSFORMERS UP TO 600 KVA
749. PRINTED CIRCUIT BOARD
750. PVC WIRES & CABLES
751. RE-CONDITIONING OF PICTURE TUBE
752. RESIN CAST CT & PT (1 KV)
753. SEMI CONDUCTOR DEVICE
754. SEMI CONDUCTORS FOR TRANSISTORS & DIODES
755. SETTING UP OF A VIDEO STUDIO
756. SMOKE DETECTORS
757. SOLAR CELLS
758. SOLAR MODULES
759. SOLAR PHOTO VOLTAIC SYSTEM
760. SOLDER FLUXES
761. SOLAR WATER HEATING PANELS
762. STEEL FURNITURE & ELECTRICAL APPLIANCES
763. STEREO AMPLIFIERS
764. STEREO CASSETTE RECORDERS/PLAYERS
765. STREET LIGHT FITTINGS SURGE SUPPRESSOR
766. TANTALUM CAPACITORS
767. TEFLON COATED ELECTRIC CABLE
768. TELEMEDICINE (DISTANCE HEALTH CARE) (Rs. 5000/-)
769. TELEPHONE CORD/CABLE
770. TELEPHONE (PUSH BUTTON TYPE)
771. TELEPHONE (PUSH BUTTON & CORDLESS)
772. TELEVISION (CTV & B/W)
773. TELEVISION (3-D)
774. TELEVISION DEFLECTION COMPONENTS
775. TELEVISION SIGNAL BOOSTERS
776. TELEVISION TUNERS
777. TRACTION BATTERIES
778. TRAINING INSTITUTE OF MEDICAL TRANSCRIPTION
779. TRANSFORMER FOR B/W TV
780. TRANSFORMER FOR VOLTAGE STABILIZER & E.H.T
781. TRANSMISSION POWER LINE FITTING
782. TRANSMISSION TOWER FITTING
783. TV AUDIO EQUIPMENT CABINETS & THEIR ASSEMBLING UNIT
784. UN-INTERRUPTED POWER SUPPLY (U.P.S)
785. VARIABLE FREQUENCY
786. VARIABLE VOLTAGE A.C. DRIVE
787. VIDEO CASSETTES (COMPLETE MANUFACTURING & ASSEMBLING)
788. VIDEO CASSETTES RECORDER (V.C.R)
789. VIDEO FILM STUDIO
790. VOLTAGE REGULATOR FOR AUTOMOBILES
791. VOLTAGE STABILIZERS
792. VOLTAGE STABLIZER & T.V. GAIN BOOSTER
793. WAX AND CHEMICAL COATED, BRAIDED TINSEL WIRE
794. WEBSITE DESIGN & E-MAIL REGISTERING
795. WELDING ELECTRODES
796. WIND ENERGY POWER PROJECT (10 MW)
796A WIRES (METAL)

FOOD, AGRO FOOD, PROCESSED FOOD, AGRO PLANTATION , CULTIVATION, FARMING, DAIRY/MILK, TOBACCO/PAN MASALA, BREWERY & DISTILLERY, EDIBLE OILS, EOU FOOD PRODUCTS AND ALLIED PRODUCTS

797. ALCOHOLIC BEVERAGES & VENEGAR FROM COCONUT WATER
798. ALCOHOL DRINKS FROM ETHYL ALCOHOL BY MIXING OF VARIOUS FLAVOURS
799. ANTI SCALE COMPOUND FOR ADDING INTO SUGAR JUICE BOILING
800. APPLE JUICE CONCENTRATED & DEHYDRATED FRUIT & VEGETABLES
801. ARTIFICIAL FISH MEAL FOR POULTRY FEED
802. AUTOMATIC BISCUIT PLANT
803. BABY CEREAL FOOD AND MILK POWDER
804. BACTERIA FOR CANE JUICE
805. BAKER'S YEAST
806. BAKERY INDUSTRY
807. BANANA PUREE
808. BEER & WINE
809. BEER PLANT (BREWERY)
810. BIDI
811. BIDI & CIGARETTE
812. BISCUIT PLANT

813. BREAD (AUTOMATIC PLANT)
814. BLACK PEPPER (SPICES)
815. BREAD AND BISCUITS
816. BREEDING FARM
817. BROILER CHICKEN
819. BUTTON MUSHROOM CULTIVATION & PROCESSING
820. CANNING OF RASAGULLAS IN METAL CANS
821. CAFFEIN FROM TEA WASTE
822. CANNING OF FRUITS & VEGETABLES
823. CASEIN AND BY-PRODUCTS
824. CASHEW FRUIT JUICE FROM CASHEW FRUIT APPLE
825. CASHEWNUT KERNEL EXTRACTION FROM CASHEWNUT FRUIT
826. CASHEWNUT SHELL LIQUID & KERNEL PROCESSING
827. CASHEW FENI
828. CATECHEU (BY CHEMICAL PROCESS)
829. CATTLE FEED FROM TAPIOCA
830. CHEWING & BUBBLE GUM
831. CHICKEN/SHEEP MEAT PROCESSING
832. CHOCOLATE (MILK)
833. CIGARETTE AND BEEDIES
834. COCOA BUTTER FROM COCOA MASS
835. COCONUT PRODUCTS & BY PRODUCTS PROCESS COMPLEX
836. COLD/SOFT DRINKS
837. COLLECTION OF MILK AND MILK MAKING POWDER
838. COLLECTION OF MILK AND PACKING IN POLYTHENE POUCH (1/2 KG.1 KG. & 2 KG.)
839. CONDENSED MILK (SWEETNED)
840. CONFECTIONERY INDUSTRY (TOFFEE & CANDY, SEMI-AUTOMATIC PLANT)
841. COUNTRY LIQUOR FROM MOLASSES
842. CIGARETTE
843. DAIRY FARM AND DAIRY (MILK) PRODUCTS (PASTEURISED MILK, BUTTER, GHEE, PANEER)
844. DAIRY FARM TO PRODUCE MILK & PACKING IN POUCHES (50%) & CAN(50%)
845. DAIRY FOR MILK PROCESSING
846. DAIRY FARM (BUFALO)
847. DAL (PULSE) MILL UNIT
848. DEHYDRATION OF CARROT & GARLIC
849. DEHYDRATION & CANNING OF FRUITS & VEGETABLES
850. DEHYDRATION OF FIGS
851. DEHYDRATION OF FRUITS AND VEGETABLES
852. DEHYDRATED ONIONS AND ONION POWDER
853. DRY ICE BY BREAKING OF AIR
854. DRYING OF RED CHILLIES, HALDI, DHANIA, AND GREEN PEAS
855. EGG POWDER (40,000 EGGS PROCESSING PER DAY)
856. EXPORT OF PROCESSED FOODS AND MARINE PRODUCTS
857. FISH CANNING & POUCHING
859. FISH FARMING (PRAWN & OTHER MARINE PRODUCTS)
860. FISH MEAL
861. FLOUR MILL AND MUSTARD OIL
862. FOOD COLOUR & ORASTED GROUNDNUT GRAM PEAS, ETC IN POUCHES
863. FROG LEGS PROCESSING
864. FROZEN MEATS PROCESSING
865. FOOD FLAVOURS (WHISKY) VODKA, GRAPE, BUTTER SCOTCH)
866. FOOD PRODUCTS COMPLEX (DEHYDRATED ONIONS, GARLIC POWDER & FLAKES, CATTLE FEED, TOMATO POWDER, TOMATO PRODUCTS, CANNED FRUITS & VEGETABLES, TOMATO PURE, GROUN NUT OIL, REFIND OIL, DEHYDRATED GRAPES, BANANA POWDER & WAFFERS)
867. FRUIT JUICE, JAM, JELLIES & ALLIED PRODUCTS
868. FRUIT JUICE, PICKLES PROCESSING AND CANNING
869. FRUIT JUICE MAKING & PACKING IN PLASTIC CONTAINER/POUCHES
870. FRUIT PROCESSING (JAM & JELLIES)
871. FRUIT PULP & JUICE CONCENTRATES
872. FRUIT & VEGETABLE DRYING (FREEZE DRYING METHOD)
873. GOAT & SHEEP FARMING
874. GRAM DALL/PULSE MILL
875. GRAPE DEHYDRATION
876. HARD BOILED CANDY (TOFFEE & CANDY)
877. HERBAL CIGARETTES
878. HONEY PROCESSING & PACKAGING
879. ICE CREAM OF DIFFERENT FLAVOURS
880. ICE CREAM STABILIZER
881. ICE MAKING PLANT
882. INDIAN MADE FOREIGN LIQUOR (I.M.F.L)
883. INSTANT FOOD (IDLI MIX, DOSA MIX, GULAB JAMUN MIX)
884. INSTANT FOOD (INSTANT FOOD & FAST FOOD PARLOUR)
885. INSTANT NOODLES
886. INSTANT TEA
887. INSTANT TEA FROM BLACK TEA
888. INTEGERATED STARCH BAKING POWDER/YEAST INDUSTRY
889. IODIZED SALT
890. IODIZED SALT (ORDINARY MOISTURE-LESS/FREE FLOWING IN PLASTIC BAGS AND CONTAINERS)
891. JAM, JELLIES, FRUIT JUICE & ALLIED PRODUCTS
892. KATHA AND CUTCH
893. KHANDSARI SUGAR
894. KHANDSARI SUGAR & IMFL
895. LACTIC ACID FROM WHITE SUGAR BY FERMENTATION PROCESS
896. LACTOSE & BY PRODUCTS PROCESSING FROM MILK
897. LIQUID GLUCOSE AND ITS BYE PRODUCTS
898. MACRONI AND VERMICILLI
899. MALT EXTRACTION FROM BARLEY
900. MANGO PROCESSING (MANGO PULP, JUICE & SLICES)
901. MAYUR BRAND TYPE CHEWING TOBACCO
902. MINERAL WATER
903. MILK PRESERVATION & MARKETING TO WHOLE SELLERS (INPOUCH PACKING BY UHT TECHNOLOGY)
904. MILK PROCESSING AND PACKAGING OF MILK PRODUCTS
905. MILK PRODUCTS (CASEIN, LACTOSE, GHEE & WHEY POWDER)
906. MILK TOFFEE
907. MINI FLOUR MILL
908. MINI SUGAR PLANT
909. MISRI (PEARL SUGAR CANDIES)
910. MODERN RICE MILL
911. MURABBA
912. MUSTARD OIL EXTRACTION & REFINING
913. MUTTON TALLOW
914. NAMKEEN INDUSTRY (BHUJIA, CHANA CHUR ETC.)
915. NAMKEEN & SWEETS
916. NON-BASMATI RICE FROM PADDY
917. OLEORESIN, ESSENTIAL OIL, DYES & POWDER OF SPICES
918. OLEORESIN EXTRACTION FROM DIPTERO-CARPUT TURMINATUS AND PINUS KHASYANA
919. OLEORESIN EXTRACTION FROM CHILLI
920. PAN MASALA AND POUCH

Apart from the above mentioned reports EIRI is also having other most lucrative projects (as many as 30,000). You just name it and we have that report.

MAKING
921. PAN MASALA, TOBACCO, ZARDA & KIMAM
922. PANEER FROM MILK
923. PAPPAD PLANT
924. PAPAIN FROM PAPAYA (PAPAYA LATEX)
925. PECTIN FROM MANGO PEEL PECTIN FROM APPLE POMACE
926. PHYTO TEA (HERBAL TEA)
927. PICKLES AND SAUCES
928. PICKLES MURABBA ETC. (VEG. & NON. VEG.PICKLES)
929. PIGGERY MEAT PROCESS
930. PINE-APPLE JUICE PREPARATION & PACKAGING
931. POTATO CHIPS/WAFFERS
932. POTATO POWDER
933. POUCH FILLING & PACKAGING OF EDIBLE OIL & GHEE
934. POULTRY FEED
935. PROCESSED FOODS & SPICES (EOU)
936. PROCESSED READYMADE FOOD
937. PROCESSING OF FRUITS & VEGETABLES
938. RABBIT FARMING
939. RASGULLAS MAKING & CANNING IN METAL CANS
940. READY TO EAT PROCESSED COOKED FOOD
941. READY TO EAT SNACK FOOD (CRAX, ROLL & BALL TYPE)
942. RICE & CORN FLAKES
943. ROASTED/SALTED/ MASALA,CASHEW NUTS, ALMONDS & PEANUTS
944. ROLLER FLOUR MILL
945. SALT LICKS FOR CATTLE
946. SAUSAGES FOOD CASING
947. SOFT DRINKS
948. SOFT DRINKS ESSENCES
949. SOFT DRINKS (NON CARBONATED) MANGO, LICCHI, PINEAPPLE FLAVOURS FROOTI TYPE IN TETRAPACK)
950. SOFTY ICE CREAM CONES (FULLY AUTOMATIC)
951. SOFT/COLD DRINKS (COLA, ORANGE, LEMON ETC. FLAVOURS)
952. SOYABEAN PRODUCTS
953. SOYA MILK & PANEER
954. STARCH & ALLIED PROPDUCT FROM BROKEN RICE
955. STRAWBERRY CULTIVATION & PROCESSING
956. SUGARCANE JUICE PRESERVATION
957. SUGAR CUBES FROM CANE SUGAR
988. SUGAR PLANT
989. SWEET AROMA BETEL NUT
990. SYNTHETIC TALLOW
991. TAMARIND JUICE POWDER
992. TEA & COFFEE PROCESSING & PACKAGING
993. TOFFEES, GOLIES, CANDY (HARD BOILED)
994. TOMATO PRODUCTS
994. TRADING BUSINESS OF SPICES & PAN MASALA
995. TUITY FRUITY
996. VODKA FROM POTATOES
997. WINE, BRANDY, WHISKY & CHAMPAGNE
997. WINE FROM DATES
998. YEAST FROM MOLASSES
999. ZARDA, KIMAM NO. 60,90,120,160,240,300 & 400 (TOBACCO)
1000. ZARDA-ZAFRANI (BABACHHAP TYPE)

GUMS & ADHESIVE

1001. ACRYLIC ADHESIVE
1002. ADHESIVE (FEVICOL TYPE)
1003. ADHESIVE BASED ON POLYURETHANE
1004. ADHESIVE FOR BAND AID (JOHNSON & JOHNSON TYPE)
1005. ADHESIVE INDUSTRIES (LAMINATED, STICKER,DDL & OTHER TYPES)
1006. ADHESIVE FOR GASKET (LIQUID/PASTE)
1007. GUAR GUM
1008. GUM BOTTLE (PVC)
1009. GUM FOR PASTING LABELS
1010. OFFICE PASTE
1011. RUBBER ADHESIVE
1012. SURGICAL ADHESIVE PLASTER

LEATHER & LEATHER PRODUCTS

1013. HANDMADE LEATHER
1014. LEATHER AUXILLARIES & CHEMICALS
1015. LEATHER DYES
1016. LEATHER WASHERS
1017. LEATHER BOARD FROM LEATHER WASTE
1018. LEATHER FOR UPHOLSTRY (SOFA)
1019. LEATHER GARMENTS
1020. LEATHER GOODS
1021. LEATHER SHOES
1022. LEATHER SHOE & CHAPPAL
1023. LEATHER SUITCASES, BRIEFCASES & TRAVELLING BAGS
1024. LEATHER GOODS AND GARMENTS
1025. LEATHER GARMENTS, SHOE & CHAPPAL
1026. LEATHER TANNING
1027. LEATHER TANNING & GARMENTS (EOU)
1028. SHEEP SKIN PICKLING PLANT
1029. SHOE UPPER
1030. SPORT SHOES (PLASTIC)

MISCELLANEOUS PRODUCTS

1031. AGARBATTI (INSENCE STICK)
1032. AGARBATTI (Mosquito Repellent)
1033. AGARBATI BAMBOO STICK
1034. AGARBATTI SYNTHETIC PERFUMERY COMPOUND
1035. AIR FRESHNER (ODONIL TYPE)
1036. AIR TAXI
1037. AMUSEMENT PARK
1038. ANODIC ALUMINIUM LABEL
1039. AQUACULTURE PRAWN FARMING (100% EOU)
1040. AQUA CULTURE SHRIMP FARMING (100% EOU)
1041. ARTIFICIAL FLOWERS
1042. ARTIFICIAL JEWELLERY
1043. ASBESTOS YARN
1044. ASH TRAYS FOR MARUTI VEHICLE
1045. AIR BUBBLE PACKAGING
1046. ASPHALTIC ROOFING SHEET (METAL COMPONENTS)
1047. AUTOMATIC BOOK BINDING
1048. ALKYD RESIN
1049. APPLE JUICE CONCENTRATE
1050. BALL POINT PEN FEFILLS (JOTTER TYPE)
1051. BANK BRANCH BUILDING
1052. BANQUET HALL
1053. BIO-COAL BRIQUETTES FROM AGRICULTURAL CELLULOSE WASTE
1054. BOOT CREAM/POLISH
1055. BUFFING & POLISHING COMPOUND
1056. BRASS BADGES BY ETCHING
1057. BRIQUETTED FUEL FROM AGRO WASTE
1058. BRIQUETTING OF LIGNITE COAL

Above all the Detailed Project Reports are available at *"ENGINEERS INDIA RESEARCH INSTITUTE"*. 4449, Nai Sarak (D), Main Road Delhi - 110 006
• Ph : 91-11-23918117, 2391 6431, 23840361, 31082370 • Fax : 91-11-2391 6431
• E-Mail : eirisidi@bol.net.in

1059. BUFFALO HORN TIP, HOOF
1060. BANQUET HALL
1061. BUTTON
1062. CALCINED PETROLEUM (C.P) COKE
1063. CANVAS SHOES
1064. CANVAS SHOES, JUNGLE BOOTS
1065. CARBON BRUSH, BRUSH HOLDER & SLIP RING
1066. CEMENT SHEETS WITH COIR FIBRE & OTHER SEGMENTS
1067. CERAMIC TILES (GLAZED) BY DOUBLE FIRING/HEATING
1068. CHILDREN RECREATION CENTRE
1069. COAL BRIQUETTES
1070. COLD STORAGE & ICE
1071. COLD STORAGE FOR FRUITS AND VEGETABLES
1072. COMPRESSOR (HERMETIC) FOR AIR CONDITIONER
1073. COSTUME JEWELLERY/ IMITATION JEWELLERY
1074. DECORATIVE LAMINATED SHEET (SUNMICA)
1075. DIAMOND CUTTING & EXPORTS
1076. DRINKING STRAW FROM PROPYLENE
1077. ENGINEERING COLLEGE
1078. ENTERTAINMENT CLUB
1079. FASHION TECHNOLOGY INSTITUTE
1080. FAST FOOD PARLOUR
1081. FAST FOOD (INSTANT FOOD & FAST FOOD PARLOUR)
1082. FIRE EXTINGUISHERS (SODA ACID TYPE)
1083. FISH NET
1084. FLORICULTURE (CUT FLOWER ROSE) WITH GREEN HOUSE
1085. FLOOR COVERING SHEET
1086. FILM STUDIO (VIDEO)
1087. FLUSH DOOR, CHIP BOARD, WOOD WOOL & OTHER INSULATING BOARDS
1088. GAS DETECTORS OF L.P.G
1089. GEMS MANUFACTURING
1090. GLASS BOTTLE BY SCRAP
1092. GOAT & SHEEP FARMING
1093. GOLD ELECTROPLATING
1094. GOLD JEWELLERY (E.O.U)
1095. GOLD PLATED SILVER JEWELLERY & CUTLERY
1096. GRANITE SLAB AND TILES
1097. GREEN HOUSE
1098. HARD CHROMIUM PLATING
1099. HEALTH CLUB AND BEAUTY PARLOUR CUM HAIR SALOON WITH SONA BATH
1100. HEALTH CLUB CUM BEAUTY PARLOUR TRAININGINSTITUTE
1101. HORN TIP,HOOVE BUTTON
1102. HOSPITAL
1103. HOSPITAL (100 BEDS)
1104. HOSPITAL (200 BEDS)
1105. ICE MAKING PLANT
1106. IMITATION AND COSTUME
1107. JEWELLERY (NECKLACE, EARRINGS EAR TOP ETC.)
1108. INITMATE SCENT CHEMICALS FROM ALL TYPES OF FLAVOUR
1109. INVESTMENT CASTING
1110. JUTE, COIR, GLASS ROPE/ SUTLI
1111. JUTE TWINE
1112. L.P.G BOTTLING PLANT
1113. L.P.G REGULATOR (DOMESTIC PURPOSE)
1114. LAMINATED PARTICLE BOARD & HARD BOARD
1115. LAMINATED SAFETY AND TOUGHENED GLASS
1116. LEASING & HIRE PURCHASE
1117. LICHEN (CHARILA)
1118. MANILA ROPES
1119. MEDICAL COLLEGE
1120. MATCH UNIT FROM WAXED PAPER
1121. MEDIUM DENSITY FIBRE BOARD
1122. MELAMINE CROCKERY
1123. MINERAL WATER
1124. MINI CEMENT PLANT
1125. MIRROR SILVER, GOLDEN, PINK, BLACK & SMOKES
1126. MODERN ADVERTISING AGENCY WITH DTP & FILM STUDIO
1127. MOTEL/SMALL HOTEL
1128. MULTI COLOUR PRINTING
1129. MULTI STOREY COMMERCIAL COMPLEX ALONGWITH RESIDENTIAL AND DELUX FLATS FOR FOREIGN TOURISTS & REVOLVING RESTAURENT AT THE TOP
1130. MULTIPLE LAMINATION INDUSTRY
1131. MUSHROOM GROWING AND PROCESSING (BY DEEP FREEZING METHOD)
1132. NEWS PAPER PRINTING
1133. NICKEL LINED INDUSTRIAL SCREEN
1134. OFFSET COLOUR PRINTING PRESS (SIX COLOUR)
1135. OFFSET PRINTING PRESS
1136. P.C.C ELECTRIC POLES
1137. PHOTOGRAPHIC DEVELOPER & FIXER
1138. PVC EXTRUSION PROFILE (DOOR & WINDOWS)
1139. POP-CORN
1140. PHOTO ETCHING OF S.S.
1141. PRE STRESSED CEMENT CONCRETE PIPES
1142. PILFER PROOF CAPS
1143. PILFER PROOF CAPS AND CROWN CAP
1144. POUCH MAKING & GRAVURE PRINTING (ROTO PRINTING)
1145. POULTRY & FISH FARMING (INTEGERATED UNIT)
1146. PRINTING OF TIN SHEETS
1147. READYMADE GARMENTS
1148. RESTAURANT
1149. ROSE PLANTATION AND ROSE OIL EXTRACTION
1150. ROTOGRAVURE PRINTING
1151. SAFETY BELTS
1152. SAFETY MATCHES
1153. SHOE LACES
1154. SILK COCOON CULTIVATION (GROWING OF SILK COCOON WARM)
1155. SILK SCREEN PRINTING FORMULATIONS FOR PLASTIC, PAPER & CLOTH
1156. SPIKENARD (JATAMANSI)
1157. STENCIL COATING SOLUTION
1158. SUGAR CANDY (MISRI)
1159. SUGAR CANE PLANTATION
1160. SUGAR CANE JUICE PRESERVATION
1161. SURAT ZARI
1162. SYNTHETIC SHOES & SOLES
1163. TEA PACKAGING INDUSTRY
1164. TENNIS BALLS
1165. THREE STAR HOTEL
1166. TRAVELLING AGENCY
1167. TRAYS, TROLLEYS FOR HOSPITAL WITH SCRATCHLESS COATING
1168. WAX EXTRACTS (TANNING POWDER)
1169. WIRE ROPE SLINGS
1170. WOOD WOOL SLAB
1171. WOODEN CANE FURNITURE WITH EXPORT POTENTIAL
1172. WOODEN FURNITURE
1173. WOODEN PANEL INCLUDING KILN SEASONING
1174. WOODEN FURNITURE
1175. WATCH CASE BUFFING
1176. WATCH DIAL
1177. WRIST WATCHES
1178. WATCHES (ELECTRONIC)
1179. ZEDOARY (KACHUR)

EDIBLE OILS, ESSENTIAL OILS LURICATIING OILS, GREASES, VEGETABLE OILS, WAXES, CAMPHOR, PERFUMES & PERFUMERY COMPOUNDS AND REFINED OILS ETC.

1180. AROMATIC PERFUMERY COMPOUND
1181. AEROSOL
1182. AGARBATTI PERFUMERY COMPOUND
1183. BEES WAX MANUFACTURE
1184. CAMPHOR
1185. CARDANOL FROM CASHEW NUT SHELL LIQUID
1186. CASTOR OIL
1187. CASTOR OIL DERIVATIVE OLEORESINS
1188. CHILLI OIL
1189. CITRONELLA OILS
1190. CLOVE OIL
1191. CONCENTRATE OF ROSE JASMINE & LILY ETC.
1192. COLOURED FLAME CANDLE

1193. CANDLES (SEMI-AUTOMATIC)
1194. CORN OIL (MAIZE OIL)
1195. DEHYDRATED CASTOR OIL
1196. EUGENOL FROM CINNAMON LEAF OIL
1197. EXTRACTION OF ESSENTIAL OIL (CARDAMON, JEERA, AJOWAN, GINGER OILS ETC. & PACKAGING OF GROUND SPICES)
1198. EXTRACTION OF JASMINE ESSENCE
1199. EXTRACTION OF ESSENTIAL OILS BY SUPER CRITICAL FLUID METHOD FROM FLOWERS, HERBS & SPICES
1200. EUCALYPTUS OIL
1201. EXTRACTION OF OIL FROM OIL SEED EXPANDEREXTRUSION TECHNOLOGY)
1202. FAT LIQUOR SULPHATED OIL
1203. FLAVOURS FOR FOOD
1204. GARLIC OIL & POWDER
1205. GINGER OIL, SANDALWOOD OIL AND NAGARMOTHA OIL
1206. GINGER OIL
1207. GINGER OIL & GINGER DUST
1208. INTEGERATED WAX COMPLEX
1209. IONONE FROM LEMON GRASS OIL
1210. JASMINE & LILLY FLOWER OIL
1211. LEMON GRASS OIL
1212. LIQUID PARAFFIN
1213. LUBE OIL & GREASE
1214. LUBRICATING OIL
1215. MENTHOL CRYSTALS
1216. MENTHOL OIL & CRYSTAL
1217. MICRO CRYSTALLINE WAX
1218. MUSTARD OIL (EDIBLE OIL)
1219. OIL FROM ARTEMISIA HERBS
1220. PALM OIL CRUSHING UNIT
1221. PAN MASALA
1222. PARAFFIN WAX
1223. PARAFFIN WAX FROM SLACK WAX
1224. REFINED OIL-SUN FLOWER OIL, GROUNDNUT OIL, STAFF FLOWER OIL & COTTON SEED OIL
1225. REFINED VEGETABLE OIL
1226. RECLAMATION OF USED ENGINE OIL
1227. RICE BRAN OIL (R.B.O)
1228. ROSE OIL EXTRACTION
1229. SMOKE LESS CANDLE
1230. SPICE OIL & OLEORESINS
1231. SOLVENT EXTRACTION PLANT (OIL CAKE BASED)
1232. SYNTHETIC ALMOND OIL
1233. SYNTHETIC TALLOW
1234. SYNTHETIC GHEE
1235. VEGETABLE OIL EXTRACTION & REFINING
1236. WADDING OIL (100%) FOR WADDING OF COTTON HOSIERY CLOTH IN DYEING PROCESS
1237. WAX EMULSION FOR TEXTILE
1238. WAX FLOOR POLISH

PAINT, ENAMEL, SOLVENTS, THINNERS, INKS & VARNISH

1239. ACRYLIC EMULSION PAINTS
1240. ALUMINIUM PAINT
1241. AUTOMOBILE PAINTS
1242. BALL POINT PEN REFILL INK
1243. BITUMINIOUS ROAD EMULSION
1244. BITUMEN
1245. BITUMINIOUS FELTS FOR WATER & DAMP PROOFING
1246. BITUMINIOUS ROAD EMULSION RAPID MEDIUM & SLOW SETTING
1247. BUFFING & POLISHING
1248. CEMENT PAINT FOR WHITE & GREY CEMENT

1249. DISPERSANT
1250. DRY DISTEMPER
1251. DRY DISTEMPER & CEMENT PAINT
1252. DUPLICATING INK BLACK FOR GESTNER DUPLICATOR
1255. EMULSION PAINTS (WATER BASED)
1256. HAMMERTONE PAINT
1257. INSULATING VARNISH & WIRE ENAMEL
1258. IRON OXIDE PIGMENTS
1259. INSULATING VARNISH (POLY VINYL BUTYRAL BASED, FFC GRADE)
1260. LIME COLOUR (CEMENT COLOUR)
1261. SYNTHETIC RED OXIDE FOR FLOORINGS
1262. SOLVENT & THINNERS
1263. MARKING INKS (WATER PROOF)
1264. METAL NAPHTHANATE (AS DRIER FOR PAINTS)
1265. N.C.PUTTY
1266. OFFSET PRINTING INK
1267. OIL BOUND DISTEMPER PAINT
1268. PAINT BRUSHES
1269. PAINT REMOVERS
1270. PAINT INDUSTRY
1271. PAINT & VARNISH
1272. PICTURE VARNISH
1273. POWDER COATING PAINT
1274. PRINTING INKS (OFFSET, FLEXO & ROTO GRAVURE)
1275. PRIMER PAINT & ENAMEL PAINT
1276. PUTTY & WATER PROOFING PAINT
1277. PRINTING INKS (FLEXO-GRAPHIC INK)
1278. PUTTY (METAL CASEMENT)
1279. RED OXIDE PRIMER (ANTI CORROSIVE)
1280. REFRECTORY PAINT (GRAPHITE BASED)
1281. SCREEN PRINTING INKS
1282. SILK SCREEN PRINTING INK FORMULATION FOR PLASTIC, PAPER, CLOTH
1283. STAMP & PAD INK
1284. STOVING PAINT
1285. SPIRIT SOLUBLE MALEIC RESIN
1286. TEXTURE PAINT
1287. THINNERS AND ITS ALLIED PRODUCTS
1288. TONER INK
1289. VARNISH THINNER (SOLVENT)
1290. VACUUM METALLIZING LACQUERS
1291. WOOD PRIMER

PHARMACEUTICAL, DRUGS, AYURVEDIC/HERBAL COSMETICS & MEDICINES, HOMOEOPATHIC MEDICINES, DISPOSABLE SYRINGE, DENTAL COLLEGE & FINE CHEMICALS ETC.

1292. AROMATIC PILLS
1293. ASPIRIN
1294. AYURVEDIC PAIN BALM OINTMENTS
1295. AYURVEDIC CHURAN AND TABLETS
1296. AYURVEDIC TABLETS (HAJMOLA TYPE)
1297. AYURVEDIC/HERBAL PHARMACY
1298. AYURVEDIC SHERBATS
1299. AYURVEDIC PRODUCTS
1300. BULK DRUGS (E.O.U)
1301. BLOOD BAGS
1302. CALCIUM GLUCONATE
1303. CAPSULE, TABLET & INJECTION WITH MODERN INSTRUMENTS
1304. CASHEW FENI
1305. CHLOROQUINONE PHOSPHATE (BULK DRUGS)
1306. CLINICAL THERMOMETER
1307. DENTAL CLINIC

1308. DENTAL COLLEGE
1309. DENTAL GRADE EUGENOL
1310. DEXTROSE MONOHYDRATE, LIQUID GLUCOSE
1311. DEHYDRATED ONION & ONION POWDER
1312. DEXTROSE POWDER (ANHYDROUS FROM STARCH)
1314. DEXTROSE SALINE SOLUTION
1315. DISTILLERY (I.M.F.L)
1316. DISPOSABLE NEEDLES FOR SYRINGES
1317. DISPRIN
1318. DISTILLED WATER
1319. EMPTY HARD GELATINE CAPSULES
1320. FILLING & PACKING OF CAPSULES
1321. GLUCOSE - D - POWDER
1322. GLYCERINE
1323. HERBAL COSMETICS
1324. HERBAL SHAMPOO
1325. HERBAL HAIR OILS (AYURVEDIC)
1326. HOMOE & BIO-MEDICINES WITH MOTHER TINCTURE
1327. HOMOEPATHIC MEDICINES
1328. HYPODERMIC NEEDLES
1329. I.V. FLUIDS
1330. IBUPROFEN
1331. INFUSION & TRANSFUSION SETS (I.V. SET)
1332. INJECTABLE FOR PHARMACEUTICALS
1333. INJECTION AMPOULES PACKAGING BOX
1334. INTEGERATED SURGICAL COTTON
1335. ICE MAKING PLANT
1336. ICE & COLD STORAGE
1337. LACTOSE & BY PRODUCTS PROCESSING FROM MILK
1338. LICHEN (JATAMANSI CHARILA)
1339. LIQUID GLUCOSE AND ITS BY-PRODUCTS
1340. L-LYSINE MONOHYDRO CHLORIDE
1341. LIQUID GLUCOSE FROM POTATOES
1342. MEDICAL COLLEGE
1343. NICOTINE FROM TOBACCO WASTE
1344. OINTMENT-AYURVEDIC (YELLOW & WHITE)
1345. PHARMACEUTICAL AND FOOD GRADE GELATINE
1346. PHARMACEUTICAL INDUSTRY (TABLETS, CAPSULES, LIQUID, GEL, OINTMENT POWDER INJECTABLE)
1347. PHARMACEUTICAL UNIT (EOU) WITH FORMULA TIONS, INJECTABLES, ETC. PYRIDINE & DERIVATIVES
1348. SALT (IODIZED SALT)
1349. SALINE & INJECTION WATER
1350. SALINE WATER & DEXTROSE SOLUTION (I.V.FLUID IN PLASTIC BOTTLES)
1351. SORBITOL
1352. STARCH (MAIZE)
1353. SURGICAL ADHESIVE PLASTER
1354. SURGICAL BANDAGES
1355. SURGICAL GLOVES
1357. SURGICAL COTTON
1358. SURGICAL COTTON AND BANDAGE
1359. SYNTHETIC CAMPHOR POWDER
1360. TABLETS & CAPSULES
1361. TISSUE CULTURE
1362. TINCTURE FROM RECTIFIED SPIRIT
1363. TRIMETHOPIME
1364. VETERENARY MEDICINES (ONLY FORMULATIONS)
1365. VITAMIN 'C', SORBITOL' ANHYDROUS DEXTROSE, STARCH

PULP, PAPER, STRAW/GREY BOARD, KRAFT PAPER, PACKAGING, PAPER CARRY BAGE, PAPER FROM AGRO WASTE & STATIONERY ETC.

1366. AMMONIA PAPER
1367. AUTOMATIC BOOK BINDING
1368. ADHESIVE (FEVICOL TYPE)
1369. ALL PIN & GEM CLIPS
1370. CARBON PAPER
1371. CARD BOARD
1372. CARBON LESS PAPER
1373. CELLPHANE PAPER
1374. COMPUTER FORMS & SECURITY PRINTING PRESS
1375. CORRUGATED BOARD & BOX (PRINTED & LAMINATED)
1376. CORRUGATED BOARD AND BOXES FROM FROM CARD BOARDS
1377. CORRUGATED CARTONS FROM PLAIN PAPERS
1378. CORRUGATRED PACKING & MATERIAL (BULB & TUBES PACKING)
1379. DESK TOP PUBLISHING
1380. DEFOAMING AGENT FOR PAPER PLANT
1381. DRINKING STRAW PAPER
1382. D.T.P CUM OFFSET PRESS
1383. EGG TRAYS
1384. EXERCISE NOTE BOOK, REGISTER AND PAD
1385. FLEXOGRAPHIC INK
1386. GREETING CARD BY OFFSET PRESS
1387. HAND MADE PAPER FILTER PAPER
1388. HARD BOARD
1389. INJECTION AMPOULES PACKAGING BOXES
1390. INSULATIING PAPER
1391. KRAFT PAPER
1392. KRAFT PAPER FROM BAGASSE
1393. LAMINATED PACKAGING PAPER WITH PRINTING
1394. LAMINATION & COATING ON PAPER
1395. M.G. PAPER FROM WASTE PAPER
1396. MILL PAPER FROM WASTE PAPER
1397. MILL BOARD FROM RICE & WHEAT STRAWS
1398. MILL BOARD FROM WASTE PAPER
1399. MINI PAPER PLANT FROM SISAL
1400. MINI PAPER PLANT
1401. MULTI WALL PAPER SACKS
1402. NEWS PAPER FOR CHILDREN
1403. NEWS PRINT PAPER FROM RICE STRAW BAGASSE
1404. NEWS PAPER CHILDRENS
1405. NEWS PRINT PAPER
1406. OFFSET AND TREADLE TYPE PRINTING PRESS
1407. MILL BOARD BASED ON RICE STRAW
1408. PAPER AND BOARD FROM STRAW
1409. PAPER & PAPER PRODUCTS
1410. PAPER ENVELOPES
1411. PAPER CARRY BAGS
1412. PAPER BOARD CARTON
1413. PAPER CONES FOR LOUD SPEAKERS
1414. PAPER FROM AKRA
1415. PAPER FROM BAGASSE WITH CORRUGATED BOARD & BOXES
1416. PAPER FROM BAMBOO
1417. PAPER GLASSES FOR BEVERAGES
1418. PAPER FROM RICE HUSK & WHEAT HUSK
1419. PAPER FROM TREE BARK, EUCALYPRUS WOOD
1420. PAPER PRODUCTS
1421. PAPER PLANT (WHITE WRITING & NEWS PAPER FOR PULP & WASTE PAPER)
1422. PAPER PLATES, PAPER GLASS
1423. PAPER CONES & TUBES
1425. PAPER PLANT WITH DTP & PRINTING & PUBLISHING UNIT
1426. PAPER BASED PHENOLIC SHEET
1427. PAPER CUP FOR ICE CREAM
1428. PAPER TUBES SPIRAL WINDING COMPOSIT CONTAINER
1429. PAPER LABLE FOR BEER BOTTLES
1430. PARTICLE BOARD & BLACK BOARD WITH SANDING & LAMINATION OF PARTICLE BOARD
1431. PARTICLE BOARD FROM RICE HUSK
1432. POUCH FILLING & MAKING FOR TOMATO SAUCE
1433. POUCH MAKING &

GRAVURE PRINTING
1434. PROCESSING OF PAPER FOR FEEDING IN COMPUTER
1435. PULP FROM BAMBOO & WOOD
1436. PAPER FILES
1437. PLAYING CARDS
1438. ROSIN SIZING AGENT (FOR PAPER PLANT)
1439. SAND PAPER
1440. SANITRY NAPKINS
1441. SILICON COATED PAPER
1442. STENCIL PAPER
1443. STRAW BOARD AND GREY BOARD
1444. STRAW BOARD & MILL BOARD
1445. STRAW BOARD AND PAPER BOARD
1446. TISSUE PAPER FACIAL
1447. TISSUE MOIST TOILETERY CLEANSING TISSUE AND RELATED PRODUCTS
1448. TISSUE PAPER ROLLS
1449. TETRA PACK FOR MILK PACKAGING, GHEE & OTHER LIQUIDS
1450. TOILET PAPER ROLLS
1451. TOILET PAPER & NAPKINS
1452. WAX COATED PRINTED PAPER
1453. WET FACE FRESHNER TISSUE
1454. WHITE WRITING & PRINTING PAPER
1455. WRITING & PRINTING PAPER (PAPER MILLS)

PLASTIC, B.O.P.P, ACRYLIC, DISPOSABLE PLASTIC PRODUCTS, PET PRODUCTS, P.V.C, H.D.P.E, P.P, L.D.P.E., P.U, A.B.S, THERMOFOARMING, MASTER BATCHES, & POLYMER AND RUBBER PRODUCTS, TYRE, TUBE, ADHESIVE, SHEET, COIR & MANY OTHERS

1456. ABS GRANULES FROM ABS SCRAPS FROM OLD T.V. CABINETS, WHITE GOODS ETC.
1457. ACRYLIC BEADS
1458. ACRYLIC COPOLYMER EMULSION
1459. ACRYLIC LATEX
1460. ACRYLIC SHEET
1461. ACRYLIC SHEET & MOULDED PRODUCTS
1462. ACRYLIC TEETH
1463. AUTO TUBES
1464. AUTO FLAPS FOR TRUCKS & BUSES
1465. AUTO TYRES & TUBES
1466. BABY BOTTLES (PLASTIC) WITH WHITESILICON RUBBER NIPPLES
1467. B.O.P.P. FILM
1468. B.O.P.P. PRESSURE SENSITIVE SELF ADHESIVE TAPE
1469. BABY NIPPLE (SILICON)
1470. BABY NIPPLE (BIG SIZE)
1471. BALLOON PLASTIC ADVERTISING
1472. BLISTER FILM PVC
1473. BLISTER PACKAGING & POUCH PAKAGING
1474. BLOW MOULDING PLASTIC CONTAINER
1475. COATING ON METALIZED POLYESTER FILM/METALISED PAPER/ ALIMINIUM FOIL
1476. COATING ON PLASTIC (ELECTROLYSIS) & GLASS
1477. COIR FOAM (RUBBERISED)
1478. COLOUR COATING ON PLASTICS
1479. COLOUR MASTER BATCHES FOR VARIOUS PLASTICS
1480. CYCLE TYRES AND TUBES
1481. DISPOSABLE PLASTIC CUPS GLASSES, ETC.
1482. DISPOSABLE PLASTIC SYRINGES & NEEDLES
1483. DISPOSABLE PLASTIC SYRINGES
1484. DOUGH MOULDING COMPOUND (D.M.C)
1485. EPOXY RESIN
1486. EXPANDED POLYESTRENE MOULDING (THERMOCOLE)
1487. F.R.P AUTO, SCOOTER ROOFS & CEILINGS
1488. F.R.P PRODUCTS (HELMET, WASHBASIN SHEETS, ROOFING SHEETS)
1489. FIBRE REINFORCED PLASTIC (HIGH PRESSURE MOULDING WITH SMC BMC AND DMC)
1490. FIELD RUBBER CONVERTED TO THE 60% LATEX RUBBER
1491. FLEXIBLE P.U. FOAM
1492. FORMALDEHYDE CROCKERY & OTHER ITEMS
1493. FORMALDEHYDE RESIN (UREA, PHENOL, MELEMINE)
1494. GASKET SHEET
1495. GUM BOTTLE (PVC)
1496. GLASS BEADS
1497. HDPE COATED PAPER SACK
1498. H.D.P.E. BAGS
1499. H.D.P.E. CONTAINERS (BLOW MOULDING)
1500. H.D.P.E. CONTAINER, POLY JARS BY INJECTION MOULDING (FOOD GRADE)
1501. H.D.P.E. JERRY CANS
1502. HDPE MANUFACTURING FROM ETHYLALCOHOL
1503. H.D.P.E PIPE AND FITTINGS
1504. H.D.P.E. PIPES
1505. H.D.P.E PRINTED BAGS
1506. H.D.P.E TWINES AND ROPES
1507. H.D.P.E. & L.D.P.E PIPES AND FITTINGS
1508. H.D.P.E/PP BOX STRAPPING
1509. H.D.P.E/PP WOVEN SACKS USING PLAIN LOOMS
1510. HOLOGRAM STICKERS-3D
1511. H.M BAG PLANT WITH PRINTING UNIT
1512. HAWAI CHAPPALS (RUBBER)
1513. I.V PLASTIC BOTTLE
1514. ICE CREAM CUP (PLASTIC)
1515. INJECTION MOULDED AUTO COMPONENTS
1516. INJECTION & BLOW MOULDED PLASTIC PRODUCTS
1517. INJECTION MOULDED PLASTIC PRODUCTS
1518. INTEGERATED COMPLEX ESTER'S & ALLIED PRODUCTS (D.O.P, D.B.P, & ETHYL ACETATE, BUYTL ACETATE, WIRE ENAMELS, JELLY CABLE COMPOUND)
1519. L.D.P.E. (LOW DENSITY POLY ETHYLENE) GRANULES FROM VIRGIN (L.D.P.E. RESIN)
1520. INTEGERATED SURGICAL RUBBER GOODS INDUSTRY
1521. INJECTION MOULDED PLASTIC BALLS
1522. L.D.P.E FROM ETHYL ALCOHOL
1523. LDPE MOULDED PRODUCTS
1524. LAMINATION OF COEXTRUSION MULTILAYER FILM IN ROLL FORM
1525. LATEX RUBBER
1526. LATEX RUBBER CONDOM
1527. MASTER BATCHES (COLOURED, P.V.C, L.D.P.E, H.D.P.E, ETC.)
1528. MELAMINE FORMALHYDE RESIN
1529. MOULDED LUGGAGE
1530. MULTI-LAYER (3 LAYER BAGS)
1531. MULTI-LAYER (3 LAYER) FILM WITH LAMINATION & PRINTING
1532. OIL SEAL
1533. PET BOTTLE/CONTAINERS
1534. PET BOTTLES FROM PRE FORM
1535. PET BOTTLE & MINERAL WATER
1536. PET PRE-FORM FROM PET RESIN
1537. PET PRE-FORM CUM PET BOTTLES
1538. PET PRE-FORM PET BOTTLES CUM MINERAL WATERS
1539. POLY CARBONATE RESIN
1540. PTFE COMPONENTS
1541. PU/PVC SOLE FOR SPORT SHOE BY IMPORTED M/C.
1542. PVC BATTERY SEPARATOR
1543. P.V.C COMPOUNDS (FRESH)
1544. P.V.C COMPOUNDS (SCRAP)
1545. P.V.C ELECTRICAL INSULATING TAPE
1546. P.V.C. EXTRUSION PROFILES
1547. P.V.C FITTINGS
1548. P.V.C FLEXIBLE FUSIBLE POWDER HEAT FUSIBLE POWDER
1549. P.V.C GRANULES (FOR

INSULATION & SHEETS GRADES)
1550. P.V.C GRANULES FROM PVC SCRAPS (WITH POLLUTION CONTROL)
1551. P.V.C HOSES
1552. P.V.C LEATHER CLOTH
1553. P.V.C FLEXIBLE PIPES
1554. P.V.C PIPES AND FITTINGS
1555. POLYTHENE BAGS (PRINTED)
1556. PVC PLASTICS FILM SHEET SOFT/RIGID
1557. PVC RESIN AND COMPOUND
1558. PVC RULAR
1559. PVC STABLIZERS (SINGLE PACK SYSTEM)
1560. PVC WIRE AND CABLES
1561. PAPER BASED PHENOLIC SHEET FOR ELECTRICAL
1562. PHENOL FORMALDEHYDE RESIN
1563. PHENOLIC RESIN
1564. PLASTIC BEADS FROM PLASTIC SCRAPS
1565. PLASTIC BUTTONS
1566. PLASTIC CANS
1567. PLASTIC COLLAPSIBLE TUBE
1568. PLASTIC CORRUGATED SHEET & BOXES
1569. PLASTIC FILM AND SHEETS WITH PRINTING FLEXO & ROTO/LDPE/HDPE/PP/HM/PVC
1570. PLASTIC FILTER MASTER BATCH & OTHER MASTER BATCHES FOR VARIOUS PLASTICS
1571. PLASTIC JERRY CANS
1572. PLASTIC GRANULES OR POWDER FROM PLASTIC SCRAP
1573. PLASTIC INJECTION MOULDED T.V. CABINETS
1574. PLASTIC ITEMS MANUFAC TURE FROM POWDER MELAMINE
1575. PLASTIC GOODS
1576. PLASTIC PIPES & TARPAULINES
1577. PLASTIC SHEET FROM SCRAP
1578. PLASTIC PLANT (BLOW MOULDING & INJECTION MOULDING)
1579. PLASTIC PRODUCTS (GOLD, SILVER, NICKEL)
1580. PLASTIC TOYS
1581. POLYESTER BEADING
1582. POLYESTER FILM
1583. POLYTHENE BAGS & AUTOMATIC PRINTING
1584. POLYTHENE PRINTED BAGS
1585. POLYURETHANE FOAM AND ITS PRODUCTS
1586. PROPYLENE FILM (PRINTED) & BAG MANUFACTURING
1587. PLASTIC MATS
1588. RAINBOW COLOUR ON PVC FILM & SHEET
1589. RED MUD PVC PIPES AND FITTINGS
1590. RE-RUBBERISED OF SOLID TYPE
1591. RESIN COATED SAND REXINE
1592. REXINE CLOTH & ALLIED PRODUCTS
1593. RUBBER ADHESIVE
1594. RUBBER AUTO PARTS
1595. RUBBER BELTING
1596. RUBBER MOULDING UNIT INCLUDING LINING RUBBER SHEETING
1597. RUBBER RECLAIMING
1598. RUBBER ROLLERS FOR TEXTILE MILLS & PAPER INDUSTRIES
1599. RUBBER & PLASTIC SHEETS. MATS & FLAPS
1600. RUBBER SHEET AND ALLIED HOSPITAL RUBBER GOODS
1601. RUBBERIZED PVC GASKET
1602. RUBBERISED COIR
1603. RUBBER COMPOUND FOR AUTOMOBILES
1604. SAFETY BELTS
1605. SILVER AND GOLD PLATING ON PVC AND NYLON-6
1606. SILICONE RUBBER NIPPLES/ TEATS
1607. SPECTACLE FRAMES (PLASTIC)
1608. SPUNGE RUBBER
1609. SURGICAL EXAMINATION GLOVES
1610. SYNTHETIC PEARL COATING ON POLYSTYRENE BEADS
1611. SYNTHETIC RUBBER ADHESIVE
1612. TEFLON MANUFACTURING
1613. TEFLON TAPE
1614. TEFLON TAPES & CABLES
1615. THERMOCOLE SHEET AND MOULDED PRODUCTS EXPANDED POLYESTERENE EXTRUSION PROFILES
1616. THERMOFORMED PACKAGING (BLISTER PACKAGING & POUCH PACKAGING)
1617. THERMOPLASTIC POLYURETHANE
1618. THERMOFORMED CUPS, PLATES & GLASS WITH HIPS SHEET
1619. THERMOCOLE
1620. THERMOCOLE BASED DISPOSABLE GLASS, CUPS & PLATES
1621. TOOTH BRUSHES
1622. TOY BALLOON, DECORA TIVE & INDUSTRIAL BALLOONS
1623. TREAD RUBBER
1624. TYRE RETREADING (HOT)
1625. TYRE RETREADING BY COLD PROCESS
1626. TYRE TUBES & FLAPS
1627. TYRE & TUBES
1628. UNSATURATED POLYESTER FOR REXINE
1629. V-BELT AND FAN BELT
1630. VINYL ASBESTOS AND PVC WALL PAPER
1631. VITON (FLUORO ELASTOMER)

SOAP, COSMETICS & PERFUMS

1632. ACID SLURRY, SYNTHETIC DETERGENT POWDER
1632. ACID SLURRY
1633. AGARBATTI SYNTHETIC, PERFUMERY COMPOUND
1634. AFTER SHAVE LOTION
1635. ANTISEPTIC CREAM
1636. BETA IONONE
1637. BLEACHING POWDER
1638. BLUE DETERGENT POWDER
1639. CLEANING POWDER (VIMTYPE)
1640. COLD CREAM
1641. COLOURED FLAME & PERFUMED CANDLES (RED, BLUE, GREEN FLAME)
1642. COSMETIC INDUSTRY (MODERN)
1643. COSMETIC INDUSTRY (SHAMPOO, SPRAY PERFUME, TALCUM POWDER
1644. DETERGENT POWDER (ARIEL TYPE)
1645. DETERGENT POWDER (NIRMA TYPE) FULLY AUTOMATIC PLANT
1646. DETERGENT WASHING POWDER
1647. FISH OIL SOAP
1648. GLYCERINE TRANSPARENT SOAP
1649. HAIR REMOVING CREAM
1650. HERBAL COSMETICS
1651. HERBAL SHAMPO & CREAM
1652. HERBAL/AYURVEDIC COSMETICS
1653. INCENSE POWDER, INCENSE STICKS & INCENSE CAKE
1654. OPTICAL WHITENERS
1655. ROSE OIL EXTRACTION
1656. SHAMPOOS (COCONUT OIL BASED COLD PROCESS)
1657. SHAVING CREAM
1658. SINDUR (KUMKUM)
1659. SOAP COATED PAPER
1660. SPRAY DRIED DETERGENT POWDER
1661. STAIN REMOVER
1662. TALCUM POWDER (FACE & TOILET POWDER)
1663. TOILET AND HERBAL SOAP
1664. TOOTH PASTE & POWDER
1665. WASHING DETERGENT POWDER AND WASHING SOAP
1666. WASHING POWDER LIQUID DETERGENTS, LOTION & SHAMPOO

TEXTILE INDUSTRIES, READYMADE GARMENTS, COTTON, DYEING, BLEACHING, CLOTH, HOSIERY, POWER LOOM, HAND LOOM, WOOLLEN, SILK, SOCKS, SURGICAL COTTON & MANY OTHERS

1667. ANGORA RABBIT WOOL
1668. BUCKRAM
1669. CANVAS SHOES, JUNGLE BOOT, BOOT RUBBER KNEES & BOOT COMBAT
1670. CARPET FROM COTTON WASTE
1671. CERAMIC THREAD GUIDE
1672. COTTON BUDS/SWABS
1673. COTTON FROM WASTE YARN
1674. COTTON ROLLS
1675. COTTON SPIDERS FOR LOUD SPEAKERS
1676. DENIM CLOTH
1677. DENIM CLOTH (INTEGERATED UNIT WITH BLEACHING, DYEING AND PRINTING)
1678. DISPERSENT FOR TEXTILE
1679. DYEING & BLEACHING
1680. DYEING OF HANK YARN
1681. EMULSIFIER FOR WOOL BATCHING OIL
1682. EMBROIDERY ON FABRICS
1683. GARMENT DYEING, WASHING & STITCHING (JEANS, JACKETS, SKIRTS & SHIRTS)
1684. GOVES KNITTING
1685. GUNNY BAGS
1687. HDPE WOVEN SACKS
1688. HDPE TARPAULINS USING PLAIN LOOM WITH LAMINATION
1689. HDPE/PP WOVEN SACKS USING CIRCULAR LOOMS
1690. HOSIERY CLOTH (COTTON) PROCESSING (BLEACHING, DYEING, FINISHING OF CLOTH)
1691. HOSIERY INDUSTRY
1692. HOSIERY MERCERISING
1693. HOSIERY PRODUCTS LIKE VEST, BRIEF, T-SHIRTS & SOCKS
1694. JACQUARD FABRICS
1695. JUTE COIR, GRASS ROPE/ SUTLI MAKING
1696. JUTE FELT
1697. JUTE TWINES
1698. KNITTED FABRICS
1699. LAMINATED JUTE BAGS
1700. LAMINATION OF HDPE WOVEN CLOTH (JUTE,COTTON, PAPER)
1701. NYLON YARN CRIMPING, DOUBLING AND BLEACHING
1702. PIGMENT BINDER FOR TEXTILE PRINTING
1704. POLYESTER RESIN FOR WIRE ENAMEL
1705. POLYESTER RESIN
1706. POLYESTER YARN FROM WASTE POLYESTER ZIP FASTENERS
1707. POWER LOOM
1708. READYMADE GARMENTS & HOSIERY
1709. READYMADE GARMENTS MERCHANDISE
1710. READYMADE GARMENTS & COVERS
1711. READYMADE GARMENTS & EMBROIDERY OF GOWNS, SHIRTS, BLOUSES, T-SHIRTS ETC. (ONLY LADIES)
1712. READYMADE SALWAR SUIT
1713. RECOVERY OF NYLON FROM NYLON WASTE
1714. ROTARY PRINTING AND DYEING ON COTTON, SYNTHETIC TEXTILE
1715. SANITARY NAPKINS
1716. SCREEN PRINTING ON COTTON CLOTH
1717. SEWING THREAD REELS & BALLS MAKING INDUSTRIES
1718. SCREEN PRINTING ON COTTON, POLYESTER & ACRYLIC
1719. SHAWLS (WOOLLEN)
1720. SHOE LACES
1721. SILK FABRICS ON HANDLOOM
1722. SOCKS KNITTING
1723. SPINNING, DOUBLING DYEING MERCERISING & BLEACHING OF COTTON YARN
1724. SPINNING & CARDING OF WOOL INTO YARNS
1725. STARCH BOOK BINDING CLOTH
1726. SURAT JARI
1727. SURGICAL COTTON & BANDAGE
1728. SYNTHETIC TEXTILE INDUSTRY(SUITING, SHIRTING, SAREES) TERRY CLOTH
1729. T-SHIRTS
1730. TOWELS, BED SHEET COVERS
1731. TERRY TOWEL
1732. TERRY FABRICS WEAVING UNIT
1733. TEXTILE AUXILLIARIES & CHEMICALS
1734. TEXTILE BLEACHING, DYEING & FINISHING & PRINTING OF COTTON FABRICS
1735. TEXTILE (HOSIERY)
1736. TEXTILE MILL
1737. TEXTILE DYEING & PRINTING
1738. TEXTILE PRINTING (JOB WORK)
1739. TEXTILE PIGMENT PRINTING BINDER
1740. TOWEL (TERRY)
1741. VELVET CLOTH BY FLOCKING PROCESS
1742. VISCOSE STAPLE FIBRE
1743. WADDING OIL (100%) FOR WADDING OF COTTON HOSIERY CLOTH IN THE DYEING PROCESS
1744. WEAVING OF DASUTI CLOTH WITH PRINTING, DYEING, EMBROIDERY & FINISHING
1745. WASHING OF JEANS & OTHER GARMENTS
1746. WORSTED WOOLLEN YARN CLOTH
1747. ZARI GLITTER SALMA SITARA OF PLASTIC FILM

INFOTECH/IT, HOSPITALITY, HOSPITAL, COLLEGE, SCHOOL, MEDICAL, ENTERTAINMENT CLUB, WARE HOUSING & REAL ESTATE, PROJECTS

1748. AMUSEMENT PARK
1749. AMUSEMENT PARK CUM WATER PARK
1750. BANQUET HALL
1751. CALL CENTER (DOMESTIC)
1752. CALL CENTER (INTERNATIONAL)
1753. CHILDREN RECREATION CENTRE
1754. COLD STORAGE
1755. COMMUNITY HALL
1756. COMPUTER EDUCATION INSTITUTE
1757. COMPUTER SOFTWARE
1758. COLLEGE
1759. CYBER CAFE
1760. DENTAL CLINIC
1761. DENTAL COLLEGE
1762. DIAGONOSTIC CENTRE
1763. E-COMMERCE/BUSINESS
1764. E-SCHOOL (Rs. 5000/-)
1765. ENGINEERING COLLEGE
1766. ENTERTAINMENT CLUB
1767. ENTERTAINMENT CLUB, HOLIDAY RESORT, 4 STAR HOTEL, AMUSEMENT PARK CUM WATER PARK, MUSHROOM & ITS PRODUCTS, FISH FARMING, LAKE FOR BOATING, DEER PARK
1768. FASHION TECHNOLOGY INSTITUTE
1769. FAST FOOD PARLOUR
1770. FIVE STAR HOTEL
1771. FOOD PARLOUR
1772. FRANCHISE TRAINING PROGRAMME FOR IIT & ENGINEERING ENTRANCE EXAMS.
1773. GOLF COURSE
1774. HEALTH CLUB, BEAUTY PARLOUR
1775. HEALTH CLUB AND FITNESS CENTER
1776. HEALTH RESORTS
1777. HOLIDAY RESORTS
1778. HOLIDAY RESORT CUM

ENTERTAINMENT CLUB WITH 4 STAR HOTEL
1779. HOSPITALS
1780. ICE CREAM PARLOUR
1781. INTERNET SERVICE PROVIDER (I.S.P.)
1782. MEDICAL COLLEGE
1783. MEDICAL COLLEGE, HOSPITAL & RESEARCH INSTITUTE
1784. MEDICAL TRANSCRIPTION CENTRE
1785. MENTAL RETARDATION HOSPITAL & CEREBRAL PALSY
1786. MOTEL/SMALL HOTEL
1787. MULTISTOREY COMMERCIAL COMPLEX
1788. MULTISTOREY RESIDENTIAL COMPLEX
1789. NURSERY SCHOOL
1790. NATURE CARE CENTRE
1791. NURSING HOME
1792. ONLINE SHOPPING MALL (RS. 5000/- REPORT)
1793. PORTAL
1794. REHABILITATION CENTRE FOR AGED & NEEDY PERSONS
1795. RESIDENTIAL CUM COMMERCIAL COMPLEX
1796. RESTAURANT
1797. RESTAURANT WITH PUB
1798. SCHOOL (PRIMARY)
1799. SCHOOL (HIGHER SECONDARY)
1800. THREE STAR HOTEL
1801. TOURIST CLUB
1802. TRAINING INSTITUTE FOR MEDICAL TRANSCRIPTION
1803. VIDEO FILM STUDIO
1804. WARE HOUSE
1805. WEBSITE DESIGN & E-MAIL REGISTERING

AGRO BASED INDUSTRIES

1806. COAL BRIQUETTES FROM AGROWASTE
1807. FURFURALFROM RICEHULL
1808. MUSHROOM CULTIVATION & PROCESSING (BUTTON)
1809. MUSHROOM GROWING & PROCESSING WITH AIR CONDITIONING
1810. MUSHROOM CULTIVATION & PROCESSING UNIT DEHYDRATION & PACKAGING OF OYSTER & PADDY STRAW MUSHROOMS
1811. ORGANIC MANURE
1812. PAPAYA CULTIVATION
1813. PAPAYA & TOMATO CULTIVATION
1814. PROCESSING & UTILISATION OF COCONUT
1815. PROCESSING OF SHEEP HAIR TO PRODUCE WOOL

BAKERY, CONFECTIONERY & FOOD PRODUCTS

1816. AGROLACTOR SOYA MILK
1817. APPLE FRUIT JUICE WITH CANNING BOTTLING
1818. AYURVEDIC SHARBAT
1819. BAKERY UNIT (PASTRIES, BREAD, BUNS, CAKE, TOFFEE ETC.)
1820. BAKING POWDER
1821. BANANA & ITS BY PRODUCTS
1822. BANANA POWDER
1823. BANANA WAFERS
1824. BANANA CULTIVATION
1825. BEER INDUSTRY
1826. DEHULLING OF JAUN FOR BEER
1827. BEER & WINE
1828. BEER, ALCOHOL, IMFL
1829. BESEN PLANT
1830. BISCUIT PLANT
1831. BREAD & BISCUIT PLANT
1832. BOTTLING PLANT COUNTRY LIQUOR FROM RECTIFIED SPIRIT
1833. BRANDY
1834. BREAD RUSKS
1835. CANNED FRUITS & VEGETABLES
1836. CANNING & PRESERVATION OF MEAT
1837. CANNING & PRESERVATION OF VEGETABLES
1838. CANNING OF MANGO PULP & MANGO SLICES
1839. CARBONATED BEVERAGS
1840. CASHEW FENI
1841. CASHEW NUT (DRIED & FRIED)
1842. CATTLE BREEDING
1843. CATTLE BREEDING & DAIRY FARM TO PRODUCE MILK
1844. CATTLE FEED FROM TAPIOCA
1845. CHEWING GINGER & AMLOKI
1846. CHEWING GUM
1847. CHILLI SAUCE
1848. CHILLI POWDER
1849. CHOCOLATE
1850. CIDER PLANT
1851. COCOA POWDER
1852. COCOA BUTTER & COCOA POWDER
1853. COCONUT SHELL POWDER
1854. COCONUT WATER
1855. COCONUT SWEET (WATERY)
1856. COCONUT MILK POWDER (DEHYDRATED)
1857. COCONUT PRODUCTS & BY PRODUCTS (INTEGRATED PLANT)
1858. COLD DRINK
1859. CURRY POWDER
1860. DAIRY FOR MILK PROCESSING (GHEE, BUTTER & PANEER)
1861. DAIRY PRODUCTS
1862. DAIRY PRODUCTS MILK PACKAGING IN POUCH (GHEE, BUTTER, ETC.
1863. DAIRY FARM TO PRDUCE MILK WITH PACKAGING (COW)
1864. DAIRY FARM TO PRDUCE MILK WITH PACKAGING (BUFALLOE)
1865. DAIRY FARM & MILK PRODUCTS
1866. DAL MOTH, CHANACHUR & BHUJIYA
1867. DEHYDRATION OF FRUITS & VEGETABLE
1868. DESICCATED COCONUT POWDER FROM COCONUTS
1869. DEHYDRATION & CANNINGOF FRUITS & VEGETABLES
1870. DRY FRUIT ROASTING & PACKAGING
1871. DRYING OF RED CHILLIES, HALDI, DHANIYA, PEAS & GROUND NUT
1872. EGG POWDER
1873. FISH CANNING IN TIN & POUCHES
1874. FISH DEHYRATION (DRYING OF FISH)
1875. FISH MEAL
1876. FISH PROCESSING (BEAST FREEZING PROCESSES)
1877. FLAVOURS FOR FOOD INDUSTRIES
1878. FLOUR MILL (ROLLER)
1879. FROZEN MEAT
1880. FOOD DEHYDRATION (FRUITS & VEGETABLES)
1881. FRIED & ROASTED GROUND NUT, GRAMS, PEAR ETC.
1882. FRUIT JUICE MAKING & PACKAGING IN PLASTIC CONTAINER
1883. FRUIT JUICE IN TETRA PACK (DRINKS)
1884. FRUIT JUICE, SQUASHES, SAUCE & KETCHUP, JAM, JELLY, VINEGAR ETC.
1885. GARLIC FLAKES
1886. GARLIC POWDER
1887. GHEE & BUTTER
1888. GINGER (PULVERISED)
1889. GINGER GLAZING & PRESERVATION
1890. GINGER STORAGE
1891. GINGER PROCESSING
1892. GINGER OIL & GINGER DUST
1893. GINGER POWDER (DRY) & OLEORESIN
1894. GRAPE DEHYDRATION
1895. GRAPE CULTIVATION
1896. GRAPE JUICE
1897. HONEY PROCESSING & PACKAGING
1898. ICE CREAM & ICE CANDY
1899. ICE CUBE
1900. INVERT SUGAR
1901. IDLI MIX, DOSA MIX SAMBHAR MIX, VADA MIX, GULAB JAMUN MIX
1902. INSTANT COFFEE & INSTANT TEA

1903. INSTANT NOODLES
1904. INSTANT SOUPS
1905. IODIZED SALT FROM CRUDE SALT
1906. JAM CHUTNEY PICKLES & SQUASHES
1907. KATHA MANUFACTURING
1908. LECITHIN (SOYA BASED)
1909. LEMON & ITS PRODUCTS
1910. MACARONI MANUFACTURING
1911. MACARONI, SPAGHETTI, VERMICELLI & NOODLES
1912. MAIZE & ITS BY PRODUCTS MALTING PLANT
1913. MANGO PAPPAD (AAM PAPPAD)
1914. MANGO POWDER RIPE
1915. MANGO POWDER
1916. MANGO PROCESSING & CANNING (MANGO PULP)
1917. MEAT PROCESSING (CHICKEN MUTTON)
1918. MEAT PROCESSING (BUFFALO)
1919. MENTHOL BOLD FROM MENTHOL FLAKES
1020. MILK POWDER
1921. MILK POWDER & GHEE
1922. MILK POWDER, GHEE & SPICES
1923. MILK PRESERVATION & MARKETING TO WHOLE SELLERS
1924. MILK PRESERVATION & MARKETING TO WHOLE SELLERS (IN POUCHES)
1925. MILK TOFFEE MANUFACTURES
1926. MINERAL WATER
1927. MINERAL WATER IN POUCHES
1928. MINI FLOUR MILL ATTA MAIDA, SUJI & WHEAT BRAN
1929. MITHAI/HALWAI (SWEET & NAMKEEN)
1930. MUTTON PROCESSING
1931. PAN MASALA (MEETHA, SADA, ZARDA) MAKING & PACKING
1932. PAN MASALA AND POUCH MAKING
1933. PANEER (CHEESE)
1934. PAPAD & BARIYAN
1935. PAPAD PLANT
1936. PEPSICOLA IN POLYTUBES
1937. PETHA PACKAGING
1938. PICKLES
1939. PIGGERY/MEAT/CHICKEN PROCESSING
1940. PINE APPLE JUICE CANNING
1941. POTATO & ONION POWDER
1942. POTATO & ONION FLAKES
1943. POTATO CHIPS
1944. POTATO GRANULES
1945. POUCH FILLING FOR SAUNF SUPARI ILAICHI ETC.
1946. PRESERVATION OF RAWS MANGO JUICE
1947. PROCESSED CHEESE & MARINE PDTS.
1948. PULP FROM TARMARIND
1949. READYMATE PROCESSED FOOD
1950. RICE & CORN FLAKES
1951. RICE BASMATI (TRADING)
1952. RICE POLISHING & PACKAGING IN POUCH
1953. ROASTED/SALTED/MASALA/ CASHEW NUTS ALMONDS & PEA NUT
1954. ROLLER FLOUR MILL

INFOTECH/IT PROJECTS

1955. MEDICAL TRANSCRIPTION
1956. E-COMMERCE
1957. CYBERCAFE
1958. INTERNET SERVICE PROVIDER (ISP)
1959. COMPUTER EDUCATION CENTRE
1960. PORTAL (WEBSITE DESIGN)
1961. CALL CENTRE

TERMS AND CONDITIONS

FOR INDIA

1. Please ask for Quotations of Each *Market Survey Cum Detailed Techno Economic Feasibility Report.* Payable in advance through Draft/M.O./Cash in favour of 'ENGINEERS INDIA RESEARCH INSTITUTE', Delhi. Delivery by Regd.post within 2 Days. (Postage Free)

2. Ask for the Hi-Tech Projects Monthly magazine. Each Magazine covers many Project Profiles for selection of Industry.

FOR OVERSEAS

1. Please ask for Quotations in US $ of Each *Market Survey Cum Detailed Techno Economic Feasibility Report.* Payable in advance through Draft/M.O./Cash in favour of 'ENGINEERS INDIA RESEARCH INSTITUTE', Delhi. (Payable in India) Delivery by Regd.post within 4 Days.

2. Ask for the Hi-Tech Projects Monthly magazine. Each Magazine covers many Project Profiles for selection of Industry.

ENGINEERS INDIA RESEARCH INSTITUTE

4449, Nai Sarak (D), Main Road, Delhi - 110 006 (India)
Ph:. 91-11-23918117, 23916431, 23840361, 31082370
Fax: 91-11-23916431 E-Mail : eirisidi@bol.net.in
Website:www.startindustry.com
Also at : 4/27, Roop Nagar, Near Roop Nagar No. 1 School, Delhi - 110 007 (India) Ph:. 23840361